Interpretive Labor

Interpretive Labor

Experimental Music at Work

KIRSTEN L. SPEYER CARITHERS

OXFORD
UNIVERSITY PRESS

Oxford University Press is a department of the University of Oxford.
It furthers the University's objective of excellence in research, scholarship,
and education by publishing worldwide. Oxford is a registered trade mark of
Oxford University Press in the UK and in certain other countries.

Published in the United States of America by Oxford University Press
198 Madison Avenue, New York, NY 10016, United States of America.

© Oxford University Press 2025

All rights reserved. No part of this publication may be reproduced, stored in a retrieval system,
transmitted, used for text and data mining, or used for training artificial intelligence, in any form or
by any means, without the prior permission in writing of Oxford University Press, or as expressly
permitted by law, by license or under terms agreed with the appropriate reprographics rights
organization. Inquiries concerning reproduction outside the scope of the above should be sent to the
Rights Department, Oxford University Press, at the address above.

You must not circulate this work in any other form
and you must impose this same condition on any acquirer

Library of Congress Cataloging-in-Publication Data
Names: Speyer Carithers, Kirsten L., author.
Title: Interpretive labor : experimental music at work / Kirsten L. Speyer Carithers.
Description: [1.] | New York : Oxford University Press, 2025. |
Includes bibliographical references and index.
Identifiers: LCCN 2024038496 (print) | LCCN 2024038497 (ebook) |
ISBN 9780197698778 (hardback) | ISBN 9780197698785 (paperback) |
ISBN 9780197698792 (epub) | ISBN 9780197698815 (digital-online)
Subjects: LCSH: Music—21st century—Performance. | Music—Performance—Philosophy
and aesthetics. | Avant-garde (Music) | Music—Labor productivity.
Classification: LCC ML457 .S (print) | LCC ML457 (ebook) |
DDC 781.4—dc23/eng/20240909
LC record available at https://lccn.loc.gov/2024038496
LC ebook record available at https://lccn.loc.gov/2024038497

DOI: 10.1093/9780197698815.001.0001

*This book is dedicated to everyone who puts in the work,
especially my parents, my sister, and my dearest love.*

Contents

Acknowledgments	ix

INTRODUCTION: EXPLORING INTERPRETATION, ENGAGING WITH LABOR — 1
INDETERMINACY, IMPROVISATION, AND EXPERIMENTALISM — 6
CHAPTER OVERVIEWS — 11

1. THE VALUE OF INTERPRETIVE LABOR — 14
THE THEORETICAL STAKES OF "INTERPRETIVE LABOR" — 16
   On Interpretation — 17
   On Labor — 21
EXPERIMENTAL NOTATION: AN IMPETUS FOR INTERPRETIVE LABOR — 30

2. THE "EXECUTIVE" MODEL: COMPOSERS AS BOSSES — 40
REALIZATION AND AUTHORSHIP: WRITING, TRANSLATING, WORKING — 42
THE EXECUTIVE FUNCTION IN *CARRÉ* — 48
   Reading *Carré*: Indeterminacy and Score Production — 48
   Working Procedures: Realizing *Carré* — 54
   Translational Labor in *Carré* — 56
THE EXECUTIVE FUNCTION IN *PLUS MINUS* — 62
   Reading *Plus Minus*: Indeterminacy — 62
   Realizing *Plus Minus*: Performances — 67
   Translational Labor in *Plus Minus* — 76
CONCLUSION: THE EXECUTIVE MODEL TODAY — 79

3. THE "SCIENTIST" MODEL: THE COMPOSITION STUDIO AS LABORATORY — 86
MEET PETR KOTÍK — 86
ON CHANCE AND INTERPRETATION — 90
   Kotík on (and Resisting) Interpretation — 94
   The Composer as Scientist — 98
THE COMPOSER AS SCIENTIST, II: HILLER — 111
CONCLUSION: MUSICAL SCIENTISTS PAST AND PRESENT — 115

viii CONTENTS

4. THE "ADMINISTRATOR" MODEL: "WOMEN'S WORK"
AND NEW-MUSIC COORDINATORS 121
   GENDER AND LABOR 122
   ORGANIZATIONS 126
      Center of the Creative and Performing Arts 126
      Avant-Garde Festivals of New York 131
   LABOR AND GENDER 137
   CONCLUSION: THE ADMINISTRATOR MODEL TODAY 141

5. THE "HACKER" MODEL: SUBVERSION IN THEORY AND
PRACTICE 145
   CARDEW ON INTERPRETATION 149
   ON THE HACK 153
   COMPOSING *TREATISE* 156
   PERFORMING *TREATISE* 160
      Creative Associates, 1966 161
      QUaX, 1967 167
      S.E.M./Creative Associates, 1970 170
   CARDEW, HACKER, VERSUS STOCKHAUSEN, VECTORALIST 173
   MUSIC-MAKING AS HACKING 179
   CARDEW'S POLITICS AFTER *TREATISE* 181
   CONCLUSION: MUSICAL HACKING 183

6. THE "GAMER" MODEL: GAMES, PLAY, AND
OTHER LUDIC EXPERIMENTS 190
   INTRODUCTION: EXPERIMENTAL MUSIC AND
      LUDOMUSICOLOGY 190
   MODDING 193
   THE WORK OF ART IN THE AGE OF USER-GENERATED
      CONTENT 198
   EXPERIMENTAL MUSIC AS A SHARING ECONOMY 211
      Subversive Sharing/Subversive Play 215
   CONCLUSION: MUSICAL GAMES AS TECHNOLOGIES 223

CONCLUSION: INTERPRETIVE LABOR BEYOND
EXPERIMENTALISM 229
   INTERPRETATION AS LABOR 233

Bibliography 239
Index 253

Acknowledgments

I am grateful to a veritable army of people who have aided, abetted, and improved this project. First: the team at Oxford University Press, with special mention to Norm Hirschy for providing an incredibly positive experience for this nervous first-time author, and to Laura Santo for patient guidance through manuscript preparation. Erin Maher provided stellar indexing and proof-reading. Thank you to the anonymous reviewers who assessed earlier versions of this project; their insightful feedback helped to shape some substantial improvements to the text. (Of course, any remaining issues are entirely my own.)

I am grateful to a number of people for their assistance with providing and/or serving as primary sources: Gabriela Krchňáčková for information on the history of the Ostrava Center for New Music; both Jan Williams and Petr Kotík for sharing scores, correspondence, and their valuable time; Jim Bohn for generously allowing me to reprint his flowchart for the Hiller program in Chapter 3; and to the lovely Renée Levine Packer for allowing me to interview her multiple times about her experience, for sharing archival material, and for general support of my interest in administrative labor. Thank you also to everyone in the various ensembles and other organizations discussed throughout the book. As I hope to have made clear, you all deserve praise (and, frankly, a terrific salary) for your work!

Huge thanks to the publishers who have allowed reprints of score excerpts, without which my discussions of *Carré*, *Plus Minus*, *Treatise*, and *Teaching and Learning as Performing Arts* would have been much more clumsy: Claudia Patsch at Universal Edition, Klaudia Wojtczak at Buchhandlung Walther König GmbH & Co. KG; Lauren Windsor at Faber Music; Marybeth Coscia-Weiss at Edition Peters; and Mora Martínez Basualdo at Peter Freeman, Inc.

To the intrepid librarians and archivists who keep all of us musicologists afloat: you are amazing. At SUNY/University at Buffalo: John Bewley, Deborah Chiarella, and Nina MacClean; Hannah Pacious at the Smithsonian American Art Museum; Catie Huggins, Scott Krafft, and Greg MacAyeal with Northwestern University Libraries; and my wonderful colleagues James

X ACKNOWLEDGMENTS

Procell and Matt Ertz at the University of Louisville. Also at U of L, I have had the good fortune of working with a fantastic School of Music writing group: Devin Burke, Kimcherie Lloyd, Rebecca Long, Amy Acklin, and Ulrike Präger; I'm likewise grateful for the encouragement of supportive colleagues Chris Brody, Allison Ogden, Jerry Tolson, Krista Wallace-Boaz, and Teresa Reed. To Ryan Dohoney, whose role as my dissertation advisor shaped many of the ideas that have made their way into this book, I am forever grateful for your mentorship and support. My own students, especially in the Music & Labor seminar, are also an incredible source of inspiration and encouragement.

Finally, I thank my dear family and friends. My amazing sister Bethany inspires me, and always has. I am grateful for my wonderful in-laws, Jackie and Jim. My own parents, John and Daryl, continue to model the values of care, humility, and hard work. To my girls Shannon, Emily, and Amanda: I am so glad we were thrown together as undergrads and that we remain sisters and friends; I treasure each reunion with you. And finally, to my sweetie, Ben: like so many people, we have both been tested over these past few years, and I am still, and always, thanking my lucky stars that you are by my side through it all.

INTRODUCTION

EXPLORING INTERPRETATION, ENGAGING WITH LABOR

As a college undergraduate, I was fortunate to participate in a wide variety of music ensembles, including bands, choirs, orchestra, an early-music ensemble, an Afro-Caribbean ensemble, and chamber groups. One type of experience that particularly stands out in my memory is orchestral playing for operas and musical-theater productions. On February 25 and 26, 2000, my peers and I donned our concert black (standard attire for such an event), took our seats in the small pit area below the stage in Kobacker Hall on the campus of Bowling Green State University, and settled in for performances of W. A. Mozart's *Le Nozze di Figaro*.[1] At that point, I had been a music major for a couple of years and was becoming familiar with the sound of big-C Classical music, including spending some lesson time on 18th-century sonatas and on excerpts from Mozart's oboe concerto. I had only played in bands before starting college, though, so I was still getting accustomed to the norms of orchestral participation—even such basic elements as tuning the group, knowing where to sit depending on variations in wind instrumentation, and watching string players work out bowings—and I was terribly inexperienced in terms of playing in a way that was stylistically appropriate for the time period of the composition. In one particularly chastening moment during a rehearsal, I jumped into Susanna's *andante* aria "Deh vieni, non tardar," in a brisk two, only to have the poor soprano (and the conductor) look at me like I had just grown an alien head: it hadn't occurred to me that a movement in 6/8 time could be taken in a leisurely six. Lacking suitable knowledge of the repertoire at hand, I instinctively tried to draw on my limited background—the 6/8 time signature must mean a march tempo!—and, frankly, flailed.

By the time of the first performance, I'd like to think that we had prepared sufficiently and were able to interpret the score appropriately, but that

---

[1] "The Marriage of Figaro," *Digital Gallery*, BGSU University Libraries June 16, 2020. digitalgallery.bgsu.edu/collections/item/28304.

Interpretive Labor. Kirsten I. Speyer Carithers, Oxford University Press. © Oxford University Press 2025.
DOI: 10.1093/9780197698815.003.0001

2 INTERPRETIVE LABOR

certainly did not happen overnight (and probably no thanks to me, in any case). We needed numerous rehearsals to work on tempi, stylistic expression, coordination with the singers on stage, and a host of other elements. Before the dress rehearsals with the full ensemble, we had sectionals and worked on some of the numbers, especially the overture, with just the orchestra. Before that, each person spent time in the practice room (and probably also lessons), working on specific sections of the score. Most of the ensemble had more experience than I, thankfully, and were therefore able to mask my artistic immaturity. In the end, under the baton of Dr. Emily Freeman Brown, we were collectively able to present a convincing iteration of *Figaro*.

In contrast to the relative comfort of educational ensembles, such as my experience with the opera orchestra, the musicians of the postwar avant-garde lacked most of the institutional guardrails that can help keep things on track. While many of its participants benefited from conversations with one another, there were few other resources: no textbooks, performance-practice treatises, conservatory programs, or archived videos. This paradigm directly contributed to the ways artists have engaged with so-called experimental music, and subsequently shaped my understanding of the era under consideration in this book. While much has been written about musical interpretation, broadly speaking, scholars and critics have been somewhat less engaged with questions about interpretive procedures in experimental or avant-garde performance, and it is toward that phenomenon that I have been drawn, over and over. My curiosity was first piqued right around the same time as that *Figaro* performance. Perhaps I should not admit this in print, but I was not exactly the most engaged student in my undergraduate music history courses—until, that is, we started talking about artistic projects undertaken in the postwar era. It really was as if a switch had been flipped, and I was fascinated, wanting to know more about what had happened and why. (This was not a sophisticated curiosity: my thoughts were along the lines of "This is weird! What were they thinking?!")

Fittingly, the more specific orientation of my ongoing research, including the present book, began with a chance encounter just a couple of years later. In one of the courses for my master's degree, I was randomly assigned a class presentation on the topic of "indeterminacy." While my peers in the class who were assigned other subjects gathered copious published sources, my preparation was hampered by the dearth of available scholarship. At the start, I was especially frustrated by the limited available resources because the assignment required a teaching demonstration of the subject, and unlike most of my colleagues who presented areas well-covered in textbooks, "my" topic was not even mentioned in *The New Grove*.[2] What I wouldn't have given for an in-progress copy of Rebecca Kim's dissertation! In retrospect, of course, I cannot imagine it any other way; once I picked up a copy of Cage's book *Silence*, I was hooked.[3]

In the intervening years, my life took some unpredictable turns, including several years of employment in finance, which culminated in a position managing an audit and compliance team for a large mortgage company. After further graduate study, I am now fortunate to work in higher education, and have all the while continued to develop increasing curiosity about the relationships between musical performance and economic issues. This book, then, has been shaped by my own interdisciplinary professional experience and likewise aims to advance a multifaceted theoretical framework. My primary contribution, and the central theme, is an idea that I am calling *interpretive labor*: the creative work of realizing something that has indeterminate components. In the following chapters, I develop an account of this theory through five models, represented by five types of experimental-music practice. The concept of Interpretive Labor, I contend, both directly reflects actual financial circumstances and also serves as a useful metaphor for broader labor relations. I argue that the rise of ambiguously notated (i.e., indeterminate) compositions coincides with changes in labor more generally, showing how they reflect the socioeconomic and other cultural conditions of these works' creators and realizers and often forshadow the present economic paradigm.

To illustrate these ideas, I rely on a handful of interrelated locations and institutions and the artists whose lives became entangled with them: Buffalo, New York, including the Creative Associates (a term for fellows of the Center of the Creative and Performing Arts at the State University of New York at Buffalo); cultural centers in New York City, including Carnegie Hall and the Bohemian National Hall; Prague and Ostrava, Czech Republic, and the Ostrava Days Festival and Institute; and other spaces where "new music" has been fostered. Some key players include the ensembles QUaX and S.E.M., and composer-performers Petr Kotík, Cornelius Cardew, and Karlheinz

---

[2] As of June 2023, *The New Grove Dictionary of Music and Musicians*, later incorporated into the expanded *Oxford Music Online*, still lacks a standalone entry for "indeterminacy," although the term increasingly appears in entries for specific musicians.

[3] Rebecca Y. Kim, "'In No Uncertain Musical Terms: The Cultural Politics of John Cage's Indeterminacy" (PhD diss., Columbia University, 2008). John Cage, *Silence: Lectures and Writings* (Middletown, CT: Wesleyan University Press, 1961).

4   INTERPRETIVE LABOR

Stockhausen. Throughout the chapters, we will find Creative Associates and the S.E.M. Ensemble performing Petr Kotík's work, Kotík performing Cardew, Cardew performing Stockhausen, and so on. To borrow a phrase from literary theorist Sandra Bermann, this complex network both shapes and proves a "relational identity, made of encounters."[4] At the same time, I should note that this specific network is rather homogeneous in terms of geography and culture. The present text lays out the theory of Interpretive Labor through the lens of Euro-American experimentalism, with much of the historical activity having taken place in and around New York State, specifically, and I want to be clear that this is just one of many possible networks that could fruitfully illustrate this theoretical framework. One of my long-term hopes for this research is that it will prompt scholars who specialize in additional groups and genres to consider how and why artists have invested so much of themselves in the interpretive project, broadly speaking. Through this text, I want to encourage other music researchers to think about labor: What work is involved in making a performance? How can we, and why should we, make this a part of our dialogue more regularly?

In addition to musicology and labor studies, this project is also deeply grounded in a theoretical framework indebted to continental philosophy and critical theory. Throughout the chapters, for example, I draw on different aspects of hermeneutics, ultimately synthesizing several concepts into a working model of Interpretive Labor informed by the work of Heidegger, Derrida, and Gadamer.[5] Throughout the text, I incorporate a number of related concepts that spark new insight into experimental-music repertoire: the relationship between work and play, circulation networks and their peripheries, and concealed power structures.[6] By interrogating these thinkers' assumptions and conclusions as related to the material substance

---

[4] Sandra Bermann, "Performing Translation," in *A Companion to Translation Studies*, ed. Sandra Bermann and Catherine Porter, Blackwell Companions to Literature and Culture (Chichester, England: Wiley-Blackwell, 2014), 293.

[5] Cf. Martin Heidegger, *Being and Time*, trans. Joan Stambaugh, rev. Dennis J. Schmidt (Albany: State University of New York Press, 2010); Jacques Derrida, "What Is a 'Relevant' Translation?" *Critical Inquiry* 27, no. 2 (Winter 2001), 174–200; Jacques Derrida, *Specters of Marx: The State of the Debt, the Work of Mourning and the New International* [1993] (Hoboken, NJ: Taylor and Francis, 2012); Hans-Georg Gadamer, *Truth and Method*, trans. Joel Weinsheimer and Donald G. Marshall, 2nd rev. ed. (New York: Continuum, 1994); Hans-Georg Gadamer, *Philosophical Hermeneutics*, trans. David E. Linge (Berkeley: University of California Press, 1976).

[6] For two recent and dynamic texts informing both specific theoretical constructs and my engagement with cross-disciplinary thinking, see William Cheng, *Sound Play: Video Games and the Musical Imagination* (Oxford: Oxford University Press, 2014) and Brigid Cohen, *Musical Migration and Imperial New York: Early Cold War Scenes* (Oxford: Oxford University Press, 2022).

of composition and performance history, I knit together a rich account of the economics of indeterminacy. The book as a whole combines interpretation, realization, subversion/hacking, and circulation into a narrative of performing indeterminacy, using both present and historical accounts. Drawing on these experimental/indeterminate artistic practices, I illuminate the power structures and labor demands that are hidden within contemporary composition.

To perform a conventional musical composition such as a symphony, sonata, or chamber work, artists complete a fairly proscribed, if extensive, set of tasks. This typically includes years of training on a particular instrument or voice type; gaining specialized experience in the relevant ensembles, genres, and/or musical styles; practicing the specific piece; gathering with an audience in a designated space for the concert; and finally performing the piece. For chamber musicians working on, say, a mid-19th-century piano trio, they will likely consider its stylistic similarities to Lieder and other pieces from the same period, using those examples to shape phrasing, note lengths, dynamic contrast, and other expressive elements. A violinist preparing a concerto might focus first on the most technically challenging passages, working up to the expected speed and dexterity, while also considering how to shape any lyrical phrases and to blend smoothly with the accompanying ensemble. Musicians in a professional jazz combo will probably consider the recordings they have heard and the jam sessions they have participated in— maybe in a lab band in college or a previous gig—when translating the lead sheet or chart into a dynamic new performance. All of these musicians draw upon their educations and experiences to transform dots and lines on a page into a meaningful sonic experience. In other words, they are called upon to interpret the notation before them. These activities—cognitive, creative, and embodied—take *effort*. Musicians invest time and energy to develop the skills and artistry expected of them, typically by engaging in long-term study, practice, and preparation in addition to the most "visible" portion of their careers: that is, performances. For all of these artists, these activities are components in a system of labor and work that have too long gone unrecognized.

In reflecting on the scope and methods of this project, I keep returning to the idea of a precarious economy of knowledge. To be sure, the overall structure of this document indulges my taxonomic leanings, and this is but one type of investigation into labor and music. I have found that I am drawn to this model-based approach, and to discussions of terms whose meanings

6   INTERPRETIVE LABOR

are perhaps best left flexible, because it was challenging to truly tease out experimental artists' expectations for their most extreme compositions and to understand the performance practice of this repertoire. Again, when I first started digging into the work of avant-garde composers as a new graduate student, I felt that the idea of indeterminacy was not being given the attention it deserved within musicological literature.[7] In the years since then—well over a decade now—this repertoire and much related to it has congealed into a subfield called experimental-music studies. While there has been an absolute wealth of important and well-crafted research in this area, two concerns arise: first, since it is a fairly new field, its scholarship tends to emphasize specific case studies rather than broader theories; and second, it seems to have sidestepped some of the (admittedly tedious) task of defining itself and its vocabulary.[8] I have always enjoyed organizing things—sorting, classifying, labeling—and this simple pleasure seemed well-suited for an account of musical indeterminacy. On the other hand, as Dörries notes in a discussion of biological research, "Model organisms, apparatuses, and key terms constitute transient patterns, *guiding* as well as *constraining* researchers in the course of their investigations."[9] Clearly, there are potential pitfalls to a model-based project: rely too much on the archetypes and risk shoehorning in important practices that don't naturally fit; try to cover all possible scenarios and lose the clarity that makes a model desirable in the first place. Given the forward-looking and promising state of experimental-music studies, though, I felt that it was worth the risk. Ideally, this theory of Interpretive Labor, with its attendant models and definitions, will contribute to this emergent discourse and raise matters for future application.

INDETERMINACY, IMPROVISATION, AND EXPERIMENTALISM

If interpretation is present in most or all forms of artistic expression, and if interpretive work is a form of labor, the concept of Interpretive Labor might

---

[7] The music history assignment mentioned above also inspired my (rather simple, descriptive) thesis: "The Network of Influence: New York Artists and the Indeterminate Works of John Cage, 1951–1978" (MM thesis, Bowling Green State University, 2005).

[8] Of course, this work is extremely valuable, as well. Much of the "case study" scholarship has already proven indispensable to the field.

[9] Emphasis added. Matthias Dörries, "Life, Language, and Science: Hans-Jörg Rheinberger's Historical Epistemology," *Historical Studies in the Natural Sciences* 42, no. 1 (February 2012), 75.

productively be applied to a massive range of musical practices. This text, though, emphasizes the world of so-called experimental music (or "contemporary classical," or "the avant-garde"; its labels are varied and often fuzzy). Why? As I hope to make clear, it is especially well suited for this inquiry: its compositions (if one wants to call them that) are often inherently ambiguous, rendering the degrees and kinds of interpretation quite extreme.[10] I also focus on indeterminacy and other experimental phenomena because I find labor to be under-theorized thus far in studies of avant-garde art. In no way is this emphasis meant to suggest that postwar classical experimentalism is somehow better or more valuable than other forms of music; in fact, interpretive labor is present in essentially all music-making, especially in forms relying on improvisation—including much of the world's musics beyond this limited Euro-American scope—and in practices with any level of power imbalance among the music's participants. My aim is for this specific study to provide theoretical framing that may prove useful for scholar-practitioners in many other artistic circles, from jazz experts working with "fake books" to Carnatic musicians passing along their knowledge in lessons.

By focusing on this specific context, though, much essential music-making of the same era will be left out. To that end, it would be irresponsible to discuss experimental music without pointing toward some of the underlying biases and assumptions that scholars have unearthed—biases that have shaped my own education and preparation for writing this book. A significant source of tension explored in recent musicological scholarship is the racial exclusion faced by Black musicians, especially within avant-garde institutions. John Cage's problem-laden association with African American art forms, for example, dates back to at least 1940, when he accompanied modern dance classes at the Cornish School in Seattle. That year, as recounted by Tamara Levitz, he created music to accompany Syvilla Fort's piece *Bacchanale* for her graduate recital. Fort "expressed African-American social struggle by embracing modernism through movements that in her time were understood as being quintessentially 'African,'" and Cage developed what he thought was a suitable musical correlate: a piano prepared to sound like a marimbula, an Afro-Cuban instrument that Cage had encountered in Henry Cowell's class.[11] In the next decade, Cage appropriated jazz recordings in an

---

[10] By this, I mean that performers frequently have to make a lot of choices about how the piece should sound, and also that this repertoire lacks a well-documented performance-practice tradition akin to that experienced in most conservatories for common-practice-period works.

[11] Tamara Levitz, "Syvilla Fort's Africanist Modernism and John Cage's Gestic Music: The Story of *Bacchanale*," *The South Atlantic Quarterly* 104, no. 1 (Winter 2005), 129.

8   INTERPRETIVE LABOR

early experiment with magnetic tape. After having sampled 42 jazz albums into the tape collage *Imaginary Landscape No. 5* (1952), he referred to its components as "timbres which are unmusical or distasteful."[12] According to Rebecca Kim, this and Cage's experiences with Joseph Jarman and the Association for the Advancement of Creative Musicians (AACM) frame his well-known and problematic relationship with jazz. As posited in Kim's work, Cage intentionally rejected jazz in the 1950s not because it conflicted with the aesthetic goal of non-intention, as he had claimed, but because he had unsatisfying personal interactions with specific African American musicians, and he extrapolated those feelings onto the entire genre of jazz.[13]

Because Cage was such a central figure in experimental-music scholarship published before, say, the last 20 years, his position had an outsize influence on which ideas received scholarly and critical attention. As a corrective to this, recent research explores a much more diverse set of institutions and perspectives. For example, the AACM is becoming better recognized for its important position in histories of the postwar avant-garde. Founded on the south side of Chicago in the 1960s, it presently describes itself as "a collective of musicians and composers dedicated to nurturing, performing, and recording serious, original music" who include in their mission "to provide an atmosphere conducive to the development of its member artists and to continue the AACM legacy of providing leadership and vision for the development of creative music."[14] The most prominent scholarly voice on the group is that of George E. Lewis, a musicologist, performer, composer, and longtime member of the group. He has created both a voluminous academic text and an experimental multimedia opera about the AACM, the premiere of which I was fortunate to attend at the 2015 Ostrava Days festival.[15] Participants in the early days of the group debated the meaning of originality, the issue of "seriousness," and the goals and vision for the group, as they established an organization for mutual support of one another's creative work.

---

[12] John Cage, "Composition as Process: Changes," in *Silence: Lectures and Writings*, cited in Rebecca Y. Kim, "John Cage in Separate Togetherness with Jazz," *Contemporary Music Review* 31, no. 1 (February 2012), 63.

[13] Kim, "John Cage in Separate Togetherness," 64.

[14] This is not unlike the Black Arts Repertory Theater and School, founded by Amiri Baraka (then LeRoi Jones) in Harlem the same year (https://www.aacmchicago.org/about-us). See also John Pippen, "The Boundaries of 'Boundarylessness': Revelry, Struggle, and Labour in Three American New Music Ensembles," part of the "Boundaries of the New: American Classical Music at the Turn of the Millennium" forum, *Twentieth Century Music* 16, no. 3 (2019), 424–44.

[15] George E. Lewis, *A Power Stronger than Itself: The AACM and American Experimental Music* (Chicago: University of Chicago Press, 2008) and *Afterword: The AACM (as) Opera* (2016).

INTRODUCTION 9

Upon being formally chartered as a non-profit in Illinois in 1965, the AACM announced its birth in the Chicago *Defender*, and the musicians set to work producing concerts and recordings.[16]

As Lewis points out, "The 'AACM model' stresses a composer-improviser orientation and the importance of asserting the agency, identity, and survival of the African-American artist."[17] He cites a 1973 profile by co-founder Muhal Richard Abrams and trumpeter John Shenoy Jackson, which asserts: "The Black creative artists must survive and persevere in spite of the oppressive forces which prevent Black people from reaching the goals attained by other Americans. . . . Black artists must control and be paid for what they produce, as well as own and control the means of distribution."[18] While the nine purposes listed in its founding documents do not specifically mention race,[19] it was clearly a major factor shaping the priorities for the nascent organization. If its early members had been welcomed into the largely white institutions that supported other experimental and avant-garde artists, they would not have needed to create their own organization, figure out how to pursue funding opportunities, and otherwise handle all of the logistics that were ultimately placed on their shoulders. But because these artists took on that work, the AACM has become a vital, inspirational force for creative artists in numerous fields across experimental sound, free improvisation, jazz, and everything in between, providing an intellectual and cultural home for multiple generations of musicians.

George E. Lewis, in his watershed 1996 article on improvisation, rightly questions the biases informing decisions to exclude important jazz musicians from histories of "contemporary" music. Occasionally, his frustration rises to the surface: in discussing an ill-conceived interview between Cage and jazz critic Michael Zwerin, he describes it as "two white males prepar[ing] to discuss 'the trouble with black people.'"[20] As Lewis makes clear, improvisatory practices—such as those at the heart of the birth and development of jazz and other forms of Black music-making—are every bit as important as any other musical practice in the history of 20th-century music.

---

[16] George E. Lewis, "Experimental Music in Black and White: The AACM in New York, 1970–1985," *Current Musicology*, nos. 71–73 (Spring 2001), 106.

[17] George E. Lewis, "Improvised Music after 1950: Afrological and Eurological Perspectives," *Black Music Research Journal* 16, no. 1 (Spring 1996), 111.

[18] Muhal Richard Abrams and John Shenoy Jackson, "Association for the Advancement of Creative Musicians," *BlackWorld* 23, no. 1 (November 1973), 72, cited in Lewis, "Experimental Music in Black and White."

[19] Lewis, "Experimental Music in Black and White," 105–6.

[20] Lewis, "Improvised Music after 1950," 104.

10 INTERPRETIVE LABOR

Lewis, Kim, and Levitz, among others, have therefore produced invaluable scholarship on the role of race in experimental-music studies, fostering critical engagement with indeterminacy/improvisation in its many iterations and demonstrating the extent of racially-motivated disenfranchisement, both historical and historiographical. The case studies in the present book existed concurrently with the rise of bebop, free jazz, and other forms of Afro-modernism, and were undoubtedly influenced by those developments. In other words, Black American "serious" music, and its attendant forms of interpretive labor, merit careful and sensitive research. Scholars like George E. Lewis, Ingrid Monson, Matthew D. Morrison, and others have created (and are continuing to produce) important work that addresses these issues and will surely become foundational for future study.[21]

The investigation of musical experimentalism through the lens of Interpretive Labor raises questions about whether and how musicians' experiences track with increasing anxiety about unrecognized (and therefore uncompensated) work more broadly. Likewise, there are numerous factors to consider when placing these musical performances in dialogue with (music) history more broadly, not least of which are the strong political provocations of much indeterminate music. Composers such as John Cage and Cornelius Cardew's scores and writings served to disrupt the prevailing composer–performer relationship. As their ideologies shifted, there seems to have been a corresponding shift in the degree or kind of artistic freedoms given to—or pushed onto—performers.

One might argue that all performed music has some element that is indeterminate as the score or orally transmitted source version is translated into a fresh iteration. That person would receive no quarrel from me; it is not at all feasible to produce fully identical copies of any piece of music.[22] While it can be a fun philosophical game to imagine realizations without variation, it should not be too controversial to suggest that most performances of music involve some degree of difference from other realizations of the same work,

---

[21] Ingrid Monson, *Saying Something: Jazz Improvisation and Interaction* (Chicago: University of Chicago Press, 1997); Matthew D. Morrison, "Race, Blacksound, and the (Re)Making of Musicological Discourse," *Journal of the American Musicological Society* 72, no. 3 (Fall 2019), 781–823.

[22] Even digitally created and recorded sounds will have some minute variation in the ambient characteristics of the space in which they are reproduced, unless every environmental parameter is duplicated. Even then, one could make the case that the audience has changed, or if the same individuals are hearing it again, that the audience's perception has changed because they already heard it once, and so on, ad infinitum. Primarily, though, I am most interested here in live performance, for which it is even more difficult to replicate every precise condition.

INTRODUCTION   11

and that these different iterations do not by their very existence dismantle the work's identity. A "work" may exist as an entity regardless of when, where, and if it is performed; to quote Richard Littlefield, it is "a finished man-made product, a self-sufficient entity . . . that exists beyond the place and time of its creation."[23] It is both an idea and an incarnation of that idea, and as such, it is open to—sometimes slight, sometimes great—variation when brought to life. In at least one important respect, though, the scope of this project is distinct from the sort of casual, everyday indeterminacy that results from slight fluctuations in performance parameters. Rather, I intentionally focus on works where either compositional or performer indeterminacy is a *defining* component.

CHAPTER OVERVIEWS

Chapter 1, "The Value of Interpretive Labor" introduces the theory and philosophy underpinning my research, focusing on foundational work in interpretation and in labor. It also reviews some of the types of musical writing—that is, notation—that have been most salient in terms of developing this account of experimentalism, to prepare readers for the specific compositions investigated in Chapters 2, 3, 5, and 6. Each of the following five chapters introduces one model of Interpretive Labor, shares some of the artistic practices that have shaped my thinking on that model, and considers how we might apply the model to current or future paradigms of music-making.

In Chapter 2, "The Executive Model: Composers as Bosses," I consider the compositions *Plus-Minus* and *Carré* by Karlheinz Stockhausen (1928–2007), drawing on the accounts written by his assistant, English composer Cornelius Cardew (1936–81). In this case, I conceptualize the relationship between composers and those who realize their works in terms of the capitalist executive system, and specifically engage with the idea of outsourcing. Stockhausen here is like a manager in the neoliberal present: identifying (and exploiting) workers who can handle the day-to-day grunt work while

---

[23] Richard Littlefield, "The Silence of the Frames," in *Music/Ideology: Resisting the Aesthetic*, ed. Adam Krims, Critical Voices in Art, Theory, and Culture, Saul Ostrow, series editor (Amsterdam: G + B Arts, 1998), 213. For a classic text on the development of the "work concept," see Lydia Goehr, *The Imaginary Museum of Musical Works: An Essay in the Philosophy of Music*, rev. ed (Oxford: Oxford University Press, 2007).

12   INTERPRETIVE LABOR

taking credit for efficiently taking care of business. This model is informed by philosophical aspects of translation, decoding, and realization, and raises concerns about how these presuppose a "right" answer or a "proper" interpretation.

Chapter 3, "The Scientist Model: The Composition Studio as Laboratory," discusses Petr Kotík (b. 1942), who founded and directed two experimental music ensembles in Prague in the 1960s and in 1969 joined the Creative Associates at the University at Buffalo, where he formed the S.E.M. Ensemble. To think about composition as a scientific practice, Kotík and Lejaren Hiller (1924–94) are brought into conversation. Chance is significant here, as is its interpretation. Envisioned here as a synthesis between strict realization and subversive hacking, this chance-informed interpretation is a means of grappling with the undefined, of making sense of indeterminate elements. This chapter argues that certain compositional acts, especially those incorporating chance/aleatory techniques, are directly comparable to the actions of research scientists in laboratories, and discusses how this labor shapes the development and sound of the related compositions.

Chapter 4, "The Administrator Model: "Women's Work" and New-Music Coordinators," considers the management of new-music ensembles. Drawing on archival materials of organizations and events like the ONCE Festivals (1961–68), the New York Avant-Garde Festivals (1963–1980), and the Center of the Creative and Performing Arts in Buffalo (1964–1980), I demonstrate the extent to which (primarily women) coordinators like Charlotte Moorman and Renée Levine Packer have facilitated significant institutions for new music. This type of interpretive labor demands competence in numerous skills, like the affective labor of managing competing egos (e.g., of composers and performers), the translational labor of realizing directors' ideas, and the ability to manage complex systems. With this in mind, I consider how and why this might connect to the problematic notion of "women's work." Through an investigation of both historical and current institutions, we uncover hidden labor and establish a conceptual framework for improving the recognition of these essential roles.

Chapter 5, "The Hacker Model: Subversion in Theory and Practice," reads the creation and life of Cardew's composition *Treatise* as a reaction to his experience working on Stockhausen's *Carré*. This chapter introduces the history and criticism of "hacking" as related to computer coding, its ramifications in popular culture, and subversive forms of labor, including rebellious practices in and beyond music. I argue here that hacking is not simply a problem to be solved, but actually a polyvalent term (and concept) that celebrates creative labor and community formation in ways that are particularly valuable for musicians.

Chapter 6, "The Gamer Model: Games, Play, and Other Ludic Experiments," examines manifestations of the most liberal form of Interpretive Labor, in which any participant may freely realize a score. This is most closely associated with the Fluxus movement, although a number of other artists (ONCE, Creative Associates, etc.) should be included, as they are here. This chapter develops the idea of user-generated content as a bridge between music and the information age, and addresses the problem of capitalizing on "voluntary" labor from users. This chapter also argues that this form may actually require the most work in terms of interpretive labor; with no guidelines, all performance decisions must be made and carried out as/if the performer is the creator/composer.

Finally, in the Conclusion, "Interpretive Labor beyond Experimentalism," I provide applications of Interpretive Labor to repertoires and practices outside the scope of this book, demonstrating its explanatory power beyond this relatively specific context. This section further considers ways to rethink interpretation and work in the 21st century, including connections to "influencer" culture and the normalization of the gig economy. This opens up Interpretive Labor, allowing us to reflect on playing with labor and playing with interpretation, both of which suggest the postmodern fluidity characterizing present-day creative practices.

1
THE VALUE OF
INTERPRETIVE LABOR

This project documents the social and working relationships among several international artists active between 1960 and the present, it introduces new voices and questions into the field of "experimental music studies," and it emphasizes the question of labor, which is a crucial but little-discussed aspect of artistic practice. The chosen case studies—including an English-born communist who started his international musical career with a hyper-controlling German mentor, a Czech-born performer-composer who emigrated to the United States and became a leader within the contemporary music scene, and a group of Rockefeller-funded postgraduates at the Center of the Creative and Performing Arts in Buffalo—expand the present boundaries of the field. More importantly, they provide an opportunity (and an obligation) to foreground the perspectives of actual working musicians: the performers who labor, often for little or no recognition, to interpret difficult pieces of experimental music. The overlapping networks investigated here also give us more tools for understanding the economic, social, and cultural forces at work throughout the Cold War era, and help provide nuance to the varied and fraught political issues woven throughout these histories, including the issues of labor, representation, and recognition. Indeed, the amount and types of work required of performers indicates parallels with other systems of labor and compensation. These problems are not unique to experimental or avant-garde musical circles, and in fact take on new urgency in our current late-capitalist economy. Individuals and corporations desperately need to work out the kinks in economies of creative labor, such that they can fairly serve their increasingly connected super-users and other "content creators." As participants stumble toward that goal, an understanding of this earlier creative labor might provide something of a roadmap—or at least some warning signs.

Many of the terms and concepts discussed throughout this book have had multiple meanings, depending on the time and place in which they have

Interpretive Labor. Kirsten I. Speyer Carithers, Oxford University Press. © Oxford University Press 2025.
DOI: 10.1093/9780197698815.003.0002

been used; likewise, various researchers and theorists have put these ideas into operation in service of a wide array of agendas. The following, therefore, lays out the questions and concerns driving my work on musical labor, and provides some background on the implications (and applications) of the areas of focus therein. My objective is twofold: to examine what it means to engage in the act of interpretation, and to align indeterminate-music performance with developing theories of labor. By "indeterminate," I mean compositions in which one or more significant aspects—for example, pitch, duration, voices or instruments used, and so forth—are left open. These characteristics may remain unspecified by the composer and therefore must be chosen by the performer(s), or they may be chosen using some type of chance procedures during the process of composition.[1] This repertoire was largely developed from the 1950s into the 1970s (and beyond, to a lesser extent), and while it varies widely, it is frequently marked by unconventional musical notation, up to and including scores consisting solely of text or pictures. For performer-indeterminate repertoire, in contrast to most conventionally notated music, each performance differs greatly depending on the decisions made, and a piece may become unrecognizable even to its own composer.[2] Realizers of these works must be fluent not only in reading notational systems of varying types but also in the oral traditions that govern many details of realization. Lacking the formal, institutionalized training that has long been established for common-practice repertoire, they rely on encounters with other new-music performers, workshops with composers and directors, and other sorts of ad hoc guidance. At the same time, special demands are placed on audience members experiencing "experimental" music, as well. Even people with significant prior exposure—performer or audience—may not have a strong analytical or aesthetic framework for a given performance, given the diversity of approaches. This is both exciting and, sometimes, difficult to navigate.

The relationships among composers, performers, and audiences therefore constitute micro-economies for the work of interpretation. All three groups negotiate their connections to the musical work and to one another before,

---

[1] This term has been deployed to describe varying types of music, from fully notated works composed using chance procedures to open-to-interpretation pictographic or text-only "scores." For this project, I focus primarily on music in which one or more substantial aspects are left up to the performer-realizers in order to emphasize the work required of performers, but all manner of indeterminacy is brought into the models introduced below and in each of the following chapters.

[2] See, for example, the account in David Grubbs, *Records Ruin the Landscape: John Cage, the Sixties, and Sound Recording* (Durham, NC: Duke University Press, 2014), 73.

16 INTERPRETIVE LABOR

during, and after performances, and this is most challenging when there is limited precedent tempering expectations. To put it differently, much of the music discussed in this book was meant to surprise and disrupt. While this has many benefits, it also means that its participants were unable to draw on the standardized performance practice and normative expectations of most other "classical" music, such as the Mozart opera discussed in the Introduction. In that case, I was able to infer expectations around musical style and interpretation because I had already encountered similar pieces and because I was intimately familiar with the notational system. In experimental works, performers rarely have this luxury. A demanding form of interpretation, then, becomes necessary to realize the scores.

In the following chapters, I will argue that composer–performer–audience relationships are also reflected in and deeply connected to economies writ large, partly by engaging with emergent theories of labor developed in response to cultural work and affective labor, the proliferation of hidden work as wrought by digital media, and the attendant post-Marxist critiques thereof. Before digging into specific forms of labor and the music-related practices that reveal them, the remainder of this chapter aims to establish the foundation on which interpretive labor—as a concept, and as a politics—stands.

THE THEORETICAL STAKES OF "INTERPRETIVE LABOR"

> The politics of information, the history of knowledge, advance not through a critical negation of false representations but a positive hacking of the virtuality of expression. Representation always mimics but is less than what it represents; expression always differs from but exceeds the raw material of its production.
>
> —McKenzie Wark, *A Hacker Manifesto*[3]

As a framework for investigating music, the concept of Interpretive Labor is a new way of thinking about the actual practices involved in making experimental or avant-garde music. In part, this is because discussions of this repertoire tend to focus on aesthetic questions or on examinations of the compositional techniques employed. These are worthwhile areas of inquiry;

[3] McKenzie Wark, *A Hacker Manifesto* (Cambridge, MA: Harvard University Press, 2004), 91.

however, they do not necessarily account for the demands placed on realizers of experimental music. Performers often invest comparable effort into the performance as do the composers of the score, and arguably more, in some cases—for example, in open-ended text scores that lack even basic instructions or guidelines. In order to examine the phenomenon of this work (and I mean that in the sense of labor, effort, and exertion both physical and cognitive), I will focus on three primary theoretical areas that shape the investigations in the following chapters: first, the question of interpretation itself; second, issues of labor; and finally, the general philosophical and political stance motivating my subsequent inquiry.

On Interpretation

While labor is a central subject of this project, it goes hand-in-hand with an investigation of interpretation. Suggestive of a host of interrelated meanings, from explanation to representation, from signification to translation, interpretation is concerned with meaning itself. The analysis of interpretive procedures, that is, hermeneutics, is necessarily critical to my project. My conception of interpretation is indebted to the work of political scientist Michael Loriaux, who distinguishes between two basic definitions for hermeneutics in its earliest iterations. He writes,

> The first, which one might call "mere translation," places the reader, conceived unproblematically as capable of reading and understanding, before a text that, written in a foreign language or in an allegorical style, is unclear. Hermeneutics in this encounter seeks clarity and accuracy. The second, for which one might, for purposes of distinction, reserve the term "interpretation," places the reader, whose mortality and limitations might be acknowledged, before a text that claims to reveal and clarify a mystery. Hermeneutics in this encounter seeks to disclose *alêtheia*, truth or revelation (from *lêthô*, to be unseen; *lêthê*, a place of oblivion in the underworld).[4]

In what follows, I will maintain a distinction between interpretation and translation, focusing on the former as a dynamic process by which to reveal

---

[4] Michael Loriaux, "Hermeneutics," *The Encyclopedia of Political Thought*. First published 15 September 2014. Wiley-Blackwell. DOI: 10.1002/9781118474396.wbept0465.

18 INTERPRETIVE LABOR

something about a text (literary or otherwise), and translation as a subset of this larger category. In some ways, though, this terminology is imperfect, as one might reasonably argue that translation itself is never a simple matter of replacing text with other text; it, too, requires foundational knowledge and a process of investigation grounded in experience. In the second chapter, translation is investigated in greater detail, and placed into relief against realization in particular. For the purposes of this introductory discussion, though, I will concentrate on interpretation, the broad category that will prove to envelop realization, translation, and other forms of engagement with documented material (that is, texts).

One challenge for musicologists attempting to engage with theories of meaning and interpretation—in whatever form—is that much of the foundational work in hermeneutics was closely tied to literary theory. Therefore, part of my task is to tease out which aspects of these ideas are relevant, and within those, to determine which, if any, go beyond analogy toward directly applicable concepts. To that end, various philosophers, for example, Johann Gottfried von Herder and other 18th-century thinkers, will be brought into the discussion, especially in considering issues of translation. Herder (1744–1803) seems to have been among the first Germanic philosophers to acknowledge that people of different times and places vary greatly in beliefs and concepts.[5] Given this phenomenon, sometimes called the principle of radical difference, interpretation is enormously difficult, especially across significant temporal distance.[6] While this may seem obvious now, it is an important idea to keep in mind, especially in the context of musical performance. This may take the form of gaps in time between composition and realization, or geographical and cultural difference, or even subtle aesthetic leanings. The more dissimilar are a composer and his/her interpreter, the more labor will be involved in decoding the score into a convincing rendition.

My work is more closely connected to 20th-century philosophy, including the work of Martin Heidegger, Michel Foucault, and Jacques Derrida. In *Sein und Zeit* (Being and Time, 1927), Heidegger reveals interpretation as a second phase beyond simply understanding. Here, understanding is itself

---

[5] This idea also, of course, underpins the long history of Relativistic thinking, which had already been developing for centuries by the time of Herder's writings. Cf. Eva Piirimäe, "Berlin, Herder, and the Counter-Enlightenment," *Eighteenth-Century Studies* 49, no. 1 (Fall 2015), 71–76.

[6] Johann Gottfried von Herder, *Philosophical Writings*, trans. and ed. Michael N. Forster (Cambridge: Cambridge University Press, 2002), xvii.

THE VALUE OF INTERPRETIVE LABOR 19

already experiential, not theoretical—it is a way of being-in-the-world.[7] Moving even beyond this experiential understanding, interpretation then becomes a process by which something is "brought to reflective consciousness.... Interpretation makes things, objects, the fabric of the world, appear *as something*, as Heidegger puts it. Still, this *as* is only possible on the background of the world as a totality of practices and intersubjective encounters, of the world that is opened up by *Dasein*'s being understandingly there."[8] In other words, all interpretation is shaped by an individual's place in the world. An example from Barbara Bolt's work illustrates this nicely. The artist Sophie Calle received an email message in which a romantic partner broke up with her. In response, Calle enlisted the help of 107 other women who were asked to help interpret the email. Per Bolt's account, each of the women relied on the skills and experiences they had developed through their interactions with the world, to create an interpreted response in their own idioms. This is not the simple axiom that context matters, however; it begins—according to Heidegger—with our "thrownness" (*"Geworfenheit"*)—our being placed abruptly into the world in ways we didn't choose—and the fact of having been thrown underlies our interactions with the world. I read this to mean that the world already exists around us; we join it and interact with different aspects of it (perhaps multiple worlds) and thus shape the world, which will be joined by others, who will shape it, and so on. It is constantly in motion, always changing us and being changed by us, and this is what makes us *Dasein* (there-being/being-in-the-world). In my view, it is also what makes music and other arts worthwhile: through our artistic endeavors, we shape the world and in turn feed back into the endless cycle of change in which others are also participating.

Bolt argues, "For Heidegger, the central question concerning Being is not the everyday practices of human beings, but rather what such activities and practices can reveal or disclose about the Being of (human) beings."[9] In other words, the main idea is to learn about, and to experience, *Dasein* (therebeing) through the creative and other acts people engage in. What do our actions (artistic and mundane, social and cultural) *reveal* about the nature

---

[7] Jeff Malpas, "Locating Interpretation: The Topography of Understanding in Heidegger and Davidson," *Philosophical Topics* 27, no. 2 (Fall 1999), 130.

[8] Bjørn Ramberg and Kristin Gjesdal, "Hermeneutics," *The Stanford Encyclopedia of Philosophy* (Winter 2014 ed.), ed. Edward N. Zalta. https://plato.stanford.edu/archives/win2014/entries/hermeneutics/

[9] Barbara Bolt, *Heidegger Reframed: Interpreting Key Thinkers for the Arts* (London: I.B. Tauris, 2011), 26.

20 INTERPRETIVE LABOR

of existence? This process of revelation is made possible by working beyond "mere" understanding (experiential knowledge) into acts of interpretation— or, understanding something *as* something. Through experiential interaction, we begin to understand the score of Cornelius Cardew's *Treatise*, for example. Petr Kotík and his new S.E.M. group at Buffalo experienced the piece by engaging with it, by handling it. Beyond that, though, it needed to be interpreted—experienced *as* Cardew's *Treatise*, as a work of art, as a social process of working out what to do with the notation.

This bringing-to-consciousness is particularly effective, I would argue, in compositions with significant indeterminate elements. Performers cannot rely on the habits they have built over years of training, rehearsals, and performances. They have to engage second-order thinking, going beyond a general interaction, and confront the nature of the artwork itself. This engagement is a type of interpretation that is well-suited to Heidegger's philosophy. If and when the piece is experienced *as* art, *as* music, *as* a score, the participant has accepted it into his or her consciousness, and into conversation with all of the other elements of his or her (musical) life. It becomes part of the individual's experience of Being.

Returning to Loriaux, we see that Heidegger's theory of interpretation engages in the sort of socio-cultural work that bridges individuals in creative fields:

> Heidegger's critical hermeneutics endeavors to reawaken the primitive, authentic experience of *Dasein*. It exhorts the interpreter to undertake an exercise in self-reflection and self-application. Unlike Schleiermacher and Dilthey, Heidegger does not wrestle with the philosophical complexities of the hermeneutic circle. Circularity is always already inherent in the primitive care structure of *Dasein*. Circularity is to be embraced as an exercise in reflexivity, as the path to *Eigentlichkeit* [authenticity]. Heidegger's hermeneutics, like Augustine's, is a kind of pilgrimage.[10]

Through the pilgrimage, through entering the circle, an interpreter begins to understand her own situation, which illuminates the ways in which she approaches the challenging score, which later shapes her perceptions of other scores, which informs her general understanding of the repertoire, and so on. This spins out in broader levels and back into more specific aspects of

---

[10] Loriaux, "Hermeneutics."

interpretation, all the while developing both a vocabulary and a basic conceptual framework for the process of interpretation.

In the five "model" chapters that follow, musical actors' voices will be addressed wherever possible, including both musicologists and the composer-performers whose stories make up the material of the project. Cornelius Cardew and Petr Kotík, in particular, have written and spoken thoughtfully on the subject of interpretation, and discussion of their ideas is incorporated into their respective chapters. In addition, music scholars such as Abigail Chantler, Morag Josephine Grant, and Tobias Pontara, all writing for the *International Review of the Aesthetics and Sociology of Music*, have variously engaged with questions of musical versus general hermeneutics, using semiotics to define "experimental" versus "new" music, and critical interpretation, respectively.[11] Their ideas, to some extent, intersect with the issues of interpretation under consideration and will be addressed where appropriate.

On Labor

The question of work within the arts is old and highly complex. As musicologists like Timothy Taylor and Andrea Moore have argued, though, it is perhaps more problematic today, under the guise of neoliberal capitalism, than it ever has been previously.[12] One such challenge is the tension between the traditional institutions of concert music (whose expensive production costs rely on patronage and government subsidies) and the economic realities of the post-bubble early 21st century. Moore notes that "union orchestras in the United States have not been immune to widespread efforts to reduce the economic and political power of trade unions, whose economic protections of their members have been denigrated as standing in the way of economic progress, or as detrimental to workers' 'freedom.'"[13] Likewise, boards of directors for orchestras have cited waning income from investments and declining ticket sales as factors requiring them to reduce the

---

[11] Abigail Chantler, "Revisiting E. T. A. Hoffmann's Musical Hermeneutics," *International Review of the Aesthetics and Sociology of Music [IRASM]* 33, no. 1 (June 2002), 3–30; Morag Josephine Grant, "Experimental Music Semiotics," *IRASM* 34, no. 2 (December 2003), 173–91; Tobias Pontara, "Interpretation, Imputation, Plausibility: Towards a Theoretical Model for Musical Hermeneutics," *IRASM* 46, no. 1 (June 2015), 3–41.

[12] Timothy D. Taylor, *Music and Capitalism: A History of the Present* (Chicago: University of Chicago Press, 2016).

[13] Andrea Moore, "Neoliberalism and the Musical Entrepreneur," *Journal of the Society for American Music* 10, no. 1 (February 2016), 36. See also Robert J. Flanagan, *The Perilous Life of*

22 INTERPRETIVE LABOR

pay and other benefits for their musicians, with even major groups like the New York Philharmonic "run[ning] deficits every season since 2001–02."[14] Union musicians and those who represent them have railed against such cuts. While some top orchestra members claim that high salaries are necessary to attract and retain the best performers, smaller groups are fighting for subsistence-level compensation.[15] American Federation of Musicians (AFM) attorney Kevin Case claims that the situation is "a full-fledged assault on protections for musicians that took decades to achieve." He continues,

> Perhaps most disturbing, however, is the response from some orchestra managers and board chairs to the argument that players, faced with these draconian measures, will pack up and leave. The message is simple and blunt: we don't care. Go ahead and leave. After all, you're totally replaceable; we'll just hire one of those fantastic kids coming out the conservatories. This message is being delivered with stunning candor. The chairman of one major orchestra demanding huge cuts noted the "quite remarkable" number of music-school graduates, characterizing it as "a large supply." Another manager acknowledged a "risk" that his players would "find their way to another place" if forced to accept management's demands, but shrugged it off: "those who can leave will." Yet another board chairman told one departing principal that he wouldn't care unless nine or ten players left—and then, only because it might be "bad PR."[16]

Symphony Orchestras: Artistic Triumphs and Economic Challenges (New Haven, CT: Yale University Press, 2012).

[14] Michael Cooper, "It's Official: Many Orchestras Are Now Charities," *New York Times* online, November 15, 2016, https://www.nytimes.com/2016/11/16/arts/music/its-official-many-orchestras-are-now-charities.html. In Pittsburgh, which saw a 2-month strike in 2016, "the symphony's Board of Trustees Chair Devin McGranahan said in a statement Sept. 30, when the strike began, that a wage reduction was necessary to deal with a financial crisis that could force the symphony to close in mid-2017 when it would be at risk of running out of cash. Symphony officials have said they are facing a $20.4 million deficit over the next five years." Mark Kanny, "Pittsburgh Symphony Strike Eats into Revenue," *Pittsburgh Tribune-Review* online, October 23, 2016, http://triblive.com/aande/music/11347194-74/symphony-strike-musicians.
[15] For example, the Hartford Symphony leadership faced a complaint from the National Labor Relations Board (NLRB) in in 2015 over a proposed cut in "guaranteed performances and rehearsals . . . by about 40 percent for core musicians of the orchestra, dropping their yearly salary from a little over $23,000 to below $15,000. Musicians would also have to be available for daytime rehearsals and performances, which would be a hardship for many musicians who have day jobs." Ray Hardman, "Federal Complaint Says Hartford Symphony Orchestra Failed to Negotiate with Union," WNPR Connecticut online, September 10, 2015, http://wnpr.org/post/federal-complaint-says-hartford-symphony-orchestra-failed-negotiate-union#stream/0.
[16] Case is a violinist, attorney, founder of Case Arts Law, and, since 2015, General Counsel for the International Conference of Symphony and Opera Musicians. Kevin Case, "The Commoditization

THE VALUE OF INTERPRETIVE LABOR   23

In the issues cited here, we feel the urgency of including labor in our engagements with music: without doing so, we risk further detachment from the economic conditions of musical experience, and worse yet, we enable exploitation of musical practitioners. But what is meant by "exploitation" in this context? How is labor to be conceptualized within a theory of interpretation? This text aims to address these questions in the following chapters.

Along with the specific question of musically interpretive work and the attendant risks therein, broader labor issues—especially in creative endeavors—continue to press urgently. In the United States in the 21st century, income inequality is an especially notable problem. The headlines are dismaying: chief executives of corporations, even those that fail to turn a profit, are showered with massive compensation packages including millions of dollars in salaries and bonuses, while the employees doing most of the work receive comparatively little. Among companies on the S&P 500 (a leading market index compiled by Standard & Poor's), average 2014 compensation for U.S. CEOs topped $22 million, or 373 times the salary of the "average production and non-supervisory worker."[17] While the overall ratio has improved somewhat in the last 10 years, a report from the Institute for Policy Studies identifies 100 companies on the S&P 500 where the CEO-to-worker pay gap is over 600-to-1.[18] Some analysts and economists argue that such extravagance is justified in the name of competitiveness, citing the resulting tournament-like environment as a means of fostering employees' contributions to the company.[19] Meanwhile, working Americans in various industries are struggling to make ends meet. Sixteen percent of part-time workers and 4% of full-time employees are classified as "working poor," or those whose incomes remain below the federal poverty level.[20] As

of Symphony Orchestra Musicians" (2012), online at http://www.caseartslaw.com/perch/resources/article-re-commoditization.pdf

[17] Tim Mullaney, "Why Corporate CEO Pay Is So High, and Going Higher," *CNBC*, May 18, 2015, http://www.cnbc.com/2015/05/18/why-corporate-ceo-pay-is-so-high-and-going-higher.html. This has slowed somewhat in the intervening years; as of 2022, median pay was $14.8 million/year. At 6.1% inflation and median pay for workers at those top 500 companies at $77,178/year, though, "it would take that worker 186 years to make what a CEO making the median pay earned just last year." Alexandra Olson, "CEOs Got Smaller Raises: It Would Still Take the Average Worker 2 Lifetimes to Make Their Annual Pay," *NPR NewsHour* (May 31, 2023).
[18] Institute for Policy Studies, "Executive Excess 2023" report (Washington, DC: IPS, 2023).
[19] Andrew D. Henderson and James W. Fredrickson, "Top Management Team Coordination Needs and the CEO Pay Gap: A Competitive Test of Economic and Behavioral Views," *The Academy of Management Journal* 44, no. 1 (February 2001), 98–99.
[20] "Who Are the Working Poor? [2013 data from the Bureau of Labor Statistics]," published by the Center for Poverty Research at the University of California, Davis, http://poverty.ucdavis.edu/faq/who-are-working-poor.

24 INTERPRETIVE LABOR

researchers Howard and Paul Sherman put it, "[in] terms of income, there are two Americas: the enormous class of employees and the tiny class of capitalists."[21] These issues, while less discussed in creative fields, underpin economic problems in these areas—that is, the arts—as well.

Relatedly, with the rapid expansion of Web 2.0, internet users have increasingly created and posted much of the "content" that we now "consume." Back in 1999, chat-room moderators called Community Leaders (CLs) made waves when they asked the U.S. Department of Labor to determine whether they should have been paid by America Online (AOL), for whom they invested hours hosting chat sessions in exchange for free or discounted memberships to the site.[22] When the investigation got dropped, a large group of CLs brought a class-action lawsuit against the company and later settled out of court.[23] Like these moderators, other "volunteer" contributors like bloggers and review-writers have begun banding together to seek compensation for their efforts.[24] In this, I see an important parallel with the fraught economics of musical performance; musicians have long felt the tension between performing "for the love of it" and earning a living wage. Because of the long history of artistic activities as hobbies, lines can easily be blurred between work and play, resulting in exploitation.[25]

At the core, I am interested in labor as a cultural practice, informed by various aspects of economic and social theory. As with my work on interpretation, I aim to develop a promiscuous conceptual framework, as will be made evident throughout the remaining chapters.[26] Some general ideas, though,

---

[21] Howard J. Sherman and Paul D. Sherman, "Why Is This Cycle Different from All Other Cycles?," *Journal of Economic Issues* 42, no. 1 (March 2008), 257.

[22] Lisa Margonelli, "Inside AOL's 'Cyber-Sweatshop,'" *Wired* (October 1, 1999).

[23] According to AOL's own *Annual Report*, "The parties to all of the Community Leader-related lawsuits have agreed to settle the lawsuits on terms that did not result in a material incremental expense or material payment by the Company in 2009. The court granted preliminary approval of the settlement on February 2, 2010. The Company does not expect to make any additional payments related to this matter." America Online, *Annual Report* (2009), p. 96. Another report lists the settlement at $15 million. Mark W. Batten, Elise M. Bloom, and Fredric C. Leffler, "Misclassifying Workers as Independent Contractors: The Price of Independence," Proskauer Rose LLP, 26 (online at https://www.proskauer.com/insights/download-pdf/1691).

[24] Brendan James, "Unpaid Huffington Post Bloggers Actually Do Want to Get Paid," *International Business Times* (February 18, 2016); Laura Northrup, "Yelp Reviewers File Class Action Lawsuit, Want to Get Paid," *Consumerist* (August 12, 2014).

[25] This certainly may be financial, but is more commonly socio-cultural exploitation, an expansion of the classical Marxist idiom discussed below.

[26] In addition to mirroring the diverse aspects of experimental music, this approach is pursued in an effort to achieve balance between positivist data presentation and critical sociological theorizing, or what Dahlhaus might judge "vulgar Marxist" analysis. Some reasons for adopting this eclectic methodology are outlined usefully in James Hepokoski, "The Dahlhaus Project and Its Extra-Musicological Sources," *19th-Century Music* 14, no. 3 (Spring 1991), 244–45.

shape the more detailed analyses in Chapters 2 through 6; first among these is a soft spot for Marx's critique of the structures of capitalism and the abuses of power engendered therein. Sociologist Mathieu Desan writes:

> [F]or Marx capital is doubly social in that it entails in the first instance a social relation of exploitation and in the second instance the totality of social relations that reproduce this fundamental relation's conditions of possibility. The concept of capital thus does not refer exclusively to the "economic" sphere. In fact, Marx's point is to demonstrate how even apparently straightforward "economic" phenomena are constitutively social, political, and cultural. So, whereas capital may appear here as money and there as means of production, Marx's concept of capital allows us to pierce this fetishized form and to see capital not as a thing, but as a process; and not just a process, but a process of exploitation; and, finally, not only a process of exploitation, but also a social totality.[27]

This conception of Marx's work is key for my project. The social, political, and cultural are not separate from economic forces nor are they even secondary to them; rather, they are inextricably entwined. I take this a step further, applying this to the more general concept of labor. While there are some interesting questions to consider regarding financial imbalances within experimental-music performance, most of my work in the following chapters centers on the issue of recognition: a decidedly social, political, and cultural problem. This recognition may lead to greater financial rewards (in the form of commissions, additional performance opportunities, etc.) but, more commonly, it is symbolic cultural capital that comes into play, as will be discussed in detail throughout. Labor, as I see it, cannot be separated from its social context, despite efforts by some economists to sanitize issues of work. To modify Desan, then, Marx's concept of *labor* "allows us to pierce this fetishized form and to see [labor] not as a thing, but as a process; and not just a process, but a process of exploitation; and, finally, not only a process of exploitation, but also a social totality." This emphasis on the human-interactive perhaps explains Marxism's continuing prominence in studies of the social and cultural.

---

[27] Mathieu Hikaru Desan, "Bourdieu, Marx, and Capital: A Critique of the Extension Model," *Sociological Theory* 31, no. 4 (December 2013), 322.

26 INTERPRETIVE LABOR

Management researchers Michael Rowlinson and John Hassard have argued that "Marxism has been in retreat" since the Left's high point of 1968, "when it seemed that the specter of communism had returned to haunt not just Western capitalism but state socialism as well."[28] In the period roughly coinciding with the musical experimentation discussed throughout this project, political economists were developing the field of "labor process theory," the germ of which is found in Marx, but a revival of which was set off by Harry Braverman's response to Baran and Sweezy's *Monopoly Capital* (1968).[29] In short, it differs from orthodox Marxism in its rejection of some basic aspects—namely, the labor theory of value (LTV) and a predictive "law" about profit rates falling—but at its core, it maintains the anti-management stance of Marx.[30]

In large part, what I am talking about is "cultural capital," a concept famously theorized by Pierre Bourdieu. As he defines it, capital is "the set of actually usable resources and powers,"[31] and later, capital is "accumulated labor . . . which, when appropriated on a private, i.e., exclusive, basis by agents or groups of agents, enables them to appropriate social energy in the form of reified or living labor."[32] Essentially, this is a conception of capital as a source of power, which does reflect the imbalance central to Marx's political economy. As Desan notes, though:

[W]hereas for Marx capital denotes the social relation of exploitation—that is, the extraction of surplus-labor—contained within the production of commodities, for Bourdieu capital designates an object insofar as, due to its unequal distribution within a field, it is capable of accruing benefits to its owner. In other words, capital, for Bourdieu, simply designates an exploitable object, not a social relation of exploitation. This remains a fetishized

---

[28] Michael Rowlinson and John Hassard, "Marxist Political Economy, Revolutionary Politics, and Labor Process Theory," *International Studies of Management and Organization* 30, no. 4 (Winter 2000–2001), 85.

[29] David A. Spencer, "Braverman and the Contribution of Labour Process Analysis to the Critique of Capitalist Production—Twenty-Five Years On," *Work, Employment and Society* 14, no. 2 (June 2000), 223–43.

[30] Rowlinson and Hassard, "Marxist Political Economy," 87.

[31] Pierre Bourdieu, *Distinction: A Social Critique of the Judgement of Taste* [1979], trans. R. Nice (Cambridge, MA: Harvard University Press, 1984), 114.

[32] Pierre Bourdieu, "The Forms of Capital," in *Handbook of Theory and Research for the Sociology of Education*, ed. J.G. Richardson, trans. R. Nice (New York: Greenwood Press, 1986), 241. In other writings, such as *Reproduction in Education, Society, and Culture*, with Passeron [1970], Bourdieu offers slightly different explanations of capital.

conception of capital as a thing. . . . [B]y capital Bourdieu seems to mean simply any resource insofar as it yields power.[33]

So, while Bourdieu has perhaps wrongly been recognized as extending Marxist economic theory into the socio-cultural sphere (because Marx was already concerned with socio-cultural issues; his entire theory seeks to explain them),[34] Bourdieu's work does bring to the surface the problem of power. Likewise, if we excuse Bourdieu's imprecise use of terms like "capital" and "profit" and either consider them as metaphors or substitute less overburdened terms, his ideas become increasingly effective at explaining social relations such as those discussed in this text. By conceiving of capital in this broader way, that is, as a social relation, we focus on the question of power and hierarchy, which will be especially important when theorizing the relationship between Stockhausen and Cardew, for example, or any other composer–realizer relationship in which one party feels exploited in some way. Bourdieu's cultural capital is not just recognition of one's talents or social standing; it is also a component in the system of social resources—the socio-cultural economy—and as such, already always suggests the problem of hierarchy.

Finally, referents for capital and labor obviously shift over time. Marx's primary frame of reference was industrial production; now, in the information age, we are faced with knowledge as a form of (or, more radically, replacement for) capital. Media theorist McKenzie Wark argues,

That the vectoralist class [that is, those who control information] has replaced capital as the dominant exploiting class can be seen in the form that the leading corporations take. [. . .] Their power lies in monopolising intellectual property—patents, copyrights and trademarks—and the means of reproducing their value—the vectors of communication. The privatisation of information becomes the dominant, rather than a subsidiary, aspect of commodified life.[35]

---

[33] Desan, "Bourdieu, Marx, and Capital," 331–32.

[34] Cf. Jacques Bidet and Anne Bailey, "Questions to Pierre Bourdieu," *Critique of Anthropology* 13–14 (1979), 203–8; Robert Boyer, "Pierre Bourdieu, a Theoretician of Change? The View from Regulation Theory" [2004], in *The Institutions of the Market: Organizations, Social Systems, and Governance*, ed. A. Abner and N. Beck (Oxford: Oxford University Press, 2008), 348–97; Desan, "Bourdieu, Marx, and Capital," 318–42.

[35] Wark, *A Hacker Manifesto*, 12.

28 INTERPRETIVE LABOR

We might, then, think of musical knowledge as "capital" (both in terms of cultural capital and monetary wealth). Musicians who are financially and/or popularly successful become the bearers of knowledge. They are the experts, the ones who have trained and mastered the craft of performance. But— and this is an important distinction—do they *own* this information? Unlike Wark's "vectoralist" class, performers typically lack the structural and institutional means to actually control the movement of information.[36] Rather, music directors and other coordinators typically play this role. In selecting repertoire for concerts and festivals, they determine what musical information enters into the public discourse and becomes part of the known repertoire. While there are certainly exceptions, as will be discussed further in the following chapters, the labor of directors tends to be recognized more readily than does that of performers, and in this way, they echo imbalances in power between those who create content (e.g., computer programs, news stories, even restaurant reviews) and those who control its dissemination (e.g., multi-national media conglomerates). This is not to say that directors of new-music festivals are particularly well compensated (or even fairly recognized, necessarily) but that any hierarchical relationship has the potential for an imbalance of labor. Theoretical questions like those of Wark, Bourdieu, and Marx remind us to be on guard for these issues: Who has the power? Who is doing the work? Thus, the conception of labor running through this project is rather fluid: yes, I refer to actual financial economy, but also to its metaphorical extension—political economy, recognition, cultural capital, and so on.

One event that provides a framework for contemporary labor history is a 1977 conference on international labor, including the "work humanization" movement. At that time, as reported by the Industrial Relations Research Association, companies were beginning to make efforts to improve the quality of life for their employees during the workday. One key component of this discourse is "codetermination," which in this case means that workers are represented in decisions made at the enterprise level. Here, George Elton Mayo's transformative work plays into the post-Taylorist economy: as Barbash notes, "Mayo described a social man interested in work as a collaborative experience."[37] For chamber ensembles of any type, collaboration and

---

[36] To some extent, they do have this power, passing along knowledge through music lessons; this maintains a performance practice through oral tradition. However, I have in mind a more expansive type of control, in which musical knowledge is transmitted more broadly.

[37] At the same time, Mayo evidently limited his findings to specific types of workers who fit his own biases; for more, see Melissa Gregg, *Counterproductive: Time Management in the Knowledge*

codetermination would seem to be ideal aspects of intra-group relations, and perhaps are even more pronounced when facing works with unconventional notation.

In media studies, researchers address the role of digital technologies on new forms of labor, and their ideas are useful for thinking about new directions in theories of work. For example, I will later adapt elements of hacker and gamer theory—such as questions of hierarchy, subversion, and play—into productive theories about the activities and mindsets of experimental musicians. In a 2009 conference, participants met at the New School to discuss labor as manifested in online activity. One presenter, Ayhan Aytes, traces the function of cognitive labor[38] from the mid-19th century to the present, arguing that since cognitive tasks can now be fragmented and divided through digital crowdsourcing, the workers performing these tasks are faced with a "cultural state of exception" in which they are detached from the results of their work and therefore outside the realm of community.[39] This helps to shape an understanding of the division of labor between composer and performer: to what degree is the information fragmented, and to what extent does that foster or discourage a sense of cooperation between them? That problem is most obvious in a work such as Cage's *Atlas Eclipticalis*, where the actions taken by the orchestra musicians can be overridden by whoever controls the mixing board.[40] Of course, this merely represents one end of the spectrum, with true collaboration on the other end and a range of intermediary situations in between. Aytes's formulation provides one way of thinking about the various levels of cooperation between and among the participants in indeterminate music.

Economy (Durham, NC: Duke University Press, 2018), especially 40–47. Jack Barbash, "The Work Humanization Movement: U.S. and European Experience Compared," in *Labor Relations in Advanced Industrial Societies: Issues and Problems*, ed. Benjamin Martin and Everett M. Kassalow (Washington, D.C.: Carnegie Endowment for International Peace, 1980), 184.

[38] That is, mentally taxing work, such as solving calculus problems or coding complicated computer programs. Philip Kitcher's work addresses the ways cognitive labor is divided within scientific communities, and has served as a springboard for research in the social sciences and philosophy of science, in particular. Philip Kitcher, "The Division of Cognitive Labor," *The Journal of Philosophy* 87, no. 1 (January 1990), 5–22.

[39] Ayhan Aytes, "Return of the Crowds: Mechanical Turk and Neoliberal States of Exception," in *Digital Labor: The Internet as Playground and Factory*, ed. Trebor Scholz (New York: Routledge, 2013), 79–97.

[40] See Benjamin Piekut's account in "When Orchestras Attack! John Cage Meets the New York Philharmonic," in *Experimentalism Otherwise: The New York Avant-Garde and Its Limits* (Berkeley: University of California Press, 2011), 20–64.

30 INTERPRETIVE LABOR

Likewise, Michel Bauwens's account of peer-commons production raises interesting questions for experimental-music performance. He calls for a model of a peer-to-peer network that builds and sustains a commonly held knowledge base, which could have useful applications in developing a performance practice (or practices) for indeterminate music. If we think of performance practice as a form of production—which I find to be a valuable and necessary shift of perspective in this project—it seems fitting to substitute it in Bauwens's conditions for a new mode of operation, which he defines as "the crisis of the old model of production and the availability of a working alternative that can perform better while solving a number of systemic problems plaguing the current dominant form of production."[41] Through the detailed descriptions of compositions and the ways in which they have been realized, this text and others like it contribute to an emergent working alternative; namely, a collaboratively produced body of knowledge that will—I hope—be useful to individuals and ensembles grappling with this repertoire. I envision in the future a set of documents and other resources, including this book, that can be consulted as reference material for a whole spectrum of indeterminate compositions: some form of collectively produced archive of experimental-music practices and approaches.

EXPERIMENTAL NOTATION: AN IMPETUS FOR INTERPRETIVE LABOR

Before the proliferation of indeterminacy in the middle of the 20th century, there were a few scattered efforts, although most were likely novelty acts: choose-your-own-adventure constructions meant to entertain amateur European musicians in their parlors.[42] Later, with the simultaneous development of experimental forms and the new notational systems to support them, the 20th century saw a dramatic and rapid increase in chance and other indeterminate explorations.

In the years leading up to the works discussed in detail in this text, a handful of influential composers began to experiment with indeterminacy. Those associated with the so-called New York School took varying approaches, from new forms of nonspecific notation to works using carefully

---

[41] Michel Bauwens, "Thesis on Digital Labor in an Emerging P2P Economy," in *Digital Labor*, 210.

[42] Stephen A. Hedges, "Dice Music in the Eighteenth Century," *Music and Letters* 59, no. 2 (April 1978), 180–87.

THE VALUE OF INTERPRETIVE LABOR   31

managed chance operations. Earle Brown engaged thoughtfully with the issue of notation, arguing that the recent excursions into graphic and other pictorial notations were actually part of a long history of shorthand types, rather than a break with history—aside from the most recent attempts at strict control.[43] His ideas were brought to life in *Folio* (1952–53), a set of compositions with unique visual representations, and in the following year's *4 Systems*, a set of lines of varying lengths and thicknesses accompanied by the following instructions: "May be played in any sequence, either side up, at any tempo. The continuous lines from far left to far right define the outer limits of the keyboard. Thickness may indicate dynamics or clusters." Brown identified Charles Ives and Henry Cowell as important predecessors to his own solutions to the problems of conventional notation, and rightly so, but things reached a tipping point in the 1950s when composers and performers began engaging with experimental systems of writing in earnest.

Ideas such as mobile (or "open") form were taking hold elsewhere. The Third Piano Sonata (1956–57) of Pierre Boulez was planned with five movements, to be arranged into "eight possible trajectories," and the portions that have been published include optional passages, while still maintaining close control over the musical material.[44] Likewise, Karlheinz Stockhausen had already made some forays into this area, most famously with *Klavierstuck XI* (1956). Its score is made up of 19 self-contained sections of notated music, the order of which is supposed to be selected at random by the performer during the performance. To connect the sections, the pianist is bound to the tempo, dynamics, and type of attack indicated at the end of the previously played section.[45] Notably, while the performer is able to control the order of things, the composition has a finite number of possible realizations, and the material is thus primarily limited by the composer. Of course, much more has been written about such developments undertaken

---

[43] Earle Brown, "The Notation and Performance of New Music," *The Musical Quarterly* 72, no. 2 (1986), 180–201. This article is "an edited version of lectures given by Earle Brown in Darmstadt in 1964."

[44] Zbigniew Granat, "Open Form and the 'Work-Concept': Notions of the Musical Work after Serialism" (PhD diss., Boston University, 2002), 40.

[45] Galia Hanoch-Roe, "Musical Space and Architectural Time: Open Scoring versus Linear Processes," *IRASM* 34, no. 2 (December 2003), 148. Also, as blogger Ed Chang points out, "The use of random eye-contact does bring a few questions to mind, though . . . I think a performer would naturally have certain 'non-random tendencies' after he/she has become familiar with all of the [sections]. Is it possible for a pianist to be truly random after becoming intimately familiar with the piece? Or perhaps, Stockhausen expects sub-conscious factors and familiarity to affect the choices." Ed Chang, "Klavierstuck XI," *Stockhausen—Sounds in Space* (blog), June 12, 2015, http://stockhaus enspace.blogspot.com/2015/06/klavierstuck-xi.html.

32 INTERPRETIVE LABOR

in both the United States and in Europe in the 1950s; in brief, though, indeterminacy was very much becoming part of the vernacular of musicians associated with avant-gardism.[46] In the early scholarship, writers fell into two primary "camps": composers who issued defenses of their work, and critics who struggled to situate those works within some framework with which they were equipped to assess them. In the 1960s, composers such as Earle Brown, Roger Reynolds, and Cornelius Cardew explained what indeterminacy and chance meant to them, and even into the following decade, terms were being defined in contradictory ways.[47] "Indeterminacy," "aleatory," and "chance"—related but not synonymous terms—were gradually explored and codified, yet even as of 2023 the primary English-language music reference work lacks an entry for "indeterminacy," and fails to provide a sufficient account in the article on "aleatory" to which the reader is referred.[48]

That reference text notwithstanding, this repertoire is experiencing a surge in scholarship, as evinced by numerous well-researched, theoretically engaging recent works. In fact, researchers of experimental music have enacted a much-needed shift toward diverse, critical engagement. The 1990s saw the inauguration of a significant debate over the relationship between improvisation and the experimental art-music establishment. Composer/performer/scholar George Lewis's article on postwar "real-time forms of musicality" signaled this change, taking musicologists to task for limiting discourse on experimentalism to "a particular group of postwar music-makers who come almost exclusively from either European or European-American heritage."[49]

---

[46] Lukas Foss, "The Changing Composer–Performer Relationship: A Monologue and a Dialogue," *Perspectives of New Music* 1, no. 2 (Spring 1963), 45–53; James Pritchett, "The Development of Chance Techniques in the Music of John Cage, 1950–1956" (PhD diss., New York University, 1988); William G. Harbinson, "Performer Indeterminacy and Boulez's Third Sonata," *Tempo*, New Series, no. 169 (50th Anniversary 1939–1989, June 1989), 16–20; Michael Nyman, *Experimental Music: Cage and Beyond*, Music in the Twentieth Century (Cambridge: Cambridge University Press, 1999).

[47] See Brown, "The Notation and Performance of New Music," 180; Roger Reynolds, "Indeterminacy: Some Considerations," *Perspectives of New Music* 4, no. 1 (Autumn/Winter 1965), 136; Cornelius Cardew, "Notation: Interpretation, etc.," *Tempo*, New Series, no. 58 (Summer 1961), 21; and Frank W. Hoogerwerf, "Cage contra Stravinsky, or Delineating the Aleatory Aesthetic," *IRASM* 7, no. 2 (December 1976), 235–47.

[48] Paul Griffiths, "Aleatory," *Grove Music Online, Oxford Music Online* (Oxford University Press).

[49] Lewis, "Improvised Music after 1950," 101. The debate did have some predecessors. As early as 1963 improvisation was being discussed by composers; see the report on the Festival of Contemporary Arts at the University of Illinois, which included a roundtable called "Approaches to Improvisation." Ben Johnston, "Letter from Urbana," *Perspectives of New Music* 2, no. 1 (Autumn–Winter 1963), 137–41. See also the lengthy 1982 forum on improvisation in *Perspectives of New Music*, with contributions from a number of active composer-performer-improvisers. Barney Childs, Christopher Hobbs, Larry Austin, Eddie Prévost, Keith Rowe, Derek Bailey, Harold Budd, Lee Kaplan, Vinny Golea, Elliott Schwartz, Larry Solomon, Malcolm Goldstein, John Silber, Davey

It is this debate that seems, at least in part, to have helped to steer experimental music studies toward its current, more inclusive state. In subsequent years, scholars have taken up the call for a corrective, helping to put improvisation, indeterminacy, and experimentalism into conversation in ways not previously attempted. For example, certain strands of jazz and avant-garde art music coexisted—apparently happily—within articles on improvisation by David Borgo and Matthew Sansom.[50] Of course, accounts of improvisation have a long history within ethnomusicology and its predecessor, comparative musicology, including in journal articles, monographs, and edited collections.[51] As stated by Bruno Nettl, improvisation is "music making with a special immediacy," and as such it inspires a wealth of approaches.[52] Several of these have been published in the field's leading journals, including articles on a vast array of geographic locations and practices.[53] Oxford has also published two volumes on improvisation in their handbook series, under the umbrella of "critical improvisation studies." As noted by the publisher, these texts include a "wide range of perspectives, with contributions from more than 60 scholars working in architecture, anthropology, art history, computer science, cognitive science, cultural studies, dance, economics, education, ethnomusicology, film, gender studies, history, linguistics, literary theory, musicology," and 10 other fields.[54] Clearly, the study of improvisation has undergone a significant expansion.

Williams and Pauline Oliveros, "Forum: Improvisation," *Perspectives of New Music* 21, no. 1/2 (Autumn 1982–Summer 1983), 26–111.

[50] David Borgo, "Negotiating Freedom: Values and Practices in Contemporary Improvised Music," *Black Music Research Journal* 22, no. 2 (Autumn 2002), 165–88; Matthew Sansom, "Imaging Music: Abstract Expressionism and Free Improvisation," *Leonardo Music Journal* 11 (2001), 33.

[51] See, for example, Gabriel Solis and Bruno Nettl, eds., *Musical Improvisation: Art, Education, and Society* (Urbana: University of Illinois Press, 2009); Bruno Nettl, ed. with Melinda Russell, *In the Course of Performance: Studies in the World of Musical Improvisation* (Chicago: University of Chicago Press, 1998); Paul Berliner, *Thinking in Jazz: The Infinite Art of Improvisation* (Chicago: University of Chicago Press, 1994); and Ingrid Monson, *Saying Something: Jazz Improvisation and Interaction* (Chicago: University of Chicago Press, 1996).

[52] Bruno Nettl, preface to Gabriel Solis and Bruno Nettl, eds., *Musical Improvisation: Art, Education, and Society*, ix.

[53] See, for example, Laudan Nooshin, "The Song of the Nightingale: Processes of Improvisation in dastgāh Segāh (Iranian Classical Music)," *British Journal of Ethnomusicology* 7 (January 1998), 69–116; Rolf Groesbeck, "Cultural Constructions of Improvisation in Tāyampaka, a Genre of Temple Instrumental Music in Kerala, India," *Ethnomusicology* 43, no. 1 (Winter 1999), 1–30; Ali Jihad Racy, "The Many Faces of Improvisation: The Arab Taqāsīm as a Musical Symbol," *Ethnomusicology* 44, no. 2 (Spring 2000), 302–20; Nicholas Gray, "Of One Family? Improvisation, Variation, and Composition in Balinese Gendér Wayang," *Ethnomusicology* 54, no. 2 (Spring/Summer 2010), 224–56; and Hettie Malcomson, "Cuban Flute Style: Interpretation and Improvisation," *Ethnomusicology Forum* 24, no. 3 (Fall 2015), 478–80, among others.

[54] George E. Lewis and Benjamin Piekut, eds., *The Oxford Handbook of Critical Improvisation Studies, Volume I* (Oxford: Oxford University Press, 2016).

34 INTERPRETIVE LABOR

Outside of improvisation studies, as well, scholars have engaged with diverse theoretical and methodological schemes for experimental or avant-garde art-music. In her 2008 dissertation, Rebecca Kim outlines approaches to scholarship on John Cage in particular, noting a marked uptick since the composer's death in 1992 and welcoming a critical turn that has shaped my own thinking about Cage and others.[55] Benjamin Piekut's work, both in articles and in the volume *Experimentalism Otherwise*, has helped to expand the subfield of experimental music studies.[56] I most admire that he takes seriously the activities of so-called experimental musicians, seeing them as worthy of serving as iterations of significant theoretical concerns. Elsewhere, Tamara Levitz's work opens up experimental music studies to issues of embodiment: the physical circumstances of performance and the ways in which its physicality engenders meaning in both music and dance.[57] This concern for materiality, likewise, informs my own work, especially as it relates to both physical and financial economic conditions of composition and performance.

This project also necessitates careful consideration of the types of notation with which performers are faced, and the ways those systems place new demands on their interpreters. Numerous aspects of experimental-music performance function as oral traditions and are thus absent from the notation. Within any improvisatory/indeterminate practice, significant components of the work remain outside the scope of its written record. Even those parts that do become committed to paper serve, as Amy Stillman argues, both prescriptive and descriptive aims, noting: "musical texts are capable of entextualizing different states of musical expression—of ideas to be realized, conveyed prescriptively, as well as practices engaged in the process of realization, conveyed descriptively."[58] Accounts of musical notation, especially those that attempt to capture traditions with strong oral/aural traditions, require thoughtful treatment. A brief overview of notational systems is set out below, with more detailed discussions of specific pieces contained within each of the "model" chapters that follow.

---

[55] Kim, "In No Uncertain Musical Terms," 3–20.

[56] Piekut, *Experimentalism Otherwise*.

[57] This is a particularly useful direction for Cage's work, given the close relationship between modern dance and his compositions. Tamara Levitz, "David Tudor's Corporeal Imagination," presented at the Getty Research Institute Symposium, "The Art of David Tudor" (2001) and "Syvilla Fort's Africanist Modernism," 123–49.

[58] Amy Ku'uleialoha Stillman, "Textualizing Hawaiian Music," *American Music* 23, no. 1 (Spring 2005), 90.

The most comprehensive text to date is Andrea Valle's *Contemporary Music Notation: Semiotic and Aesthetic Aspects*, which engages closely with the music of 1950–70.[59] That said, as of this writing, I would argue that the notation *is* the literature of much of this repertoire, in much the same way that one might study the poetry or drawings of an ancient era. Based on extant sources, I identify five main types of scores used in experimental or avant-garde repertoire: mobile, graphic, figural, poetic, and verbal.[60] Since there are discrepancies among scholars regarding the labels for such systems, the following suggests some definitions and representative works.[61] First, mobile (or modular) scores are most similar to conventional common-practice-period notation. Sections of music are fully notated (meaning the music is represented through symbols including staves, clefs, noteheads and stems, dynamic markings, accidentals, and so on). Instead of reading the score continuously from left to right, though, the various sections may be reordered according to instructions given by the composer, or as determined by the performer. A frequently cited example of this type is Stockhausen's *Klavierstuck XI* (1956).

Graphic scores, like conventional and mobile scores, involve a visual field that represents both time (usually horizontal) and pitch (vertical), but leave other parameters unspecified. These works may be notated on a graph, such as Morton Feldman's *Projection 1*, in which relative pitch is indicated through the use of small squares and rectangles inside boxes. The level of indeterminacy in this system might at first suggest a different kind of relationship between sign and action, and to some degree, that is correct. Instead of each symbol representing a specific audible result (for example, a short sound on the pitch A played pizzicato and quietly on a violin), it now represents a range of possibilities. Depending on the specific composition, this range may be more or less open. In *Emmett Williams's Ear* by Dick Higgins, the score consists of small images stamped on staff paper. While the pictograms of hearts and stars may require imaginative interpretation, their placement

---

[59] Andrea Valle, *Contemporary Music Notation: Semiotic and Aesthetic Aspects*, trans. Angela Maria Arnone (Torino: De Sono Associazione per la Musica, 2018).

[60] These are in addition to the standardized "Western art music" notation that has become relatively codified. Of course, a wide array of sophisticated notational systems have been in use across the world for centuries; the focus here is on types of writing that are most prevalent in the repertoire under discussion in the following chapters.

[61] Sources for these works include the John Cage Collection, Northwestern University Music Library; the Charlotte Moorman Collection, Deering Library of Special Collections at Northwestern University; and "MsC 518: Manuscript Register, Alternative Traditions in the Contemporary Arts, The A. M. Fine Collection," Special Collections Department, University of Iowa Libraries.

36 INTERPRETIVE LABOR

still indicates pitch and temporal placement. As in conventional notation, the score as a whole represents a prescriptive document, translatable from visual cues into audible sounds, and the relationship maintains a correlation between the horizontal and vertical axes.

In contrast, what I call figural notation is a visual representation in which images are not bound by a pitch/time grid. A beautiful example is Toshi Ichiyanagi's *The Field*, rendered in embossed paper with performance notes. More cryptic, because it lacks instructions, is Albert Fine's *Supermarket Song for George Brecht*. That score consists of small abstract drawings, along with stamps from a grocery store. The manuscript is drawn on a postcard which reads, "this piece is for the same orchestration as Mahler's 8th, or for george brecht—AF."[62] In these compositions, the relationship between sign and action becomes yet more tenuous. Without being tethered to pitch and time, the performer assumes great responsibility for devising a means of interpretation.

Poetic scores consist of text that, much like a figural score, suggests some abstract idea or state of mind, but does not directly prescribe an action. *Dream*, by Richard Maxfield, reads, "You will/ I am going to mind the rainbow/ The I." In both figural and poetic notations, the sign of the score is evocative rather than direct. Finally, verbal scores also make use of text, but are prescriptive. Examples range from the charming (Nam June Paik, *Half-Time*)[63] to the absurd (again Nam June Paik, *Gala Music for John Cage's 50th Birthday*)[64] to the silly but harmless (Alison Knowles, *Salad*).[65] The imperative tone—the fact of its prescriptiveness—removes the sign altogether. If understood as direct instructions for action (and this is open to some debate), these works have no need of a sign. There is no act of interpretive translation between some representative symbol and some related but distinct action, except in the nominal sense that language is representative. In line with other

---

[62] Albert M. Fine, Series II, folder A-191, John Cage Collection, Northwestern University Music Library (n.d.).

[63] "half-time/ or/ a piece for the peace./ play on the first July/ 12 o'clock noon (Greenwitch mean time)/ the tonika-accord of c. major/ for/ 10 minutes./ thinking that/ someone, somewhere/ in the world/ is/ playing/ exactly same time/ exactly same sounds." All spelling and punctuation as in the original.

[64] The piece begins, "on monday sleep with elisabeth taylor/ on tuesday sleep with brigitte bardot/ on wednesday sleep with sophia loren/ on thursday sleep with gina lorobrigitta/ on friday sleep with pascale petit/ on satur day sleep with malyrin monroe." All spelling and punctuation as in the original.

[65] The manuscript is a portion of a notepad with hand-written, detailed instructions (for specific named performers) on how to prepare a vegetable salad in the performance space.

experimental repertories, works using these notational systems are not necessarily performable as written.

One additional system encountered is the schematic. Several composers, including Max Neuhaus and Frederic Rzewski, developed methods for documenting various technological components used in their works, such as loudspeakers, circuitry, and electronic amplifiers. These, I would argue, are not musical scores in the sense applied above. They signify a static arrangement of physical artifacts. If nothing else, a musical work requires sound in time; therefore, a musical score must suggest some aspect of temporality.[66] Of course, these categories fail to account for the numerous works that occupy the fringes and borders of multiple score types; in the piece *Snows*, for example, artist Carolee Schneeman uses a timeline with verbal and pictographic indications. However, it does seem useful to establish a base-line classification, from which notational systems can be further grouped in analogue to Peirce's semiotic.[67] If graphic notation is analogous to an icon—is self-resembling in its visual map of pitch and time—then the other score types can be assessed as well. Mobile and common-practice notation suggest both icons and symbols: within the pitch/time grid, there is no actual connection between a dot on a staff and the sound of the note, but we recognize the relationship because it is conventional to do so. Finally, figural and poetic scores might be indices of their sounds. They bear no resemblance to their objects, but have a real connection to them because performers make it so.

What these notational explorations do have in common is that they all are a type of subversion of the conventional understanding of a musical score. Each type and each work threaten to destabilize the "Western Art Music" literary paradigm, and with it, the primacy of the composer as an authority figure. Thus, it was not only experimental sounds and performance practices but also the notation used to spark those sounds and practices, that constituted a form of knowing rebellion—a type of hacking—among the avant-garde.

***

To a large extent, in this text I am attempting to marry ethno/musicology, hermeneutics, and critical theory into an account that accurately and

---

[66] Again, the definition of music has a fraught and fascinating history, especially under the weight of the mid-century challenges represented in the repertoire under investigation here. I adopt the "sound in time" parameter in keeping with what tends toward a broadly inclusive definition.

[67] Charles Sanders Peirce, "A Sketch of Logical Critics," in *The Essential Peirce: Selected Philosophical Writings, Vol. 2 (1893–1913)*, ed. the Peirce Edition Project (Bloomington and Indianapolis: Indiana University Press, 1998), 460–61.

38   INTERPRETIVE LABOR

fairly represents the practices of hard-working experimental musicians. As Habermas argued, hermeneutics needs critical theory. It is not universal, as Gadamer had argued; it needs a standard of validity, by which it can "serve the purpose of emancipation and social liberation."[68] My approach may often be descriptive and taxonomic, but the spirit of my work owes much to Derrida's account of the always-provisional nature of meaning. "The word, the *logos*, is the bearer of traces that implicate it in a textual, contextual, and intertextual network of signifieds that forever 'haunt' the text. The text in context engenders multiple interpretations, rather than one 'universally correct' interpretation. And yet, though the network submerges expression in equivocation, it is the condition of possibility of the text's ability to convey meaning."[69] As in linguistic texts, meaning in musical texts is also always provisional, deferred in time, and open to playful interpretation; this will be argued (explicitly and not) throughout the following chapters. In addition, the actual circumstances of interpretive work can be understood in terms of the hermeneutics of suspicion shaped by Marx, Nietzsche, and Freud ("the world, as a web of human meaning and practice, is saturated by illusions and systematic self-deception. If human being is self-interpretative by nature, the aim of interpretation is not simply to disclose the possibilities for a more authentic existence but to uncover the *systemic or social mechanisms* through which the logic of self-deception is sustained.")[70] What kinds of deceptions are enabled through this work will be teased out in the following chapters.

Some useful questions to keep in mind throughout this text are these: Where is the indeterminacy? Who created it and what does it require? Who has to deal with it, why was it used, and what kind of indeterminacy is it? The answers indicate where we can find the labor, the *work*. The theory of Interpretive Labor can be boiled down into a set of guiding questions:

- Who creates the indeterminacy and who has to respond to it?
- What tools are available to the interpreter(s)?
- How, and how well, has the interpreter been prepared for this work?
- What kind of recognition/reward is granted in exchange for the work?
- Is this recognition/reward commensurate with the labor required/ expected?

---

[68] Ramberg and Gjesdal, "Hermeneutics."
[69] Loriaux, "Hermeneutics."
[70] Emphasis added. Kristin Gjesdal, "Hermeneutics," *Encyclopedia of Political Theory*, ed. Mark Bevir, vol. 2 (Thousand Oaks, CA: SAGE Reference, 2010), 618–19.

Wherever a text is intentionally left incomplete (for example, in the Basic Score of Stockhausen's *Carré*, the chance procedures used by Kotík, the ambiguous notation of Cardew), there is some kind of work that has to be done to translate the text into a sounding thing. In some cases, this is done by the composer (Kotík working through his own chance-based systems); in others, by collaborators (Stockhausen/Cardew); and in still others, by performers (as in Cardew's *Treatise*). How do their demands and expectations differ based on this idea? Can we interpret that to say something about their personalities, aesthetics, assumptions, identities? What does it say about each piece, each practice, and each artist to consider on whom they relied to do the work?

At its core, this project is grounded in a simple belief: that people deserve to be recognized and compensated for the work that they do. What exactly that means will be examined throughout the chapters that follow. Beyond the scope of experimental music, my investigation also sheds light on what it means to be a performer of another person's work in more general terms, whether that takes the form of a jazz chart, classical ballet choreography, or any other artistic phenomenon. Indeterminate pieces, in their inherent ambiguity, require a significant degree of performer–composer collaboration, but all performance involves—demands, even—interpretive labor.

2

THE "EXECUTIVE" MODEL

COMPOSERS AS BOSSES

In the mid-2000s, I worked for a large financial-services corporation. At that time, one of the major initiatives was transferring several functions from teams in the United States to a new service center in Southeast Asia.[1] I was not privy to the financial gains enabled by this change, but compensation costs in that country, at least in manufacturing, were approximately $2–3/hour in U.S. dollars at the time, or approximately 10% of the U.S. rates.[2] Perhaps unsurprisingly, this was not an isolated incident. Much rhetoric and hyperbole permeate accounts of offshoring, outsourcing, and related actions, but most analysts agree that jobs, in substantial numbers, have been and are being shifted toward places where costs are lower. Companies like Apple, Inc., have made headlines for the allegedly abysmal working conditions of their overseas suppliers' employees,[3] and have since begun efforts to "address shortfalls and take immediate action to resolve any issues we find."[4] Mega-retailer Walmart has promised to "increase its sourcing of American-made products by $50 billion over the next ten years," a staggering number but roughly only 1% of its total projected sales for that same period.[5] *The Wall Street Journal* reported in 2012 that the 35 largest U.S. multinational

---

[1] In line with non-disclosure requirements, some details of this account are intentionally left vague.

[2] "Hourly compensation (labor cost) is the average cost to employers of using one hour of employee labor in the manufacturing sector. Compensation includes (1) pay for time worked, (2) directly paid benefits, and (3) employer social insurance expenditures and labor-related taxes." International Labor Comparisons Program, *Charting International Labor Comparisons: 2012 edition* (U.S. Department of Labor and U.S. Bureau of Labor Statistics, September 2012), 30.

[3] Many of the issues underlying Chinese production for Apple and other U.S.-based multinationals are laid out in Chak Kwan Chan and Zhaiwen Peng, "From Iron Rice Bowl to the World's Biggest Sweatshop: Globalization, Institutional Constraints, and the Rights of Chinese Workers," *Social Service Review* 85, no. 3 (September 2011), 421–45.

[4] https://web.archive.org/web/20150814063623/http://www.apple.com/supplier-responsibility/our-suppliers/.

[5] Hiroko Tabuchi, "Walmart's Imports from China Displaced 400,000 Jobs, a Study Says," *The New York Times* (December 9, 2015).

Interpretive Labor. Kirsten I. Speyer Carithers, Oxford University Press. © Oxford University Press 2025.
DOI: 10.1093/9780197698815.003.0003

corporations had added many new jobs in the previous two years, but that almost 75% of those jobs were "overseas."[6]

Perhaps not surprisingly, the "transition," as it was euphemistically called by my managers, coincided with a period (2000–2007) in which the country taking over these operations for us experienced more employment growth than nearly all other countries, with gains of nearly 3%, and during which the United States, Japan, and a number of other developed nations saw net declines in overall employment.[7] The bank's transfer of functions was not without its challenges. There were language and cultural barriers, time zone issues, expensive international travel for middle managers overseeing the new teams' development, and so on, but these were--I presume--offset by the gains achieved through lower labor costs.

If I might be forgiven a brief personal aside: I do want to be clear that I am not arguing against global economic development. It is crucial for workers in every country to have the types of opportunities that bring education and training, financial stability, and potential for advancement. I also don't envy anyone who has to make strategic decisions about how and where to distribute jobs, because each position in one place means lost potential for that position in every other place. It is a treacherous balancing act. All that said, however, it is important to be aware of the issues of present-day global economics and to consider the long-term effects of such actions. As Timothy Taylor notes, citing Foucault, "neoliberalism is not simply an economic system but an organizing ideology that shapes thoughts, practices, and self-conceptions."[8] The paradigm of neoliberal capitalism means that the impact of U.S.-based corporations will be felt far beyond their headquarters in ways that--while possibly beneficial in the short term--have the potential to disrupt and permanently alter the sociocultural fabric of those newly enfolded locations.

At the bank, middle managers were tasked with running financial-services operations cost-effectively, which they did in part by demanding regular "scorecards" on our new offshore co-workers, while executives in the background made the overarching decisions and called the shots on the budget. In this way, the situation with my former employer was actually quite similar to an arrangement between two composers who worked on the orchestral

---

[6] Scott Thurm, "U.S. Firms Add Jobs, but Mostly Overseas," *The Wall Street Journal* (April 27, 2012).

[7] International Labor Comparisons Program, *Charting International Labor Comparisons*, 20.

[8] Taylor, *Music and Capitalism*, 46.

42 INTERPRETIVE LABOR

composition *Carré* (1959–60). In that instance, a person considered to be important (Karlheinz Stockhausen) received a request to accomplish something complex (write a piece for large ensemble) from an entity that would fund it (Radio Hamburg). More to the point, Stockhausen himself handed off the repetitive, mundane work of realization to his assistant at the time, Cornelius Cardew; he effectively *outsourced* it. And like the managers and executives, Stockhausen took full credit for the resulting creation.[9]

The key elements of Stockhausen and Cardew's collaboration, then, include a basic imbalance of power and recognition. In this case, two individuals contributed substantial time and energy, but only one was in a position to gain commensurate artistic recognition from it. Stockhausen's stance might be described as rigid, controlling, and concerned with authorship. At the same time, the bulk of the interpretive labor––that is, the work of realizing indeterminate notation––fell to Cardew.

In what follows, I will lay out details of how this piece was created, and then consider how both *Carré* and another ostensibly Stockhausen piece, *Plus Minus*, function similarly. Before turning to those examples, though, we will consider how the terms "interpretation," "realization," and "translation" might productively be interrogated and adopted in discussions of musical works with similar "executive" functions.

REALIZATION AND AUTHORSHIP: WRITING, TRANSLATING, WORKING

I find it useful to place musical indeterminacy across a spectrum of different manifestations, from chance operations to mobile forms to improvisation-prompting verbal instructions. This chapter introduces the first of five models of Interpretive Labor, falling on the end of the range in which most of the material is actually determined in advance of a performance. In this form, the interpretive work is (a) generated by a composer who provides raw material in place of a conventionally playable score and (b) produced by someone else who turns that raw material into a musical composition. To demonstrate how this functions, I will turn to a dynamic personality in the experimental-music circles of the 1960s: German composer Karlheinz

---

[9] An even more direct comparison might be made to the heads of Hollywood studio music departments in the 1930s, who at that time could win Academy Awards for film scores rather than the individuals who actually composed the music.

THE "EXECUTIVE" MODEL   43

Stockhausen (1928–2007), who takes on a form of "executive" power in some of his activities.

This type of work involves artists in leadership roles who rely on others to bring their ideas to fruition. To best account for this phenomenon—that is, musicians acting in executive capacities, especially in relation to performances of experimental music—I propose two theoretical moves. First: acknowledge the labor of those whose work is perceived to be subservient to these executive figures. For the most part, they act as co-composers or co-creators, as will be addressed in the discussion of their working methods. Second: conceptualize this specific type of labor as a process of "translation," a term that encompasses myriad activities and engenders significant philosophical considerations. In this chapter, I tease out some of the many aspects of this problem, drawing on traditional theories of translation, recent developments in translation studies as employed both within and outside musicology, and the relationships among translation, realization, and interpretation. By relying on a second artist to translate their ideas into a playable score, the first composer functions as an executive or boss, calling the shots and taking credit, but avoiding much of the "daily grind" work.

* * *

Precisely notated, overflowing with performance instructions, and led by not only a director, but *four* conductors who are themselves under the direction of the composer: these are not typical aspects of an indeterminate composition. And yet, Karlheinz Stockhausen's *Carré* incorporates all of these things. Composed in 1959–60, this work for four orchestras and choirs acts as a bridge between conventional notation and newer, more experimental forms, a piece that required substantial work to realize it into audibility. It was premiered in Hamburg in 1960, with subsequent performances including those in Berlin (1986) and more recently by Ensemble Musikfabrik at the Darmstadt Internationale Ferienkurse für Neue Musik (August 2014).[10]

In contrast to the precise and richly prescribed content of his large orchestral work, Stockhausen's *Plus Minus* suggests a very different type of indeterminacy. Composed just a few years later, in 1963, it is subtitled "2 x 7 Seiten

---

[10] As of 2022, music critic Andrew Clements notes how infrequently *Carré* was performed, compared to other pieces by the same composer. Clements, "Stockhausen: *Carré*/Kagel: *Chorbuch* Review—Thrillingly Original Rarities," *The Guardian*, July 7, 2022, https://www.theguardian.com/music/2022/jul/07/stockhausen-carre-mauricio-kagel-chorbuch-review-original-rarities.

44 INTERPRETIVE LABOR

für Ausarbeitungen" (two sets of seven pages for elaboration, or working out, or realizing) with performing forces left unspecified. Cornelius Cardew and Frederic Rzewski gave its premiere in Rome in June 1964, both on pianos.[11] Charlotte Moorman performed and recorded the piece at her Avant Garde Festival in August of the same year; this version included "a full-size robot named Robot Opera, built by Nam June Paik."[12]

Both *Carré* and *Plus Minus* demand substantial interpretive work before they can be performed. Stockhausen maintained close control over most aspects of his works, as is evident in their "scores," but at the same time, there are openings for a realizer to introduce non-Stockhausenesque ideas. This type of interpretation incorporates not only an individual artist experimenting with compositional methods but also a second artist (or group of artists) who take(s) on responsibility for the work's content in performance. I see the procedures undertaken by Cardew (for *Carré*) and composer-performers (for *Plus Minus*) as a true problem, worthy of its own philosophical and theoretical considerations. We say that these participants *realize* the work or the score, but what does that mean? The idea of realization, it seems, has become a sort of shorthand for a challenging set of interconnected issues. The discipline of translation studies will be brought to bear on this repertoire, as a means of working through some of the thornier issues between composers and their realizers. Only then will it be feasible to consider the ways in which these works fit into the broader system of Interpretive Labor.

In the hermeneutics discussed in the previous chapter, interpretation suggests a dynamic process. In contrast, I think of realization as a more restricted form of engagement: a subset of interpretation constrained by formal conventions. Interpretation, again, is a dialectical procedure, mediating between the context (training, aesthetic leanings, understanding of a particular musical idiom) and the creative action that expands that knowledge. This becomes clear if we think of it in terms of a common-practice-period music theory and analysis course: "Realize the given figured bass," the professor might instruct, and we understand that there is an expected way to do that. Within a musical context, "realization" presupposes a right answer or

[11] Robin Maconie, *Other Planets: The Music of Karlheinz Stockhausen* (Lanham, MD: Scarecrow Press, 2005), 252.

[12] Original announcement card, Annual Avant Garde Festival of New York, August 30, 1964 (originally broadcast as WBAI-FM Avant Garde Concert III, December 12 & 17, 1964), Charlotte Moorman Archive, McCormick Library of Special Collections, Northwestern University Library.

a proper interpretation, or at least a set of closely related answers bound by the conventions of the style, genre, and period. Realization, then, fits within the broader concept of interpretation, and sets up rigid structures that are waiting to be fought against. Cardew's work on *Carré* is a form of realization: he is given a partial form of notation, which he must interpret within the constraints established by the artist whose work defines the conventions of the time (in this case, Stockhausen). *Carré* is an ideal example here precisely because Cardew left an account of his working conditions, the feedback he received from the composer, and the ways he felt hamstrung by Stockhausen's rules and requirements.

Thus, even complex, avant-garde compositions of the 20th century can fit happily into a continuum of interpretive work, not as distant from extemporized Baroque accompaniments as might initially be assumed. This helps to situate what I'm calling the Executive Model of Interpretive Labor within a broad history of music in general and to see how it might be extrapolated onto other forms of musical realization. To understand the various ways this model connects with ideas outside of music, I turn to translation theory.

The academic discipline of translation studies is concerned not only with literary works––from an original written language to a second––but also with a wealth of related fields. Several universities now have departments or institutes for translation studies, some of which remain pragmatic training centers for linguists, while some are broader in scope. The year 2002 saw publication of the collection *Translation Studies: Perspectives on an Emerging Discipline*, which marked a shift from the limitations of comparative literature to an engagement with metaphorical or otherwise expanded ideas about translation.[13] A journal for the field was established in 2008, with the aim of "extend[ing] the methodologies, areas of interest and conceptual frameworks inside the discipline, while testing the traditional boundaries of the notion of 'translation' and offering a forum for debate focusing on historical, social, institutional and cultural facets of translation" a scope that includes "people

---

[13] The editor notes, "By the 1990s, translation studies had established itself as a general discipline by means of which the broad and multifaceted range of translation phenomena are investigated"; the accounts in this volume are largely adapted from a 1999 conference addressing these questions. Alessandra Riccardi, ed., *Translation Studies: Perspectives on an Emerging Discipline* (Cambridge: Cambridge University Press, 2002). This closely followed the publication of the textbook *Introducing Translation Studies: Theories and Applications* by Jeremy Munday (New York: Routledge, 2001). Munday also edited the *Routledge Companion to Translation Studies* (2009).

46 INTERPRETIVE LABOR

working in literary theory, sociology, ethnography, philosophy, semiotics, history and historiography, theology, gender studies, postcolonialism, and related fields."[14]

Certainly, writers since the earliest recorded cross-linguistic accounts have discussed the merits and pitfalls of translation; the revised edition of a scholarly compilation begins with St. Jerome's letter to Pammachius, "*De optimo genere interpretandi*," dated 395 CE.[15] In the last two decades, though, these ideas have begun to be codified into an academic discipline with a different aim. As set out by literary theorists Sandra Bermann and Catherine Porter, "the word 'translation' itself has become a metaphor for transformation or transposition of many kinds. Increasingly a site of theoretical reflection, translation's role in representing self and other in complicated hierarchies of power, in staging the performance of sexualities, in posing ethical questions, and in constructing linguistic and cultural histories has been increasingly acknowledged . . . and scholars have begun to speak of a 'translation turn' in the humanities and social sciences."[16] For Bermann, translation represents an encounter with the Other: other authors, other languages, other texts. On this latter point, she notes that "Just as all literary writing entails an ongoing iterability, along with an array of intertexts and conventions, so does the language of translation. But translation adds to this its reference to a particular prior text (or 'source'). By bringing within its scope this 'other text' with its clearly different language(s), conventions and historical context, translation dramatizes the encounter with alterity."[17] In other words, it uniquely marks a sort of boundary-space not only between texts and languages, but between the very cultural forces to which they belong. With this in mind, translation can offer up a rich set of considerations for music studies, as well. For example, the idea of the border comes into play in musicologist Brigid Cohen's work on Stefan Wolpe. There, she explores metaphors of traffic and translation as "exemplary 'boundary situations' that figured prominently in the imaginations of certain relevant intellectual communities . . . in Weimar-era Germany," situating the composer's music and writings alongside those of Walter Benjamin and Hannah Arendt, both

---

[14] *Translation Studies* journal (Taylor & Francis Online) https://www.tandfonline.com/journals/rtrs20/about-this-journal#aims-and-scope.

[15] Commonly translated as "On the best method of translating." Lawrence Venuti, ed., *The Translation Studies Reader*, 2nd ed. (New York: Routledge, 2004).

[16] Bermann and Porter, *A Companion to Translation Studies*, 1–2.

[17] Bermann, "Performing Translation," 289–90.

THE "EXECUTIVE" MODEL   47

of whom were contemporaries of Wolpe.[18] Theories of translation here provide a way to reconcile Stockhausen's compositional practice with the labor of his interpreters.

* * *

In October and November 1961, Cornelius Cardew published in *The Musical Times* a two-part report on the composition of *Carré*.[19] Writing in his native language and for a potentially sympathetic British audience, Cardew had the opportunity there to interject a wealth of personal anecdotes and opinions. At the time of the report on *Carré*, most of his language is subtle and is sometimes contradictory, but it also introduces a tone in his writing that would become increasingly polemical, culminating later in the missive "Stockhausen Serves Imperialism."[20] Because of this, the report is worthy of a close reading that teases out specific clues to his perspective. I identify three main categories of thought interwoven throughout Cardew's text: first, his ideas about indeterminacy itself; second, discussions of the processes he worked through alongside (or against) Stockhausen; and finally, issues of authorship and ownership within their collaborative project. Each of these three themes provides a frame for one of the major questions raised by the Executive Model. First, what forms does the indeterminacy take? How do the details of notation, performing forces, and so on necessitate some form of interpretive labor by its practitioners? Second, what kinds of work does it make necessary? How have those realizers

---

[18] Brigid Cohen, "Boundary Situations: Translation and Agency in Wolpe's Modernism," *Contemporary Music Review* 27, no. 2/3 (April/June 2008), 329. As I understand it, Cohen reads Wolpe's compositional voice as "translating" because he integrates personally significant but "other" artistic styles into his own works, modifying them in a way analogous to Benjamin's assertions about a translation modifying the translator's new language (discussed below). See Walter Benjamin, "The Task of the Translator," trans. Harry Zohn, in *Selected Writings, vol. I, 1913–1926*, ed. Marcus Bullock and Michael W. Jennings (Cambridge, MA: Harvard University Press, 1996), 256, and discussed again when he cites Pannwitz: "The basic error of the translator is that he preserves the state in which his own language happens to be instead of allowing his language to be powerfully affected by the foreign tongue." Benjamin, 262.

[19] Cornelius Cardew, "Report on Stockhausen's *Carré*," *The Musical Times* 102, no. 1424 (October 1961), 619–22, and "Report on *Carré*: Part 2," *The Musical Times* 102, no. 1425 (November 1961), 698–700.

[20] This was originally the title of a talk broadcast on BBC radio, a portion of which was published in the BBC periodical *The Listener* and the full text later published in Cardew's larger book. The essay on Stockhausen actually makes up less than 10% of the book by the same title. Cornelius Cardew, "Stockhausen Serves Imperialism," *The Listener* 2255 (June 15, 1972), 809, and Cornelius Cardew, *Stockhausen Serves Imperialism, and Other Articles* (London: Latimer New Dimensions Limited, 1974).

48   INTERPRETIVE LABOR

developed procedures to transform Stockhausen's symbols into a legible notational product? And finally, how do these procedures provide evidence of
an "executive" role?

THE EXECUTIVE FUNCTION IN *CARRÉ*

> When will the time finally come, when it will be possible to perform
> *Carré* carefully, with enough rehearsal time for working on details,
> for making acoustical experiments, as well as for arriving at a perfect
> balance?
>
> —Karlheinz Stockhausen (1986)[21]

Reading *Carré*: Indeterminacy and Score Production

The piece *Carré* ("square" in French) was written for an unusual ensemble: a
large orchestra and chorus divided into four smaller ensembles of instruments
and voices, each with its own conductor. It was the product of a commission
from Radio Hamburg, "conceived during Karlheinz's long flights over North
America while he was lecturing there."[22] As with many other of his works,
Stockhausen provides detailed instructions, including specifying the ideal
setup, hall size and shape, dimensions for the musicians' platforms, and height
of the conductors' podia. There are four separate scores, one for each ensemble,
and each includes a reduced notation of the other three groups' music (see excerpt in Figure 2.1).

In 1986, the composer produced an eight-page supplement to the preface
in response to a Berlin performance, in which he criticizes aspects of the
setup and performance. For example, he notes, "a series of circa 7 concerts
with performances of *Carré* should have been programmed," and "the audience should, by no means, be seated between the podia, as happened
in Berlin."[23] Likewise, when the composer found out in 1994 that David

---

[21] Karlheinz Stockhausen, Supplement to the Preface to the score, *Carré* [published in response
to the September 1, 1986, performance], online at http://www.karlheinzstockhausen.org/pdf/
CARRE_English.pdf.

[22] Cardew, "Report on Stockhausen's *Carré*," 619.

[23] It is difficult to imagine any orchestra devoting seven consecutive performances to such a demanding (in every sense) work. http://www.karlheinzstockhausen.org/carre_english.htm.

THE "EXECUTIVE" MODEL   49

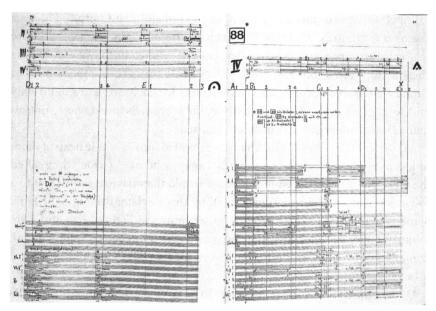

Figure 2.1 Karlheinz Stockhausen/Cornelius Cardew, *Carré* (Orchestra I, pp. 96–97). Reproduced, with permission, from Karlheinz Stockhausen, *Carré*. Vienna: Universal Edition, 1960.

Robertson, the director of the Ensemble Intercontemporain, was planning to perform the work, he wrote to Robertson, advising that the choir needed to be amplified and pushing for a particular way of arranging the microphones and speakers. He concludes, "Please fight for this amplification: it will be hard ('money'...), but the music is the most important!"[24] Of note for this piece is the unconventional arrangement of the musicians and audience. The four orchestra-and-chorus groups are situated in a square (hence the title) surrounding the audience, with the conductors not in the corners of the room, but in the center of each wall, between two orchestras (see Figure 2.2). Stockhausen specifies in the score that the "favourable hall" is 25 meters by 25 meters square (corresponding to the dimensions of the hall used for the premiere in Hamburg), with each group of performers on a platform measuring 5.25 meters by 12 meters, and 50 centimeters high. The instrumentation includes some unconventional additions for an orchestra, such as bass

---

[24] Letter from Karlheinz Stockhausen to David Robertson (Ensemble Intercontemporain, October 1994), reprinted at http://www.karlheinzstockhausen.org/carre_english.htm.

50   INTERPRETIVE LABOR

trumpet, three saxophones, and amplified cimbalom and harp.[25] The four chamber orchestras, while similarly voiced, are not identical. *Carré*'s score also calls for a percussion setup that is large relative to the size of the orchestra (tom-toms, bongos, cowbells, cymbals, hi-hats, gongs, tam-tams, "Indian" bells, bass drums, and snare drums for each orchestra), and only mid-to-high strings (no basses). In total, the score calls for 4 conductors, either 32 or 48 singers, and 77 instrumentalists.

As Cardew describes it, Stockhausen provided him "a whole heap of more or less hieroglyphic notes, including 101 snappy items"[26] (which they called the Basic Score) that the young assistant would then have to translate into a rough score of more conventional notation; this was later fixed into the Final Score. These notes from the composer, as shown in Figures 2.2a and 2.2b, took the form of a type of graphic notation, which indicated pitch material, dynamics, movement around and between the four chamber orchestras, and other aspects of the music.

Of the limited literature on this piece, most is concerned primarily with its place among Stockhausen's moment-form works, or with his sound spatialization requirements; for example, French aesthetics scholar Elena de Bértola mentions the work in passing in her doctoral thesis on kinetic art.[27] The first edition of Robin Maconie's "guidebook" volume, *The Works of Karlheinz Stockhausen*, includes the piece in a discussion of moment form; this was cited by Jonathan Kramer a couple of years later.[28] Even in the 21st century, the overall shape of the piece seems to be of most interest. *Carré* receives an entire chapter of Zbigniew Granat's 2002 dissertation, but here again this is in the context of analyzing the work's form. Notably, Granat does describe some selected "moments" or sections, and includes brief excerpts of the score to illustrate these, which are welcome additions to the literature.[29] Also, given that project's scope of exploring "openness" in music, the emphasis chosen is

[25] The published score's instrument list includes "cymbalum," but Stockhausen's setup notes refer to "the strings of the cimbalom."

[26] Cardew, "Report on Stockhausen's *Carré*," 619. Cardew does not explain his use of the modifier "snappy," but it seems to refer to the discrete icons or small graphic figures shown in Figure 2.2.

[27] There is a diagram of the hall setup (placement of orchestras and conductors) in an excerpt of the thesis that was published in a 1972 journal, but the composition itself is not discussed at all. Elena de Bértola, "On Space and Time in Music and the Visual Arts," *Leonardo* 5, no. 1 (Winter 1972), 27–30.

[28] Robin Maconie, *The Works of Karlheinz Stockhausen* (London: Oxford University Press, 1976) (2nd ed. published in 1990); Jonathan D. Kramer, "Moment Form in Twentieth Century Music," *The Musical Quarterly* 64, no. 2 (April 1978), 177–94.

[29] Granat, "Open Form and the 'Work-Concept'"; see especially chapter 4: "An Unending Moment: Karlheinz Stockhausen's *Carré*," 68–90.

THE "EXECUTIVE" MODEL 51

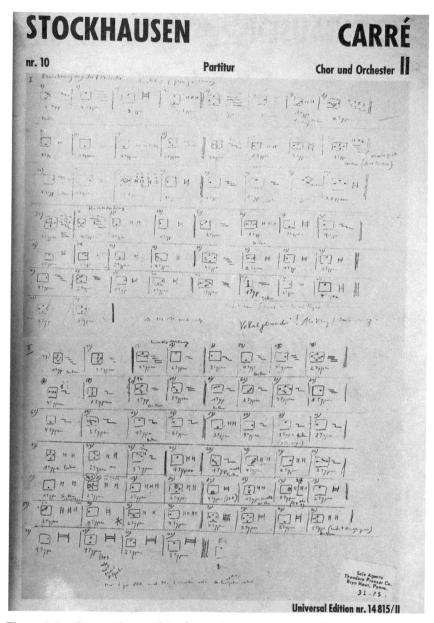

Figure 2.2a Cover, Chor und Orchester II. Reproduced, with permission, from Karlheinz Stockhausen, *Carré*. Vienna: Universal Edition, 1960.

52   INTERPRETIVE LABOR

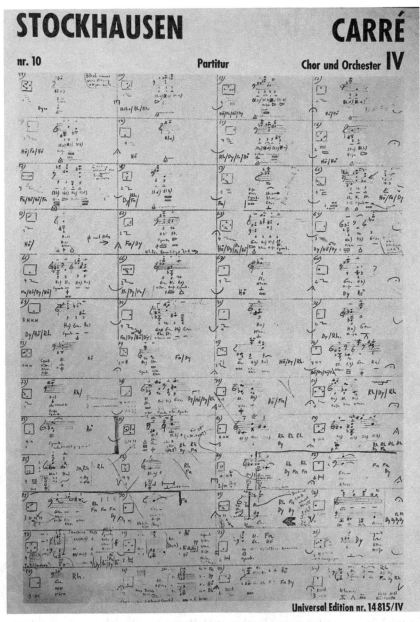

Figure 2.2b Cover, Chor und Orchester IV. Reproduced, with permission, from Karlheinz Stockhausen, *Carré*. Vienna: Universal Edition, 1960.

THE "EXECUTIVE" MODEL   53

perfectly sufficient. However, there is one point with which I must take issue. Granat claims, "composition itself is no longer viewed as a creative act in the Romantic sense but rather as a collaboration. . . . Similarly, the notion of the performance of the work as controlled by a single conductor is now replaced with a new concept of interpretation based on the interaction of four independent conductors."[30] As I will attempt to demonstrate, Stockhausen retained a death grip on his own position of authority for *Carré*, and neither Cardew nor the co-conductors working with them were allowed anything like independence.[31] If anything, Stockhausen reinforced the Romantic ideal of the iconoclastic creative artist, while apparently misleading some later scholars into thinking he valued communal leadership.

For *Carré*, then, the type of indeterminacy introduces a second actor, such that we now have both composer and collaborator (or, more precisely here, assistant or employee) investing their time and energy into creating a piece of music. In the *Musical Times* essays, Cardew makes two oblique references to indeterminacy by engaging with a sort of Cagean philosophy of acquiescence. Toward the beginning of Part I, he explains a potential procedure for true collaborative composition among two or more musicians, which he contrasts with the way it was actually handled by Stockhausen and himself. At the end of this summary––in which he advocates for mailing drafts of a score back and forth until no participant makes any more changes––Cardew writes, "I . . . would embark on [this idea] with anyone who cared to collaborate with me, though I cannot answer for the results. And it is this which indicates the great merit of the idea, that it is 'dilettante' and entered into with free love and acceptance of no matter what eventuality––like abandoning the project, or shooting your collaborator, or never finishing it."[32] This "acceptance of no matter what eventuality" is reminiscent of, and perhaps directly quoting, Cage's professed approach to indeterminacy around that time.[33]

---

[30] Granat, "Open Form and the 'Work-Concept,'" 88.

[31] In Stockhausen's absence, though, the situation is different; present-day conductors would experience a more collaborative form of interaction. Granat's claim to its *composition* as collaboration, though, remains a mischaracterization.

[32] Cardew, "Report on Stockhausen's *Carré*," 619.

[33] Cage had addressed this multiple times by 1961, including several instances of which Cardew may have been aware: published in London in 1955, he had written, "no knowing action is commensurate, since the character of the knowledge acted upon prohibits all but some eventualities . . . . An experimental action, generated by a mind as empty as it was before it became one, thus in accord with the possibility of no matter what," in "Experimental Music," *The Score and I.M.A. Magazine* (London, 1955); and more directly, the phrase "no matter what eventuality" is repeated 16 times in the 1958 Darmstadt lecture "Indeterminacy." Both are reprinted in *Silence: Lectures and Writing*, 13–17 and 35–40.

54 INTERPRETIVE LABOR

Later, Cardew discusses the distinction between the Basic Score (Stockhausen's symbolic/graphic notation) and the Final Score, claiming that manifestations of Stockhausen's personality are evident only in the Basic, and so a realizer could potentially create a version that rendered Stockhausen's "personality" insignificant in the final product. He notes, "I would hazard the opinion that it is lack of faith in these manifestations that would lead Karlheinz to oppose the release of such a score. ('Release' is the right word: the score leaves your hands and *anything* may happen to it. . . .)."[34] While Cardew does not refer directly to indeterminacy per se, he does hint at the tension between compositional control and the life of a piece once it has been notated in some manner. Here, Cardew seems open to the possibilities of an unanticipated result, even excited about them, while he associates Stockhausen with a much more rigid approach.

Working Procedures: Realizing *Carré*

Much of Cardew's *Musical Times* report on *Carré* consists of explanations of how he and Stockhausen worked through various tasks to create the piece and prepare for its first performance. The basic procedure was that Stockhausen created a large number of shorthand notations that indicated a few pitches, a dynamic level, the instrument family (e.g., woodwind), and the "movement between the orchestras." For about three months, beginning in April 1959, Cardew worked out realizations for these notations at Stockhausen's home "from 3 pm till dinnertime." At the end of that three-month period, when Cardew understood the rough score to be just about complete, Stockhausen decided to add sections of contrasting material. This caused the rough-score completion to be pushed back until March of the following year. Throughout the realization work, Cardew was, in his words, "aided, irritated, confused, encouraged and sometimes even guided" by the composer, who gave advice, provided notes, and explained the signs given in the Basic Score.[35] This may be one of the few cases in all of art music where one can speak fairly confidently of the composer's intentions, since Stockhausen so frequently weighed in on the interpretive work being attempted by his young assistant.[36] Despite

---

[34] Cardew, "Report on Stockhausen's *Carré*," 620. Emphasis in original.

[35] Cardew, 619.

[36] This is further supported by the sketches for the work. These include 2 pages by Stockhausen and 27 pages by Cardew, with annotations by Stockhausen. The 114-page manuscript is attributed to both composers and dated April–July 1959. Karlheinz Stockhausen, *Carré für 4 Orchester und Chöre, Werk Nr. 10, Manuskript- und Skizzen-Kopien* (Kürten: Stockhausen-Verlag, 1983).

THE "EXECUTIVE" MODEL   55

the collaborative nature of the work, though, Cardew notes in the report that his access to the piece was subsequently withdrawn.

Composer–performer interactions were not always so strained, of course. While Cardew recognized and became frustrated with the imbalance of power between them, other performers seemed eager to contribute to works by living composers. Percussionist Jan Williams, who trained at Eastman and the Manhattan School of Music and later joined the faculty of the University at Buffalo, notes:

> The question came up quite often of whether, given the level of input you, as a player, had in the production of a new piece, whose piece is it? Should your name not appear as the co-composer? Maybe you came up with a lot of the sounds or you put them together within a framework. My reaction to that question was, of course it's the composer's piece because he or she is the one who literally conceived the piece in the first place. I always felt that no matter how open a form it is or how sketchy it is as a piece, our input as performers is just that: a performer's input. I don't consider myself a composer. I never did. And I never approached it that way and never got upset, because I felt my input was important and made the piece really work. But I didn't "compose" it.[37]

The issue of co-composition, revisited throughout this text, remains one of the most important questions for indeterminate works, as it brings to light the sometimes hidden power dynamics among and between musicians. Returning to Cardew and Stockhausen, this issue would inform an increasingly antagonistic tone, finally exploding in the aforementioned essay "Stockhausen Serves Imperialism."[38]

For the premiere in Hamburg in 1960, which was broadcast on local radio and for which the dress rehearsal was (thankfully) recorded, Cardew arrived in time for the rehearsals, 10 days before the performance.[39] In addition to some last-minute copying of one of the orchestra's parts, both composers attended sectional rehearsals, where groups met by instrument groupings (brass, wind, strings, percussion, and combinations of these) and with the

---

[37] Jan Williams in interview with Jonathan Hepfer, *Percussive Notes* 8 (February 2007), n.p.
[38] This will be discussed in detail in the "Hacker" chapter.
[39] Karlheinz Stockhausen, *Gruppen/Carré*, Mauricio Kagel, Karlheinz Stockhausen, Andrzej Markowski, and Michael Gielen, conductors; Chor und Sinfonie-Orchester des Norddeutschen Rundfunks Hamburg (Deutsche Grammophon 137 002).

56 INTERPRETIVE LABOR

four chamber orchestras individually. Throughout this process, things went well, up until they tried to put all four orchestras together in the large exhibition hall where the performance was to take place. Cardew notes,

> my job was supposed to be flitting among these cubicles [where each orchestra would be recorded separately] adjusting the balance of the four microphones for each orchestra, and then the balance of the four orchestras together in the fifth cubicle, meanwhile running out into the main hall every few seconds to give detailed instructions as to who was too loud and too soft, and too early and too late, among 108 musicians . . . and all this carrying a heavy armful of four full scores each opened at the right page. But what happens when you want to turn a page?[40]

He seems frustrated with the work expected of him: not only did he have to manage the balance issues, identifying problems and communicating with the conductors, but he also had to meet the physical demands of the job: wielding the massive score documents and running back and forth among the chamber orchestras. This is an aspect of labor not frequently considered in music literature, but is an important component. Playing instruments, conducting, stage setup––all of these activities require a serious investment of energy and bodily engagement.

Translational Labor in *Carré*

In the composition of *Carré*, the primary act of translation resides between the composer and his realizer: Cardew had to translate Stockhausen's shorthand into more conventional notation so it could be read by the choral and orchestral musicians. What happens during the process of translation? To think about this more carefully, both classic texts and more recent theoretical work can be mobilized in useful ways. Walter Benjamin's text "The Task of the Translator" figures prominently in numerous later accounts.[41] Written

---

[40] Cardew, "Report on Stockhausen's *Carré*," 699–700. One gains a material appreciation for this labor when studying *Carré* today; the published score weighs nearly 20 pounds.

[41] As noted by de Man in 1983, "this text by Benjamin on 'The Task of the Translator' is a text that is very well known, both in the sense that it is very widely circulated, and in the sense that in the profession you are nobody unless you have said something about this text." Paul de Man, "'Conclusions' on Walter Benjamin's 'The Task of the Translator,'" Messenger Lecture, Cornell University, March 4, 1983, reprinted in *Yale French Studies* 97 (2000), 10–35.

THE "EXECUTIVE" MODEL   57

in 1921 as the foreword to his own translation of Baudelaire, this short piece introduces several relevant ideas. For one, he identifies the special relationship between translation and the translator's own native language: "While a poet's words endure in his own language, even the greatest translation is destined to become part of the growth of its own language and eventually to perish with its renewal. Translation is so far removed from being the sterile equation of two dead languages that of all literary forms it is the one charged with the special mission of watching over the [waning] of the original language and the [pain or suffering] of its own."[42] Translation, in other words, actively changes the new language into which the original text is being placed. It is impossible to create an exact, one-to-one mapping between source and new, and so the text--through its translation--shapes the second language. It introduces ideas and concepts that had not previously been a part of that language, thereby stretching it, molding it into new forms, just as Cardew's contributions to *Carré* introduced novel elements to Stockhausen's compositional language that would not have existed had Stockhausen realized it himself. Benjamin further argues for translation as evidence—or even as enactment--of the afterlife of a work of art, an idea with considerable appeal for music. In reference to important works of world literature, he claims that "translation marks their stage of continued life. The idea of life and afterlife in works of art should be regarded with an entirely unmetaphorical objectivity."[43] We might conclude by extension that--like a linguistic translation of a text--a fresh interpretation of a musical text serves the same function. Without contemporary performances of the works of Bach or of Hildegard, they would be relegated to the fate suffered by dusty old volumes in so-called dead languages, crumbling and forgotten.

Returning to Cardew's two-part report in *The Musical Times*, its most illuminating aspect is the wealth of small comments alluding to issues of the authorship and ownership of *Carré*. Throughout the essays, he introduces sometimes subtle, sometimes direct references to his working relationship with Stockhausen, and through this language, provides insight into a developing political stance in which he would become vocal about distrusting authority. At a very basic level, he refers to the other composer nearly throughout as "Karlheinz"; using his first name suggests familiarity, if not

---

[42] Words in brackets are suggested by altering Zohn's translation, as informed by de Man's lecture on the subject, cited above. Benjamin, "The Task of the Translator," 256.

[43] Benjamin, "The Task of the Translator," 254.

58   INTERPRETIVE LABOR

disrespect, especially since he refers to other composers discussed (e.g., Cage, Wolff, and Bussotti) by their surnames. Cardew also frequently states that he disagreed with whatever Stockhausen was doing. For example, he notes that he and David Tudor both felt that the material for the Basic Score, unrealized, could be published as a score in its own right. In contrast, he states, "Karlheinz on the other hand would probably oppose the idea strongly. This score, if published, would be the score of a piece for four orchestras by Karlheinz Stockhausen and no mistake about it."[44] Later, in discussing the instrumentation, he says that he would have preferred to use a different balance between brass and woodwinds, that the overall chamber-orchestra groupings had "a slight wrongness of scale," and that the "strings lacked all initiative."[45]

Two other major aspects of the piece are emphasized, both relating to the piece's overall form. First, Cardew explains how he and Stockhausen determined timings for each of the short sections by imagining the sounds in real time, and notes that the conductors could follow the same procedure rather than using the timings marked in the score. He writes, "I could never really regard [the timing numbers] as binding (they were not *composed*), and I personally would have liked the conductors to have felt free to ignore them in all cases except those where they actually found they had to refer to them in order to get an idea of what the music was about."[46] Elsewhere, he criticizes the quantity of cuts made in the final rehearsals, as well as the rushed treatment given to many remaining portions of the score. In his words: "Many groups—even where there were no cuts—were reduced to less than half their planned length, so very little (or let's say much less than I would have liked) remained of the perfect stillness of the original conception. . . . I am of course offering only my own personal and prejudiced and exaggerated impression."[47] This use of the "personal/personally" qualifier emphasizes Cardew's distance from Stockhausen, marking them as separate individuals and reinforcing his position as an artist with valid opinions of his own.

Finally, I identify a set of comments that all connect to the idea of compositional authority and Cardew's own compromised position in that regard. Just after the opening salvo, he begins, "when I was actually involved

---

[44] Cardew, "Report on Stockhausen's *Carré*," 620.
[45] Cardew, "Report on Stockhausen's *Carré*," 621.
[46] Cardew, "Report on Stockhausen's *Carré*," 622.
[47] Cardew, "Report on Stockhausen's *Carré*," 700.

in the collaboration with Stockhausen on 'his' *Carré* . . . I spent some of the afternoons when work on it seemed pointless, thinking of possible or sensible forms that a collaboration could take."[48] Cardew's use of scare quotes is significant: he acknowledges that Stockhausen's name is on the piece, but immediately draws the reader's attention to its contested authorship. Even more boldly, he later compares it to "any other piece I have written," as if he were the sole composer.[49] Even in banal explanations, he interjects comments indicating his contributions: "the whole piece does unfold within a space of 4 ½ octaves, with only occasional excursions, for which Karlheinz was not responsible," and about the chorus, "I wrote their notes and Karlheinz their nonsense, later laboriously copied according to the rules laid down by the International Phonetics Association."[50] Cardew seems to want to ensure that he is not blamed for the limited range of the piece, nor for the singers' text.

The last issue is what Cardew calls "personality," a topic he discusses several times. To return to an example introduced earlier, he identifies the distinction between the Basic Score and the Final Score. He writes,

> Let us look for manifestations of personality in the piece. There are doubtless many in the Basic Score . . . which label it incontrovertibly STOCKHAUSEN, but these manifestations are in the Basic Score, and not necessarily in the Final Score. That is to say that were the realizer to approach the Basic Score with sufficient boldness, these manifestations could become insignificant—intentionally concealed, or unintentionally ignored. I, for one, would certainly now approach the task in this fearless spirit.[51]

His general philosophy about the piece, his approach to realizing this indeterminate notation, has thus been transformed during the long process of his "collaboration" with Stockhausen. This is explained more thoroughly in the following paragraphs: "I think Karlheinz does want his music to be a certain way, and it is as a result of this that he has constantly exerted his personality in coaching performances of his works . . . thus he has evaded the necessity of finding an adequate formalization of his ideas." In other words,

---

[48] Cardew, "Report on Stockhausen's *Carré*," 619.
[49] Cardew, "Report on Stockhausen's *Carré*," 620.
[50] Cardew, "Report on Stockhausen's *Carré*," 621.
[51] Cardew, "Report on Stockhausen's *Carré*," 620.

60 INTERPRETIVE LABOR

as long as he can communicate his wishes verbally in rehearsal and performance, Stockhausen can avoid developing a sufficient system of notation that addresses all possible questions of interpretation.[52] Cardew continues,

> It is in this role—that of breathing down the performer's neck—that you find him exerting his personality in *Carré*: his advice to me while working on the Basic Score, his copious notes and hieroglyphics accompanying the Basic Score, his elucidations of the signs used in the Basic Score, these were the strongest manifestations of personality in the complex process which we loosely term *Carré*. And in fact I did work at the score all the time keeping his intentions in mind, though my own "personality" tended more and more to interfere as the work progressed. The sections which were finally cut in the performance were either ones in which my personality conflicted with his—or seemed to—or ones which manifested virtually no personality at all.[53]

"Personality" in this context appears to refer to something like style or compositional or authorial voice, or how exactly the general indications in the Basic Score were being translated into specific iterations of a given musical gesture. In converting the notational shorthand into a score legible to others, both Cardew and Stockhausen had to work though all possible results, or at least those that would have been apparent to them at that time, and decide how best to pin down a particular version.

Cardew seems genuinely frustrated that *Carré* "realiz[ed] only a fraction of its musical potential," and describes ways it could be taken further. While he claims that the working rapport between himself and Stockhausen was basically genial, he pulls no punches throughout the two-part report, chipping away at the notion of *Carré* as a fruitful collaborative project. He also makes the most of the opportunity to convey his own ideas about the piece, even–– or especially—where they contrast with what Stockhausen required, going so far as to suggest that the other composer himself did not know precisely what he wanted. "With *Carré*," he writes, "it seemed that not even Karlheinz

---

[52] I see this as the artistic side of what Christopher Fox calls Stockhausen's "megalomania," which grew out of his attention to detail. Fox notes that as the composer "became more famous ... promoters would be presented with lists of demands, specifying everything from the colour of the microphone cables to the size of the composer's bed. He also started to make fixed versions of several open-form works." Christopher Fox, "The Flat-Pack Stockhausen," *The Guardian* (July 12, 2010).

[53] Cardew, "Report on Stockhausen's *Carré*," 620.

THE "EXECUTIVE" MODEL   61

was convinced of the validity of the indications in the score," and with that undermines Stockhausen's authority yet again.[54] By invoking acquiescence, by highlighting his own contributions, and by engaging with this critical language, Cardew labors to negotiate authoritative space for himself.

In a self-reflexive piece on working with Herder's texts, Philip Bohlman emphasizes "translational otherness," or the idea that translators try to reveal meaning hidden in works from vastly different times and/or places, which in turn reveals the otherness of the translator himself. Bohlman argues that the act of translation—at least for texts of great cultural import (the Bible, folk songs, and epics, for example)—is responsible both for creating new texts and for collapsing history:

> History, too, as the temporal horizon within which translations emerge and acquire their meaning, is collapsed and neutralized in a discourse that imagines translation as the "recovery" of an original meaning or as a technique that aims at restaging the effect the source text has on its readers. Translation, in these discourses, becomes *the very erasure of time and difference* from the scene of writing.[55]

For Bohlman, translation has revelatory power because of its deep connections to two contrasting texts, and therefore to issues of self and other; these are "articulations . . . of difference, not unlike Ricoeur's notion of foreignness, which emerges when self and other become inseparable through encounter."[56] In the work of Bohlman, Sandra Bermann, and Brigid Cohen, then, translational procedures serve to reinforce or enact our states of separation. The border, the encounter with the Other—these are all allied with Cardew's uneasy relationship with Stockhausen.[57] Instead of writing a composition himself, and being credited for that creative labor, Cardew is instead relegated to the role of anonymous translator.[58] His labor is hidden, and

---

[54] Cardew, "Report on Stockhausen's *Carré*," 700.

[55] Philip V. Bohlman, "Translating Herder Translating: Cultural Translation and the Making of Modernity," in *The Oxford Handbook of the New Cultural History of Music*, ed. Jane F. Fulcher (New York: Oxford University Press, 2011), 507 (emphasis added).

[56] Bohlman, "Translating Herder Translating," 507.

[57] That uneasy relationship certainly goes in both directions; given the tone and content of Cardew's report, one can imagine that Stockhausen had plenty of frustrations with his assistant, as well.

[58] Of course, Cardew ameliorated that situation by writing the two-part report in the *Musical Times* and through other writings; however, that recognition was originally largely hidden by Stockhausen.

62 INTERPRETIVE LABOR

he knows it. Stockhausen executes his authorial power such that Cardew's writing amounts to labor under erasure.

THE EXECUTIVE FUNCTION IN *PLUS MINUS*

Reading *Plus Minus*: Indeterminacy

Composed in 1963, Stockhausen's *Plus Minus* allows for unspecified performing forces (solo or small ensemble) and has an unspecified duration. Its score includes seven pages of symbols, seven pages of pitch material, and numerous prefatory instructions (six pages each in German and in English translation in the published version).[59] According to Robin Maconie, it was originally created as an exercise in Stockhausen's composition class at the Cologne New Music Courses (Kölner Kurse für Neue Musik), which he directed from 1963 to 1968. In fact, Maconie claims that "If *Plus Minus* were written today, logically it would be written as an intelligent-computer program which, having been set up with the appropriate form-scheme and note-page combinations, would then be able to configure the music according to the rules in general terms for an operator to reject or modify at will. As a compositional game it probably operates at a level too elevated and abstract for most composers; it is certainly a game for initiates, and ultimately for the 'Magister ludi' himself."[60]

With Maconie's description in mind, the work's notational material makes a little more sense. The score for *Plus Minus* includes many symbols that must be interpreted; one recent interpreter went so far as to call it "a sort of flat-pack composition," evidently a reference to the do-it-yourself assembly required when one purchases furniture from a big-box store.[61] Each of the seven pages of pitches includes two or three staves of basically conventional notation in treble and/or bass clef, and each of the seven pages of symbols includes 53 boxes containing shapes such as triangles, circles, and various lines (see Figure 2.3).[62] These are supplemented by several pages of performance directions, some of which affect multiple parameters. For example, see the instructional note in Figure 2.4.

---

[59] Karlheinz Stockhausen, *Plus Minus* (London: Universal Edition, 1965).
[60] For the record, I take issue with Maconie's characterization that the piece is "too elevated . . . for most composers." Maconie, *The Works of Karlheinz Stockhausen*, 156–57.
[61] Fox, "The Flat-Pack Stockhausen."
[62] Stockhausen, *Plus Minus: 2 x 7 Seiten für Ausarbeitungen* (Vienna: Universal Edition, 1963).

THE "EXECUTIVE" MODEL 63

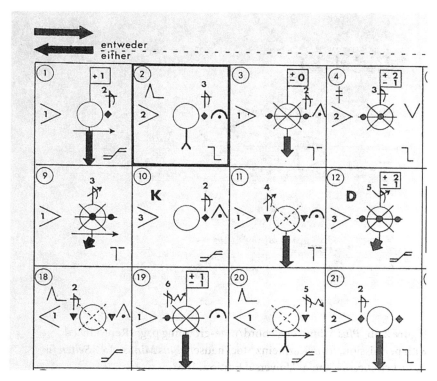

Figure 2.3a *Plus Minus*, one symbolic notation page. Reproduced, with permission, from Karlheinz Stockhausen, *Plus Minus: 2 x 7 Seiten für Ausarbeitungen*. Vienna: Universal Edition, 1963.

This is just one of 35 instructions prefacing the remainder of the score. Others range from simple and direct ("A page of symbols is to be applied to each page of notes") to those requiring more cognitive effort (e.g., "If no transposition of Zentralklang [central sound] and (or) Nebennoten [secondary notes] takes place, the highest note of the chord and (or) the (parenthetical) note of reference for the Nebennoten is to be identified with the highest note of the chord and (or) with the note of reference of the previous event; but it is also possible to insert the chord and the Nebennoten as they last appeared.")[63]

---

[63] Some German terms are left untranslated in the English version of the instructions in the published score; translations are provided here in brackets. Stockhausen, *Plus Minus*, 11–13.

64 INTERPRETIVE LABOR

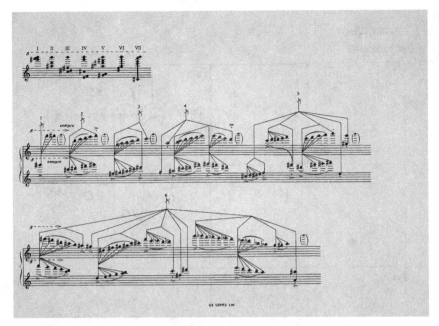

Figure 2.3b *Plus Minus*, one chord/note-grouping page. Reproduced, with permission, from Karlheinz Stockhausen, *Plus Minus: 2 x 7 Seiten für Ausarbeitungen*. Vienna: Universal Edition, 1963.

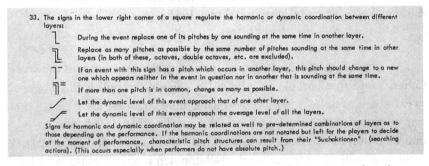

Figure 2.4 *Plus Minus*, performance instruction number 33. Reproduced, with permission, from Karlheinz Stockhausen, *Plus Minus: 2 x 7 Seiten für Ausarbeitungen*. Vienna: Universal Edition, 1963.

THE "EXECUTIVE" MODEL   65

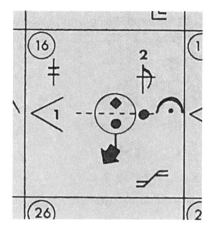

Figure 2.5a *Plus Minus*, detail, n.p. Reproduced, with permission, from Karlheinz Stockhausen, *Plus Minus: 2 x 7 Seiten für Ausarbeitungen*. Vienna: Universal Edition, 1963.

To convert Stockhausen's documentation into a musical score, the realizer has a number of tasks to complete. After reading all of the instructions and getting familiar with the symbols and the order in which they need to be addressed, one begins by choosing one of the seven symbol pages and one of the seven chord pages (or more than one of each, if creating a longer version). In addition, up to seven "layers" of these pairings may be presented simultaneously. Within each symbol page, Stockhausen includes seven types of events; there is one iteration of an event in each of the 53 boxes on each page. These event types are designated by the arrangement of accessory notes to the central sound (as shown in Figure 2.5). For example, event 16 fits into the fifth type of event, where the central, accessorized sound is followed by an "accessory" note.

Once each of these types has been identified on the chosen symbol page, all of the boxes associated with that type are matched with a chord from the page of pitch material. From there, one consults the instructions to interpret each of the other symbol types: hairpins indicate "degrees of change... of register, dynamic level, or duration of the event"; the vertical line with two hash marks (above, just below the circled number 16) indicates "periodic rhythm, also trills, tremoli and repetitions"; the horizontal dashed line through the central sound indicates "sounds, soft, with precise pitches, if possible related to all parts of an event"; the thick arrow below it dictates to "start immediately after the beginning of the next event in another layer"; and so on. Once

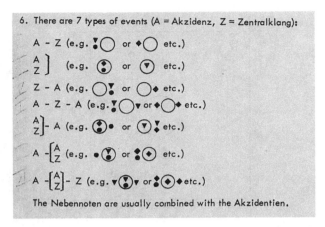

Figure 2.5b *Plus Minus*, detail, n.p. Reproduced, with permission, from Karlheinz Stockhausen, *Plus Minus: 2 x 7 Seiten für Ausarbeitungen*. Vienna: Universal Edition, 1963.

all aspects of the event have been worked out, the next consecutive event box is realized in the same manner, until all 53 (or 106, or 159 . . .) boxes have been translated into musical notation.

Christopher Fox, with John Snijders, undertook a realization of the score for the Ives Ensemble in the late 1990s. He explains that the title is apt:

> The appearance of a plus or minus number [in the flag above the central-sound symbol] affects all subsequent appearances of that event-type. +1, for example, above a particular event-type means that at its next appearance there will be an extra helping of the event; -1 means that there will [be] less of it. An accumulation of minus numbers will lead to the annihilation of that event-type and the replacement of its *Zentralklang* [central sound] and *Akzidentien* [accidentals, accessories] by what Stockhausen calls "negative band," sounds in "obvious opposition to the corresponding positive layers." . . . The plus/minus flags have a radical effect on the music. On the plus side they extend events, generating a sort of looping hiatus as events grow; on the minus side they lead to the introduction of the "negative bands" and can eventually make events disappear. [. . .] Negative-minded realisers can kill the piece, the over-positive can encourage disproportionate growth.[64]

---

[64] Christopher Fox, "Written in Sand: Stockhausen's *Plus Minus*, More or Less," *The Musical Times* 141, no. 1871 (Summer 2000), 19.

THE "EXECUTIVE" MODEL   67

Fox also cautions against mistaking *Plus Minus* for "just another early sixties 'graphic score,'" as he had done as a postgraduate teacher of a new-music class years earlier. Unlike, say, Feldman's *The King of Denmark*, it would be impossible to perform this piece from the composer's published score, making a real-time realization.[65] There is simply too much to work out, too many complex and interrelated rules, or as Fox describes it, it is "a score which is deliberately designed to be unperformable until weeks of work have been expended on the production of a performing version."[66] As will be discussed in the following section, performers who want to realize *Plus Minus* invest tremendous cognitive effort into creating a usable score. Its indeterminacy, while allowing for some degree of individual style, is ultimately constrained by the labor-intensive rules governing its production.

Realizing *Plus Minus*: Performances

A concert program dated April 29, 1967, includes five compositions, the oldest of which is Elliott Carter's 1948 Sonata for Cello and Piano. The remaining pieces date from the 1960s, including Stockhausen's *Plus Minus*, which makes up the entire second half of the program.[67] This was an Evenings for New Music event, organized by the Center of the Creative and Performing Arts under the direction of Allen Sapp and Lukas Foss at the State University of New York at Buffalo. Presented in the Albright-Knox Art Gallery auditorium, the Creative Associates who performed that evening included oboist Andrew White, percussionist (and later artistic director and resident conductor of the Creative Associates) Jan Williams, and 30-year-old Cornelius Cardew. According to the program, this was the "first United States performance" of *Plus Minus*, although a realization of it had in fact been made and recorded nearly three years earlier in New York City, evidently unbeknownst to the Buffalo group.[68] Critic Thomas Putnam's response to the lengthy Creative Associates performance was tepid, at best, stating only: "Also on the program was Stockhausen's 'Plus Minus' which was composed for this performance by Cornelius Cardew, [Edward] Burnham and Williams."[69] Putnam's verb

---

[65] Morton Feldman, *The King of Denmark* (Glendale, NY: C.F. Peters, 1965).

[66] Fox, "Written in Sand," 22.

[67] Evenings for New Music concert program, April 29, 1967, Music Department Notebooks (no index), University at Buffalo, SUNY, Music Library.

[68] Broadcast September 12, 1964, by New York radio station WBAI, it was performed by cellist Charlotte Moorman and Nam June Paik's "Robot Opera," as part of the New York Avant Garde Festival. Charlotte Moorman, *Cello Anthology*, 4-disc set, NMN 064BOX (Italy: Alga Marghen, 2006).

[69] Thomas Putnam, "'New Music' Evening," *Buffalo Courier Express* (April 30, 1967).

68 INTERPRETIVE LABOR

choice ("composed") is likely a nod to the program note, provided not by Stockhausen but by Cardew:

> I began composing this piece several years ago and have now reached the third page. Things are slowing down; at this point it takes me 26 minutes to play only four events. So I decided to hand on [sic] the esoteric information obtained by me in the course of my work to my two percussionist friends, Jan Williams and Ed Burnham (both of whom come relatively fresh to the art of composition), in the hope that they might wring some less somber constellations from the complex mass of data and directives originally provided by Mr. Stockhausen. This evening's performance consists of simultaneous presentation of their work and mine.[70]

Like most concerts in this series, the program was repeated a few days later at New York City's Carnegie Recital Hall, where critics, sadly, were less kind. While Howard Klein notes that "the small, in-group audience seemed to enjoy everything," he also deeply misunderstands *Plus Minus*, claiming that "Thinking . . . may be too strong a word for what went on Tuesday night at Carnegie Recital Hall . . . for these flights into improvisation and chance seemed to require more intuition on the part of the player and listener than working the brain." Worse yet, he states that the length of Stockhausen's piece "tested the endurance of the ear drum and the patience of the victim."[71]

The program for the 1967 Buffalo performance is unfortunately devoid of notes about the instrumentation used, but an archival recording survives. Its catalog listing indicates the use of percussion, piano, and electronic organ, with the latter instrument used for one of the negative bands in that 31-minute performance.[72] The recording clearly captures the sounds of a marimba, wood blocks, a xylophone, a whistle, some distorted recorded sounds, and the keyboard instruments played by Cardew, among other percussion instruments indicated in Jan Williams's valuable sketches.[73] Williams and Burnham had determined the instrumentation and division of the score, and

---

[70] Cornelius Cardew, program note for Evenings for New Music concert no. 31, April 29, 1967. Music Department Notebooks (no index), University at Buffalo, SUNY, Music Library.

[71] Howard Klein, "'Tic' by Albright and 'Plus Minus' End Music Series," *New York Times* (May 4, 1967).

[72] A note within the sketches reads "PLAY ORGAN" above section 12 of the realization. Jan Williams Collection of Annotated Scores (1950–1999), Mus. Arc. 10.1, Box 13, Item 175, Folder 7, University at Buffalo Music Library.

[73] Creative Associates Evenings for New Music Catalog, 1964–1980, University at Buffalo Music Library, 18.

THE "EXECUTIVE" MODEL   69

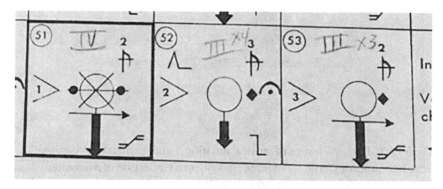

Figure 2.6 Excerpt from *Plus Minus* symbol page, annotated by Jan Williams and/or Edward Burnham and/or Cornelius Cardew in 1967. Folder 7, Jan Williams Collection of Annotated Scores (1950–1999), Mus. Arc. 10.1, Box 13, Item 175. University at Buffalo Music Library. Reproduced with permission.

worked with Cardew on other aspects of their version.[74] In their annotations and sketches (excerpts shown in Figures 2.6–2.8 below[75]), we can actually see their translational process at work, as the symbols from Stockhausen's pages are mapped over, the event boxes are paired with corresponding pitch material in preparation for the next step, and the instructions are worked out to create the score to be used in performance.

Cardew had actually performed a short version of *Plus Minus* already in Rome—the same year as the Moorman-Paik performance at the Avant Garde Festival (AG Fest)—along with Rzewski. This was the first known public performance.[76] According to Virginia Anderson, "both composers tried to manipulate Stockhausen's instructions to their own ends while 'playing the game' by observing the rules, as they resented Stockhausen's control," and argues that Cardew further "satirized" *Plus Minus* in his piece *Solo with Accompaniment* (1964).[77] About the premiere, Maconie writes,

---

[74] Jan Williams, personal communication (May 5, 2016).
[75] Figure 2.6: Folder 7, Figure 2.7: Folder 6; Figure 2.8: Folder 1. Jan Williams Collection of Annotated Scores. Reproduced with permission.
[76] Fox, "Written in Sand," 19.
[77] "Feeling the healthy composer's reluctance to compose another man's music, [I] decided to bring all elements as quickly as possible into the negative sphere." Cornelius Cardew, "Stockhausen's *Plus-Minus*," *London Magazine* (April 1967), 87, cited in Virginia Anderson, "'Well, It's a Vertebrate...': Performer Choice in Cardew's *Treatise*," *Journal of Musicological Research* 25, no. 3–4 (2006), 300.

70   INTERPRETIVE LABOR

Figure 2.7 Three measures of musical notation, hand-written by Williams, Burnham, and/or Cardew. Folder 6, Jan Williams Collection of Annotated Scores (1950–1999), Mus. Arc. 10.1, Box 13, Item 175. University at Buffalo Music Library. Reproduced with permission.

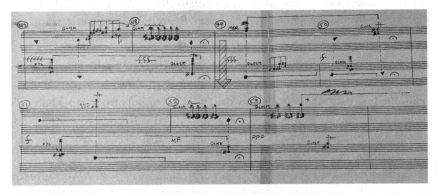

Figure 2.8 Manuscript score excerpt of the material sketched above, hand-written by Williams, Burnham, and/or Cardew. Folder 1, Jan Williams Collection of Annotated Scores (1950–1999), Mus. Arc. 10.1, Box 13, Item 175. University at Buffalo Music Library. Reproduced with permission.

In 1964 Frederic Rzewski and Cornelius Cardew prepared a version of *Plus-Minus*—one page each—for two pianos. Both decided to use an accessory instrument to perform the "negative-band" music which appears when a "central sound" is eliminated from play. Rzewski decided on a cluster played on harmonium, while Cardew opted to play static noise found between stations on a transistor radio. Stockhausen, who was not consulted on the matter and who was not particularly enamoured of either sound source, nevertheless expressed approval of the result.[78]

---

[78] Maconie, *The Works of Karlheinz Stockhausen*, 162.

THE "EXECUTIVE" MODEL   71

This "approval" is noted in the third volume of Stockhausen's *Texte zur Musik* (1963–70), in which he notes that he was fascinated by the sounds created by Cardew and Rzewski. Stockhausen writes,

> Sounds and sound combinations that, while recognizing their use by other composers, I had personally avoided . . . were now being brought by performers *into my music*, and in exact accordance with the functional sound requirements laid down in the score. The result is a highly poetic quality, reached as a result of the way *Plus Minus* is constructed.[79]

Stockhausen, then, approved of his own construction of the piece, and not necessarily of the interpretive, translational work done by Cardew and Rzewski, but he did have a generally positive reaction to the recording of their performance.

In contrast, Stockhausen seemed less enamored of Charlotte Moorman, perhaps for her handling of some documents she had borrowed for the Avant Garde Festival. A letter dated October 15, 1964, reads:

> Dear. Miss Moorman,
> I still expect—according to our agreement—book of my Texte II and tapes of Originale. Please send it TO-DAY!
> K. Stockhausen[80]

If the text were not brusque enough to make his point, the composer also hand-wrote this in black marker, in print large enough to fill an entire sheet of paper.

Surviving documents from the *Plus Minus* performance at that festival reveal some of the challenges presented by Stockhausen's raw material. On August 30, 1964, Moorman gave a cello recital as the opening event in the second annual festival, accompanied by Nam June Paik and Terry Jennings. The performers of this version are listed in the program as "c moorman and robot," and there are accompanying notes to indicate that the realization was done by Paik, and that the performance was the world premiere.[81] For 99

---

[79] Emphasis added. Karlheinz Stockhausen, *Texte zur Musik*, vol. 3, ed. Dieter Schnebel (Cologne: DuMont Buchverlag, 1971) [since 1991, published by the Stockhausen-Verlag, Kürten], cited in Maconie, *Other Planets*, 252.

[80] Charlotte Moorman Archive, folder 34, McCormick Library of Special Collections, Northwestern University Library.

[81] Given the Cardew-Rzewski premiere, this is inaccurate. Program booklet in Charlotte Moorman Archive, folder 43.

72   INTERPRETIVE LABOR

cents, interested audience members could gather in Judson Hall, greeted by Paik's latest technological creation, which he called Robot Opera. A hand-written note on Peter Moore's photograph proof pages indicates that that audience included George Maciunas, Max Neuhaus, and Allan Kaprow—artists associated with the playful experimental semi-group Fluxus, who will be discussed in the following chapters. Moore's stunning photographs provide vivid, intimate images of the concert, including Moorman per-forming, audience members mingling in the lobby during intermission, and Paik's robot on stage. Just as importantly, Moorman also kept the three sketchbooks for Paik's realization of *Plus Minus*, stapled booklets of manu-script paper with notations on treble and bass clefs. One such page is shown below in Figure 2.9.

On some pages of the sketches, the top staff is marked "Robot" and the lower staff "Tape"; on others, there are no such indications. Many sections show one notehead per staff, with a squiggly diagonal line between them to in-dicate glissandi played on the cello. In addition to these three booklets, Moorman and Paik also archived several versions of prose about the realiza-tion, noting in part,

> The MUSIC GRAPH of PLUS MINUS can demand a unique place in its in-tegrity and originality in today's music graphic rush-hours. Paik's realization of Stockhausen's symbols resulted in cello glissandos of every variety and velocity played by Miss Moorman and pizzicatos played by Paik's robot "Robot Opera." Electronically controlled by a 30 channel wireless system, this robot waved its hat, twirled its left breast, lit up its nose, revolved its propelled eyes, twisted its abdomen & even walked—forwards, backwards and in all directions.[82]

Even with all of this documentation, though, it is difficult to determine the precise working procedures for making that realization. One mystery resides on the back of a barely legible draft of a letter from Moorman to Stockhausen, written while she was preparing for the *Originale* performance as part of the AG Fest. Stamped June 29, 1964, the faintly written note reads, "Ronald Thomas is working hard on Plus-Minus & went to Coudersport, PA to make the tape & will be back 8th Wednesday."[83] Thomas, now primarily a

---

[82] The last sentence is crossed out in one of the three versions of this text. Score documentation [no folder number], Charlotte Moorman Archive.

[83] Charlotte Moorman Archive, folder 34, McCormick Library of Special Collections, Northwestern University Library.

Figure 2.9 Two pages of manuscript for *Plus Minus*, hand-written by Charlotte Moorman and/or Nam June Paik in 1964. Score documentation [no folder number], Charlotte Moorman Archive, McCormick Library of Special Collections, Northwestern University Library.

jazz-influenced keyboardist who describes *Plus Minus* as "a formidable and valuable discipline," was at that time studying with Stockhausen.[84] Oddly, there is no mention of his contribution within the program book for the festival. While the sketches mention use of tape, it may have been omitted in the end. Most likely, though, whatever sounds were produced on the tape recording would have made up the "negative band" material, to be sounded during specified interruptions ("At 0 a negative band is to be heard during the interruption; at -1, -2 etc., the negative band is itself interrupted once, twice, etc., according to the duration of the subtracted parts in question").[85]

According to music theorist Alcedo Coenen, *Plus Minus* is similar to *Spiral*, *Kurzwellen*, and others that he identifies as "process-plan pieces":

---

[84] Ron Thomas, autobiography, http://www.ronthomasmusic.com/bio.html.
[85] Karlheinz Stockhausen, *Plus Minus*, 12.

74 INTERPRETIVE LABOR

The main element is the process, being a musical structure in which elements are transformed. The main parameter involved is change (*Veränderung*), which is expressed in terms of increase or decrease, concerning any parameter in relation to some other event. In these scores this is mostly found notated in terms of plus, minus, and equal signs.... The scores are meant to be worked out by the musicians themselves, interpreting these signs in relation to some chosen source. *Plus-Minus* and *Spiral* are the most abstract examples of this meta-music idea; every version of these pieces is a new piece in itself; the process of composition has become part of the performance.[86]

Given this reading, it may not be surprising that there have been relatively few documented performances of this piece, and almost none that attempt to realize all seven pages of pitch material.[87] Returning to Christopher Fox's recent account——which provides valuable insight into the decisions made and contributing factors in his and John Snijders's 1999 translation of Stockhausen's score——we find that the two realizers differed in several ways in their approach. This serves to illustrate the areas of indeterminacy in the piece: for example, choosing instruments, how to indicate time, and even how much of the notation to work out for the performers and how much to leave flexible.[88] Despite the abundant instructions, making a realization is no straightforward task. For example, the end of note 31 states that "insertions should be clear announcements or memories [*Erinnerungen*] foreign to the context."[89] What does the composer mean by "memories"? This particular note explains where to insert events from certain pages into blank squares on other pages, so the material has just been worked out. Should it be revised to fit with some memory of another sound? As Fox recalls,

Anyone wanting to make music from [*Plus Minus*] has to be willing to spend hours deciphering the symbols, and then many more hours translating each constellation of symbols into something that musicians can actually

---

[86] Alcedo Coenen, "Stockhausen's Paradigm: A Survey of His Theories," *Perspectives of New Music* 32, no. 2 (Summer 1994), 213.

[87] As of 2000, only one known version had been made using the complete score. Fox, "Written in Sand," 20.

[88] "I had brought a rather more British attitude to my realisation, effectively composing out any performer freedom and providing instead a prescriptive solution of Stockhausen's puzzle." Fox, "Written in Sand," 20.

[89] Stockhausen, *Plus Minus*, 13.

read. . . . It took months, a process of trial and error in which I would translate a few symbols, discover I had misunderstood an instruction and have to start all over again. . . . It was a strange experience. I was composing, yet not writing my own music, referring every decision back to Stockhausen's instructions, some of them quite ambiguous.[90]

One ambiguous note is that of the "negative bands." It reads in part,

To represent 0 and negative numbers acoustically two so-called negative bands of sound should be added to each layer (one to the Zentralklänge, the other to the Akzidentien). All parameters (e.g., duration, pitch, dynamics, timbre, location in space etc.) may be included in the distribution of negative assignments. The negative bands should be in obvious opposition (e.g., very soft, undefinable) to the corresponding positive layers.[91]

Fox and Snijders, like Cardew and Rzewski, used two different noise sources for the "negative band," in this case choosing recordings of tearing paper and spoken-word material in a collage of different languages, respectively.

In every instance of realization, the piece makes significant demands on anyone who wants to engage with it, no matter their expertise in performance or composition, or both. In the Hacker chapter, I will consider subversive responses to this phenomenon, especially Cardew's, but note also Gavin Bryars and John Tilbury's "painstaking irreverence" (pace Fox) toward the score, which was an alternate way of dealing with the demands of its detailed instructions. On the other hand, Fox notes:

Why did John [Snijders] and I persevere? . . . a perverse pride in the extraordinary lengths to which we were going to bring Plus minus to life again—if obsessive characters like John and I weren't prepared to make the effort, who are? . . . [we] became ever more aware of the quality of thought that had gone into the creation of the score. There are ambiguities, some of which one or both of us deliberately exploited, but Stockhausen has created a remarkably coherent, provocative and complex theoretical environment within which realisations can grow.[92]

---

[90] Fox, "The Flat-Pack Stockhausen."
[91] Stockhausen, *Plus Minus*, 12.
[92] Fox, "Written in Sand," 22. The work's title is not italicized in this source.

76   INTERPRETIVE LABOR

Elsewhere, Fox explained his motivations more succinctly: "*Plus Minus* comes from the middle of a 20-year period in which Stockhausen invented some of the most extraordinary music of the last century. Working on the score was like having a composition lesson with him at the height of his powers."[93]

Throughout the performances discussed here--Cardew/Rzewski, Moorman/Paik, Williams/Burnham/Cardew, and Fox/Snijders--the participants engaged in co-composition, not only with their collaborators for their individual performances, but with Stockhausen himself. The kinds of work done by these musicians shows that--beyond the broader form of realization, which is itself a form of broader interpretation--co-composition is a demanding form of labor. This is reflected both in the extant materials that document their procedures and in comments by some of these individuals. As Cardew stated in the program note for Buffalo, "I began composing this piece several years ago," and again, Fox said "I was composing."[94] These statements are unambiguous. In the case of *Plus Minus*, to an extent greater than in most other musical works, the information provided by the composer has to be translated into notation before it can be performed.

Translational Labor in *Plus Minus*

What of the sort of work being undertaken by interpreters of indeterminate forms? Is their labor different from that of performers who have a precise text? Sandra Bermann, who draws surprising connections between such disparate writers as Walter Benjamin, J. L. Austin, Jacques Derrida, and Judith Butler, identifies the issue of *performing* translation. This perspective is particularly apt for the ideas under consideration in this chapter, as it emphasizes the *doing* of translation: performing translational acts. The work being done by all who realize *Plus Minus* is direct in this way. This is not translation as metaphor; this is translation as action. Here, Barbara Godard's conception of "transformance" is apt, especially in the labor of realizing *Plus Minus*. This new term combines performance, translation, and transformation, emphasizing that translators are "active participant[s]

---

[93] Fox, "The Flat-Pack Stockhausen."
[94] Cardew, program note for Evenings for New Music concert no. 31; Fox, "The Flat-Pack Stockhausen."

THE "EXECUTIVE" MODEL   77

in the creation of meaning, who advance a conditional analysis."[95] Any realization of *Plus Minus* necessarily includes performance, translation, and
transformation. One cannot simply open the published score and begin to
play. The provided notation has to be transformed from a sort of map with
various directional indications and side-trips in order to be legible as a piece
of music. The new version of the piece, arrived at after substantial work and
thought, is translated from the page into audible sound in performance.
Translation happens in layers here: first from Stockhausen to the realizers,
then the realizers to the performers, then the performers to the audience.
While this is not so different from many indeterminate compositions, *Plus
Minus* does require an unusual degree of interpretive work on the part of
its realizers. Again, its translators are "active participant[s] in the creation of
meaning"; the original composer gives up some control over the meaning
of the piece, a fact that would be increasingly exploited by musicians in later
performances.[96] Returning to the ideas of borders, through its performativity,
translation is politicized (or, more accurately, it is always already political,
but by conceiving of it as an action, we more readily recognize it as political).
The translator becomes acutely aware of the boundary between the self and
the other as s/he works through the steps of making a translation of a text,
and this holds true for both linguistic and musical texts.

Alongside Godard's "transformance," perhaps the most applicable account
of translation for this project can be found in Derrida's 1998 lecture "Qu'est-
ce qu'une traduction 'relevante'?" In his typically circuitous language,
maintained productively in Venuti's English translation, Derrida interrogates
the word *relève* (relevant, answerable, to answer, "the most right, appropriate,
pertinent, adequate, opportune, pointed, univocal, idiomatic, and so on").[97]
While his primary emphasis is on the questions of translatability or untrans-
latability and of tensions between aiming for the letter (literalizing) or the
spirit (free) of the original, these issues are bound up in questions of language itself. One tiny branch of this thought—almost an aside—encapsulates
the problem under consideration throughout this chapter: Derrida connects
the terms "translation," "transit," "traveling," "travailing—which in French,

---

[95] Barbara Godard, "Theorizing Feminist Discourse/Translation," *Tessera* 6 (1989), 50, cited in
Bermann, "Performing Translation," 293.
[96] This phrase also from Godard's "Theorizing Feminist Discourse/Translation."
[97] Derrida, "What Is a 'Relevant' Translation?," 177.

78 INTERPRETIVE LABOR

of course, is labor (*travailler*—to work).[98] Translation, then, moves through movement itself into labor; translation in action is work.

To step back onto solid ground for a moment, interpretation as translation also implies (and embodies, enacts) social and cultural encounters. The core significance of translation is that it always activates this borderline between two entities, two authors/artists. Glossing Benjamin, Cohen writes, "Translation serves to come to terms with conditions of cultural plurality in a way that benefits from contact with cultural difference."[99] In other words, translational procedures help us to identify similarities between ourselves and others, thus productively negotiating difference. Bohlman argues, "Translation endows cultural history with moral responsibility."[100] Not only are we tasked with fairly representing these (temporal, geographical) differences, but we also ought to be mindful of the ways our translations might be read in the future. Finally, we return to Bermann: "Translation is not merely the interpretation that a translator performs on a literary or social script. Rather, translation itself—and particularly its encounter with otherness—becomes a model for ethical and political action. In this sense, 'performing translation' allegorizes an ethical, and politically effective, comportment."[101] Translational acts, then, are far from some neutral mapping of one language onto another. Instead, they involve moral, ethical, and political *work*. For artists realizing Stockhausen's works *Carré* and *Plus Minus*, though, that work must be excavated from its hidden place. Otherwise, Stockhausen the executive gets to keep all of the authorial credit.

***

The indeterminate elements in both pieces discussed here are the product of a particular stance on the composer's part, namely, that of an individual in a position of authority. In *Carré*, Stockhausen has handed off the responsibility of realizing his sketches to a qualified worker, who then translates the notes, comments, and other feedback into a more permanent—and more legible—form. In *Plus Minus*, this procedure is one step further removed, in that the realizers may actually be the performers (or some other person/ group who prepares a score for them), rather than one individual working

---

[98] "The word is not only *in* translation, as one would say in the works or in transit, *traveling, travailing,* in *labor.*" Derrida, "What Is a 'Relevant' Translation?," 177; emphases in original.

[99] Cohen, "Boundary Situations," 330.

[100] Bohlman, "Translating Herder Translating," 519.

[101] Bermann, "Performing Translation," 293.

THE "EXECUTIVE" MODEL   79

closely with the composer. With these arrangements in mind, the concepts of realization and translation take on a new urgency: they are absolutely crucial to understanding the labor involved in these compositions.

CONCLUSION: THE EXECUTIVE MODEL TODAY

To revisit the key components of Interpretive Labor, introduced in Chapter 1:

1. The indeterminate situation is created by Stockhausen, and must be dealt with by his assistant.
2. Cardew is given an almost overwhelming amount of oversight. Guidance includes verbal, written, and visual feedback, which is essentially constant during the working process.
3. Cardew knows the system pretty well, but his understanding is constantly "improving" or being refined through the feedback from Stockhausen.
4. Recognition for his contributions is almost nil, at least as formally documented. Stockhausen's name is on the score; Cardew has to make his own recognition through the publication of the "Reports," later writings, and so forth. In the published score for *Carré*, Cardew is mentioned but given very little credit, as discussed below. Likewise, in a six-page discussion of the piece in Maconie's handbook, he receives only one terse sentence: "The writing-out of *Carré* from the composer's sketch plans was undertaken by Cornelius Cardew in 1959."[102] There is no discussion of what that actually meant, no elaboration apart from citing Cardew's *Musical Times* report in the footnote. Looking ahead to the Hacker model, I would like to suggest that subversive reactions often come into play when there is a serious imbalance of power. Talented, knowledgeable agents (whether intelligence or customer service) feel the weight of oppression by the ruling entity and act out. It is no coincidence that the term "agent" is used in these contexts.
5. The ratio of difficulty to recognition is imbalanced, suggesting that it may not have been worth the effort. Thinking of this collaboration in terms of a return-on-investment analysis, it likely was not worth it for Cardew to have taken on this assignment. He, as the so-called

---

[102] Maconie, *The Works of Karlheinz Stockhausen*, 96.

80 INTERPRETIVE LABOR

agent, has very little power and receives insufficient recognition for doing much of the hard work, while the manager/composer/person-in-power gets credit and financial compensation for achieving the goal.[103] Stockhausen does mention him in the note preceding the published score to *Carré*, but it reads: "The score was worked out in 1959 *in collaboration with my assistant* at that time, Cornelius Cardew, who notated it *with me* according to *my* plans, drawings, daily instructions and corrections."[104] In this brief sentence, there are four distinct linguistic indicators of power over Cardew: (1) it is not that Cardew worked out the score, it is that Stockhausen worked out the score "in collaboration with" someone; (2) Cardew is identified not as a composer, but as "my assistant"—and he further qualifies him as his assistant only "at that time" [*damaligen*], not as anyone with a long-term relationship; (3) Cardew notated it "with me," as if the younger composer were incapable of managing notation by himself and (4) Stockhausen points out the extent to which Cardew required hand-holding with "daily instructions and corrections."

So, here we have a composer with a strong ego—hardly a notable situation. What is different here is the mode of interaction, the relationships between him and those who worked alongside him to produce legible texts based on his ideas. This is not unheard of in the visual arts; for example, I find it instructive that Damien Hirst's minimalist paintings, produced by poorly paid assistants, are unironically treated as an investment strategy in the journal of the International Honor Society in Economics.[105] However, this sort of relationship is unusual in the arts, especially in musical composition, perhaps apart from film scoring. In some ways, an artist like Stockhausen is exactly

---

[103] Cardew's payment for being Stockhausen's assistant is unknown, but I posit that he would not have complained so much about the process if he had been happy with his compensation. Or perhaps he was just difficult.

[104] "Die Ausarbeitung entstand 1959 unter Mitwirkung meines damaligen Assistenten Cornelius Cardew, der gemäß meinen Plänen, Zeichnungen, täglichen Instruktionen und Korrekturen die Partitur mit mir notierte." Karlheinz Stockhausen, *Carré* (Vienna: Universal Edition, 1960), ii (emphasis added).

[105] Marjorie May Haight, "Value in Outsourcing Labor and Creating a Brand in the Art Market: The Damien Hirst Business Plan," *The American Economist* 56, no. 1 (Spring 2011), 78–88.

THE "EXECUTIVE" MODEL   81

the type of "dictator" or "monster" against which John Cage claimed to re-coil.[106] I do not intend to conflate the practices of Stockhausen with either the danger and violence of truly totalitarian dictators or the profit-driven moral ambivalence of capitalist leaders, but rather to bring these functions into conversation, in order to tease out what precisely is happening in this type of indeterminate realization.

If Stockhausen's role is that of the executive, and his realizers the exploited laborers, what does that mean beyond their unique relationships? For one thing, it enables us to watch out for that paradigm in other eras and with other individuals. Perhaps the clearest example today is German composer-provocateur Johannes Kreidler's 2009 performance-art piece *Fremdarbeit* for flute, cello, keyboard, percussion, electronics, and moderator.[107] Briefly, the premise is that Kreidler received a generous (by new-music standards) com-mission for a new work, and used just a small fraction of the funds to hire a Chinese composer ("Xia Non Xiang") and an Indian computer programmer ("Ramesh Murraybay") to create the four movements in the style of his other compositions. In performance, he acts as a "moderator," commenting on the procedure undertaken, complaining about the inadequacies of the work done by Xiang and Murraybay, and tossing off likely intentionally offensive comments: for example, "China is well known for plagiarism."[108] Not sur-prisingly, the piece has triggered strong and varied reactions. In October 2013, I attended the Kreidler concert co-sponsored by The Goethe-Institut Chicago and Ensemble Dal Niente, where the Q & A after the concert spiraled out into a tense but productive discussion. In discussing a performance in London the following year, a critic with the British political magazine *New Statesman* claimed that "any disapproval the audience might have felt for the composer's methods was destabilised by his spoken-word sections, as he reminded us of the role of assistants in the visual arts––is *Fremdarbeit*

[106] He refers here to compositions, not composers, but the idea is apt: "The fact that these things that constitute it [the *Music of Changes*], though only sounds, have come together to con-trol a human being, the performer, gives the work the alarming aspect of a Frankenstein monster. This situation is of course characteristic of Western music, the masterpieces of which are its most frightening examples, which when concerned with humane [*sic?*] communication only move over from Frankenstein monster to Dictator." John Cage, "Composition as Process, II. Indeterminacy," in *Silence: Lectures and Writings*, 36.

[107] Typically translated into English as "Outsourcing"; transliterated more precisely as "Foreign Work," although that seems to obscure the politically charged implications of the shorter title in the United States. See discussion of the term as it applies to Germany in Martin Iddon, "Outsourcing Progress: On Conceptual Music," *Tempo* 70, no. 275 (January 2016), 39, note 7.

[108] Johannes Kreidler, moderator's introduction to *Fremdarbeit*, cited in Iddon, "Outsourcing Progress," 39.

82 INTERPRETIVE LABOR

exploitative in a way that the work of Damien Hirst or Roy Lichtenstein is not?"[109] When the piece was presented at the International Computer Music Conference, on the other hand, "after 5 minutes of the piece the Chinese delegation left the hall, leading to discussions all night long with the festival chief"--a perfectly understandable response.[110]

The concept of exploitation merits a closer look. For most contemporary applications of the idea, I adopt the stance of so-called neo-Ricardians toward Marx's labor theory of value (LTV), if only because their critique expands the meaning of exploitation.[111] Under orthodox Marxism, that term refers to the value of surplus labor:

> During the second period of the labor-process, that in which his labor is no longer necessary labor [that is, required for subsistence], the workman, it is true, labors, expends labor-power; but his labor, being no longer necessary labor, he creates no value for himself. He creates surplus-value which, for the capitalist, has all the charms of a creation out of nothing. This portion of the working-day, I name surplus labor-time, and to the labor expended during that time, I give the name of surplus-labor. . . . The rate of surplus-value is therefore an exact expression for the degree of exploitation of labor-power by capital, or of the laborer by the capitalist.[112]

Thus, if it took eight hours to complete the work necessary for subsistence, and a worker continued at his or her post for a total of nine hours, that additional hour was extracted as surplus-value, or exploitation: an extra hour of labor for the capitalist (e.g., factory owner) who stood to benefit from that work. While this was an important initial conception of workers' "extra" work beyond that necessary for continuous production as predicted, it is limited to work within a specific mode of production. According to neo-Ricardian economics, in contrast, "exploitation is no longer seen as the extraction of

---

[109] I would disagree that Hirst's "art" is not exploitative, as discussed above. Alexandra Coghlan, "Sounds from the Sweatshop," *New Statesman* 143, no. 5213 (June 6, 2014), 59.

[110] Johannes Kreidler, "The Culture of Copying: Monetary Value and Exploitation," interview with Julian Day, *Runway: Australian Experimental Art*, n.p., http://runway.org.au.

[111] A reference to neoclassical theories of value and distribution, named for David Ricardo (1772–1823). See Heinz D. Kutz and Neri Salvadori, "Neo-Ricardian Economics," *The New Palgrave Dictionary of Economics*, 2nd ed., ed. Steven N. Durlauf and Lawrence E. Blume (London: Palgrave Macmillan, 2008).

[112] Karl Marx, *Capital: A Critique of Political Economy, Vol. I: The Process of Capitalist Production*, trans. from the third German edition by Samuel Moore and Edward Aveling, ed. Frederick Engels (New York: International Publishers, 1967), 217–18.

THE "EXECUTIVE" MODEL   83

surplus value in the production process. Instead, exploitation can be seen as the outcome of unequal exchanges between workers and capitalists in the market."[113] In other words, it now encompasses any situation in which the value of a worker/laborer's efforts exceeds the corresponding compensation. It is in this expanded sense that I employ the concept of exploitation.

The "market" mentioned in the quote above indicates a totality within which resources are allocated. In a balanced market, workers are paid exactly what their time is worth, and those who control the means of production ensure an even exchange of goods and compensation. In the forms of labor with which I am concerned, this really only works in a metaphorical sense. It would be unwise to insist that there is some finite quantity of conceptual artistic resources that must be allocated to participants.[114] If a given musician produces a well-respected iteration of an indeterminate work and is recognized for that performance, a second musician does not lose recognition in order to rebalance the market. Instead, we might think about the market in the sense of an analogy: a pool of water that can be topped off when it rains, or a vending machine that gets refilled regularly. In other words, this is no orthodox Marxist market. It is simply a conception of artistic practice that takes into account work, recognition, and compensation. The market includes funds for commissions, ticket fees, and other concrete financial components, but also the accumulation of recognition, prestige, and power.

As noted by journalist Laura Battle, Kreidler's work shares with other dystopian art "an interest in exposing power structures and an enjoyment of the fine line between artifice and authenticity, between criticism and complicity."[115] Indeed, if Kreidler actually did outsource the composition of his piece, he is just as guilty as any other greedy executive. Should he be absolved of this guilt simply for shining a light on the exploitative circumstances? Is he trying to suggest that it is acceptable to perpetuate abuse in the name of art, in the name of bringing greater attention to abuse? Or is this just another charlatan, making a name for himself by loudly and publicly latching on to the most outrageous issues of the day? I am inclined to agree with Martin Iddon, who questions whether the entire thing is made up and is part of the piece itself. Like Kreidler's other well-known performance-art piece, *product*

---

[113] Rowlinson and Hassard, "Marxist Political Economy," 89.

[114] Of course, grants and other funding sources are limited, but this expanded notion of exploitation includes issues of recognition/cultural capital, as well.

[115] Laura Battle, "It's the Sound of the Left, All Right," *The Financial Times* (May 31, 2014), 12.

84 INTERPRETIVE LABOR

placements, it has the potential to be fiction.[116] After questioning the alleged names of the two "collaborators," Iddon notes:

> Perhaps, one might argue, Kreidler has simply concealed the "real" identities of the Chinese composer and Indian programmer by giving them pseudonyms. Yet there is no need to have provided images of them save for the illusory ring of truth these provide. Furthermore, once one's scepticism has been aroused it seems obvious that a much simpler, easier solution exists than the one which the complete score of *Fremdarbeit*—including the moderator's sections—describes, which is to say that the piece was written, in all of its specifics, by Kreidler himself. In this sense, the performance of *Fremdarbeit* has a similar relationship to the whole piece, the theatre piece which *Fremdarbeit* is, to that which the fixed media piece *product placements* has to the theatrical action *product placements*.[117]

Importantly, while *Fremdarbeit* as fiction does ease Kreidler's complicity in an unfair economic system, it does not eliminate its problematic position. In contracting out to workers in China and India (or at least portraying that situation), Kreidler "does nevertheless still produce colonial stereotypes . . . . Though individuals remain unexploited within *Fremdarbeit*, its discourse repeats a colonial one; the other subjects it depicts are fictional functions of the musical theatre, but they represent recognisable stereotypes."[118] This was not an accident. In the documentary, Kreidler claims that his audience called the "plagiarism" of the two workers "just crap," but notes that the work done by "Xiang" (perhaps really by himself) was quite good, so the alleged audience reaction "clearly illustrated that powerful stereotypes are at work."[119] Not only is the "outsourcing" itself likely a fiction, but perhaps also is the perpetuation of stereotypes. On the other hand, doing something ironically is still doing it.

To close this consideration of executive and exploitative labor in music, let me draw one last parallel between Kreidler and Stockhausen. Stockhausen,

---

[116] This is a video work in which Kreidler purportedly filled out over 70,000 copyright-permissions forms to use audio samples in a short work, brought those forms to GEMA (the German office for permissions), and intercut footage of this action with calls to GEMA, a staged press conference about the legal status of copying, and commentary by a copyright attorney.

[117] Iddon, "Outsourcing Progress," 46.

[118] Iddon, "Outsourcing Progress," 48.

[119] "Vollständige Dokumentation der Kompositionsaktion 'Fremdarbeit' (Full documentary of the Performance Piece 'Fremdarbeit' ('Outsourcing') by Johannes Kreidler). Es spielt das Ensemble Mosaik Berlin." Uploaded to YouTube by Johannes Kreidler on November 26, 2009.

THE "EXECUTIVE" MODEL   85

in a lecture given in 1971, says, "I tell my own students, if you want to become famous just take a magnifying glass and put it up to my scores, and what you see there, just multiply that for five years. For example, if you see snare drums, then you start composing around twenty pieces only for snare drums. Snare drums of all different sizes: for fifty snare drums, for twenty, for thirty—snare drums on the roof, snare drums in the basement...."[120] Like Kreidler's 70,200 license-permission request forms in *product placements*, this is "expansio ad absurdum," to borrow Iddon's phrase.[121] It succeeds in making its rhetorical point in both instances: Kreidler draws attention to draconian copyright laws in Germany (and elsewhere), and Stockhausen positions himself as a person of influence. Likewise, in the documentary-video version, musicologist Marie-Anne Kohl, interviewed after a performance, says that the issue of exploitation is "polarized" in the piece, that "that is what Kreidler is exposing and what he's doing. He's playing the role of master."[122] Stockhausen and Kreidler, masters of their under-recognized workers and masters of their reputations, both embody the role of the late-capitalist executive. Through this model of Interpretive Labor, the depth of the imbalance is made clear. For Stockhausen, indeterminacy was given to (or, rather, imposed upon) his assistants, performers, realizers, co-composers—despite his apparent sole ownership of the resulting composition.

[120] Karlheinz Stockhausen, "Musical Forming: Composing Statistically," lecture filmed by Allied Artists, London 1971, reproduced in *Stockhausen on Music: Lectures and Interviews*, compiled by Robin Maconie (London: Marion Boyars, 1989), 52.
[121] Iddon, "Outsourcing Progress," 38.
[122] Attributed as Anne Kohl. "Vollständige Dokumentation der Kompositionsaktion 'Fremdarbeit.'"

3

THE "SCIENTIST" MODEL

THE COMPOSITION STUDIO AS LABORATORY

An original work of art, one that does not imitate anything, has many challenges to overcome. It is difficult to judge or classify, and at first, no one is sure of its worth. The artist is on guard, looking critically to find its shortcomings. Often, he does not know what is going on or where it is leading to. But his struggle gives a specific energy to the work, it makes it exciting and interesting to pursue, despite the fogginess and contradictions that it often generates. The tensions and questions the new work generates are exactly what make it attractive . . .

—Petr Kotík[1]

MEET PETR KOTÍK

"I'm going to use you," the conductor says, striding toward the front of the performance space. Having known each other for all of a minute and a half, I suppress a raised eyebrow and smile in a way that I hope conveys respect and curiosity. This is Petr Kotík, composer, flautist, and director of the S.E.M. Ensemble, and he wants me to assess the balance between the piano, percussion, and the rest of the ensemble during a rehearsal of his composition *Nine + 1*. Scored for flute, clarinet, trumpet, horn, a handful of strings, and the aforementioned piano and drum set, it was commissioned in 2013 for the "Ensemble Europa" series at WDR (Westdeutscher Rundfunk) Cologne.[2] I am in New York City in April 2015 to observe rehearsals and performances by the groups Ostravská Banda (established in 2005) and the S.E.M.

---

[1] Petr Kotík, program-magazine *Ostravské Dny [Ostrava Days] 2015*, 15.
[2] http://www.semensemble.org/about/petr-kotik.

Interpretive Labor. Kirsten I. Speyer Carithers, Oxford University Press. © Oxford University Press 2025.
DOI: 10.1093/9780197698815.003.0004

THE "SCIENTIST" MODEL   87

Ensemble (est. 1970) and its orchestra (1992), all of which were founded by Kotík.

In this concert series, the groups are honoring the 50th anniversary of the Association for the Advancement of Creative Musicians (AACM). As noted in press for the events, the finale "features major works for symphony and chamber orchestra by composers associated with the AACM—Muhal Richard Abrams, Roscoe Mitchell, George E. Lewis and Henry Threadgill—as well as works by John Cage, Christian Wolff and Petr Kotík."[3] The Tuesday concert, for chamber groups of varying makeup, included compositions by Mitchell and Lewis, along with the aforementioned *Nine + 1* and some other short pieces. Wednesday's event was an unusual double-bill of compositions for full orchestra, followed by a lengthy improvised piece created by Abrams, Lewis, and Mitchell. The concerts in the AACM50 series—four in total—are co-sponsored by Interpretations,[4] the S.E.M. Ensemble, Roulette Intermedia, the Czech Center New York at Bohemian National Hall, and the Ostrava Center for New Music.

As discussed in the Introduction, the AACM was founded in Chicago in 1965, and is the subject of two major works by polymath George E. Lewis: both a hefty academic text and a one-act opera, the staged version of which had its out-of-town preview at the 2015 Ostrava Days festival.[5] It has clearly been a vital inspirational force for creative artists in numerous fields, across experimental sound, free improvisation, jazz, and everything in between, including the ensembles founded by Petr Kotík. One might wonder how a Czech musician, known primarily for his fully notated, aesthetically neo-medieval compositions, might have become involved in its advocacy and celebration. In fact, Kotík has had a number of interactions with members of the group, beginning decades ago. The AACM saxophonist and composer Roscoe Mitchell had several of his works premiered by the S.E.M. Ensemble, in renowned venues such as Alice Tully Hall and the Prague Spring Festival, dating back to at least the mid-1990s.[6] For the 2015 events, S.E.M.'s involvement seems to have been initiated by baritone singer Thomas

---

[3] http://www.semensemble.org/aacm50.

[4] Contact information for the Interpretations series leads to Mutable Music, directed and produced by baritone singer Thomas Buckner, who also performed on the April concerts. The 2014–15 season, according to its website, consisted almost entirely of the four AACM tributes, one of which was a Buckner feature.

[5] Lewis, *A Power Stronger Than Itself* and *Afterword: The AACM (as) Opera*.

[6] http://aacm-newyork.com/roscoemitchell.html; also, personal correspondence with Petr Kotík, February 23, 2016.

Figure 3.1 Muhal Richard Abrams, Roscoe Mitchell, and George E. Lewis performing. Photograph by the author. Bohemian National Hall, New York, NY, April 29, 2015.

Buckner. According to AACM member and co-founder Muhal Richard Abrams, Buckner originally approached him with the idea of a tribute concert in honor of AACM's 50th anniversary with compositions written for the singer by AACM members.[7] That initial concert took place on March 19, 2015, but the idea was also expanded into a four-concert series, including the two with the Orchestra of the S.E.M. Ensemble and members of Ostravská Banda, held at the end of April.

Already in this brief vignette, we gain glimpses of labor- and compensation-related issues that might frame the following investigation. The concerts took place at the Bohemian National Hall (Figure 3.1), a large, recently renovated building on the affluent Upper East Side of Manhattan. Built in 1896 "with contributions from the newly arrived immigrants," it

---

[7] Interview with Muhal Richard Abrams, George E. Lewis, and Petr Kotík, WKCR New York, April 14, 2015.

houses the member organizations of the Bohemian Benevolent and Literary Association (BBLA), as well as the Czech Consulate General and the Czech Center New York. As of 2001 its ownership was transferred from the BBLA to the Czech government, enabling its expensive renovation.[8] As stated on the welcome page of its website, "the mission of organizations residing in the Bohemian National Hall is the promotion of Czech culture, business and traditions as well as the building of a cultural and social dialog between the Czech and American public."[9] Along with the resident institutions, there are also several spaces that can be rented for conferences, cultural events, business meetings, and so forth, and it was because of this cultural and economic history that the concert series directed by Petr Kotík could be held in that space. Other financial structures are important here, too, especially the concert underwriting itself. Singer Thomas Buckner's access to resources has allowed him to shape a number of different musical endeavors. He has commissioned vocal compositions from numerous avant-garde composers, including Robert Ashley, Christian Wolff, Alvin Lucier, and Phill Niblock, among others. He founded two record labels, 1750 Arch Records and Mutable Music, on whose recordings he appears.[10] In addition, he has produced the Interpretations series for over 20 years, and it was through this initiative that the AACM50 events came to fruition.[11] The central performing group in this AACM series, the S.E.M. Ensemble, is supported by numerous grants and donations as a registered not-for-profit; that group will be discussed in greater detail below.

In short, the various economic systems at play, from individual artists underwriting compositions through commissions, to new-music series with multiple types of sponsors, to the donations that made appealing performance spaces possible, all contribute to a veritable ecology of financial support. This network, in turn, is only possible through the labor of the people who help to produce it, both fundraisers working directly today and the individuals whose historical labor enabled future donors' contributions. While this is certainly a very different form of labor than the interpretive work that forms the core of this project, it is at least as important as that work, for without it, there might be no performances to discuss.

---

[8] http://www.bohemiannationalhall.com/index/bbla/lang/en.

[9] http://www.bohemiannationalhall.com/index/index/lang/en.

[10] http://www.thomasbuckner.com/beta/?page_id = 72.

[11] I might be so bold as to quote "he who has the gold makes the rules"; nearly every season has included a concert featuring Buckner himself. Details at http://www.interpretations.info.

90   INTERPRETIVE LABOR

ON CHANCE AND INTERPRETATION

In the present chapter, I establish the second of five primary models of Interpretive Labor. The current investigation falls toward the more conservative end of the spectrum of indeterminacy, where most musical material is carefully controlled, where the notation largely follows the conventions of the common-practice period, and where performers' actions are almost entirely driven by detailed signs from composers. In fact, there is not much indeterminacy present in the compositions, as most of the interpretive work actually manifests within the composer him- or herself. Chance comes into play only during the compositional process. Therefore, this is largely a self-inflicted form of labor, by and for the composer.

A number of musicians have engaged with the use of chance-based operations while composing. John Cage is likely the best-known example, as his work with *I Ching*–derived hexagrams has been well documented, but he was certainly not the first or last to employ aleatory methods.[12] Compositional indeterminacy may include a number of techniques: throwing dice, tossing coins, or consulting oracles, among others. Chance operations present real decision-making for whoever is creating the piece: for example, does a "6" rolled on a die mean to play mezzo-piano? Or to use a marimba? As Cage noted in 1978, "Most people who believe that I'm interested in chance don't realize that I use chance as a discipline. They think I use it—I don't know—as a way of giving up making choices. But my choices consist in choosing what questions to ask."[13] As a case study in this chapter, to investigate the use of chance procedures, I turn to composer/performer/director Petr Kotík. His work provides a useful counterpoint to the often-cited and well-studied repertoire by Cage. As will become apparent later in the chapter, both artists share similar values for several aspects of music-making, and their kindred

---

[12] "Aleatory" is used here in its limited sense: that of incorporating an element determined by chance (e.g., dice) rather than by human control. Cage began to use chance techniques in the early 1950s, when he became familiar with the *I Ching*, or *Book of Changes*, a book of ancient Chinese philosophy, through his student Christian Wolff. Cage first used it to organize the elements of his piano work *Music of Changes* (1950–1951). David Nicholls, "Getting Rid of the Glue," in *The New York Schools of Music and Visual Arts*, ed. Steven Johnson. Studies in Contemporary Music and Culture (New York: Routledge, 2002), 23. He went on to employ various chance techniques—including charts of potential sounds in the *Sixteen Dances* (1950–1951) and point-drawing in *Music for Carillon* (1952–1954)—in numerous works through 1957. James W. Pritchett, "The Development of Chance Techniques in the Music of John Cage, 1950–1956" (PhD diss., New York University, 1988), 88, 217.

[13] Richard Kostelanetz, ed., *Conversing with Cage* (New York: Routledge, 2003), 17.

voices raise provocative questions about how we read musical scores and experiences.

In addition to concerns about chance as a compositional strategy, this chapter is largely devoted to a model of Interpretive Labor built on that very method. For this, I see Kotík as an ideal protagonist for the concept of interpretation, which itself underpins Interpretive Labor, the central problem of this project as a whole. The theoretical framework of interpretation is envisioned in this case as a synthesis between the strict realization grounding Stockhausen's work, discussed in the previous chapter, and the subversive "hacking" underlying Cardew's reactions, as discussed in Chapter 5. Interpretation, for composers engaging with chance techniques, is a means of grappling with the undefined, of making sense of indeterminate elements; this process imbues responses to visual art, poetry, and other creative actions in addition to music. In my view, interpretation always requires foundational knowledge—stylistic, aesthetic, and conceptual knowledge—that acknowledges the original creator's ideas and values, and it also incorporates a creative process that might be stifled under the rubric conceptualized as transcription or transliteration.[14] It is an active process that manifests as a partnership among composer, performer, and director, and it serves as a dialectic bridge between prescription and openness. This investigation will be grounded in aspects of hermeneutics, particularly drawing on ideas originally established by Herder and Heidegger.

At this time, published sources on Petr Kotík are scant, with just a short entry in the *Grove*, a few paragraphs in Renée Levine Packer's excellent book on the Buffalo program, and a handful of interviews, mainly in Czech music journals, so a short side-trip into biography may be useful for readers unfamiliar with his work.[15] Following this account, I will turn to Kotík's own words about his music and about various processes of sounding, as an entry point for investigating the complex and multi-faceted concept of interpretation. The type of interpretive work being done by Kotík rests largely within a scientific framework. A number of composers have used techniques borrowed from the so-called hard sciences to create music. Simplified, that meant putting forth a hypothesis, testing it, making adjustments, retesting,

---

[14] This is discussed in detail elsewhere in conjunction with the Cardew–Stockhausen relationship.
[15] Ivan Poledňák, "Kotík, Petr," *Grove Music Online, Oxford Music Online*; Renée Levine Packer, *This Life of Sounds: Evenings for New Music in Buffalo* (Oxford: Oxford University Press, 2010); specific journals cited throughout the chapter.

92 INTERPRETIVE LABOR

and so on.[16] This model of Interpretive Labor is largely built on both Kotík and Lejaren Hiller's compositional methods, not only because both used chance techniques but also because of their specific working procedures and the language used to describe their methods.[17] Their scientific (or scientistic) practices in the middle of the 20th century come on the heels of the "machine aesthetic" of Weimar-era German artistic production.[18] Encompassing practices like electronic-music production as well as 12-tone composition and other forms of serialism, this *Neue Sachlichkeit* (New Objectivity) is associated with the visual arts and music as distancing technique from anxieties of de-stabilization.[19]

Through this discussion, I also bring attention to Kotík's merit as an artist and thinker, as well as his roles within overlapping new-music networks, drawing out latent ideas about creative interactions among composers and performers and the ways those relationships fit into the system of Interpretive Labor. Because he has been (and still is) active as a professional performer, director, composer, and festival figurehead, he provides an unusual opportunity to trace the labor inherent in several different positions. In what follows, I will shine a light on these multiple roles and the ways they fit with theories of both work and interpretation.

Born in 1942, Petr Kotík studied music formally both in his hometown of Prague and in Vienna from the mid-1950s to the mid-1960s. He studied flute performance at the Prague Conservatory from 1956 to 1962, and at the Music Academy in Prague from 1966 to 1969. He also studied composition in Prague with Vladimír Šrámek and Jan Rychlík between 1960 and 1964.

---

[16] Of course, the idea of a monolithic scientific method that serves all understanding is hardly adequate; however, this simple model, still frequently taught in basic natural sciences courses, is a useful baseline for more complex forms of inquiry. See, for example: Dan Wivagg, "The Dogma of 'The' Scientific Method," *The American Biology Teacher* 64, no. 9 (November–December 2002), 645–46; Scott B. Watson and Linda James, "The Scientific Method: Is It Still Useful?," *Science Scope* 28, no. 3 (November–December 2004), 37–39; and Ronald A. Brown and Alok Kumar, "The Scientific Method: Reality or Myth?," *Journal of College Science Teaching* 42, no. 4 (March–April 2013), 10–11, among others.

[17] As discussed later, scientific thinking also permeates other musical practices of the era, especially in electronic experiments.

[18] This phrase from Thomas Patteson, *Instruments for New Music: Sound, Technology, and Modernism* (Oakland: University of California Press, 2015), 22.

[19] See, for example, Richard W. McCormick, *Gender and Sexuality in Weimar Modernity: Film, Literature, and "New Objectivity"* (New York: Palgrave Macmillan, 2001), 41; see also Sergiusz Michalski, *New Objectivity: Painting, Graphic Art and Photography in Weimar Germany 1919–1933* (Köln: Taschen, 2003); Stephanie Barron and Sabine Eckmann, eds., *New Objectivity: Modern German Art in the Weimar Republic, 1919–1933* (Los Angeles: Los Angeles County Museum of Art, 2015); and (among other accounts) the many musicological responses to Adorno's *Philosophie der neuen Musik* (Frankfurt-am-Main: Europäische Verlagsanstalt, 1958).

THE "SCIENTIST" MODEL   93

During the period 1963–66, he continued his composition lessons at the Akademie der Musik und Darstellende Kunst in Vienna, studying with Karl Schieske, Hans Jelinek, and Friedrich Cerha.[20] Kotík cites John Cage and R. Buckminster Fuller as influences, but not artists or thinkers whose style he aims to borrow; rather, they seem to have provided conceptual space that became useful in his own compositions.[21] As explained in an autobiographical statement, although "Kotík studied fundamentals of composition, both privately in Prague and later at the Vienna Academy of Music, his technique is self-made and has very little to do with commonly used methods."[22] Thus, he identifies primarily as self-taught in composition.

While Kotík was training in composition in Europe, he also continued to perform in Prague, Vienna, and Warsaw throughout the 1960s. It had not been easy for him to leave what was then Czechoslovakia. As Levine Packer writes, "In the early 1960s, there were only a few holes in the Iron Curtain . . . Warsaw and Vienna were two."[23] Through his contacts in new-music circles in those two cities, he learned about the Center of the Creative and Performing Arts (CCPA) at the University at Buffalo/SUNY. In 1968, Lejaren Hiller—who had by then taken over as co-director of the Center—met Kotík in Warsaw, and they began to discuss arrangements for a fellowship in Buffalo. Hiller and John Cage, with whom he had worked closely for a few years by then, wrote recommendations on Kotík's behalf, as he wanted to be granted immigrant rather than refugee status; he would later argue that his primary reason for moving had been professional.[24] By his own account, he did not confirm his decision to leave Europe until the fall of 1969. His group, QUaX, was supposed to have performed in Berlin that year, but "the Prague authorities" banned their travel, effectively canceling the concerts.[25] This seems to have been the last straw, prompting him to move abroad, where he would be free from such constraints.

In 1969, due to the turbulent political circumstances, he had to leave abruptly while the Czech borders were temporarily opened. Shortly thereafter, his then-wife Charlotta and their infant son Tomas, who had stayed behind in Prague, made their way to the United States to join him for his post with

---

[20] http://www.semensemble.org/about/petr-kotik.
[21] Biographical statement, program book for Ostrava Days 2015 Festival, 65.
[22] "Petr Kotík Biography," personal communication received February 23, 2016.
[23] Levine Packer, *This Life of Sounds*, 98.
[24] Tereza Havelková, "Petr Kotík's Umbilical Cord," *Czech Music* 2003-1 (January/February 2003), 9.
[25] Petr Bakla, "Petr Kotík: As a Composer, I've Always Been a Loner," *Czech Music* 2 (2011), 5–6.

94 INTERPRETIVE LABOR

the Creative Associates (CAs) of the CCPA.[26] His first performance there was in December 1969, and he quickly jumped into a busy performing schedule, discussed in more detail below. A second son, Jan, was born in Buffalo in 1972. The Kotíks remained in that city for several years after the end of his Creative Associates appointment, further establishing his recently founded S.E.M. Ensemble. In 1977, Kotík became an American citizen.[27]

Petr Kotík's longstanding engagement with the musical avant-garde means that his activities illuminate important aspects of the work involved in performances of this repertoire. How are these events funded? How are programming decisions made? What sorts of determinations have to be sorted out to transform an indeterminate score into a sonic experience? It is with these questions in mind that we can begin to assemble the current type of Interpretive Labor, that is, a form of labor related to scientific practices, broadly conceived.

Kotík on (and Resisting) Interpretation

There is something appealingly antagonistic about an artist who claims to reject the fields of analysis and aesthetics outright, and this calls for a deeper investigation. As introduced in his 2011 discussion with Petr Bakla and reinforced in our conversation in 2015, Kotík's position is that

> [t]he majority of musicologists believe that everything can be rationally analyzed, that each aspect in a composer's work is a result of some deliberate decision, which can be deciphered. I have never understood the premises of musical analysis, it never made much sense. Varèse completely rejected analysis. He claimed it murdered music. The problem is that the effort to find rational explanations creates the wrong frame of reference and that leads nowhere.[28]

---

[26] Levine Packer, *This Life of Sounds*, 98. Charlotta Kotík, great-granddaughter of the first president of independent Czechoslovakia (Tomas Garrigue Masaryk), had to use a different first name during communist rule because she had been named for her great-grandmother, the first lady. Kay Grigar, "Charlotta Kotik: An Exceptional Czech New Yorker," Radio Praha, October 12, 2005, transcript at http://www.radio.cz/en/section/czechstoday/charlotta-kotik-an-exceptional-czech-new-yorker.

[27] "Petr Kotík," in *The Harvard Biographical Dictionary of Music*, ed. Don Michael Randel (Cambridge, MA: Harvard University Press, 1996).

[28] Bakla, "Petr Kotík," 8–11.

THE "SCIENTIST" MODEL   95

I will return to this question later, but for the moment, suffice it to say that Kotík advocates for trusting one's creative intuition, which he sees as opposed to rational analysis.[29] Likewise, he interprets the field of aesthetics as oppressive, calling it too "a form of cultural ideology." To summarize the explanation in the 2011 Bakla article cited above: he aims to avoid the judgments of beauty, of what people "ought to like (or dislike)." He seems to be more interested in artists making original statements, rather than creating what people might like. He questions even composers' abilities to assess the work of other composers, or visual artists to judge visual artworks. Instead, he says, personal relationships are better ways to determine "who the artist is and how serious he is."[30] These individual connections enable a person to develop a deeper, more intuitive understanding of the art being created, no matter the genre.

Kotík's compositional procedures and stance toward aesthetics resonate with philosopher Joseph Margolis's account of objectivity. Margolis notes, referring to Kuhn and Feyerabend, that even hermeneutic relativism depends on

> what I may now call interpretation in the "constituting" sense. I mean the sense in which we concede that the characterization of what ... is treated as objective in the way of reported data (on a theory) is also viewed, *without disturbing the other*, as "interpretively" formed by the enculturing processes of that particular society—and hence the sense in which it is impossible to claim to have arrived at an assuredly *neutral* account of such data, free from any "construction," which we may *then* interpret for this or that purpose.[31]

Scientific data, Margolis seems to say, is already always interpretation. In service of his defense of relativism, Margolis insists on separating physical properties and what he calls intentional properties, or (to radically simplify) material aspects versus produced aspects. This second type, found in complex artworks, is not bound by a fixed determinism, but "*determinable* only

---

[29] As noted by Ryan Dohoney, this aligns Kotík with the "Bergsonian spirit" inherent in the modernist project of other artists associated with the avant-garde. See Ryan W. Dohoney, "The Anxiety of Art: Morton Feldman's Modernism, 1948–1972" (PhD diss., Columbia University, 2009); cf. S.E. Gontarski, "'What It Is to Have Been': Bergson and Beckett on Movement, Multiplicity, and Representation," *Journal of Modern Literature* 34, no. 2 (Winter 2011), 65–66.

[30] Bakla, "Petr Kotík," 11–12.

[31] Emphasis in original. Joseph Margolis, "Relativism and Interpretive Objectivity," *Metaphilosophy* 31, no. 1/2 (January 2000), 213.

96 INTERPRETIVE LABOR

in being open to being interpretively *determined*."[32] Kotík's work, and that of other composers creating works with chance, gets caught in between these two forms. The working procedures aim to foreclose second-order interpretation through their commitment to scientific "objectivity," but since the product is still an artwork, it must remain interpretable.

Again, interpretation cannot happen without a substantial degree of foundational knowledge. It is a procedure by which artists engage with a written text (e.g., a score), and draw on their training, their understanding of the author/composer, and other experiences. However, it is not "mere" transliteration or one-to-one mapping; it is also a deeply creative endeavor that incorporates the performer's own input, ideas about the piece, and—as Kotík said—"a real education, that comes through one's own initiative."[33]

One crucial element of musical interpretation, as aligned with Kotík's ideas, is that of genre. This term suggests "a set of general purposes and rules which [the text] aims to realize."[34] Musically speaking, it tends to be mobilized to refer to some set of musical works that share stylistic traits such that they can be grouped analytically and/or by their sociocultural associations. This relates to Kotík's argument about performing Cage (and others), in that one needs to have a core level of competence with the basic framework being used. One cannot enact an appropriate interpretation of a work without first respecting the underlying assumptions of the composer's work, including its "general purposes and rules." It is also necessary to be cognizant of the pull to simply reproduce what is already comfortable. Cage himself would likely cite this as the most important component of interpretation. Interpretation, then, is subject to a dialectical pull, as is indeterminacy itself.

As I see it, the model of interpretation as dialectics continues to thrive in Petr Kotík's work, as well. In an interview published in 2003, he explains:

> In music there are two aspects to interpretation: the first is the note record and the second, which is just as important, is the tradition of performance, something we call style, that leads straight to the composer. Only when a tradition is interrupted and vanishes from consciousness, do we discover how imperfect and incomplete the note record is. The most important thing, the quality that makes a score into a work of music, is not something

---

[32] Margolis, "Relativism and Interpretive Objectivity," 222.

[33] Bakla, "Petr Kotík," 8.

[34] Michael N. Forster, "Herder's Philosophy of Language, Interpretation, and Translation: Three Fundamental Principles," *The Review of Metaphysics* 56, no. 2 (December 2002), 352.

we shall actually find in any note record. . . . The very notion that you can buy the sheet music without knowing anything about it and can read everything out of the notes and instructions is just as nonsensical as the idea that you could learn to play the flute on a correspondence course, by email. That is not the way music is done.[35]

This view is not surprising, coming from a musician who, for much of his career, identified as a performer first and a composer second. To play any piece of music effectively, one must understand the stylistic context of the piece at least as well as the bits that get written down. This is why performers spend years training with private instructors, participating in masterclasses with respected players, listening to recordings, and becoming enculturated as members of studios. All of the subtle nuances of realizing a composition—where to breathe, how long to hold this tenuto, how short to make that staccato (if such indications are even notated)—all of these details inform the reason gifted performers are often called "interpreters" of a given repertoire.

This is all fairly straightforward. What might be contentious here is Kotík's assertion that performing the avant-garde music of, say, John Cage requires the same type of stylistic knowledge as does the music of any other composer of notated music, such as Beethoven.[36] As has been argued in recent musicological literature as well as by Kotík here, Cage actually had very specific ideas about how his compositions should be played. Because this seemed to contradict ideas presented in his writings, though, performers who did not have close relationships with him tended to use his open notations as excuses to make realizations that he never would have condoned.[37] Regarding Cage's best-known collaborator, the pianist and later electronic-music composer David Tudor, Kotík notes,

Their connection was perfect and Cage deliberately left some things open. But of course this presents us with a problem today and perhaps it rather destroys Cage's work to the point where it won't be possible to resurrect it . . . Although [Cage's social-ideological beliefs] worked well as far as

---

[35] Petr Kotík, in Havelková, "Petr Kotík's Umbilical Cord," 10.

[36] Havelková, "Petr Kotík's Umbilical Cord," 10.

[37] See the accounts in, for example: Piekut, *Experimentalism Otherwise* and Ryan Dohoney, "John Cage, Julius Eastman, and the Homosexual Ego," in *Tomorrow Is the Question: New Directions in Experimental Music Studies*, ed. Benjamin Piekut (Ann Arbor: University of Michigan Press, 2014).

98 INTERPRETIVE LABOR

artistic strategy was concerned, they were damaging in relation to the practical situation, above all the practicalities of interpretation.[38]

In other words, the notation used by Cage in its various forms was effective only insofar as it was being read by an expert in the underlying style. In this way, it is just like any other notation of any other composer. Given the extent to which Cage's scores have traveled beyond the small circle of people he envisioned as performers, he would certainly have been surprised, and later bothered, by some of the ways these works have been interpreted.[39]

What of interpretation, then? If the "note-record" is necessarily always incomplete, performance demands careful study, and eventually understanding, of the broader context of the piece. It calls for hands-on experience with the piece, others like it, dissimilar works by the same artist, and so on. Once again, interpretation is effective only insofar as it incorporates a way-of-being that is suitable for the composition (and the interpreter). Kotík emphasizes the "tradition of performance," which might also be thought of as its situated context. This tradition may be grounded in rules memorized for various types of repertoire or stylistic periods, but it must also go beyond that. It encompasses a give-and-take between the performer and the piece, drawing on the entirety of that person's experience as a musician. It may begin with realization, but must work through the challenging process of breaking through that restraint, sometimes taking it too far, to find the point at which a "true" interpretation has been achieved.

The Composer as Scientist

Petr Kotík's compositional style is fairly difficult to classify. As Petr Bakla wrote in 2011: "Straddling the divide between European and American culture gives his work a peculiar breadth."[40] Of course, the idea of a unified or monolithic culture within spaces as massive as Europe or the United States (or, worse yet, the Americas generally) is absurd, but I think the journal's editor uses this phrase here to make a rhetorical point about the diversity of the composer's output. Many of Kotík's pieces are notated for variable

---

[38] Havelková, "Petr Kotík's Umbilical Cord," 10.

[39] Now, of course, we might argue that those "outsider" performers had every right to do what they wanted with them, leaving Cage himself to deal with his own inconsistency.

[40] Bakla, "Petr Kotík," 2.

ensembles, in which different performances may include more or fewer of the multiple lines and which may be played on different instruments each time, depending on which parts are chosen and by whom. He has written quite a lot of instrumental chamber music, from straightforward string quartet instrumentation to the idiosyncratic combination of alto flute, English horn, clarinet, bassoon, viola, and cello. There was a substantial amount of vocal music composed in the 1970s and early 1980s, setting texts written by Gertrude Stein and Buckminster Fuller, and he returned to Stein for the libretto of his opera *Master-Pieces* (2014–15). Although the majority of his compositions are for small- to medium-sized ensembles, he has also written a few orchestral works, and this repertoire has grown since he founded the Orchestra of the S.E.M. Ensemble in the early 1990s.

Kotík conveys an approach to composition that I find refreshingly, if unusually, pragmatic. For example, in the early 2000s, he had programmed Stockhausen's *Gruppen* in the Czech festival Prague Spring. When he wanted to continue doing so in subsequent years in Ostrava, he chose to program only works for three orchestras, but was unable to find enough pieces to make a full program. Not wanting to perform *Gruppen* twice (as had been done in previous circumstances) or play older repertoire (as he had done with a Gabrieli piece in the first festival), he decided to compose *Variations for 3 Orchestras* (2003–05).[41] This apparent practicality also comes out in the account of his decision to begin composing for voice: the singer Julius Eastman had joined his S.E.M. Ensemble in Buffalo, so he "had to include voice in [his] new piece for the group."[42] Similarly, he notes that the text for this first vocal composition—lectures by Gertrude Stein—was found essentially by accident. Walking by a bookstore while on tour in Albany, he saw the book by the entrance, bought it, and read a bit of it before bed that night. In his own words, "the choice of text wasn't inspired by some 'brilliant' idea; it just happened."[43] The language here is particularly illuminating, because it suggests that he is resistant to the idea of inspiration, but at the same time, he has been quite vocal about the importance of trusting one's own creative intuition.[44] In this story, he seems to choose these words to deliberately downplay his own agency in selecting that particular text, but of course he chose

---

[41] Kotík: "There's nothing worse than performing something twice." Interview with the author, August 29, 2015.

[42] Bakla, "Petr Kotík," 8.

[43] Bakla, "Petr Kotík," 8.

[44] Interview with the author, August 29, 2015.

100 INTERPRETIVE LABOR

to go into the bookstore, to pick up that book, to purchase it, and to use it for the new composition for the S.E.M. Ensemble.

Kotík's self-described compositional process employs a method that he began developing in the 1960s. His technique, he writes,

> can be described as a process in which chance and intuitive steps alternate in a game-like fashion, one influencing the other. Strategies and limitations are at the core of the method, which has the objective of triggering processes that are unpredictable yet correspond to the envisioned result. The struggle in working toward this almost unattainable ideal constitutes what Kotík regards as composition.[45]

What this actually means, in practice, is much more precisely controlled than might at first be imagined. In this account, "chance" refers to calculations of probability, rather than some looser, more improvisational meaning. In the early 1960s, with his composition teacher and dear friend Jan Rychlík, he had analyzed other composers' scores, identifying statistical patterns for the pitch relationships, and this was in turn developed into a compositional technique for his own works.[46] He explains,

> The process of chance is an integral part of my method, not something that stands separately. Chance operations I use have a direction and are partially controlled. I then take the result and proceed to work on my own. The way I compose could be called a game. It's a kind of dialogue between the results of my method and my reaction to it, intuitively correcting, editing and introducing other elements in a quasi-improvised way. This result can be further processed by the method, which can set off a chain of more intuitive interventions. It's like moving a piece on the chessboard—a predictable move leads to an unpredictable reaction, which requires further action, etc.[47]

Therefore, his use of chance operations functions somewhat similarly to the procedures undertaken by Cage in the late 1950s: developing a set of parameters for determining musical material (pitch, duration, etc.) and

---

[45] http://www.semensemble.org/about/petr-kotik.
[46] Petr Kotík seminar, Ostrava Days 2003, August 12, 2003.
[47] Bakla, "Petr Kotík," 8. An in-depth discussion of gaming and game-like activities can be found in the final "model" chapter of this book.

THE "SCIENTIST" MODEL 101

expanding that out into systems. Unlike Cage, however, he is forthcoming about the additional steps taken to change the material after having run it through the system. As I and others have noted elsewhere, Cage actually altered a number of his works, both musical and visual, to suit his taste, while trying to maintain the illusion of detachment.[48]

For approximately the last three decades, Kotík has used "a computer-generated chain of events based on Markov's probability sequences," which are employed in an "editing process" whereby some type of extant graphic material is altered.[49] This source material comes from some unusual places. Kyle Gann writes that "the lines in many of his early works are drawn from a bunch of graphs he found in the early 1970s; the graphs belonged to a science professor friend who was throwing them away, and charted response times to alcohol in experiments with rats. Kotík was charmed by the shapes and used them for years, so that the chantlike lines constitute a kind of 'found melody.'"[50] The composer confirms this in one of his composition seminars: "In 1971 I began composing music based on graphs, which were derived from physiological experiments with rat tissues. . . . When I decide on the strategy for a new piece, on its scale, on the form and the process of deriving my pitches, I work with graphic tools. It can almost be described as graphic design."[51] (This, of course, provides a parallel with Cardew, who actually was a graphic designer by trade and brought that skill to bear on scores like *Treatise*.)[52] For Kotík, though, this is the behind-the-scenes part, the work that might, in earlier scholarship, have been called pre-compositional work.

---

[48] Willemien Froneman, "'Composing According to Silence': Undecidability in Derrida and Cage's *Roaratorio*," *International Review of the Aesthetics and Sociology of Music* 41, no. 2 (December 2010), 293–317; Stewart Buettner, "Cage," *International Review of the Aesthetics and Sociology of Music* 12, no. 2 (December 1981), 141–51; and my "Cagean Aesthetics and the Rhetoric of Indeterminacy," talk at the AMS Midwest conference, Northwestern University, October 5, 2013.

[49] Petr Kotík seminar. This is explained as follows: "A process which depends on the preceding event only is an example of a simple *Markoff* [sic] *process*, and the corresponding sequence is called a *Markoff chain*." Lejaren A. Hiller Jr. and Leonard M. Isaacson, *Experimental Music: Composition with an Electronic Computer* (New York: McGraw-Hill, 1959), 71 (italics in original). Along with Hiller, Iannis Xenakis (1922–2001) was another important figure working with probability and algorithms in musical composition. See, for example, Kevin Jones, "Compositional Applications of Stochastic Processes," *Computer Music Journal* 5, no. 2 (Summer 1981), 45–61, and Sergio Luque, "The Stochastic Synthesis of Iannis Xenakis," *Leonardo Music Journal* 19 (2009), 77–84.

[50] Kyle Gann, "Petr Kotík's *Many Many Women*: A Monument from the 1970s," CD liner notes for remastered album *Petr Kotík: Many Many Women* (Dog W/A Bone, 2000), n.p.

[51] Petr Kotík seminar.

[52] Cornelius Cardew, *Treatise Handbook* (London: Hinrichsen, 1971).

102 INTERPRETIVE LABOR

Once the source scheme has been determined, the pitch material is identified using whatever strategy has been chosen. From there, the process is less clearly defined, although he does try to avoid anything he can predict too easily. In a statement that begins so incongruously as to be one of my favorite composer quotes of all time, he explains,

> For me, composition is not something where skill is a big issue. In fact, I have somewhat of a problem with it. When I continue working with a certain method, my skill improves, and as I start to become more in control of the material, I gradually lose interest in that particular method because of the predictability. As I get better, I start to be able to predict the results. Making a composition is for me a working process, it is not something like making or creating a fixed object. There is nothing more exciting for me than being surprised by the result of that process, of putting something in motion that corresponds to my vision yet is unpredictable. Acquiring too much skill makes the process more and more predictable and less and less interesting. It begins to feel like I am manipulating the material.[53]

This idea of a process rather than a product becomes evident in the number of compositions for which he has completed later revisions. For example, *There Is Singularly Nothing* (1971–73) was revised in 1995, and the orchestral "Fragment," premiered at Lincoln Center in 1998, later functioned as the first section of *Music in Two Movements* in 2002, and was re-worked for a 2011 performance. Likewise, the composition dates for the piece *Reiterations and Variables*, programmed on the December 2015 concert at the Paula Cooper Gallery, are listed as 1972–2015.[54] One gets the sense that his works are never finished, and yet he is not particularly attached to them; they are things that need to be made. In fact, he has said, "I don't believe that making art is something personal. I don't believe the world is that interested in me as a person. I want to be left alone. This is why I have no desire to push myself through my work. That would feel out of place. I have always felt like this, even before I was able to express it."[55] Along the same lines, he wrote in 2014: "My work is not about what I like or dislike; it is about what I feel that should be done, what I should do regardless of whether I like it or not."[56]

---

[53] Petr Kotík seminar.
[54] http://www.semensemble.org (retrieved December 1, 2015).
[55] Petr Kotík seminar.
[56] Petr Kotík, "Artist Statement," Foundation for Contemporary Arts grant recipient archive, http://www.foundationforcontemporaryarts.org/recipients/petr-kotik.

THE "SCIENTIST" MODEL   103

This, perhaps, echoes Cage's well-known ideas about doing what needs to be done, and appears to be one of the first affinities Kotík felt with the older composer.[57]

∗ ∗ ∗

Throughout all of this discussion of Kotík's compositional methods and attitudes, a picture begins to emerge of an individual laboring to free himself from the grip of subjectivity. His commitment to creating objects in a regulated, disciplined manner suggests affinity with a wider modernist project, which is further congruent with broader shifts in scientific inquiry itself. As recently as 2004, Joseph Hanna wrote that "it is generally agreed that one of the distinguishing virtues of science is its objectivity."[58] While Hanna immediately problematizes that claim in the remainder of this article, he points up an important aspect of the "science" label to which I am pledged. In their account of the history of science, Daston and Galison identify three main phases of objectivity, each aligned with but not limited to a particular historical era.[59] The first, truth-to-nature, is the paradigm of perfected realization. Its aim is to capture the "essence" of an object rather than every detail. (In music, we might think of Schenkerian analysis: the procedure seeks to identify ancillary aspects that can be set aside in favor of the broad structural elements.) In mechanical objectivity, the second form, the scientist works in service of accuracy. Since no detail can be dismissed, this removes the scientist from the "process of rendition."[60] Finally, emerging in the 20th century, they identify trained judgment; this is beholden in Burnett's phrase to the "deepening professionalization of scientific 'experts' and their increasingly important service to political decision making in the last hundred years."[61] As I see it, composers working with chance—Kotík, Cage, Hiller—may have felt an affinity with the "mechanical objectivity" of photography or film, for example, but really end up fitting better into the "trained judgment" role.

---

[57] Kotík explained: "the texts by Cage were the most interesting thing in the book [the 1958 *Darmstadter Beiträge*, which had been given to Kotík by Luigi Nono in 1960 in Prague]. One of the main ideas that he proposed was that one shouldn't put oneself into the work one does. 'Making music is not about what I want, it's not about me. It is about what needs to be done. Nothing personal'—this is how I can paraphrase what I read. This immediately captivated me. Getting rid of one's intentions: focusing on the music, not on oneself." Petr Kotík seminar.

[58] Joseph F. Hanna, "The Scope and Limits of Scientific Objectivity," *Philosophy of Science* 71, no. 3 (July 2004), 339.

[59] Lorraine Daston and Peter Galison, *Objectivity* (New York: Zone Books, 2007).

[60] Dana Wilson-Kovacs, "*Objectivity* [review]," *Critical Quarterly* 51, no. 3 (October 2009), 124.

[61] D. Graham Burnett, "The Objective Case: A Review of *Objectivity*," *October* 133 (Summer 2010), 136.

104 INTERPRETIVE LABOR

The recent tools of science—charts, graphs, and schemata—are brought to bear on musical practices, and they require an expert to interpret the data.

To align these artistic and scientific movements with Interpretive Labor, consider the fundamental questions of the theory.[62] First, who creates the indeterminacy and who has to respond to it? In this case, the answer to both questions is the same: the composer. Kotík himself defines the parameters by which chance will be employed, and is also responsible for interpreting the results of those decisions. There is no assistant tasked with translating codes into legible music notation, no requirement for performers to decide on durations, pitches, or rhythms. Instead, in this type of interpretive labor, the composer exerts control over the artistic material rather than over his interpreters. In addition, Kotík's approach involves a continuous process of testing and adjusting. For this reason, I am calling this model the "scientist" type, in reference to the basic scientific method.[63] Just as an individual observes some aspect of the universe, creates a hypothesis, tests, and modifies, so too chance procedures allow composers to identify some musical idea, propose ways to make it audible, test it using a chance-based system, and adjust it as needed, based on those results, and repeat the test-and-modify procedure until it reaches a "stable" state. Composers can also use this method without incorporating chance procedures, but the use of chance makes the results more difficult to predict. Openness to the unknown makes it experimental. As Hanna notes, too,

> Intuitive processes of informal reasoning [have been transformed] into more formal, algorithmic methods of calculation. . . . None of these developments eliminates the role of discursive human reasoning (*implicit practice*) in the formal and empirical sciences, but they do contribute to the *explicit objectivity* of that reasoning. The *explicit* formalization (mechanization) of lower level processes makes possible *implicit* discursive reasoning at a higher and more complex level.[64]

Kotík's processes, in shifting from the more intuitive play with charts and graphs to the use of computer-generated material, thus enables just the sort of complex reasoning that Hanna identifies.

---

[62] This set of questions is laid out briefly at the end of Chapter 1.

[63] As noted above, though, this is itself a simplification of what really happens in most scientific inquiry.

[64] Emphasis in original. Hanna, "The Scope and Limits of Scientific Objectivity," 352–53.

THE "SCIENTIST" MODEL   105

The language of the experiment is important here. While it may be even more applicable to some other avant-garde musicians of the era, it is worth noting that this repertoire as a whole has come to be known as "experimental music."[65] Various artists engaged with new ways of doing things, and sometimes this meant that the results were surprising. In many cases, though, this is neither the most useful nor the most suitable description. More often than not, the works created simply existed outside the mainstream and therefore were lumped under the umbrella of the burgeoning terminology. As John Cage explained in 1957:

> Times have changed; music has changed; and I no longer object to the word "experimental." I use it in fact to describe all the music that especially interests me and to which I am devoted, whether someone else wrote it or I myself did. [. . .]Those involved with the composition of experimental music find ways and means to remove themselves from the activities of the sounds they make. Some employ chance operations, derived from sources as ancient as the Chinese Book of Changes, or as modern as the tables of random numbers used also by physicists in research. Or, analogous to the Rorschach tests of psychology, the interpretation of imperfections in the paper upon which one is writing may provide a music free from one's memory and imagination. Geometrical means employing spatial superimpositions at variance with the ultimate performance in time may be used.[66]

At that time, then—that is, just past mid-century—numerous techniques were being explored to introduce elements of chance into the procedures of musical composition. Likewise, I think here of what Leonard Meyer called the "radical empiricist wing" of the avant-garde, or those whose work he characterized as anti-teleological. For these artists, Meyer argues, prediction cannot exist:

> What is denied in quantum mechanics and in the aesthetic of radical empiricism is not the theoretical possibility of a principle of causation, but the

---

[65] Cf., among others, Morag Josephine Grant, "Experimental Music Semiotics," *IRASM* 34, no. 2 (December 2003), 173–91; James Saunders, ed., *The Ashgate Research Companion to Experimental Music* (Burlington, VT: Ashgate, 2009); Alvin Lucier, *Music 109: Notes on Experimental Music* (Middletown, CT: Wesleyan University Press, 2012); William Brooks, "In re: 'Experimental Music,'" *Contemporary Music Review* 31, no. 1 (February 2012), 37–62; Piekut, *Tomorrow Is the Question.*
[66] John Cage, "Experimental Music (1957)," reprinted in *Silence: Lectures and Writings*, 7–12.

106   INTERPRETIVE LABOR

theoretical possibility of isolating any particular event as being the cause of another particular event. This is the case because, since the world is seen as a single continuum in which everything interacts with—is the "cause" of—everything else, there are no separable causes and effects.[67]

Unlike the more general use of "experimental" in describing newly composed music, this suggests a type of composition in which the musical results are actually unknown to the composer until they are realized in performance.

Exploratory or experimental practices were closely associated with members of several new-music networks at that time, and as the century wore on and the techniques expanded, the "experimental" label gradually became a convenient shorthand for a whole wealth of variant approaches. By the late 1990s, this had been codified concretely. Composer-saxophonist Frank Mauceri would write, "[t]he concept of experimental music is less contentious today than it was in the late 1950s,"[68] and in numerous sources since that time, the term has been applied to varied compositional techniques and styles used by many different composers, from chance-derived works to electronic music to fully notated chamber music.

* * *

Composed in 1975–78, Petr Kotík's massive work *Many Many Women* is a useful case study with which to test the "scientist" model of Interpretive Labor (Figure 3.2). As described in a biographical statement provided by the composer, "[i]n this period, Kotík stopped using general scores; the works consist instead of independently composed parts/sections that can be superimposed and combined, forming various densities, from solo to full ensembles."[69] This work, a setting of Gertrude Stein's complete novella by the same title, became, in Kotík's hands, "an innovative, exhaustive kind of contemporary plainchant with open chords."[70] This was arrived at by making extensive use of parallel perfect intervals—fourths, fifths, and octaves—overlaid on melodic material derived from the rat-tissue graphs

---

[67] Leonard B. Meyer, "The End of the Renaissance? Notes on the Radical Empiricism of the Avant-Garde," *Hudson Review* 16, no. 2 (Summer 1963), 179.

[68] However, he also argues that "[w]hen a term like 'experimental' is deployed as a category it not only creates implicit oppositions but it also takes sides, it privileges and aligns particular differences." Frank X. Mauceri, "From Experimental Music to Musical Experiment," *Perspectives of New Music* 35, no. 1 (Winter 1997), 188.

[69] http://www.semensemble.org/about/petr-kotik.

[70] Richard Kostelanetz, "S.E.M.'s *Many Many Women*," CD liner notes, n.p.

mentioned earlier in this chapter. As with other compositions of this period, including vocal works on texts by both Stein and Buckminster Fuller, Kotík carefully balanced the chance-derived material (permutations of the graphs) with intuitive adjustments. The result would later be described by Kyle Gann as "a music that floated in 'tonally atonal' chanted lines, like so many joyously random Benedictine monks seduced to a postmodern liturgy."[71] These sounds are typically produced by pairs of musicians: two sopranos, a countertenor and tenor, a baritone and bass, two flutes, two clarinets, and two trombones, although a 2013 performance substituted a trumpet for the two clarinets.[72] Recorded in 1980 by the S.E.M. Ensemble, it has also been performed on several occasions, usually in excerpted form, beginning in the mid-1970s.[73] When all 173 sections are performed, the work lasts between five and six hours, depending on tempi.

Thus, several components of the work enact indeterminacy: the number of sections performed, the instrumentation, and the transposition of the pitches, as well as the compositional method itself, which employs chance operations. Kotík's pitch and intervallic source material from this era included the charts of scientific data from the rat experiments; indeed, this fact inspired in part my turn toward the "hard sciences" as a model for this type of interpretive work. More importantly, though, the principal approach to composition is a constricted, carefully monitored form of indeterminacy. It lies at one end of the spectrum in that few elements are given to the performers to decide. As mentioned earlier, this is a self-inflicted form of labor: the composer creates the system, determines how it will be used, and is responsible for the work of turning it into a finished composition. While Kotík's works from the 1970s are apt examples of this process, they are certainly not alone. Any piece that incorporates the method, such as Cage's *Music of Changes* (1951), is also a product of the "scientist" model. In these fully notated works, nearly all of the indeterminacy, and so the interpretive labor, is undertaken by the composer himself.

I bring up Cage here again because the close connection between these two artists has been discussed and reinforced by Kotík himself, as will be developed in the penultimate section of this chapter. The question of influence,

---

[71] Gann, "Petr Kotík's *Many Many Women.*"

[72] S.E.M. Ensemble at White Box, New York, NY, June 19, 2013.

[73] Liner notes for the 2000 reissue indicate that the first partial performance took place in 1977; however, the Hallwalls Contemporary Arts Center (Buffalo, NY) has an advertisement for a December 1975 lecture-recital of sorts that was to include excerpts of *Many Many Women*. http://www.hallwalls.org/event_ephemera/277.PKotik.flyer.jpg.

108 INTERPRETIVE LABOR

Figure 3.2 Section 10 (31–32) of Petr Kotík, *Many Many Women*. © Petr Kotík, 1980. Reproduced with permission.

THE "SCIENTIST" MODEL   109

though, is evidently contentious. In discussing this idea—which he describes as confirming perhaps dormant tendencies, rather than prompting any change—he seems to correlate the conventional idea of influence with a conscious decision to construct music in a particular way. When asked in 2003 what he learned from Cage, he responded, "Recently I was asked to write something about Cage's influence on me. I was aware that what is usually described as influence is actually imitation, which actually has very little in common with influence. Unfortunately society praises people who imitate others, but imitation has never attracted me."[74] His other writings and interviews, though, certainly reveal his respect for Cage, and there are a number of productive relationships among their ideas. Foremost among these is the basic premise of interpreting (indeterminate) compositions.

While Kotík has had an international circle of associates that he refers to as friends, he identifies himself as separate from any group. He states,

> As a composer, I've always been a loner. Until recently, my work was only marginally accepted by the public. Even people I was close to, for example Rudolf Komorous, often raised their eyebrows when they saw what I was composing and also how I was composing it. I remember my mentor Vladimír Šrámek, when I first showed him my compositional method, he screamed at me: "You don't compose like this! This is no way to compose music!"[75]

Here, I am reminded of Polanyi's classic formulation: "the scientist's task is not to observe any allegedly correct procedure, but to get the right results."[76] Kotík has developed his own procedures, apart from the methods taught by his mentors, to obtain musical results that he desires (but which, according to his own anti-aesthetics stance, are not supposed to be shaped by his likes or dislikes).

Further, Kotík notes, "We are living in a culture built on the Enlightenment illusion that people know what they want. . . . One silly view you can hear from professors at all the universities is that a composer writes music he hears internally, and it is an expression of what he wants."[77] He argues instead

---

[74] My understanding is that this is a wry comment on trends in music and other cultural activities, rather than meaning that some unspecified aspect of "society" literally praises imitation. Havelková, "Petr Kotík's Umbilical Cord," 11.

[75] Bakla, "Petr Kotík," 4.

[76] Michael Polanyi, *Science, Faith and Society* (Chicago: University of Chicago Press, 1964), 40.

[77] Again, a bit of hyperbole, but shaped by his own experiences and status as a bit of an outsider. Havelková, "Petr Kotík's Umbilical Cord," 10.

110   INTERPRETIVE LABOR

that, while the music he creates is enabled by his environment, it is not a direct product of any tradition. Drawing these disparate interview responses together—with Havelková in 2003, Bakla in 2011, and my own conversations with him in 2015—I interpret this as affinity with the concept of acquiescence, preached so frequently by Cage. Of course, this was not Cage's own idea; he had lifted it from what he understood to be Zen teachings and adapted it to his own ends. The basic sentiment, though—that it is better to accept the things outside one's control—lends a sense of calm acceptance to Kotík's accounts of his own artistic experiences. While this could be interpreted as resignation or as not caring, it instead is likely a way to deal with events that could otherwise have been possibly catastrophic to a young artist: cancelation of concerts, being left out of the leading group of composers, travel bans, visa issues.

Importantly, he argues that he does not typically work with any particular objectives in mind, aside from very basic parameters. He notes, "I personally am not goal-oriented. To set priorities and goals is completely against my way of thinking. In fact, I believe that this focus on goals that young people are continually advised to have, is a grave mistake."[78] Elsewhere, he has elaborated on this, albeit somewhat cryptically, talking about how we have very few choices about things, and a lot is actually predetermined.[79] Goals, perhaps, will be interrupted anyway, so it is best to take each new experience one step at a time, live with the result, and make the next move intuitively, but informed by the environment and available resources: in composition as in life. Likewise, a science experiment would not be much of an experiment without the possibility of an incorrect hypothesis. The procedures must be as objective as possible, detached from what the researcher hopes will be the outcome. As Hans-Jörg Rheinberger writes, "Experimentation, as a machine for making the future, has to engender unexpected events. However, it also channels them, for their significance ultimately derives from their potential to become ... integral parts of future technical conditions."[80]

Kotík describes composition as follows: "Composition is writing a set of instructions on how to make music."[81] And what, for him, is music? "Music invokes a situation that can lead to meditation; a personal, poetic and

---

[78] Petr Bakla, "Ostrava Days 2007: Institute and Festival of New Music," *Czech Music* 3 (April 2007), 29.
[79] Interview with the author, August 29, 2015.
[80] Hans-Jörg Rheinberger, *Toward a History of Epistemic Things: Synthesizing Proteins in the Test Tube* (Stanford, CA: Stanford University Press, 1997), 33.
[81] Petr Kotík seminar.

intellectual meditation. It is a field of sound, which we perceive in a time space. Music is not universal, it is always specific, and the ability to 'understand' or navigate in this sound field requires education. A real education, that comes through one's own initiative."[82] This initiative to pursue an individual education will prove to be crucially important for anyone interpreting composers' works—not just Kotík's own, but those of any composer from any era. Stylistic knowledge and understanding are the basis for any convincing, successful performance, and one must put in the work—the foundational study that will later support the work of interpretation—and this, too, is a form of labor.

THE COMPOSER AS SCIENTIST, II: HILLER

In the early 1970s, Daphne Oram—co-founder and director of the BBC Radiophonic Workshop—wrote of her own book, "we shall have to ask the scientist to forgive us if we do not view his discoveries with strict scientific scrutiny; we will also need to ask the forgiveness of the composer if we attempt to bring down to earth some of his difficult aesthetics. Analogy, metaphor, and even mythology will, I hope, help us to keep our balance."[83] Throughout this text, as well, I draw on such points of comparison in an effort to demonstrate the scientific work of composers (and other musicians). A more explicit example of the scientist model can be found in the work of Lejaren (Jerry) Hiller Jr. (1924–94). Trained as a chemist—he earned the PhD in that field at Princeton—Hiller also studied composition with Roger Sessions and Milton Babbitt.[84] After a short stint as an industrial research chemist, he turned to the academy and found an intellectual home in the University of Illinois, where he remained from 1952 to 1968. During his time there, he continued working as a chemist and also began using computers for musical experiments. After a few years, he was transferred to the faculty of the School of Music, where he helped to establish the country's second electronic music studio.[85] Hiller, then, is a composer-scientist in the most ordinary, literal sense of those terms.

---

[82] Bakla, "Petr Kotík," 8.

[83] Daphne Oram, *An Individual Note: Of Music, Sound and Electronics* (London: Galliard, 1972), 7.

[84] James Matthew Bohn, "An Overview of the Music of Lejaren Hiller and an Examination of His Early Works Involving Technology" (PhD diss., University of Illinois, 1997), 3.

[85] Bohn, "An Overview of the Music of Lejaren Hiller," 5–10.

112   INTERPRETIVE LABOR

For his master's thesis project, completed while he was already on the chemistry faculty at the University of Illinois, Hiller created what would become the *Illiac Suite* (later String Quartet No. 4), the first musical work created by computer. The procedures used are explained in great detail in a 1959 book co-authored with chemistry research assistant Leonard Isaacson, whom Hiller admired as a programmer and who was sympathetic to his objectives. While Isaacson "had no formal training in music," he "had a general interest in computer applications for problem solving."[86] Each of the four movements, labeled Experiment 1 through Experiment 4, was created using a different set of parameters; the work's title comes from the name of the computer used to process these experiments (the ILLIAC I). As the numerous tables, graphs, and flowcharts (Figure 3.3) in Hiller and Isaacson's text demonstrate, they approached this project as they would any other scientific inquiry. Likewise, the structure of the book itself aligns with their other writings, for example, in natural-sciences journals; chapters are titled things like "Nature of the Problem," "Experimental Details," and "Experimental Results." As they explain, "The logic used to write a computer program differs from the logic one might ordinarily use to explain compositional problems in strictly musical terms. In planning a computer program, the first step is to design a block diagram which outlines the required logical processes. This is followed by the actual writing of the program itself."[87] One such diagram appears below.

The four experiments devised for this project were:

- Experiment One: Monody, two-part, and four-part writing (based on cantus firmi 3–12 notes in length, and using "a limited selection of first-species counterpoint rules")
- Experiment Two: Four-part first-species counterpoint (with rules "added successively to random white-note music")
- Experiment Three: Experimental music (largely chromatic music controlled by a set of rules and codes)
- Experiment Four: Markoff chain music (the most complicated; largely based on "zeroth-order harmonic and proximity" probability functions, or circumstances in which musical events (e.g., intervals) are independent of the preceding and following pitches/intervals)

---

[86] Bohn, 6; Hiller and Isaacson, *Experimental Music.*
[87] Hiller and Isaacson, *Experimental Music*, 82.

THE "SCIENTIST" MODEL   113

Surprisingly (or perhaps unsurprisingly for someone well versed in both counterpoint and probability), Hiller notes that "the actual coding of Markoff chain music was extremely simple by comparison with the programming of strict counterpoint. It was a completely efficient process, since there was no attrition resulting from the production of unusable notes; therefore, no try-again subroutine was required."[88]

While the piece is now held up as a watershed moment in electronic music, at the time, its reception was largely harsh. Hiller recalls,

> I would say the great preponderance of reaction was that I was *some sort of scientist* who should know better than to meddle in musical matters. There was a great deal of hostility, certainly in the musical world, without question. With very few exceptions . . . I'd say the hostility index was extremely high, and certainly, although it made me famous in a way, it made it very difficult too, because, I was immediately pigeon-holed as an ex-chemist who had bungled into writing music and probably wouldn't know how to resolve a dominant seventh chord.[89]

One whimsical adoption of a science-experiment approach came about a decade after the *Illiac Suite* project: namely, the use of the "musical dice game" (attributed to Mozart), realized by computer program and employed as one of seven keyboard scores within *HPSCHD*, a work created in collaboration with John Cage in the late 1960s. As with his other computer-driven works, Hiller employed code that replicated the Monte Carlo method, which is "the experimental production of random sets which are made to conform to statistical controls. . . . it is distinguished from more traditional laboratory experimentation in which significant environmental factors are systematically varied or controlled."[90] In *HPSCHD*, Hiller explains, "there are four versions in which a number of bars of the music were replaced each time before a new realization—a new 'pass'—was generated. In other words, after the first realization was finished, we entered another loop and called subroutine 'ICHING' 20 times in order to obtain 20 chance values between one and 64."[91] In all, the master programming for this piece included at least a dozen distinct

---

[88] Hiller and Isaacson, *Experimental Music*, 151.
[89] Emphasis added. Vincent Plush, "American Music Series: Interview with Lejaren A. Hiller, Jr.," manuscript (November 12, 1983), 36, cited in Bohn, "An Overview of the Music of Lejaren Hiller."
[90] Hiller and Isaacson, *Experimental Music*, 69.
[91] Lejaren Hiller in interview with Larry Austin [1968], reprinted in Larry Austin, "An Interview with John Cage and Lejaren Hiller," *Computer Music Journal* 16, no. 4 (Winter 1992), 23.

114 INTERPRETIVE LABOR

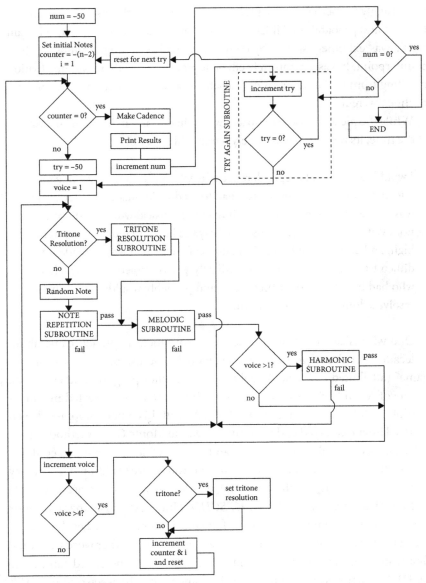

Figure 3.3 Flowchart of program used to generate four-voice counterpoint. From James Bohn, "The Music of American Composer Lejaren Hiller and an Examination of his Early Works Involving Technology" (PhD diss., University of Illinois, 1997), 144.

subroutines, each of which serves a different function: generating durations, counting musical events, determining microtonal inflection, and so on.

Hiller's truly experimental musical practices did eventually come to be recognized for their valuable contributions, and he achieved the economic and cultural capital befitting his labor. In 1968, while working on *HPSCHD* with Cage, he moved back to New York, where he became the Slee Professor of Composition at the University at Buffalo and—for several years—co-director of the Center of the Creative and Performing Arts.[92] In addition to his experiments with computer-generated music, he also composed dozens of conventional musical pieces, some for tape but many for analog instruments and/or theater.[93] While his work may be the most precisely "scientific" in terms of its procedures and even naming conventions, though, it is certainly not alone in being emblematic of a particular model of interpretive work.

CONCLUSION: MUSICAL SCIENTISTS PAST AND PRESENT

Petr Kotík and Lejaren Hiller, performers, composers, and administrators, represent crucial voices for the practice of chance-derived composition, in addition to their other accomplishments. Overall, both are key figures in experimental-music studies during the Cold War era. Regarding Kotík specifically, there are precious few artists who worked on both sides of the Iron Curtain, and even fewer who have shared their stories, let alone being still actively involved in the arts. Regarding events and institutions that are now well documented and for which we might think we have a complete account (e.g., Darmstadt, or the New York Philharmonic's performance of *Atlas Eclipticalis*), Kotík gives us a different perspective. Even for the Creative Associates at the University at Buffalo, the group that enabled his move to the United States and whose fellowship funds financed his earliest work there, he introduces a perhaps surprising critique. He notes, about the Center of the Creative and Performing Arts, "The repertoire that this relatively large and well-funded group was doing was a kind of cross between European and American new music, as it was done at the universities in the U.S., with a little

[92] Bohn, "An Overview of the Music of Lejaren Hiller," 11.
[93] Bohn, "An Overview of the Music of Lejaren Hiller," Appendix: Complete Worklist, 238–43.

116   INTERPRETIVE LABOR

bit of interesting music here and there. It was a disappointment for me."[94] In contrast, the CCPA meant, for Hiller, a welcoming respite from the hostility at Illinois, and a place where his pioneering efforts were rewarded.

As a component in the theory of Interpretive Labor, the "Scientist" model enables us to understand those works that are indeterminate primarily in their compositional procedures. The use of chance operations is a very different process from creating open-ended text scores, for example, and so it calls for a different way to conceptualize the work involved. While all indeterminate music has some degree of "unforeseen" results, the time at which those results are made evident and the individuals who labor to enact them are of course widely variant.[95] Most conventional composition, in fact, could be conceived of as a part of this model: the composer balances some extant system with intuitive adjustments until a desired score is produced. He or she is almost solely responsible for creating the piece, and the labor is theirs alone. Because of that, though, it means that the recognition tends to be theirs alone, as well. They are not obligated to share the spotlight with their interpreters. The score becomes portable in a way that more highly indeterminate compositions may not; it can later be realized in a distant time or place without a great deal of input from the composer.

In addition, Kotík's and Hiller's compositions and other musical activities illustrate a conception of interpretation that can usefully be applied to indeterminate and other experimental repertoire. Rather than trying to elucidate rules for performance, or some system of realization, many of these pieces are better served by developing a theory of interpretation that builds on its dialectic pull between the strict and the free. This tension is itself productive, and ultimately results in a synthetic model of performance. By balancing historical, cultural, and social context with specific aspects of the composition and composer, and by keeping sight of potential derailment by assumptions of familiarity, this proto-critical hermeneutics begins to take shape.

Beyond specific considerations of chance-based musical experiments, the "scientist" model can also productively be expanded to account for related ideas. As suggested above, the clearest application of scientific interpretive work can be found in the development of electronic music. From the mid-century studios associated with radio stations in Europe and Japan to

---

[94] Bakla, "Petr Kotík," 6.

[95] Hiller once said, in the context of not yet having heard sonic results of *HPSCHD*: "I wrote music for more than ten years before I heard any of it, so I've had to learn to be patient." Austin, "An Interview with John Cage and Lejaren Hiller," 22.

the modern computer-lab classrooms of the 21st century, technologically mediated composition illustrates a wide range of relevant practices. Here, the model is not merely a metaphor for creative work but rather a direct explication of the work being done: musicians develop a hypothesis (for example, what will happen when an oscillator is adjusted or a recorded sound is modified), which gets tested out in a laboratory, perhaps revised based on the results, and incorporated into a new piece or practice.

The history of electronic music is rich and varied: it encompasses developments in recording technology, manipulation of recorded sounds, sound generation by electronic means, research in acoustics, computer programming, and a whole host of other activities. Much of this work was— and still is—supported by studios. The revised *Cambridge Companion to Electronic Music* lists at least a dozen major facilities established between 1950 and 1970; a catalog from the era actually lists 148 studios in 39 countries.[96] These spaces were critically important during those early decades, as equipment was expensive and difficult to acquire. Margaret Schedel cites the Institute of Sonology (The Hague) and the Sonic Laboratory at SARC studios (Belfast) as contemporary iterations of this idea, but notes that their primary function now is to provide space for exploring music in ways that cannot be done in the home studios that have become nearly ubiquitous.[97] Now that so many musicians have access to advanced computing power on their personal devices, the studio-as-laboratory is more noticeably about community, as well as technological components that require substantial physical space. In other words, studios may have been necessary at first because there was no other place to create electronic music, but they have remained relevant throughout the late 20th century and into the 21st because they continue to provide resources that are valuable to practitioners.

We might also consider specific experiments that were undertaken in such spaces, especially those shaping the development of both musical and measurement instruments. For example, mathematician Jordan Schettler cites the influence of Wendy Carlos, whose work with the Moog synthesizer helped to

---

[96] Nick Collins and Julio d'Escriván, eds., *Cambridge Companion to Electronic Music*, 2nd ed. (Cambridge: Cambridge University Press, 2017), xvii–xx; Hugh Davies's *International Music Catalogue* (Cambridge, MA: MIT Press, 1968) is cited by Oram, in *An Individual Note*, 108.

[97] Margaret Schedel, "Electronic Music and the Studio," in *Cambridge Companion to Electronic Music*, 33–34.

118 INTERPRETIVE LABOR

improve and popularize that well-known keyboard.[98] Carlos likewise notes in the 1980s that

> the exponential growth in computers has finally expanded to include systems expressly designed for music production, editing, and performance at low enough cost to be as affordable as, say, a good grand piano. This is the first time instrumentation exists that is both powerful enough and convenient enough to make practical the notion: any possible timbre, in any possible tuning, with any possible timing."[99]

Schettler later points out that, while unconventional tunings can be determined using mathematical equations, Carlos had used experimentation to work out the pitch collections (what Schettler calls "scales") that would shape her musical creations. This work with tuning, especially, took a scientific form. Carlos's article is replete with charts, graphs, and equations showing the mathematic foundations of octave divisions and intervallic partials, championing the latest advancements in acoustic technology.[100]

In addition to shaping the evolution of the instruments themselves, musicians have of course made incredibly creative forays into writing new music using these tools. A number of excellent scholars have begun to document and interpret this history, including accounts of the Columbia-Princeton Electronic Music Center (CPEMC), first-hand discussions with practitioners, and other valuable projects. We learn about the work of artists like Halim El-Dabh and Michiko Toyama, among others, in Brigid Cohen's richly detailed monograph on the intersection between migration and artistry in mid-century New York.[101] This text is especially valuable for making significant space for musicians whose work has figured less prominently in previous histories. El-Dabh and Toyama's work at the CPEMC demonstrates the cross-cultural possibilities afforded by recording, manipulation, and other technological interventions. I also see significant value in texts such as Tara Rodgers's *Pink Noises* and Joanna Demers's *Listening through the Noise*. The former, a collection of interviews with women active in electronic music

---

[98] Jordan Schettler, "Wendy Carlos's Xenharmonic Keyboard," *Mathematics Magazine* 92, no. 3 (June 2019), 201.

[99] Wendy Carlos, "Tuning: At the Crossroads," *Computer Music Journal* 11, no. 1, Microtonality (Spring 1987), 31.

[100] "The truth of the matter is that up until now there's simply been no way to investigate beyond the standard scale within the limits of the precision of the available technology." Carlos, "Tuning," 31.

[101] Cohen, *Musical Migration and Imperial New York*.

of all kinds, revises the prevailing impression that electronics are the purview of the boys.[102] Likewise, Demers puts a new spin on its historiography, leaning into a relatively unpopular framework (aesthetics) to demonstrate electronic music's varied relationships to meaning.[103] Taken together, these three books—and other new work—provide insight into a massive array of experiments and experiences with musical technologies and the myriad ways in which creative laborers have engaged with these tools to create exciting new music.

In addition to electronic music, the scientist model also comes into play in various new types of university programs. I am thinking here of institutions like Stanford's Center for Computer Research in Music and Acoustics (CCRMA), the Qualcomm Institute (QI) at UC San Diego, and the Practice-based Experimental Epistemology (PEER) Lab, founded and run by Nina Eidsheim at UCLA. These organizations, while obviously enmeshed in the bureaucratic workings of higher education, offer time and space for participants to explore sonic phenomena. I find it encouraging that such groups receive material support from their institutions through faculty lines, equipment, and physical workspaces on campus. For example, the CCRMA directory lists approximately 30 employees, most of whom are affiliated teaching faculty.[104] Its courses, like Music 203: Audiovisual Performance and Music 285: Intermedia Lab, provide academic versions of a longstanding aspect of electronic musicking—that is, the workshop. Students in these and other classes have the opportunity to try out new ideas and to explore technologically mediated possibilities, all within the relatively low-risk environment of university coursework.

At Qualcomm, which is part of a consortium, researchers "leverage cutting-edge technology to address large-scale challenges facing the 21st century."[105] While perhaps better known for its innovations in healthcare, environmental sciences, and energy research, it has also played host to creative workers. Composer Lei Liang is "Research Artist-in-Residence" at QI, where he has developed musical works in conjunction with teams of robotics engineers. In fact, a new lab has just been announced in which the composer

---

[102] Tara Rodgers, *Pink Noises: Women on Electronic Music and Sound* (Durham, NC: Duke University Press, 2010).

[103] Joanna Demers, *Listening through the Noise: The Aesthetics of Experimental Electronic Music* (Oxford: Oxford University Press, 2010).

[104] https://ccrma.stanford.edu/faculty-staff, last accessed August 19, 2023.

[105] https://qi.ucsd.edu/about/, last accessed August 20, 2023.

120 INTERPRETIVE LABOR

will work with both graduate and undergraduate students—a promising and exciting leap into uncharted forms of music-making.[106] The PEER Lab embraces the relatively new discipline of practice-based research—a somewhat formalized type of learning by doing. Per the items featured on the Lab's homepage, participants emphasize their commitment to supporting marginalized people and ways of thinking and to transdisciplinary modes of engagement.[107] As Eidsheim notes, "In this research community, we encourage cross-sensory investigation. We regard knowledge not yet recognized by the powerbrokers of academia with the highest respect and curiosity."[108] These types of research centers seem, to me, to be the next big thing in the scientific form of Interpretive Labor: organizations that build upon the experiments of the past to propose, test, and refine the music of tomorrow.

[106] https://qi.ucsd.edu/gift-launches-lei-lab-at-the-uc-san-diego-qualcomm-institute/.
[107] https://schoolofmusic.ucla.edu/about/community-engagement/peer-lab/, last accessed August 19, 2023.
[108] https://schoolofmusic.ucla.edu/about/community-engagement/peer-lab/about-us/, last accessed August 20, 2023.

4

THE "ADMINISTRATOR" MODEL

"WOMEN'S WORK" AND NEW-MUSIC COORDINATORS

[This] is not to say that they are the beneficiaries of male enlightenment; one suspects that [Delia] Derbyshire and [Daphne] Oram were permitted to operate as they did in the 1960s because electronics was somehow considered "woman's work," like hand-stitching or macramé, background work that did not apparently threaten male hierarchies.[1]

In 2015, I was preparing for a trip to the Czech Republic for Ostrava Days, a biennial institute and festival for new and experimental music. To get a sense of what to expect, I eagerly read reviews of previous instantiations of the event. For a detailed account of the 2013 series, I turned to Boris Klepal's article in the journal *Czech Music*. The write-up provides descriptions and photographs of the nine days' worth of concerts, closing with some information about Artistic Director Petr Kotík, noting that his "organisational abilities and sheer enthusiasm keep the Ostrava Days alive. He drives the festival forward and sees to its maintaining a continuously high level."[2] There is no mention of the program's administrators at that time: coordinator Michaela Kuklová, office manager Kristýna Konczyna, or even the Ostrava Center for New Music's executive director, Renáta Spisarová.

Of course, this is just one specific article, but it got me thinking about the support systems that enable such programs to develop and thrive. Who is doing the "grunt work" that establishes, develops, and maintains such

---

[1] David Stubbs, *Future Sounds: The Story of Electronic Music from Stockhausen to Skrillex* (London: Faber & Faber, 2018), 172.
[2] Boris Klepal, "Ostrava Days: Long Concerts You Never Want to End," *Czech Music* 3 (2013), 27.

Interpretive Labor. Kirsten I. Speyer Carithers, Oxford University Press. © Oxford University Press 2025.
DOI: 10.1093/9780197698815.003.0005

122 INTERPRETIVE LABOR

organizations? How are the institutions constructed, and what kind of systems are in place to support them financially and structurally? The answers to these questions have led me to what I am calling the Administrator Model of Interpretive Labor: the role inhabited by facilitators, organizers, and support staff. New-music coordinators and administrators are just one set of workers engaging with tasks like producing and organizing events, communicating with financial backers, forecasting and managing logistics—tasks that, as it turns out, are overwhelmingly associated with women workers in the second half of the 20th century. In addition to considering the interpretive work inherent in this role, then, this chapter will also assess gender issues related to administrative functions, in this case focusing on U.S. American labor history.

GENDER AND LABOR

As I told the students in my first iteration of a class called "Women and Music," I initially resisted the idea when the topic was first suggested to me. Why should women be siloed off into a separate course, rather than being fully integrated into any other subject? Wouldn't we just be reinforcing division and tokenism? In fact, when I was a graduate student myself and was pressured to take a seminar on gender and music, I was so deeply uncomfortable with the readings listed on the syllabus and with the ideas that were going to be explored that I actually broke with my typical "teacher's pet" inclinations and begged to get out of it. I had deliberately chosen a cognate area in Critical Theory, far away from the messiness of bodies and desire; the idea of sitting in a room with my peers and talking about gender, about embodiment, and about expressing sexuality through music gave me overwhelming anxiety to the point of having a panic attack in my poor professor's office. In the following years, I developed a research agenda primarily concerned with issues of labor, experimentation, and performance practice, not with gender issues. In other words, while my curiosity has sometimes been piqued, I don't know that I would ever consider myself an expert in the field or, frankly, even someone with a longstanding commitment to research and teaching in the area of gender.

That said, as has been the case for others in historically marginalized groups, it seems that living in a particular identity sometimes means being called upon to represent that identity. As I prepared and taught two courses at my current institution in the spring of 2022 (a graduate seminar and a course for undergraduate non-music majors), both called "Women and Music," I was moved by the excellent scholarship on women's roles, and struck by just how recently developed are many of the initiatives toward equity. It was a wake-up call. Throughout the term, my students and I surveyed the history of gender roles related to music-making for performers, composers, instrument-builders, teachers, and a host of other areas. Thanks to the scholarly labor of musicological writers who came before me, I began to look ahead to the next logical steps, so that, maybe someday, we won't need to have separate courses anymore.

With that in mind, what is or was "Women's Work," and how might it relate to music? The phrase, perhaps innocuous on the surface, betrays the idea that labor is a gendered sociocultural construct. Much like musicologists, it took labor historians quite some time to engage with women's practices in any depth. When they began, their research often focused on industrial work, leaving out the majority of women wage-earners as well as most racial minorities. Writing in the late 1980s, labor historians Lois Rita Helmbold and Ann Schofield note that "before 1968, books that dealt with the history of women and work in the U.S. barely occupied one library shelf. Stimulated by the reemergence of feminism, the activism of the New Left, and the advent of the 'new' social history in the 1960s and 1970s, not only have scholars created a new literature in women's labor history, but their work has burgeoned in size and matured in conceptualization during the past twenty years."[3] Writing around the same time, Philip Scranton identifies a partition between mainstream labor history and what he calls "issue-oriented" scholarship, which "was carried forward . . . largely outside the academy. Between 1900 and 1940, these writers contributed mightily to debates about child labor, sweatshops, women's work (especially homework [sic]), industrial safety, and under- and unemployment."[4] Scranton's apparent belief that the labor of women was self-evidently separate, even in the late 1980s, suggests that there was still much work to do at that time.

Countering this stance, feminist historians began to critique the norms of their discipline, especially the assumption that work was (and must be) segregated by sex or gender. As Helmbold and Schofield summarize the

---

[3] Lois Rita Helmbold and Ann Schofield, "Women's Labor History, 1790–1945," *Reviews in American History* 17, no. 4 (December 1989), 501.

[4] Philip Scranton, "None-Too-Porous Boundaries: Labor History and the History of Technology," *Technology and Culture* 29, no. 4 (October 1988), 724.

124   INTERPRETIVE LABOR

"prevailing ideas about women's weakness"—their "presumed tolerance for tedium and their nimble fingers," "their desire for marriage and family," their assumed physical vulnerability—these factors were taken to be givens, shaping the historiography of women's labor until well into the second half of the 20th century.[5] Within Anglo-American scholarship, the gender turn transformed research and writing in labor history; however, this was not a universal change, and scholarship in and on other geographical areas (for example, China and Latin America) continued to engage more with structural issues than with gender.[6] In short, labor history's engagement with women's experiences is a recent development, and one that has much room for growth at the time of this writing. Considerations of women's roles that combine labor history and music history are, I believe, a fruitful contribution toward this goal.

Logical readers might next wonder what is interpretive about this model, and what it is doing in a book about experimentalism(s). Admittedly, the collection of traits and practices in the Administrator Model of Interpretive Labor is perhaps the least closely connected to musical experimentalism and the most universal of roles/identities among arts organizations. After all, to function as an organization requires a capable degree of administration; otherwise, the group is a "mere" collective. While this chapter focuses on activities undertaken in service of programming and performing experimentalism, the underlying work of our protagonists maps comfortably, I believe, onto similar labor by workers in other creative milieu. It might therefore provide some explanatory value for a wide range of arts organizations, including shedding light on their structures, histories, and internal dynamics.

In organizations with one or more persons "running the show," the interpretive procedures look quite different from those of, say, a clarinetist reading a composition's graphic-notation score. Whereas the latter might need to make decisions about dynamics, phrasing, use of extended techniques, or other musical parameters, the former involves largely interpersonal interpretation. For example, there are considerations about the requirements and desires of funders, directors, performers, and audiences. It is necessary to translate these viewpoints into a language common to all parties and to negotiate amongst potentially conflicting priorities. The administrator must therefore possess a clear understanding of those roles and their expectations

---

[5] Helmbold and Schofield, "Women's Labor History," 503.
[6] Peter Winn, "Labor History after the Gender Turn: Introduction," *International Labor and Working-Class History*, no. 63 (Spring 2003), 1–5.

THE "ADMINISTRATOR" MODEL   125

and be able to navigate among them—preferably in a diplomatic manner, if the organization is to achieve any long-term success.[7]

I also see financial work as an interpretive process. Arts groups are notoriously under-funded, requiring administrators to carefully manage budgets. How much can be done with minimal resources? How should funds be allocated? Where should cuts be made, if necessary? Tackling these questions requires a degree of creative labor; it demands the ability to hold multiple, competing objectives in mind simultaneously in order to weigh potential outcomes. For example, the ONCE Group, established in Ann Arbor, Michigan, in the early 1960s, was greatly aided by the work of Anne Opie Counselman Wehrer, the wife of Joseph Wehrer (who taught in the architecture school and helped with the light-and-sound productions of the Space Theatre in Ann Arbor). Anne, an actress and writer, served as the secretary of an organization called the Dramatic Arts Council (DAC) in 1960–61, and, according to Leta Miller, "would become one of the major forces assuring ONCE's success."[8]

In addition to encouraging financial support through the DAC, Wehrer also worked with potential venues for ONCE performances, arranged housing for guests, and managed, in Miller's words, "numerous logistical details." Administrative labor thus also frequently involves work that might seem mundane, repetitive, or rote. While such work has an extended history going back centuries, I find it notable that the job classification of "secretaries," with its massive growth in the mid-20th century in the United States, corresponds with the explosion of arts organizations in the same era. As university music programs, contemporary-music groups, and other parties expanded and became officially legitimized through their governing structures, they needed individuals to handle important but oft-overlooked duties, such as taking meeting minutes, typing correspondence, and posting items for the mail service—all of which was, of course, more time-consuming and labor-intensive without computers than it would be today. For multiple reasons (largely connected to class and gender), this work tends to be undervalued despite its importance.

With that in mind, I turn to the specific roles of those who manage institutions of new music: the coordinators and administrators, often

---

[7] As noted by the successful arts administrator Renée Levine Packer, "the effective administrator must be a diplomat. Diplomacy is a key attribute." Personal communication, November 15, 2023.

[8] Leta E. Miller, "ONCE and Again: The Evolution of a Legendary Festival." Essay in booklet accompanying *Music from the ONCE Festival, 1961–1966*, New World Records 80567-2, 7.

126   INTERPRETIVE LABOR

working behind the scenes. Their work involves tasks like organizing rehearsals and communicating with patrons, as well as managing concert and travel logistics for participants. To see how this works, I will briefly introduce two roughly contemporary institutions and discuss some of the individuals who developed and sustained these groups' success. Through an investigation of institutions such as these, we uncover the hidden labor of administrators and establish a conceptual framework for improving the recognition of these essential roles.

ORGANIZATIONS

While there are some similarities among groups that presented experimental/ avant-garde music in the postwar era, there is also a fair amount of diversity in terms of structure and institutional support. The following section considers the Center of the Creative and Performing Arts, a formal organization for the education and promotion of new music, and the Avant-Garde Festivals of New York, a set of relatively ad hoc events centered on performances. Existing in the same state and during mostly the same years, these two institutions nevertheless demonstrate a wide range of activities connected to the concept of administrative labor.

Center of the Creative and Performing Arts

Functioning essentially as a postgraduate program for specialists in new music, the Center of the Creative and Performing Arts (CCPA) was housed at the University at Buffalo, which had recently been incorporated into the State University of New York, or SUNY, system; the Center was active from 1964 to 1980. Including a number of well-known participants, including George Crumb, Cornelius Cardew, and Gwendolyn Sims, it was the temporary artistic home for numerous composer-performers who created new works and premiered one another's compositions.[9] The organization was established for the express purpose of providing time, space, and funding

---

[9] "If the Center could be characterized as a postdoctoral laboratory, its university base constituted a gold mine of expertise and opportunity, providing access to facilities and brainpower that many of the fellows, all of whom held faculty rank, enthusiastically exploited." Levine Packer, *This Life of Sound*, 49–50.

for creative individuals to become more proficient at making new music. Lukas Foss, in a 1963 report for the Rockefeller Foundation, notes in part that organizations should support young musicians so that they "may have leisure, concentration, facilities and outlets for such professional activities as would help [them] to find [themselves], vis. chamber music, new music, experimental music, which rarely yield remuneration."[10] (Quite so!) Upon its approval by the Foundation, a massive grant was awarded to establish and support the Center for its founding years, with the intention to have the expanding SUNY organization take over financial support in the third year.

Fortunately for the fledgling CCPA, a skilled young arts administrator had just arrived in Buffalo from New York City right around the time of the Center's establishment. Renée Levine (later Packer) served in several roles with the group, beginning with a brief stint as assistant coordinator in January 1965. In New York, Ms. Levine had worked at the Juilliard School, where she met her mentor, the modern-dance legend Martha Hill, who had founded the dance department there in 1951.[11] Recently married to violist Jesse Levine, she moved to Buffalo in August 1964, when her husband was recruited for the Buffalo Philharmonic. Lukas Foss, who was cofounder of the new Center at the university, conductor of the Philharmonic, and the Levines' neighbor, asked Renée to help with the office work for the fledgling CCPA.[12]

In the previous summer, new faculty member Richard Wernick, ostensibly a composition instructor, had been roped into handling the daily work of running the Center, including tasks like helping the first cohort of Creative Associates find places to live and ordering scores and parts for the first set of concerts, while co-director (with Allen Sapp, chair of the Music Department at the university) Lukas Foss chose which compositions would be performed and oversaw the group as a whole. As Levine Packer noted later, "it became apparent to Foss and Sapp that Richard Wernick was struggling to juggle the administrative needs of the Center by himself. There was simply too much for any one person to do."[13] Those "administrative needs," she explains, were

---

[10] Lukas Foss and Allen Sapp, "A Proposal for the Establishment of a Center of the Performing and Creative Arts with an Emphasis on New Music," cited in Levine Packer, *This Life of Sounds*, 18. For a detailed account of the establishment of the Center, see chapter 1: "The Rockefeller Years," in that text.

[11] Martha Hill research materials, Jerome Robbins Dance Division, The New York Public Library. Biography and collection information online at https://archives.nypl.org/dan/18517. Detailed information about Ms. Hill can be found in Janet Soares, *Martha Hill and the Making of American Dance* (Middletown, CT: Wesleyan University Press, 2009).

[12] Levine Packer, *This Life of Sounds*, 33–34.

[13] Levine Packer, *This Life of Sounds*, 34.

128 INTERPRETIVE LABOR

intensified by the university's new status as a state agency, by the challenges of obtaining rental parts for recently composed works, and by the lack of precedent for an institution like the Center itself. Ms. Levine quickly became an instrumental member of the organization and worked there for a decade and a half, including becoming Center Coordinator when Wernick left Buffalo in 1965 and holding that position until 1974; she was appointed Managing Director that year, staying on until 1978.[14]

The work undertaken by Ms. Levine fits into many of the categories typical of arts administrators, such as grant-writing and other financial requirements, coordinating with visiting musicians, organizing logistics for the Center's ambitious concert series, serving as the liaison with foundation officers and community figures, and managing the Center's numerous postgraduate fellows—sometimes even helping them find housing and other unofficial tasks, as had Wernick in the CCPA's first year. Broken down into smaller components, some of these tasks—taking notes, making phone calls, drafting correspondence, creating schedules, dealing with visa and union issues, answering questions—are common for those in jobs that, in the 1960s, were thought of as "secretarial."[15] At that time, nearly one-third of the working women in the United States were employed in "clerical" roles, such that approximately 70% of all clerical workers in 1965 were women. (Two decades earlier, the gender distribution for such roles had been nearly evenly split among men and women.) In the mid-1960s, only private-household workers had a higher proportion of women employees, with clerical work (stenographers, typists, secretaries, etc.) the largest public-facing categorical group by far.[16] Occupations remained largely segregated by gender at that time; among the 36 specific occupations held by at least 100,000 women in 1965, most were especially so, with only a few categories reaching anything close to an even distribution. 96% of higher of the following jobs were held by women: dressmakers/seamstresses, receptionists, housekeepers, maids, nurses, stenographers, "babysitters," telephone operators, private-household workers, and—the most populous—secretaries.[17] In other words, Levine (at

---

[14] Levine Packer, *This Life of Sounds*, 191.

[15] Specific tasks and job duties compiled from the archival materials listed below and confirmed in discussion with Ms. Levine Packer. Personal communication, November 15, 2023.

[16] United States Department of Labor (DoL), *1965 Handbook on Women Workers: Women's Bureau Bulletin No. 290* (Washington, D.C., 1965), 87.

[17] DoL, *Handbook*, 92. Incidentally, the most heavily women-held category was private-household workers, which was consistently at least 90% women, and that percentage actually increased through the first half of the 20th century. Very few people working in private homes were men. DoL, *Handbook*, 89.

least in official terms) occupied a role that was exceedingly normative for a woman in the United States at that time. While job category labels have been altered over time (discussed below), much of the administrative labor in this country is, and historically has been, undertaken by women.

During her time at the Center, Renée Levine's work expanded in scope from assistant or primarily "office work" functions to increasing responsibility for the institution's success. Already in August 1965, when she was transitioning into a recurring role for the first time (and trying to convince the leadership to provide a reasonable salary), she listed the following tasks as part of her expected workload: scheduling rehearsals, managing correspondence, making travel arrangements, managing offsite concerts, working on promotional materials, and, in her words, "the necessity of constant availability to all of the eighteen or so Creative Associates."[18] These young artists, many of whom were already well-known nationally and internationally, were energetic virtuosi with significant needs. While they were granted faculty status, none had teaching requirements; they were expected to create and perform both on campus and off, and this meant equipment rentals, transportation logistics, and other time-consuming assistance from the Center Coordinator. As funding from the initial Rockefeller grant and its renewal dwindled, her work increasingly included identifying potential funding sources, writing grant proposals, and working with various sources such as the National Endowment for the Arts, the New York State Council on the Arts, and local foundations. One of Levine's numerous memos marks another change that set the Center on precarious financial footing: "During the summer of 1968, State support for the Center was abruptly withdrawn by the University administration. . . . The Center's 10 State lines for fellowships (plus one administrator's line) were transferred to other areas. . . . To date [fall 1971], not one of these State lines has been restored."[19] By 1974, the Center was able to support only a few participants, with five full-time fellows and one half-time appointment. Throughout the intervening years, Levine managed budgets, invoices, fundraising, and other tasks, in addition to everything that might normally be expected of a "coordinator." In truth, her work involved management well before her job title caught up.

---

[18] Renée W. Levine, letter to Allen Sapp, August 25, 1965. Mus. Arc. 75, Box 5, Folder 124, University at Buffalo Music Library.

[19] Renée Levine, CCPA memo to Albert Cohen, September 10, 1971. Mus. Arc. 75, Box 6, Folder 132, University at Buffalo Music Library.

130 INTERPRETIVE LABOR

One point of tension in this history is that Renée Levine's job within the SUNY system was initially classified as a part-time "assistant to the director," with her salary drawn from a specific, and limited, funding source. Because of this, her employment remained precarious despite her importance to the institution of the CCPA—a discomfiting status that is all too familiar to the majority of academic instructional faculty today. In a letter from May 1972, she notes frustration with her lack of job security, explaining that "each year at this time I have absolutely no assurance that I will be maintained on the staff."[20] The logistics of her position's funding also meant that she was ineligible for the standard incremental pay raises that other staff received, according to the same letter. Budget documents from the time show that her salary was similar to the stipends paid out to the Creative Associates fellows, who were also, frankly, underpaid for their work.[21] Given these circumstances, it seems rather remarkable that she stayed on as "coordinator" for another two years before finally officially becoming the Managing Director.[22]

Over time, her importance to the CCPA became widely acknowledged. In 1977, Music Department Chairman William Thompson wrote,

> Ms. Levine has an intimate knowledge of every aspect of the Center's history and operation. She has acquaintance and good working relationship with key figures in local, State and Federal funding sources, arts organizations, and media centers throughout the world, as well as a distinct reputation in the field of arts management in the Contemporary scene. She is the central figure in the operation of the Center.[23]

The job description corresponding to that review maps out the enormous list of responsibilities required for this position, in the areas of fundraising, program management, project directorship for all grants, financial

---

[20] Renée W. Levine, letter to SUNYAB Music Department Chairman Albert Cohen, May 15, 1972. Mus. Arc. 75, Box 5, Folder 124, University at Buffalo Music Library.

[21] For example, the *Center of the Creative and Performing Arts 1970–72 Budget* breaks down each funding source and allocation, including production expenses, office supplies, and salaries for all positions associated with the Center. Mus. Arc. 75, Box 6, Folder 133, University at Buffalo Music Library.

[22] As she shared with me, one had to be caught up in the mission to do this work; she genuinely enjoyed working with the musicians, and this was more important than a title or salary. Personal communication, November 15, 2023.

[23] "Supervisor Comment Sheet," SUNY Non-teaching Professional Service Position Description/ Salary Justification, SUNY/Buffalo Personnel Department, 1977. Mus. Arc. 75, Box 5, Folder 125, University at Buffalo Music Library.

THE "ADMINISTRATOR" MODEL   131

management, program development, and public affairs. Specific duties range from designing budgets to negotiating fees with guest artists; from assisting Fellows with visas and contracts to organizing international tours; and even supervising Arts Management students' projects via independent study courses. Through all of this, her official title in the SUNY system remained "Assistant to the Director."[24]

In addition to her under-recognized leadership of the CCPA, Renée Levine Packer's written records are an invaluable resource. They provide a first-hand account of the wealth of concerts, rehearsals, and other related events undertaken by the Creative Associates, granting readers an insider's view of the organization. In 1973, she attended an Arts Administration institute at Harvard, where she was tasked with writing up a case study based on her work at the Center. Later projects that built on that work included a master's thesis at Johns Hopkins University, which was developed into the monograph *This Life of Sounds: Evenings for New Music in Buffalo*. In 2018, Ms. Levine Packer's papers were processed at SUNY Buffalo; these mainly consist of correspondence, along with her materials used in the preparation of *This Life of Sounds* and her second book, on the composer-performer Julius Eastman.[25] Not only did she work as a coordinator and director of the Center, then, but also she functioned as an archivist: without her memories and saved documents, we would have precious little information about the history of the CCPA.

Avant-Garde Festivals of New York

A particularly complicated case, I believe, is that of cellist and performance artist (Madeline) Charlotte Moorman. Born in Arkansas and classically trained, she has only recently been recognized as a key figure in the new-music orbit of the 1960s and 1970s.[26] Her musical education was quite

[24] "Exhibit I: Statement of New or Increased Duties," January 17, 1977. SUNY/Buffalo Personnel Department, 1977. Mus. Arc. 75, Box 5, Folder 125, University at Buffalo Music Library.
[25] Levine Packer (Renée) Papers (Mus. Arc. 75), Music Library Storage, University at Buffalo Libraries; Renée Levine Packer and Mary Jane Leach, eds., *Gay Guerrilla: Julius Eastman and His Music*, Eastman Studies in Music (Rochester, NY: Boydell & Brewer/University of Rochester Press, 2015).
[26] See, for example, the Joan Rothfuss biography, *Topless Cellist: The Improbable Life of Charlotte Moorman* (Cambridge, MA: MIT Press, 2014) and the catalog and essay collection published in conjunction with a major exhibition at Northwestern University's Block Museum of Art and NYU's Grey Art Gallery: Lisa Graziose Corrin and Corinne Granof, eds., *A Feast of Astonishments: Charlotte Moorman and the Avant-Garde, 1960s–1980* (Evanston, IL: Northwestern University Press, 2016).

132   INTERPRETIVE LABOR

conventional, including an undergraduate degree at a liberal-arts college in Louisiana, a master's degree at the University of Texas at Austin, and further studies with Leonard Rose and Lillian Fuchs at Juilliard.[27] Before that, she had played in the new Arkansas State Symphony, winning an apprentice seat as a pre-teen.[28] In New York, she played in classically oriented groups, including a season with the American Symphony Orchestra under conductor Leopold Stokowski. While there, she quickly became acquainted with the New York avant-garde, and would go on to develop an annual festival that drew some of the biggest names in the field at that time.

Before we get to the Avant-Garde Festivals, though, it is worth acknowledging that there were very few women active in that scene, a detail that shapes both Charlotte Moorman's lived experience and the reception of her work. The gender dynamics at play are perhaps exacerbated by some of Moorman's own actions, as she didn't shy away from provocative performances but rather embraced them. At the very first meeting between Charlotte and artist-composer Nam June Paik, for example, he was apparently already suggesting working with her on a striptease piece, and she was quickly "hypnotized" by him, to use her word.[29] Even when she was arrested for public indecency during a performance of Paik's *Opera Sextronique* (1967), Moorman claimed that she had to remove her clothes because she was just following the score.[30]

She repeatedly displayed deference to composers, often risking physical harm to her body—for example, by physically embracing a massive block of ice or being lifted high in the air by balloons.[31] Some concerned observers, therefore, saw her as being manipulated by male artists; others, like Philip

---

[27] Corinne Granof, "'In Times Like This': Moorman's Art in Context," in Corrin and Granof, *A Feast of Astonishments*, 4. For more details about the cellist's education and training, see the first two chapters of Rothfuss, *Topless Cellist.*

[28] Moorman's father passed away the very same month as her audition. In the wake of that and her mother's subsequent struggle with alcoholism, Charlotte was primarily raised by her grandmother, with whom she was very close. Rothfuss, *Topless Cellist*, 13–14.

[29] Moorman later stated, "[Paik] was so serious. And somehow I just became hypnotized by him, and we became partners. And we have been partners ever since." Interview from 1980 cited in Gisela Gronemeyer, "Seriousness and Dedication: The American Avant-Garde Cellist Charlotte Moorman," essay in *Charlotte Moorman: Cello Anthology*, Alga Marghen audio CD box set, Milan, 2006, n.p.

[30] On the other hand, that may have seemed like the most convincing defense at the time, although it was ultimately unsuccessful. After trying to avoid conviction by invoking the First Amendment, Moorman's attorney tried to argue that, "as an obedient interpreter of compositions, Moorman was not responsible for her nudity." Sophie Landres, "Indecent and Uncanny: The Case against Charlotte Moorman," *Art Journal* 76, no.1 (Spring 2017), 56.

[31] Jim McWilliams's *Ice Music for London/Ice Cello* (1972) and *Sky Kiss* (1968).

THE "ADMINISTRATOR" MODEL   133

Corner, said she knew exactly what she was doing and would have been angered by that characterization. In an interview in 1991, Corner argued:

> Charlotte was by no means a stupid person, she was by no means naïve, and if you had said that to her, you would have heard good old southern anger and intelligence in her defense of her position. I don't think Charlotte was a dumb goose from the South who could be exploited by us big city slickers. . . . She went wherever she wanted . . . she passionately believed in what she was doing, and she made her life choices in terms of doing that, and made a lot of sacrifices, and she put her body on the line, and she believed in it.[32]

The art critic Jill Johnston addresses these issues in some detail in an essay from 1991, which is ostensibly a memorial for the recently deceased musician. This text is littered with references to Ms. Moorman's complicated relationship to sex and gender. Johnston cites the legal opinion from the 1967 arrest for performing in only a skirt, referring to Moorman as the judge's "victim"; this characterization returns in a description of one of her last performances, a 1988 iteration of Yoko Ono's *Cut Piece*: "I saw a valiant victim in Charlotte, ever a champion of the forces that felled her."[33] Johnston also claims both that Charlotte enjoyed being "used" by the men of Fluxus and—strangely—that Charlotte's own husband had said that "she discovered sex in the 1960s and couldn't believe what she had been missing."[34] In hindsight, these comments reek of the victim-blaming and "slut-shaming" rhetoric that escalated in the 1990s and into the early internet age.[35] Much like the young women who face judgment for sharing provocative photos online, Charlotte Moorman had to walk a gendered tightrope: be attractive enough to charm the audience, but not overly so or you won't be taken seriously; be artistically adventurous, but don't stray too far from the written score; engage with performance art, but only within certain limited parameters. As Johnston explains, "there was a more insidious, more dangerous price to pay for her choice [to commit to the avant-garde over her symphony orchestra

---

[32] Gronemeyer, "Seriousness and Dedication," n.p.

[33] Jill Johnston, "Remembering Charlotte Moorman," in *Secret Lives in Art: Essays on Art, Literature, Performance* (Chicago, IL: a cappella books, 1994), 144.

[34] Johnston, "Remembering," 143.

[35] See, for example, the work of Leora Tanenbaum (e.g., *I Am Not a Slut: Slut-Shaming in the Age of the Internet* [New York: Harper, 2015]) and Meredith Ralston's *Slut-Shaming, Whorephobia, and the Unfinished Sexual Revolution* (Montreal: McGill-Queen's University Press, 2021).

134   INTERPRETIVE LABOR

job]. During the 1960s, as the so-called sexual revolution consumed our society and before the feminist movement had gained any momentum, women were an easy mark for exploitation."[36] Troublingly, Johnston seems to paint Moorman as a witting mark. Adjectives like "ready," "eager," "used," and "exposed" suggest that the essayist herself may have struggled to accept that Moorman maintained agency in these situations. Johnston's stance echoes that of several others, including Fluxus artist Alison Knowles. Knowles stated that the artist was "never . . . in a state of consciousness," and that her actions were "thoughtless": "it never broke through into a mature kind of thinking about the work, about what the work means. To think, what are you doing? And I find that at a certain point for her to redo those pieces of Paik again and again, was a bit sad, or maybe she would do it because it was the work that she was known for."[37] Knowles seems to fault Moorman for repeatedly performing the pieces in her repertoire—an action which is of course standard among working musicians in other genres. Moorman's specialization just happened to include works that challenged even the relatively progressive standards of the avant-garde, at least in the sense of their frequent invocation of human sexuality.

In conjunction with her significant work as a trendsetter in avant-garde performance practice, Moorman also displayed an aptitude for arts administration. In the early 1960s, she initiated a couple of concerts for friends, including Yoko Ono and Philip Corner, by raising funds directly and by convincing a concert agent to produce the events.[38] This was the beginning of a long and fruitful profession as an informal or unofficial impresario. One of Moorman's most important contributions to music history was her work in organizing a set of annual festivals that celebrated experimental music, held in various locations around New York City between 1963 and 1980. The first Avant-Garde Festival came together in 1963. I'll let Charlotte herself tell the origin story:

> In 1963, the composer Earle Brown came up to me, and told me about his friend Frederic Rzewski, who was supposed to be a very fine pianist. He asked me to introduce him to the concert manager Norman Seaman. So

[36] Johnston, "Remembering," 142–43. Max Neuhaus referred to Moorman's decision to turn away from the predictable classical world as "a form of musical suicide—it was much less accepted to perform contemporary music than it is now." Interview quoted in Rothfuss, *Topless Cellist*, 60.

[37] Alison Knowles interview, 1991, cited in Gronemeyer, "Seriousness and Dedication," n.p.

[38] The first such event was Kenji Kobayashi's Town Hall violin recital in 1961, produced by Norman Seaman with fundraising completed by Moorman. Rothfuss, *Topless Cellist*, 42–46.

THE "ADMINISTRATOR" MODEL   135

I took Frederic to [his] office, and Norman Seaman said, "Yes, I'll present your friend here in New York, as long as you repeat the program you did with David Tudor in Philip Corner's loft." I said, "David Tudor is in California with John Cage." "Then call him up," he said. So I called David Tudor in California, and he said he would be happy to repeat the program with me. And then John Cage said he would also do an evening. So we were really happy about that, and then he said, "Why don't you call Edgard Varèse and organize an evening of electronic music?" So we put our first festival together in twenty minutes.[39]

About a month before the 1980 interview in which she relayed that story, Moorman wrote up a slightly different version, including David Behrman and Morton Feldman among those who had "conceived the idea of a Festival of the Avant Garde for New York City." In any case, that first festival was held over six days, in Judson Hall: a site of several of the earlier Moorman/Seaman collaborations.[40] As Moorman notes in her own description of the festival series, she chose programs, contacted composers, designed brochures, addressed and stuffed envelopes, and borrowed electronic equipment—and all of that was just for the first year. She points out, too, that they all worked without pay, with the aim of "establish[ing] the festival as an annual event."[41] The first series, known as 6 Concerts '63, laid the foundation for what would become a (nearly) annual gathering of musicians, visual artists, and other creative individuals whose work pushed the boundaries of acceptability. The second festival expanded to 10 days and a longer list of composers.[42] The 1964 edition was a remarkable undertaking: five nights of recitals, followed by five nights of the multimedia extravaganza by Stockhausen called *Originale*.

Before the third festival (1965), Norman Seaman, evidently tired of losing money, dropped out as producer. This seems to have been an issue for other participants, as well; in a 1965 letter to Cage, Allan Kaprow complains about Moorman's poor management of funds during the previous year, and—in one of the more heart-breaking pieces of correspondence that I've come

---

[39] Moorman recounted this version of the founding in an interview with Grisela Gronemeyer in 1980, quoted in Gronemeyer, "Seriousness and Dedication," n.p.

[40] Rothfuss, *Topless Cellist*, 68.

[41] Charlotte Moorman, "History of the Annual AVANT Garde Festival of New York," in *Cello Anthology*, n.p.

[42] Incidentally, works programmed were all composed by men, but there was a small handful of women performers.

136 INTERPRETIVE LABOR

across—Cage is equally dismissive in his response.[43] That year presented multiple challenges: in addition to Moorman taking over sole responsibility for producing the festival, that was also the year they got kicked out of Judson Hall—the audience, following a prompt by Allison Knowles, looted neighborhood trash for furnishings for a piece by Kaprow, and this was apparently the last straw.[44] Starting in 1966, the festival was held in unusual locations: first in Central Park, then other sites around the city, including the Staten Island Ferry, a riverboat, and an infantry armory, among others.

Thanks to scholars in art history and music, we now have a fair amount of information about Moorman's activities, including her administrative work. Gratitude must also be given to Charlotte herself, who kept detailed notes and rarely threw away any papers or other ephemera. As I write this, the massive collection that makes up the Charlotte Moorman Archive is still being cataloged in the Charles Deering McCormick Library of Special Collections at Northwestern University. While a finding aid has not yet been published (as of summer 2023), library staff note that there are more than 200 boxes of materials. As a doctoral candidate, I was able to view a small portion of the collection. Archivist Scott Krafft generously allowed me to see stacks of Moorman's papers and memorabilia, some of which would make up 2016's double exhibition.[45] At the time, I was focused on notation and on musical performance, but in retrospect, this rare glimpse into yet another form of behind-the-scenes labor surely made an impression.

***

In just these two institutions, then, we see a significant range of experiences, levels of participation, and job expectations. The interpretive labor of coordinators and other administrative supporters demands competence in numerous skills, like the translational labor of realizing directors' ideas, the ability to manage complex systems, and the affective labor of navigating competing egos (e.g., of composers and performers). Some of this work is

---

[43] Kaprow wrote, in part, "Last year in spite of Charlotte's promises, a few of us lost a good bit of our personal money during the production of Stockhausen's 'Originale.' I cannot repeat this. [. . .] Charlotte means well, but her presence last year was disastrous." Letter dated May 21, 1965. Cage's reply includes, "Charlotte's we know a problem. What to do? (I gave no assurance that I would raise money.) [. . .] I swore after working with her the first year not to do it again." Letter dated May 25, 1965. John Cage Correspondence, Box 7, folder 9, Northwestern University Music Library.

[44] Johnston, "Remembering," 145; Gronemeyer, "Seriousness and Dedication," n.p.

[45] "A Feast of Astonishments" was the larger exhibition; it was also presented at New York University's Grey Art Gallery and the Museum der Moderne Salzburg. "Don't Throw Anything Out" was a companion exhibition that was presented solely in Evanston.

THE "ADMINISTRATOR" MODEL   137

straightforward, while some calls for nuanced interpretation. To build on the framework introduced earlier, I find it useful to think of this work in terms of a Facilitator or Administrator model of Interpretive Labor. This encompasses administrative tasks from taking meeting minutes to booking concert halls to developing grant proposals: work that has typically been done behind the scenes.

LABOR AND GENDER

As noted in the 1965 report of the Women's Bureau of the U.S. Department of Labor, "Social and economic developments in recent years have had far-reaching effects on the place of women in the economy. For this reason, knowledge about the work women do, the circumstances of their working, and the direction of changes in their work is essential for an understanding of American society today."[46] With that in mind, we might consider how and why the history of arts administration for new-music groups connects to the problematic notion of "women's work." Clearly, during the time period discussed here, this labor has largely been the purview of women. The evidence suggests that this is not a coincidence, but rather a widespread phenomenon that aligns with cultural norms well beyond music, and, in fact, continues to shape this industry today. While gender roles within the U.S. American workforce have certainly shifted over the past several decades, and are gradually becoming less inequitable, some startling disparities persist. For example, even as late as 2008, one of the most highly populated occupations among women working full-time and year-round in the United States was "secretaries and administrative assistants." Women made up 96.1 % of all workers in that field; only nurse midwives and pre-kindergarten teachers had a greater gender disparity.[47] Thus, when Renée Levine Packer began her tenure with the CCPA at Buffalo, when 97% of "secretaries" were women, that proportion has barely budged in the intervening 45 years.

Is there something inherently "feminine" about administrative work? Of course not, so why has it been coded that way? As of 1940, about half of all workers in clerical roles in the United States were men; by 1965, that number

---

[46] Mary Dublin Keyserling, foreword to DoL, *Handbook*, v.
[47] United States Census Bureau, Table 603: Employed Civilians by Occupation, Sex, Race, and Hispanic Origin, 2008, in the report "Section 12: Labor Force, Employment, and Earnings," in *Statistical Abstract of the United States*, 2010.

138   INTERPRETIVE LABOR

had dropped to approximately 30%. Of course, the 1950s and 1960s were a time of great change, including in employment. In 1960, 38% of women participated in the wage-earning labor market; this increased to 43% by 1970. (During the same period, men's participation hovered around 80%.) As has been well documented, during the time immediately following World War II, many women lost their high-paying (and often unionized) jobs, turning to new opportunities in education, service, and retail businesses. In many of these sectors, wages were low, accompanied by long hours and few benefits. The U.S. Department of Labor notes that the "growth of business and industry, of all kinds of services, and of government operations has brought a rising demand for workers in these occupations to handle correspondence, interoffice communications, and other forms of paperwork."[48] That explosive growth called for approximately three million laborers to manage typing, stenography, and secretarial work—and again, more than 95% of these positions were held by women as of 1965. Clearly, separation by gender not only continued into the second half of the 20th century but actually expanded rapidly. As Sonya O. Rose has argued, "laboring men and women created a working-class version of the ideology of separate spheres that redefined conceptions of working-class masculinity and femininity."[49] In other words, the idea that men gain meaning through work and public life, while women's sphere of influence is in the home, made its way into the self-identities of workers—and, by extension, to labor history itself. While Rose's quote above specifically references 19th-century labor history in England, its effects likewise reverberated across time and geography: even into the mid-to-late 20th century, the notion of "separate spheres" was still shaping understandings of gender and labor. In addition, as noted in the 1965 Handbook, "The wide disparity between the concentration of women and men workers by type of work has contributed to the difference in their earnings, in the rate of growth of their employment, and in the relative number working part time or part year."[50]

Two factors are particularly relevant to our discussion: first, a change in the language used to identify administrative work, and second, a consideration of the salaries of those workers. The issue of earnings remains a major consideration even today. While the Equal Pay Act of 1963 technically prohibits pay discrimination on the basis of sex, aggregated data shows that equity has

[48] DoL, *Handbook*, 96.
[49] Sonya O. Rose, "Gender and Labor History: The Nineteenth-Century Legacy," *International Review of Social History* 38, supplement 1 (1993), 153.
[50] DoL, *Handbook*, 85.

THE "ADMINISTRATOR" MODEL   139

not yet been achieved. As of this writing, the gender pay gap in the United States remains consistent, with women earning $0.82 for every dollar earned by men; women of minoritized races earn considerably less.[51] In every single category within the most recent report, men earn more than women, on average.[52] The closest margin is found within community/social services workers, at 94%. "Male" median earnings in this field are $46,377 per year; "female" earnings are estimated at $43,600. For jobs most closely related to the "facilitator" or "administrator" role, the gap remains larger. For example, median earnings for women in management, business, and finance are more than $20,000/year lower than for men in those fields. Among "office and administrative support occupations," the recently renamed category previously tracked as "secretaries and administrative assistants," real salaries are closer, but only because the pay is so low to begin with. The ratio is only somewhat better, with women earning about 88% of men's wages in this category.[53]

As of the 2013–17 American Community Survey, the overall population of full-time workers in the United States was 42.9% women.[54] Within that group, there are six categories that are at least 70% "female": education/training/library (70.8), health diagnosing/treating (70.9), personal care and service (74.6), health technicians/technologists (74.9), healthcare support (85.7), and our main area of investigation here, office and administrative support occupations (71.1). Apart from the "health diagnosing and treating" category, I might note that these jobs have some of the lowest typical salaries, with some—especially in service occupations—treading perilously close to the poverty line.[55] In 18 states, as of 2009, women earned only three-quarters

---

[51] United States Government Accountability Office report GAO-23-106041, "Women in the Workforce: The Gender Pay Gap Is Greater for Certain Racial and Ethnic Groups and Varies by Education Level," (Washington, D.C.: U.S. G.A.O., 2022), 2.

[52] An important limit: this data is taken from U.S. Census Bureau's American Community Survey, for which respondents are required to identify as either male or female; the data is therefore misaligned with nuanced considerations of gender identity. However, it does provide some useful general information on the U.S. labor market. U.S. Census Bureau, 2013–2017 ACS 5-Year Estimates (Washington, D.C.: U.S. Census Bureau, 2021).

[53] Median "female" earnings: $35,680; "male" is $40,414. U.S. Census Bureau, 2013–2017 ACS 5-Year Estimates. As of 2017, the weighted average poverty threshold for a family of four was $25,094, placing 6.9 million people in the "working poor" category (meaning "people who spent at least 27 weeks in the labor force . . . but whose incomes still fell below the official poverty level"). U.S. Bureau of Labor Statistics report 1079, "A Profile of the Working Poor, 2017," n.p. (Washington, D.C.: U.S. B.L.S, April 2019).

[54] Labeled as "female" in the study. U.S. Census Bureau, Report S2402, "Occupation by Sex for the Full-Time, Year-Round Civilian Employed Population 16 Years and Over," 3.

[55] The "health diagnosing and treating" category, likewise, is second only to "legal occupations" in terms of a pay gap: women earn a median $68,550 to men's $106,218. U.S. Census Bureau, Report S2412, "Occupation by Sex and Median Earnings in the Past 12 Months (in 2017 Inflation-Adjusted Dollars) for the Full-Time, Year-Round Civilian Employed Population 16 Years and Over," 1.

140 INTERPRETIVE LABOR

of men's earnings or lower. While between 2009 and 2017, the ratio for median earnings for full-time, year-round women workers improved slightly (from 78.2% of men's earnings to 80%), this still represents a difference of over $10,000 USD per year. Likewise, even in fields where the ratio is more equitable, the actual salaries tend to be among the lowest among all full-time, year-round occupations. Even among these lower-paying fields, a difference of 15 or 20 percentage points still represents several thousand dollars per year in real dollars, which has a major impact on individuals and families in these socioeconomic groups. For example, it is very difficult to accumulate savings, plan for retirement, deal with medical expenses, and so on, when a person or family is living paycheck to paycheck. A difference of $3–5k per year can, obviously, make a real difference. The fact remains that certain job categories, including those most closely related to this model of Interpretive Labor, are and have been primarily held by women, and those job categories tend to go hand-in-hand with insufficient and inequitable earnings.

These issues are particularly interesting in light of the work of Melissa Gregg, who studies productivity in relation to gender as well as to cultural issues more broadly. Drawing on 19th-century guidebooks for domestic living, she argues that the very first managers (in the modern sense) were middle-class women: women whose work not only mirrored but actually prefigured that of their male counterparts. Gregg notes, "these early documents of efficiency and labor enhancement prove that the science of management was not limited to the factory or the office at the turn of the twentieth century; productivity was also the principal logic of the household."[56] Domestic management, encompassing tasks like overseeing housecleaning staff, preparing to entertain guests, monitoring children's activities—these are not unlike some of the tasks expected of administrators for new-music groups and festivals. All involve a delicate dance between and among the facilitator and the other members of the organization; there are concerns about budgets; there is an emphasis on making sure things run smoothly. The core of this type of role is a type of management that is typically under-recognized and under-compensated—if paid at all.

---

[56] Gregg, *Counterproductive*, 33.

CONCLUSION: THE ADMINISTRATOR MODEL TODAY

I'll close by considering two mechanisms of administrative work today: the leadership of some new-music organizations in terms of gender, and the move away from separate leadership workers altogether. We might first address the state of things at present, in an attempt to consider whether this type of work is becoming more equitable. In recent years, as gender issues have become more mainstream, awareness has certainly increased and at least some organizations are taking steps to track the data and, potentially, work toward equity. The Mostly Modern Festival, established in 2018 in Saratoga Springs, New York, lists both Robert Paterson (artistic director) and Victoria Paterson (general director) as directors and co-founders.[57] The Charlotte (NC) New Music Festival/Charlotte New Music organization was established in 2012 by Elizabeth Kowalski.[58] Italy's highSCORE Festival (established in 2010) is led by artistic director Giovanni Albini and executive producer Paolo Fosso.[59] Thomas Fichter is the artistic director of TIME:SPANS, a festival "produced and presented by the Earle Brown Music Foundation Charitable Trust"; the program coordinator is Kayleigh Butcher.[60] Looking back at the Ostrava Center for New Music, it is run by Executive Director Renáta Spisarová, office manager Kristýna Konczyna, and coordinator Barbora Skálová. Now, at least, their names appear on the website alongside Petr Kotík, the longstanding artistic director.[61] This small sample demonstrates a few things: first, that there is obviously a place for women (and others in gender minorities) in leadership within arts organizations; second, that there is still a tendency to see more men than women in "artistic director" positions; and third, that it remains normative for women to hold coordinator or facilitator roles more frequently than executive roles.

In terms of gender representation among composers and directors, the 2015 Ostrava Days institute and festival included thirteen lecturers and five conductors, with just one woman involved in those roles (Jennifer Walshe); the following iteration in 2017 included the same total number of professional guest artists, with both Walshe and Kate Soper participating, giving

---

[57] https://mostlymodernfestival.org/about-the-directors, last accessed July 21, 2023.
[58] Her name does not currently appear on the organization's website, but the UNC Charlotte College of Arts & Architecture published an interview with her in its 2018 magazine. Elizabeth Kowalski, "New Music Network," *CoA + A Community* (2018), 38–41.
[59] https://www.highscorefestival.com/faculty, last accessed July 21, 2023.
[60] https://timespans.org/about/, last accessed July 21, 2023.
[61] https://www.newmusicostrava.cz/en/about-us/profile/, last accessed July 21, 2023.

142   INTERPRETIVE LABOR

women a share of approximately 12%. With a larger group of participants, the ratio appears similar for the upcoming 2023 institute.[62] The composition faculty at Tanglewood Music Center boasts the legendary Joan Tower, along with Michael Gandolfi, Osvaldo Golijov, John Harbison, and George Lewis.[63] Not incidentally, the Donne organization, based in the United Kingdom, reports that programming for orchestras is even less equitable. As of 2022, 87.7% of the compositions performed by a collection of 111 Western classical orchestras worldwide were by white men, and only 7.7% by women.[64] Given the state of gender inequity in musical programming, perhaps it should not be surprising that the organizational structures of institutions themselves have some work to do (if parity is a goal). These gaps are evidence of the durability of the "separate spheres" idea: historically, women's places have been primarily in supporting functions, rather than in the spotlight. While some strides have been made, especially for a brief moment in response to the #MeToo movement, the reckoning from such awareness has been quite weak thus far. Much more work is needed in service of an even playing field.

At the same time, I admit that I do have strong concerns about *essentializing* this into a gender issue. Yes, women's work has historically been under-recognized, and yes, the gender-based wage gap is still alive and well; however, it is also important to emphasize the contributions of all who facilitate performances of new music—of course, there have also been plenty of non-women who have taken on various administrative functions for musical institutions. One thought always at the back of my mind, in addition to how to read any "progress" that has been made, is whether this is actually a false question. At least as important, I think, is this: by emphasizing gender disparities, are we missing potential exploitation? If I celebrate that the administrations of arts organizations are increasingly gender-diverse (and I do celebrate that, to be sure), am I missing the forest for the trees?

One way institutions have changed structurally since the 1960s is that many contemporary-music organizations are now run by their own members. Instead of working with a designated individual who functions as an administrator for the group, ensemble members now frequently manage

---

[62] https://www.newmusicostrava.cz/en/ostrava-days/institute/, last accessed July 24, 2023.

[63] https://www.bso.org/tmc/composition-faculty, last accessed July 21, 2023.

[64] A few notable exceptions might be congratulated here: the Chicago Sinfonietta, the London Contemporary Orchestra, and the Chineke! Orchestra are doing particularly good work in improving the diversity of programmed compositions. See Gabriella Di Laccio, "Equality and Diversity in Global Repertoire" (England: Donne UK, 2022), https://donne-uk.org/wp-content/uploads/2021/03/Donne-Report-2022.pdf.

THE "ADMINISTRATOR" MODEL   143

their own logistics. As John Pippen explains, "Managing the labour required for gigs has led to performers taking on dual roles, operating both as musicians and as business agents of one kind or another."[65] Pippen describes musicians working out arrangements for future performances during breaks in other gigs, developing marketing materials, loading and unloading equipment—multiple forms of labor, to be sure, including the administrative. Other forms of administrative work are expected of musicians today, as well. For example, in reference to the quartet Yarn/Wire, Judy Lochhead writes: "Maintenance of all the digital media is handled, for the most part, by members of the group."[66] As funding for large institutions has dried up, much of the work that might previously have been done by a department assistant or a dedicated public-relations office now falls on the shoulders of the composers and performers themselves. In reference to another contemporary group, Ensemble Dal Niente, Lochhead notes that it "has various staff positions dedicated to making the organization run," but everyone listed in the staff directory seems to identify primarily as a composer/performer, per their biographies on the Dal Niente website; each is foremost a performing member of the group, with some logistical duties added on.[67]

The phenomenon of musicians managing their own administrative work is closely connected to what Andrea Moore calls "a gospel of entrepreneurship" within music, a shift marked by the rise in entrepreneurial training beginning in 2012.[68] One aspect of this development is this: as precarity has become more common—through gig work of all kinds—musicians and their institutions have also become implicit in normalizing forms of work previously thought to be undesirable. In place of stable employment with a dependable salary and benefits, young musicians are increasingly coached to develop "portfolio" careers, made up of multiple contingent elements such as adjunct teaching, temporary gigs, and other part-time and/or non-recurring jobs. This aspect of entrepreneurship is particularly prevalent. As Moore notes, the portfolio career is "strenuous, requiring not only the development of multiple musical and non-musical skills but an ongoing need for the musician to create and maintain his or her own opportunities, seek funding, manage shifting schedules and priorities among students and parents, and

---

[65] Pippen, "The Boundaries of 'Boundarylessness,'" 440.

[66] Judy Lochhead, "The New Music Scene: Passionate Commitment in the Twenty-First-Century Gig Economy," *Twentieth-Century Music* 16, no. 3 (2019), 416.

[67] Lochhead, "The New Music Scene," 420; https://www.dalniente.com/staff, last accessed August 4, 2023.

[68] Moore, "Neoliberalism," 34.

144 INTERPRETIVE LABOR

constantly juggle musical and financial priorities."[69] This form of entrepreneurship therefore shifts the burden of administrative labor onto each individual musician.

Contemporary entrepreneurship, while valorized for its flexibility, demands a huge amount of work, much of which is un- or undercompensated. From booking the next gig to renewing the lease on the rehearsal space, from writing marketing copy to strategizing about your ensemble's "brand identity," musicians today—not just in new-music groups, but perhaps especially pronounced there—function as their own administrative offices. Given that this scenario seems likely to continue, if not increase, for the foreseeable future, I find it crucial to acknowledge the realities of such work, so young people know what they are signing up for. Theorizing administrative tasks as a form of interpretive labor provides one mode of recognizing—even celebrating—the contributions of workers behind the scenes.

---

[69] Moore, "Neoliberalism," 39.

5

THE "HACKER" MODEL

SUBVERSION IN THEORY AND PRACTICE

The apologists for the vectoral interest want to limit the semantic productivity of the term "hacker" to a mere criminality, precisely because they fear its more abstract and multiple potential—its class potential. Everywhere one hears rumours of the hacker as the new form of juvenile delinquent, or nihilist vandal, or servant of organised crime. Or, the hacker is presented as a mere harmless subculture, an obsessive garage pursuit with its restrictive styles of appearance and codes of conduct. Everywhere the desire to open the virtuality of information, to share data as a gift, to appropriate the vector for expression becomes the object of a moral panic, an excuse for surveillance, and the restriction of technical knowledge to the "proper authorities." This is not the first time that the productive classes have faced this ideological blackmail. The hacker now appears in the official organs of the ruling order alongside its earlier archetypes, the organised worker, the rebellious farmer. The hacker is in excellent company.

—McKenzie Wark, *The Hacker Manifesto*[1]

A musical score is a logical construct inserted into the mess of potential sounds that permeate this planet and its atmosphere. That puts Beethoven and the rest in perspective!

—Cornelius Cardew, *Treatise Handbook*[2]

In spite of my best intentions, I have become a bit of a science-fiction nerd. The worlds of Star Wars, Star Trek, Marvel, Doctor Who—all of these pop-culture phenomena have become part of my own toolkit for escaping reality

[1] Wark, *A Hacker Manifesto*, 32.
[2] Cardew, *Treatise Handbook*, vii.

Interpretive Labor. Kirsten I. Speyer Carithers, Oxford University Press. © Oxford University Press 2025.
DOI: 10.1093/9780197698815.003.0006

146 INTERPRETIVE LABOR

on occasion. In the television series *Marvel's Agents of S.H.I.E.L.D.* (ABC, 2013–2020), one of the main characters is a young computer hacker called Skye. Smart, creative, and resourceful, she quickly gets caught up in events beyond anything she had imagined, and her skills must be adapted to new circumstances. In this chapter, I turn to scholarship on hacking of various types, from groundbreaking computer programmers to children at play. Throughout, I (re)turn frequently to the ideas presented in McKenzie Wark's *A Hacker Manifesto*, drawing out connections to Cornelius Cardew and other artistic interpreters.[3] Likewise, Gabriella Coleman's pioneering anthropological study of free and open-source software (F/OSS) development illuminates the intricacies of another meaning of hacking.[4] Like the fictional Skye's affiliates in the Rising Tide, these hackers are a community of creative thinkers who abide by a shared ethics of freedom and meritocracy.

By connecting interpretive labor with contemporary media studies, we can better account for works and concepts that have historically been marginalized. The power structures of performance can usefully be understood by drawing in part on theories being developed among scholars of creative work, chiefly through investigations into cognitive labor, the New Left,[5] and the rise of the hacker class. This last field of inquiry is particularly relevant concerning experimental music as a whole, and Cornelius Cardew specifically. As discussed in the Executive chapter, the relationship between Karlheinz Stockhausen and Cornelius Cardew provides evidence of a multifaceted understanding of labor. Their compositions *Plus Minus* and *Treatise*, respectively, illustrate distinct approaches to notation and, in turn, divergent stances toward performers. *Plus Minus*, nominally Stockhausen's work, demands a significant investment of time and energy: realizers must work through a series of rules and guidelines to construct a version of the piece, and to do so,

---

[3] Wark has also written on gaming, the Situationist International movement, and what might be called radicalized climate-change allegory. Her *Hacker* text is a collection of sometimes pithy, sometimes over-the-top aphorisms on the ruled and ruling classes of the knowledge economy. One caveat: while a number of the sections are quite clever and thought-provoking, the writing frequently veers toward Seussian territory. (One brief example: "Hack the lack that lacks the hack.") Despite this, the text provides ample fodder for engaging with various modes of inquiry around hacking. Wark, *A Hacker Manifesto*, 125.

[4] E. Gabriella Coleman, *Coding Freedom: The Ethics and Aesthetics of Hacking* (Princeton, NJ: Princeton University Press, 2013).

[5] Characterized by a creative, progressive agenda and antagonism toward the petite bourgeoisie, in contrast to Old Left, who resented "all social classes above the workers [sic] class: not only the privileged upper (middle) class, but also the intellectuals and well-educated groups." Beate Kutschke, "Protest Music, Urban Contexts and Global Perspectives," *IRASM* 46, no. 2 (December 2015), 332–33.

THE "HACKER" MODEL   147

they must first develop an understanding of the composer's idiosyncratic notational system. Likewise, in Cardew's *Treatise*, realizers must grapple with an unfamiliar form of notation and work hard to invent a sounding realization. I will argue, however, that there are some important differences between the forms of labor involved in performing the two compositions.

Cornelius Cardew, I will argue, is a hacker, in several of the many meanings of that term. In a 2009 article, environmental psychologists Katz and Donovan define hacking as "play, curious exploration, or as a puzzle solution that helps . . . people to better understand and control their environments."[6] It is largely in this sense that I place Cardew: he seems to delight in potential, mistrust establishment commodification, and explore possibilities that might escape the imaginations of others. Most concretely, and analogously to the computer hackers to be discussed shortly, he is an expert in the code, to the extent that he can manipulate it to his own ends. This subversion of a dominant power plays out not only in his writings but also in his compositional efforts in both Stockhausen's *Carré* (1959–60) and his own *Treatise* (1963–67). By investigating their stances toward the purpose of notation, the actual scores of both compositions, and Cardew's antagonistic writings about his one-time mentor, we gain new insight into key composer-performer issues of the 1960s. Simultaneously, these musical actors and practices illuminate the changing political landscape of labor.

***

In the early 1970s, Cardew wrote:

In bourgeois society, the artist is in the employ of capitalists (publishers, record companies), who demand from him work that is, at least potentially, profitable. And ultimately he is in the employ of the bourgeois state, which demands that the artist's work be ideologically acceptable. . . . [It] is clearly impossible to bring work with a decidedly socialist or revolutionary content to bear on a mass audience. Access to this audience (the artist's real means of production) is controlled by the state. This is why Marx and Engels say that the bourgeoisie have reduced artists to the level of wage-slaves.[7]

[6] Gregory T. Donovan and Cindi Katz, "Cookie Monsters: Seeing Young People's Hacking as Creative Practice," *Children, Youth and Environments* 19, no. 1 (2009), 198.
[7] Cardew, Introduction to *Stockhausen Serves Imperialism*, 5–6.

148 INTERPRETIVE LABOR

Throughout his career, and increasing dramatically from the late 1960s on, Cardew seems to have wrestled with his role in class struggles. A relative outsider to the socialist/communist causes—as an avant-garde composer from an imperialist nation—he may have harbored guilt about his implication in the system. In response, he railed against it in whatever ways he could, from programming Christian Wolff's *Burdocks* at the Munich Olympics in 1972 to writing dozens of political songs.[8] Although he recognized their limited power, he still argued for the importance of artists' struggles: "without a [revolutionary Proletariat] Party, every effort on the part of progressive artists to produce revolutionary art is bound to be relatively isolated and relatively ineffective. This is not to say it is wrong to make these efforts. . . . It is precisely through such struggles that political consciousness is aroused."[9] Cardew's extensive work on *Treatise*, I maintain, is just such a struggle. The focus of much of his attention throughout 1963–67, it came to represent (and present) his attitude and budding political ideology as a revolutionary artwork. It directly contradicts Stockhausen's approach in *Plus Minus* and *Carré* by refusing to limit the interpretive possibilities.

At the same time, Cardew's *Treatise* demands significant labor from those performing the piece. Without any guidelines, his interpreters have to invest a substantial amount of time and effort to determine what exactly to do with the notation in front of them. To some extent, then, Cardew is hacking not only the experimental-music system but also the idea of performer freedom itself. Like Cage, he claims to be a champion of freedom and anarchy, but simultaneously produces scores that ask an awful lot of their realizers. Unlike Cage, though, he quickly recognized that as a contradiction, and in the 1970s rejected his avant-garde compositions upon his commitment to communism and greater political activism. As noted by Taylor, Cardew identified graphic notation—which he had explored exhaustively in *Treatise*—as a trend representing the increasing *embourgeoisement* of "art" music. Graphic notation in his view had become an aesthetic object in its own right. Cardew argues generally that the artistic avant-garde is part of the imperialist superstructure. The values implicit in avant-garde art, he contends, help "to protect that [imperialist] society against radical social change."[10] In the years

---

[8] Cardew Collection, 70766-70772, British Library.

[9] Cardew, Introduction to *Stockhausen Serves Imperialism*, 8.

[10] Timothy D. Taylor, "Moving in Decency: The Music and Radical Politics of Cornelius Cardew," *Music and Letters* 79, no. 4 (November 1998), 564–65, citing Cardew, "Wiggly Lines and Wobbly Music [1976]," in *Breaking the Sound Barrier: A Critical Anthology of the New Music*, ed. Gregory Battcock (New York: E.P. Dutton, 1981), 236.

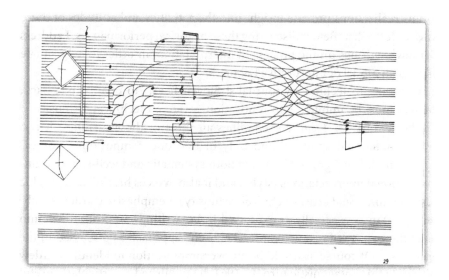

Figure 5.1 Cornelius Cardew, *Treatise* (Buffalo, NY: The Gallery Upstairs Press, 1967), 29. Reproduced with permission from Cardew, *Treatise*. Edition Peters/Faber Music, 1967.

leading up to this apparent about-face, Cardew actually took steps that, in retrospect, indicate a through-line between these two poles.

CARDEW ON INTERPRETATION

In October 1972, Cardew was invited to speak at a symposium on musical notation in Rome. He used that opportunity to outline his new, critical stance toward his own avant-garde compositions, discussing what he called "diseases of notation, cases where the notation seems to have become a malignant growth usurping an absolutely unjustifiable preeminence over the music."[11] Indeed, the notation of *Treatise* threatens to overwhelm any possibility of an easy musical experience (see Figure 5.1).

On the other hand, for a number of performers, it has been deemed worth the effort. Despite Cardew's own disavowal, it continued to be performed,

---

[11] Cardew, "Talk for Rome Symposium on Problems of Notation," in Cardew, *Stockhausen Serves Imperialism*, 80.

150 INTERPRETIVE LABOR

and its realizations provide insight into the activities and attitudes of those who undertook it. Before discussing these historical performances, I address Cardew's writings on the process of interpretation, in order to help situate this fourth model of Interpretive Labor.

According to technology journalist Steven Levy, "to qualify as a hack, the feat must be imbued with innovation, style and technical virtuosity."[12] Cardew's work on *Treatise* exemplifies all three of these qualities: it is a unique notational system found only in that one composition (innovation), it broke new ground by being both systematic and well-suited to unconventional interpretations (style), and it also evinces his skill as a graphic designer and visual artist (technical virtuosity). I emphasize Cardew's "subversive" stance, especially as expressed in his writings, in order to set into relief the rigidity of his mentor Stockhausen's approach as discussed in the previous.[13] Of course, it would be an oversimplification to identify Cardew with only this antagonistic turn. In 1961, he published a particularly useful article called "Notation: Interpretation, etc.," which is essentially a list of musings on his recent artistic activities. Amidst the commentary on contemporary notational systems and the graphic examples from Feldman, Wolff, Stockhausen, and his own compositions, Cardew relays his ideas about interpretation, in the sense of making a sounding performance. He writes, "'Musical interpretation' has become more and more a single term with less and less in common with the everyday meaning of the word 'interpret.'"[14] Unfortunately, he does not elaborate on what that everyday meaning might suggest. He continues,

Cage has re-opened the expression and utilized its implications in such fields as structure, notation, performance. His word "indeterminacy" is like a conviction: the relation between musical score and performance *cannot* be determined. If this is not realized, difficulties will always be encountered in composing, rehearsing and performing (not to mention listening). The indeterminacies of traditional notation became to such an extent accepted that it was forgotten that they existed, and of what sort they were.[15]

[12] Steven Levy, *Hackers: Heroes of the Computer Revolution* (New York: Penguin, 1994), 23, cited in Wark, *A Hacker Manifesto*, 31.

[13] Cardew seemed to want *Treatise* to be subversive, too, but in some ways it actually continued the author/executive role, as he quickly discovered. I will argue shortly that *Treatise* represents the transition between Cardew's negative hacking of Stockhausen's work and Cardew's positive hacking in the sense of contributing a to a community of like-minded creatives.

[14] Cardew, "Notation: Interpretation, etc.," 22.

[15] Cardew, 22.

I take this to mean that Cardew is interested in shifting the focus back onto notation more generally, and advocating for musicians to avoid making assumptions about what aspects of a performance are to be "filled in" by the performer. In much common-practice-period literature, for example, one might not see a *ritardando* at the end of a phrase, but conventional training suggests that it is an acceptable, perhaps expected, adjustment to make. After years of hearing it performed that way, we have forgotten that it is not technically part of the composition—or at least, it is not specified in its notation. Cardew's larger point seems to be that we identify these things as part of the work (or work-concept, although of course that term would come into use later) but that it does not necessarily have to be that way.

In contrast with Cage's commitment to indeterminacy, Cardew notes that

> much of the pointillist music of the '50s (Boulez, Berio, Goeyvaerts, Pousseur, Stockhausen, Van San, etc.) . . . seemed to exclude all possibility of interpretation in any real sense; the utmost differentiation, refinement and exactitude were demanded of the players. Just because of this contradiction it is stimulating work, and sometimes rewarding to interpret this music, for any interpretation is forced to transcend the rigidity of the compositional procedure, and music results (but the feeling is almost unavoidable that one is misrepresenting the composer!).[16]

Here, the use of "interpretation" might at first seem naïve—just the old standard meaning, as a rendering or iteration of a work. Upon closer inspection, though, Cardew distinguishes between precision in performance and "real" interpretation. What might be understood as "real"? His context here, in specifying integral-serial and/or hyper-precisely notated scores, situates these works as opposite from indeterminately notated pieces. Interpretation must be more than mere sounding. It involves some sort of creative play, or investment of the self, or liberty (or all three). He may have tongue in cheek when he claims that producing music from these scores "misrepresent[s] the composer," but that impish claim is scaffolded by years of work—work with the instructions from Stockhausen and work as a pianist, performing others' compositions. Interpretation, then, is a way to reconcile the labor of realization with the freedom to engage deeply with a piece of music.

---

[16] Cardew, 22.

152 INTERPRETIVE LABOR

Later in the same article, Cardew touches on the thorny issue of composers' intentions, a problem that was expediently (although indirectly) treated as early as the 1940s, when Wimsatt and Beardsley published "The Intentional Fallacy," whose title became a standard trope in literary criticism in the second half of the 20th century. Briefly, they challenged the prevailing assumption that to understand (interpret, perhaps?) a text, one must be able to recapture somehow what the author had planned, felt, or designed at the time of writing.[17] As with the poetry that is the object of their study, music is usually not a direct, declarative utterance, and so it, too, requires skepticism at the premise of discovering a composer's intentions. With this in mind, Cardew's later statement becomes more thought-provoking:

> I have heard people criticizing interpretations of music in a variety of ways, "he played some wrong notes, but was faithful to the composer's intention," or "he played correctly but seemed to miss the point." Such criticism disturbs me (though I have often found it valid) because it implies that there is something behind the notation, something the composer meant but did not write. In my piece [*February 1959*, excerpted in the journal] there is no intention separate from the notation; the intention is that the player should respond to the notation. He should not interpret in a particular way (e.g. how he imagines the composer intended) but should be *engaged in the act of interpretation*.[18]

A couple of issues are worth teasing out here. First, he says that those types of critical statements imply that "there is something behind the notation . . . [that] the composer meant but did not write." Of course, this cannot be disputed without risking a fall into the intentional fallacy, but at the same time, there certainly are examples where composers do not attempt to notate every aspect of a work: most compositions, probably, save the "pointillist" pieces he censured earlier. Is he just bragging about his own notational prowess, then? Without the last sentence above, we might dismiss it that way, but the end of the paragraph brings his ideas in a different direction. Here, Cardew takes the opportunity to demonstrate the dual aspect of performers: both their agency and their responsibility. This brings us back to the notion of interpretation as a dance between foundational knowledge

---

[17] W.K. Wimsatt Jr. and M.C. Beardsley, "The Intentional Fallacy," *The Sewanee Review* 54, no. 3 (1946), 468–69.

[18] Cardew, "Notation: Interpretation, etc.," 27; emphasis added.

THE "HACKER" MODEL   153

(to which the performer is responsible, and which establishes respect for the composer) and creative engagement (which frees the performer, and which establishes equivalent respect for the performer's own lifeworld).

ON THE HACK

The term "hacking" engenders a productive multiplicity of connotations. To be sure, the terms "hacker," "hacking," and "hack" all imply a set of loosely connected meanings. A *hack* can be an action or activity that alters the usual parameters of some practice, or, pejoratively, a person who does so, usually because they lack the skill to do it the right way. In its earliest recorded forms, it referred to tools used for rough chopping—to hack was to damage by means of uncontrolled blows (Chaucer: "He . . . leet anoon comaunde to hakke and hewe / the okes olde," and Shakespeare: "My sworde hackt like a handsaw").[19] Even now, this meaning has been brought into colloquial use, referring to artless mangling with a perhaps blunt instrument (e.g., overheard during a football (soccer) match: "that defender has been hacking the center forward all day, and the ref hasn't called a single foul!" or on the golf course: "I'm hacking away at everything today—can't hit a clean shot off the tee or the fringe"). In a related manner, the "Jargon File"/*New Hacker's Dictionary* claims under *hacker*: "Originally, someone who makes furniture with an axe."[20]

The most common usage today is probably that of the computer hacker. Originating in the 1960s, the modern hacker community initially coalesced around shared computer terminals, most famously at MIT's Tech Model Railroad Club and, slightly later, its artificial intelligence (AI) lab.[21] As Guy Steele has noted, though,

MIT had no monopoly on hackers. In the 1960s and 1970s hackers congregated around any computer center that made computer time available for play. (Some of this play turned out to be very important work, but hacking is done mostly for fun, for its own sake, for the pure joy of

[19] Chaucer, "The Knight's Tale," *Canterbury Tales* (c1385, Hengwrt MS.); William Shakespeare, *Henry IV, Pt. 1* II. v. 168.

[20] http://www.catb.org/jargon/html/H/hacker.html

[21] See Levy, *Hacker*; Sherry Turkle, *The Second Self: Computers and the Human Spirit* (Cambridge, MA: MIT Press, 2005); and Pekka Himanen, ed., *The Hacker Ethic and the Spirit of the Information Age* (New York: Random House, 2001).

154 INTERPRETIVE LABOR

it.) Because universities tend to be more flexible than corporations in this regard, most hackers' dens arose in university laboratories. While some of those hackers were unauthorized "random people" . . . many hackers were paid employees who chose to stay after hours and work on their own projects—or even continue their usual work—purely for pleasure.[22]

According to Katz and Donovan, *hacker*'s "most frequent—and deceptive—frame of reference in the post-9/11 security state has been in the context of computer/network security. In this context, hacking is understood as cyber crime—politically motivated or otherwise—that is a threat to national security, corporate security, and personal safety."[23] As recounted by Roger Rothman, this meaning came into popular usage in the 1980s, when "a handful of teenagers were arrested for having hacked into dozens of computers across the country. . . . In magazines and on television sets, 'hacker' became synonymous with 'computer criminal.'"[24] While the creative individuals involved in labs at MIT and elsewhere have tried to set aside the term "cracking" for criminal activity of this sort, it has not caught on, and the term "hacking" now has a multivalent collection of meanings.

In this account of experimental music, it is primarily with the MIT-originating sense of hacking that I feel most affinity for the work of performers. These early programmers developed their expertise in response to, and perhaps in spite of, the limitations placed upon them (scarcity of lab time, difficulty of communicating with other programmers, etc.). In parallel, musicians reacted to the challenges of unconventional notation by creating new modes of performance. In a similar vein, Cardew himself reacted to the stifling hand of his one-time mentor, Stockhausen, by developing a new form of musical engagement, from the notation itself to the interpretation of its symbols to the intentional lack of performance instructions.[25] In this

---

[22] Guy L. Steele Jr., "Confessions of a Happy Hacker," in *The New Hacker's Dictionary*, 3rd ed., comp. Eric S. Raymond (Cambridge, MA: MIT Press, 1996), p. xii. This book is a published version of what started as the "Jargon File," a collectively curated online collection of slang terms and their meanings.

[23] Donovan and Katz, "Cookie Monsters," 205.

[24] Roger Rothman, "Against Critique: Fluxus and the Hacker Aesthetic," *Modernism/Modernity* 22, no. 4 (November 2015), 791–92; for the original news story, see also Jake Kirchner, "Hackers Steal Legislators' Attention," *Computerworld* (September 12, 1983).

[25] As discussed in chapter 3, this is most evident in Cardew's written account of working with Stockhausen on the score for *Carré*, in which he repeatedly undermines the senior composer's authority. He also addresses this in the working notes for *Treatise*. For example: "The score was drawn out on a grid, and therefore measuring will produce boring and uniform results . . . . A measurement is made once and for all. It is stupid to repeat the process—remember playing Refrain with Karlheinz constantly re-measuring the dynamics." *Treatise Handbook*, v–vi.

THE "HACKER" MODEL   155

way, he creates—in *Treatise* especially—what later self-proclaimed hackers might call "an incredibly good, and perhaps very time-consuming, piece of work that produces exactly what is needed."[26] This second meaning for *hacking* leans toward the subversion of modern-day cracking. In many cases, the work of hackers—especially those who make the headlines today—is to break into the largely digital modes of protection that dictate corporate and personal security. Through these activities, they expose weaknesses in such systems, raising questions about their validity and effectiveness. Likewise, experimental artists have undermined prevailing musical systems: not only notation but also the longstanding composer-as-sole-author paradigm. By calling into question the attributed composer's authority, they shift the balance of power, destabilizing the expected hierarchy.

In addition, I think of the score of a composition as its source code: the fundamental set of commands and functions that drive a piece of software. When a group decides to perform *Treatise*, makes decisions about how to interpret its symbols, and jots some new symbols on the empty staves on each page of the score, they in effect alter its source code. This is a form of hacking akin to the work of developers who modify a piece of software to do something more efficiently. Coleman notes, "Although hackers hold multiple motivations for producing their software, collectively they are committed to *productive freedom*. This term designates the institutions, legal devices, and moral codes that hackers have built in order to autonomously improve on their peers' work, refine their technical skills, and extend craftlike engineering traditions. . . . [Hackers] have built a dense ethical and technical practice that sustains their productive freedom."[27] Like F/OSS developers, experimental musicians have also crafted practices that "improve on their peers' work, refine their technical skills, and extend craftlike . . . traditions." These aspects will be discussed in analysis of several performances of *Treatise* between 1966 and 1970.

What we reveal, then, are two key but contrasting conceptions of hacking, both of which play an important role in my reading of avant-gardism. First, hacking can mean a subversive stance or procedure by which a person, dissatisfied with the status quo, alters existing parameters in such a way as to cause damage. This negative hacking is seen not only in computer security breaches but also in Cardew's initial refusal to provide performance

---

[26] "hack, 2. n.," in Raymond, *The New Hacker's Dictionary*, 231.
[27] Emphasis in original. Coleman, *Coding Freedom*, 3.

156   INTERPRETIVE LABOR

instructions for *Treatise* and in his attempts to undermine Stockhausen in the realization work on *Carré*.[28] It is essentially a selfish form of labor, meant to advance the hacker's aims at the expense of others. Hacking can also have the opposite effect, as a productive method of building something new. Coleman notes that the spread of Linux and other open-source programs helped a wide audience learn about "the ethical foundations—sharing, freedom, and collaboration—of free software production."[29] This tripartite foundation, a positive form of hacking, will be seen in the myriad ways performers respond to the ambiguous notation of *Treatise* and other works. In one sense, then, Cardew's negative hacking backfires: he is just another composer exerting executive power. At the same time, his score actually leads to the positive hacking of interpretation.

***

After discussing the circumstances of *Treatise*'s composition, I will develop a history of several of its performances, exploring the personnel involved, where each event was held, and by whom it was supported. Through this, we can begin to piece together a detailed account of the networked institutions and individuals who form its early history, and to consider the ways this composition suggests multiple readings of hackerism.

COMPOSING *TREATISE*

> Hackers truly believe that it's not the words that count, but the way we get them on paper. If they gain control of the department, the way you get words on paper will be the most devious, least predictable, most costly method imaginable.[30]

Cornelius Cardew's work ranges from albums of piano solos to the "Bun" orchestral pieces to the indeterminate graphic scores of the 1960s. He famously turned away from his recent experimental works in the early 1970s, citing a new appreciation for the political teachings of Marx, Lenin, and Mao Tse-tung. By 1973, he would write, "I have discontinued composing music

---

[28] Cardew, "Report on Stockhausen's *Carré*," and "Report on Stockhausen's *Carré*: Part II."

[29] Coleman, *Coding Freedom*, 82.

[30] Patricia Caernarven-Smith, "Hackers Are Bad for Business," *Technical Communication* 35, no. 2 (May 1988), 143.

in an avantgarde [*sic*] idiom for a number of reasons: the exclusiveness of the avantgarde, its fragmentation, its indifference to the real situation of the world today, its individualistic outlook and not least its class character. . . . I have rejected the bourgeois idealistic conception which sees art as the production of unique, divinely inspired geniuses."[31] While it is now standard in the scholarship to mark the period after *The Great Learning* (1968–70) as a complete break with his earlier musical practice, I wish to argue instead that Cardew's political trajectory is actually foreshadowed in *Treatise*.

Prior to beginning work on *Treatise*, Cardew had three key experiences that were to influence that composition. One directly related aspect is that he took a course in graphic design in London in 1961; this was to shape both his career and the notation of *Treatise*.[32] Before this, he had attended concerts by American avant-gardists at Cologne, whose indeterminate works would encourage his own compositions in that area. In turn, in these pieces, Cardew's "concern for the relationship between composer and performer finds expression and this was to assume a central position in his compositions and music-making over the next decade."[33] Around the same time, Cardew began working as Karlheinz Stockhausen's assistant, working closely with him on the score for the four-orchestra piece *Carré*.

As stated by Cardew himself, he began sketches for *Treatise* in early 1963, working out preliminary material from the beginning through page 99. He writes, "To start with my idea of what the piece was to be was so sketchy as to be completely inarticulate," and in fact he would later re-compose much of the original material.[34] In the summer of that year, he put a number of pages into fair copy, although for this he used a larger format than that used for the final version of the complete piece. After some delay, seven pages were put into fair copy in December 1964, and these employed the size and format that would become final. Around the same time, the composer joined free-improvisation group AMM in London. Tilbury identifies major components of this group that were essential for Cardew: music's transience, a search for sounds, and musical dialogue:

---

[31] Cornelius Cardew, program notes to *Piano Album* (London, 1973), cited in Timothy D. Taylor, "Moving in Decency," 563.

[32] John Tilbury, *Cornelius Cardew (1936–1981): A Life Unfinished* (Essex, UK: Copula, 2008), 129–30.

[33] John Tilbury, "Cornelius Cardew," *Grove Music Online, Oxford Music Online*, accessed December 7, 2014.

[34] Cardew, *Treatise Handbook*, i.

158 INTERPRETIVE LABOR

AMM embodies a form of collective music-making in which no sounds are excluded and the essential features of which derive from first, the recognition and exploitation of music's transience ("uncatchability" was Cardew's description); second, an investigative ethos where the performers "search" for sounds and for responses attached to them rather than preparing and producing them; and third, dialogue, comprising the spontaneous interplay between players and the necessity, on the part of each individual, for heightened awareness of the contributions of others.[35]

In this second aspect, we actually see some crossover from the Scientist Model of Interpretive Labor. Cardew himself would explain,

Informal "sound" has a power over our emotional responses that formal "music" does not, in that it acts subliminally rather than on a cultural level. This is a possible definition of the area in which AMM is experimental. We are *searching* for sounds and for the responses that attach to them, rather than thinking them up, preparing them and producing them. The search is conducted in the medium of sound and the musician himself is at the heart of the experiment.[36]

In this scientific experiment, musicians are not creating sounds but are attempting to discover them, as if they exist "in nature" and simply need to be located and identified as sounds. Returning to Tilbury's list, the third facet of AMM foreshadows the interactive, game-like participation to be discussed in the following chapter: that is, in one sense, music as dialectics. He notes, "For AMM a meaningful musical dialogue came to depend above all on a deep-seated rapport between the musicians, to the extent that the full burden of meaning of an individual contribution was made manifest, even to the contributor himself, only by reference to the total sound aggregate at any given time, to the context of collective music-making."[37] These aspects of music-making together indicate that Cardew and his contemporaries in the group were activating a fresh type of engagement, not often associated with conservatory-trained artists but essential to many oral traditions. AMM, then, was a bridge.[38]

---

[35] Tilbury, "Cornelius Cardew."
[36] Cardew, "Towards an Ethic of Improvisation," in *Treatise Handbook*, xviii.
[37] Tilbury, *Cornelius Cardew*, 289.
[38] In Cardew's own words, "Joining AMM was the turning point, both in the composition of Treatise and in everything I have thought about music up to now." *Treatise Handbook*, xi.

THE "HACKER" MODEL 159

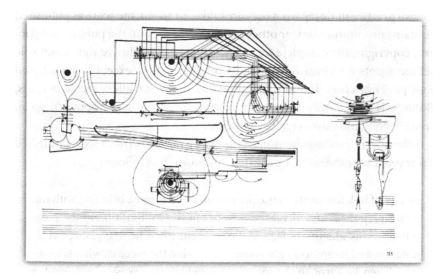

Figure 5.2 Cornelius Cardew, *Treatise* (Buffalo, NY: The Gallery Upstairs Press, 1967), 183. Reproduced with permission from Cardew, *Treatise*. Edition Peters/Faber Music, 1967.

In 1965, while in Rome on a scholarship to study with Goffredo Petrassi,[39] Cardew "pushed ahead to page 143," putting much of the score into fair copy as he went along. In the second half of the year, he returned to England, where he "worked on redrawing in the new format the first passages" copied out— that is, pages 45–51, 57–62, and 75–79—and also re-worked the intervening pages.[40] In 1966, he was invited to join the Creative Associates in Buffalo. By the time of his arrival, in October of that year, pages 45–143 were continuous and complete, and ready for performance in Buffalo, where he would write the last 50 pages in 1967.[41] In all, the score of *Treatise* is 193 pages long, with the visual content varying from just four blank staves to beautifully complex interconnected drawings (see Figure 5.2).

What is a musician to do with such a visual bounty? Cardew himself claimed that the score should "stand entirely on its own, without any form of introduction or instruction to mislead prospective performers into the

[39] Tilbury, *Cornelius Cardew*, 179–80.
[40] Chronology in Cardew, *Treatise Handbook*, i.
[41] However, his notes in the *Handbook* indicate that only the first 20 and 44 pages were read in the two New York performances in 1966.

160   INTERPRETIVE LABOR

slavish practice of 'doing what they are told.' "[42] Indeed, the score as published contains no commentary or other text at all, aside from the publication data and copyright, the complete text of which reads, "Exclusive rights and sole selling agents for Great Britain and Commonwealth (except Canada), and Europe: Hinrichsen Edition, Ltd., London. © 1967: Gallery Upstairs Press, Buffalo, N.Y., U.S.A."—not exactly helpful to performers hoping to glean some insight into how to realize the score.

When he did put together some notes for the *Treatise Handbook*, published a few years after the score, he clarified his position as follows:

> In a lot of indeterminate music the would-be performer, bringing with him all his prejudices and virtues, intervenes in the composition of the piece, influences its identity in fact, at the moment when he first glances at the notation and jumps to a conclusion about what the piece is, what is its nature. Then he turns to the instructions, which on occasion may explain that certain notations do not for instance mean what many people might at first blush expect, and these he proceeds to interpret in relation to his preconceptions deriving from the notations themselves. This is often a good thing. Since very often the notations themselves are the determining factor in the method of composition of a piece, and hence in the piece's identity and structure.[43]

In each realization of *Treatise*, performers had to "intervene in the composition of the piece," for without them it was not yet music.

PERFORMING *TREATISE*

> I, as the composer, have no idea how the piece will sound in performance. And why should I?
>
> —Cardew, "Experimental Music" (notes to concert announcement,
> London, 1965)[44]

---

[42] Cardew, *Treatise Handbook*, i.

[43] Cardew, "On the Role of the Instructions in the Interpretation of Indeterminate Music [1965]," in *Treatise Handbook*, xv.

[44] Perhaps a reference to Cage's claim from "Experimental Music: Doctrine [1955]": "Composing's one thing, performing's another, listening's a third. What can they have to do with one another?" Reprinted in *Silence*, 15.

THE "HACKER" MODEL   161

The U.S. premiere of *Treatise* was given in 1966 in Buffalo, New York. As part of the Evenings for New Music series through the State University of New York at Buffalo, a portion of *Treatise* was performed by "a good-sized chamber group" at the Albright-Knox Gallery.[45] The program was repeated three days later at Carnegie Hall. The following year, another fragment was performed by the ensemble QUaX in Prague, under the leadership of composer, flautist, and conductor Petr Kotík. It was revived when Kotík went to Buffalo, with two performances in 1970, including a multi-work event with *Treatise*, Cage's *Aria* and *Fontana Mix*, and Kotík's *Music for 3* performed simultaneously. Extant artifacts about these events, such as performers' accounts and popular-critical reception, provide insight into the working practices of musicians who were tasked with interpreting this extraordinarily open work, therefore illuminating the cultural circumstances of each realization.

Creative Associates, 1966

For the first Buffalo performance, an ensemble of 10 musicians presented a reading of the first 20 pages, with a duration of approximately 18 minutes.[46] The same group presented a longer extract, pages 1–44, at Carnegie Hall a few days later. The musicians involved were almost all Creative Associates at the University at Buffalo: Paul Zonn (clarinet), Andrew White (saxophone and electric bass), William Penn (trumpet), Klaus von Wrochem (violin), Jean Dupouy (viola), Makoto Michii (double bass), Maryanne Amacher ("halfshare of electric bass"), Jan Williams (piano), Carlos Alsina (Wurlitzer), Edward Burnham, (percussion), and Cardew himself (radio/conductor).[47] As relayed in the *Handbook*, Cardew sat in front with "his score

---

[45] John Dwyer, "Versatile Young Composers Offer New Far-Out Works," *Buffalo Evening News* (December 18, 1966).

[46] Performing forces are listed simply as "ensemble" in the CA program and catalog of recordings; however, Cardew lists the performers' names in the *Treatise Handbook*, xii. Performance timing taken from the University at Buffalo Music Library's "Evenings for New Music Catalog, 1964–1980," 15.

[47] Cardew, *Treatise Handbook*, xii. Trumpeter William Penn is not listed in either the Buffalo or New York City programs, nor is he mentioned as having performed on any of the other half dozen composition on those concerts; Cardew may have remembered incorrectly when he published the *Handbook* several years later. He did, though, perform with Cardew and some other CAs on a piece in 1967, so perhaps he was a late addition to the *Treatise* events. (University at Buffalo Music Library, "Concerts and Lectures Catalog, 1962–1981," n.p.).

162   INTERPRETIVE LABOR

placed so that all could see which page was open," and the instrumentalists watched his page turns and followed along.

Performers like Jan Williams and Eberhard Blum provide intriguing accounts of working with both Cardew and Morton Feldman, who would become Music Director of the Center a decade later. Regarding Feldman's percussion work *The King of Denmark*, composed at the same time as *Treatise*, Blum recalls:

> During his tenure at the Center of the Creative and Performing Arts in Buffalo, Jan had created a version which fully corresponded to Feldman's own conception of the work. The choice of percussion instruments, which are not determined in the score, was made by Jan according to Feldman's proposals and wishes. More than once I observed them both in the famous percussion room—Room 100 of the Music Department at the University . . .—the two of them comparing the sounds of small cymbals and triangles to make the right decision. Then Feldman said: "We are finding the definitive solution!"[48]

Similarly, Cardew expected specific responses to his purportedly open notation. Williams notes, "Cornelius . . . [said] that someone had to be responsible for the realization of each performance and that he was making the decisions in this one—'Let's do this.' Our performance of *Treatise* wasn't an anarchistic kind of improvisation; it was shaped by a hand of someone with the full understanding that subsequent shapings by another person would have completely different results, and that was fine."[49] The difference here seems to be that Cardew nudged the performers toward a particular realization for just that one performance, while Feldman's use of "definitive" suggests no such temporally adjusted leeway. On the other hand, Cardew was still the one calling the shots, rather than one of the others involved in that performance. If Cardew had really wanted to set aside his compositional authority, he could have done so by deferring to some equitable procedure for working out the realization or by suggesting that someone else select the parameters. By making those performance decisions on behalf of the group, Cardew undermines his own purportedly democratic agenda.

---

[48] So much for the stereotypical notion of indeterminacy that "anything goes." Eberhard Blum, "Notes on Morton Feldman's *The King of Denmark*," trans. Peter Söderberg, March 2008, on the Chris Villars website at http://www.cnvill.net/mftexts.htm.

[49] Jan Williams, interview with Renée Levine Packer, cited in Levine Packer, *This Life of Sounds*, 57.

THE "HACKER" MODEL   163

The December 1966 concerts included only the first portion of the score, titled *Treatise, Fragment: American Pages*. While the Buffalo press includes little detail about the performance at the Albright-Knox, the *New York Times* devotes several paragraphs to Cardew's notational experiment. Critic Theodore Strongin writes:

> The collective acumen and sensibility of 10 performers . . . resulted in a fascinating half-hour that suggested what might happen if an electroencephalograph wired for music was plugged into one's daydreams. "Treatise" was a series of mostly soft, peripheral sensations that seemed to ride the fine line between the unconscious and the waking mind. At least that was its effect. It was not at all unpleasant, nor was it boring. It was not emotional, but it was very soothing, and it did have a shape, much more than one would have expected from the composer's description in the program notes.[50]

Based on the extant recording of the Buffalo performance, I wonder how this description could be accurate. The general texture is typically quiet and without much rhythmic activity; however, this calm surface is frequently punctuated by loud outbursts from various instrumentalists. Since Cardew asserts that the same performers and methods were used for both events, it seems unlikely that the New York City performance would have had a drastically different sonic character, at least for its first 18 minutes. The first section, marked in the score with the numeral 34, was altered to comprise "17 pianissimo chords each lasting 17 seconds," half of what is designated in the notation (Figure 5.3).[51] Regrettably, these seem to have been lost on the archival Buffalo recording due to the low amplitude, and the extant version begins with dissonant figures in multiple instruments (e.g., muted trumpet and saxophone) and clocks in at approximately thirteen and a half minutes total. Unfortunately for someone trying to analyze the Creative Associates' interpretation of the score, it is terribly difficult to try to "follow along" with the score while listening to the recording. Lacking the sonic signposts that typically help us get our bearings, there is little to suggest even what page of the score might presently be audible. It seems likely, though, that pages 7–12 are

---

[50] Theodore Strongin, "Cardew's Drawing, 'Treatise,' Is Given U.S. Premiere Here," *New York Times* (December 21, 1966).

[51] Cardew, *Treatise Handbook*, xii. Jan Williams later notes that each of the numerals was read as an ensemble chord, with "each player deciding independently which notes they would contribute to the chord." Personal communication, May 5, 2016.

164 INTERPRETIVE LABOR

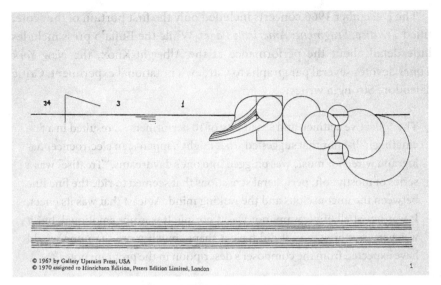

Figure 5.3 Cornelius Cardew, *Treatise* (Buffalo, NY: The Gallery Upstairs Press, 1967), 1. Reproduced with permission from Cardew, *Treatise*. Edition Peters/Faber Music, 1967.

heard beginning approximately 6 minutes into the 13-minute recording, because the sound becomes very static, with sustained pitches and just a few subtle figurations around the held chords. After about two minutes of this, there is a loud splat; is this the dots on page 12 or some other image? (And does that matter? More on this question later.)

In the remaining minutes, these interruptive figures happen more frequently and in more complicated ways, often employing extended techniques. At the end of the recording, though, we again hear quiet, sustained chords, much like what was heard in the middle section. Here, though, the score looks completely different (see Figure 5.4):

If, in fact, what we hear is pages 1–20 as specified by Cardew in the *Handbook*, there seems to be very little coordination between the graphics of the score and the sonic result that was captured on December 17, 1966. Also, if, as Jan Williams later maintained, this was not an "anarchistic" reading but was carefully guided by the composer in rehearsal, what exactly is going on here? One possibility is that the recording is poorly marked, and that we are actually hearing a different subset of the pages "read." However, if that first section was made up of 17 chords at 17 seconds each, that portion would equal about 4 minutes and 50 seconds, or the difference in duration between

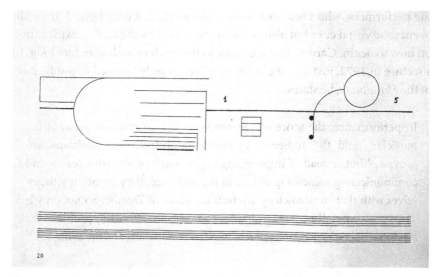

Figure 5.4 Cornelius Cardew, *Treatise* (Buffalo, NY: The Gallery Upstairs Press, 1967), 20. Reproduced with permission from Cardew, *Treatise*. Edition Peters/Faber Music, 1967.

the 18 + minutes listed in the concert catalog and the extant audio track. Since these were sustained, barely audible chords, it stands to reason that they would have been cut—perhaps unintentionally—from the recording, bringing it to the duration of over 13 minutes.

In short, it is challenging to match up the score to the audio. While this may not be terribly important from a historiographical standpoint, it does matter in the realm of performance. Many musicians turn to recordings to provide insight into a piece and to prepare their own realizations, especially if a recording was made under the supervision of the composer. For musicians who did not have the opportunity to work directly with Cardew in the 1960s, their experience with *Treatise* will involve substantial interpretive labor. Not only are potential performers denied the guidance of a set of performance instructions but they also receive little assistance from surviving sonic artifacts. As with other composers dabbling in indeterminacy, Cardew claimed these decisions in the name of "freedom," as instructions might "mislead prospective performers into the slavish practice of 'doing what they are told,'" as quoted above.[52] In practice, this places a great responsibility on

---

[52] Cardew, *Treatise Handbook*, i.

166   INTERPRETIVE LABOR

the performers, who must co-compose the work, not only bound to its idiosyncratic visual cues but also possibly frustrated by the lack of explanation on how to begin. Cardew himself came to this understanding before long. In a lecture in 1972, just a year after having "reluctantly" agreed to publication of the *Handbook*, he states:

> In performance, the score of *Treatise* is in fact an obstacle between the musicians and the audience. Behind that obstacle the musicians improvise,[53] but instead of improvising on the basis of objective reality and communicating something of this to the audience, they preoccupy themselves with that contradictory artefact: the score of *Treatise*. So not only is *Treatise* an embodiment of ... incorrect ideas, it also effectively prohibits the establishment of communication between the musicians and the audience.[54]

The "incorrect ideas" referenced here include the idea that music might exist separately from societal needs, and—more specifically—that its notation develops without recourse to the ideology of subject and ruling classes.[55] Cardew recognizes that the act of reading *Treatise* might prevent his interpreters from having a meaningful interaction with their audience. At the same time, he fails to consider that any improvisatory work, regardless of the notation, can demand that its performers become co-composers. In this way, he (unwittingly?) follows in the footsteps of his one-time mentor Stockhausen, as neither fully appreciates the interpretive labor of their realizers.

On the other hand, the Creative Associates knew (and accepted) what they were doing. Their positions meant that they were all compensated—better than many contemporary performers who had to get by without institutional support—and that they received recognition for their artistic pursuits, both among performance communities and in the press. Fifty years later, Jan Williams remembers the rehearsals as fun and "dynamic, to say the least; pretty new ground for most of us at that point in our careers."[56] Their

---

[53] A term he tried to deny, or at least problematize, in relation to *Treatise* in the intervening period. He writes, in a note dated 9.2.70, "Two years have passed since the foregoing [Introduction to the Handbook] was written. I have taken advantage of this delay in publication to include some new material, in particular the lecture on improvisation. Not that I now consider Treatise 'improvisatory' any more than I did while writing it. But it does seem (using hindsight) to have pointed in the direction of improvisation." *Treatise Handbook*, i.

[54] Cardew, "Talk for Rome Symposium," 86.

[55] Cardew, "Talk for Rome Symposium," 85–86.

[56] Personal communication, May 5, 2016.

first performance of *Treatise* would have afforded the Creative Associates the opportunity to work directly with an exciting young composer, as well as the prestige of giving the (apparent) premiere of the work. The 1966 American events, then, illuminate the conflicted politics generated by Cardew's notational experiment.

QUaX, 1967

The first known professional recording of *Treatise* was made in 1967, the year the score was finished. This version lasts 2 hours and 7 minutes, and is a live recording made in Prague, where Petr Kotík had recently founded a new ensemble that he called QUaX. Beginning in 1962, when they met at the Warsaw Autumn contemporary music festival, Kotík and Cardew had used the mail to stay in touch and exchange scores. They met up again in London in 1966; at that time, Kotík was returning home from a flute competition in England, and stayed with Cardew's friend (and later biographer) John Tilbury for several days. Kotík recalls,

> John and I visited Cornelius a few times and I received more pages of *Treatise* then. Cornelius was just about to go to America to join the Center of the Creative and Performing Arts at the University at Buffalo, New York. He was not excited about leaving London and jokingly suggested that I go in his place. I had a laugh, but the thought of it made me think about what it would be like to live in a "normal" world instead of being stuck behind the Iron Curtain.[57]

Three years later, Kotík did find himself in Buffalo, as discussed earlier. As of 1966, though, he was making do with the resources available in his hometown of Prague,[58] and that included forming a new ensemble to realize the

---

[57] Petr Kotík, "Remembering Cornelius Cardew," liner notes to Cornelius Cardew, *Treatise*, QUaX Ensemble, Petr Kotík, director (remastered recording, audio CD: mode records 205), 2008.

[58] Kotík has been vocal about his frustrations with the music scene there, noting, "Look at Prague's architecture. You won't find such richly appointed houses anywhere in the whole world, I would say. There must have been money since the mid 19th century, especially at the end of the 19th century. There must have been money pouring out of the walls. [. . .] Yet, there was not one good orchestra there. Till today there is not a hall in Prague which was built for a symphony orchestra, where you could put Mahler's orchestra. They could not find the money . . . I have to calm myself or I will start calling names . . . to build a hall for music. [. . .] The most depressing thing about Prague and the Czech environment is that it doesn't bother anyone, it doesn't bother anyone. People are not walking around being ashamed of the fact that they could not build a decent concert hall. [. . .] Janáček was

168 INTERPRETIVE LABOR

available pages of *Treatise*. Extant documents do not identify precisely which pages those were. Cardew lists it as "probably 1–44" in the *Handbook*, but in other sources (e.g., notes to the Mode recording) the authors note that the pages were unknown, except that they likely didn't include the last 50 pages. Kotík's liner notes indicate that he did not see the complete score until after his arrival in Buffalo, so the version performed in Prague could not have included all 193 pages. The first page of Kotík's copy of the score, with his annotations, indicates a 5-minute duration, suggesting that—if each page kept to a similar duration—perhaps 24–25 pages were performed.[59] The Prague concert took place on a Sunday afternoon beginning at 4:00 p.m., with the entire program running for approximately three and a half hours in the Faculty of Law Student Building.

The instrumentation used in Prague is grounds enough for studying this performance. Kotík later notes,

> I realized how confusing it must be to listen to the recording without knowing who plays on what instrument. Each of the group members performed on his own instrument: Petr Kotík, flute; Pavel Kondelík, tenor saxophone; Jan Hynčica, trombone; Josef Vejvoda, percussion; and Václav Zahradník, piano. In addition, we also had many other instruments and sound objects, sometimes treating them as sources of noise. For example, everyone had a violin (hence the string tuttis), although none of us knew really how to play the instrument.[60]

Among those "other instruments and sound objects," the group employed a Violiophone found in the attic of Vejvoda's father (composer of the *Beer Barrel Polka*) and a trumpet played with a bassoon reed. In many places, it is very difficult to determine which of the instruments is being played at any given time, largely because there is significant use of extended techniques such as multiphonics and altered timbral effects. At one point during the middle of the second hour, Zahradník (a successful jazz/pop composer and bandleader) plays a recognizable boom-chick chord pattern while singing

---

effectively prevented by the Prague garbage heap from joining the pantheon of composers of the early 20th century." Petr Kotík in interview with Ian Willoughby, Radio Praha, October 17, 2008; transcript at http://www.radio.cz/en/section/arts/petr-kotik-part-2.

[59] Image of the annotated score reprinted in liner notes for the Mode Records CD. Cornelius Cardew, *Treatise*, QUaX Ensemble, Petr Kotík, director.

[60] Kotík, liner notes to Cardew, *Treatise*, QUaX Ensemble.

THE "HACKER" MODEL   169

a popular-sounding tune (this all glossed by composer-performer Dan Warburton as "cocktail bar comping"),[61] then the strings resume their dissonant creaking, winds shriek and groan, and it sounds once again like midcentury musical barbarism.

While the sounds heard here are fascinating on their own, perhaps the most surprising aspect of this version is that Kotík felt that two hours of *Treatise* was not enough content for one concert. Also on the program: a version of Stockhausen's *Plus-Minus* and Kotík's own *Contraband*. Thus, as far back as the mid-1960s, we observe the inauguration of a crucial new-music grouping (Kotík, Cardew, and Stockhausen) that would come to shape the work of not only those three musicians but also an extended network of composers and performers. For Kotík, this concert provided an occasion for presenting one of his own compositions alongside works by Stockhausen and Cardew, thus perhaps helping to establish himself as a peer of some well-known musicians. Works like *Plus Minus* and *Treatise*, with their integral indeterminacy, also gave the newly formed ensemble an opportunity to try out new repertoire: first, to give them tools to learn one another's styles as performers,[62] and second, perhaps to avoid potential issues in performance that would have been more obvious in better-known repertoire. Performing *Treatise* accomplished some very practical goals, then: working through the intragroup politics of how performance decisions would be made, establishing Kotík as a leader, and building ensemble rapport.

Performing *Treatise* at that time also represented a significant break with the musical establishment in Prague. As recounted by Miloš Jůzl, from 1948 on, publishing was controlled by the State and musical composition was subject to the (populist) ideology of the Zhdanov doctrine.[63] In the early 1950s, states Jůzl, "new music could not have developed in these circumstances. Progress could not have been achieved in this way."[64] In the years leading up to the Prague Spring uprising of 1968, the situation became somewhat less constrained—albeit temporarily—owing to the "attrition in ideological

---

[61] Dan Warburton, untitled review, *Paris Transatlantic* online magazine (February 2009), posted on Mode Records' online catalog, http://www.moderecords.com/catalog/205cardew.html.

[62] Kotík notes, "The first thing we did [upon forming QUaX] was to rehearse *Treatise*. Session after session, we worked through the pages I had. The piece was very important for getting all of us together, musically speaking, besides having a lot of fun . . ." Liner notes to Cardew, *Treatise*, QUaX Ensemble.

[63] Andrei Zhdanov, the Communist Party's Central Committee Secretary and Politburo member, enforced Party ideology in the arts and other cultural areas.

[64] Miloš Jůzl, "Music and the Totalitarian Regime in Czechoslovakia," *IRASM* 27, no. 1 (June 1996), 41.

170 INTERPRETIVE LABOR

influence," but even the so-called new music typically meant Soviet-style mass songs, accessible choral works, and programmatic symphonies.[65] Most music being composed and performed adhered to the guidelines established by the Party, and musicians whose ideas even suggested affinity for the "decadence" of America, for example, were censured. Given these circumstances, it would have been a real risk to perform avant-garde compositions.

S.E.M./Creative Associates, 1970

A few years later, *Treatise* was undertaken again in Buffalo, this time with the help of Kotík. For the April 1970 event, members of the Center of the Creative and Performing Arts (the S.E.M. Ensemble and a few guests) presented *Treatise* simultaneously with Cage's *Aria* and *Fontana Mix* and Kotík's *Music for 3* (*Hudba pro tři*, 1964, for viola, cello, and bass). The audio recording of this concert, thankfully, has been preserved at the University at Buffalo, State University of New York, and provides insight into a performance that would be nearly impossible to replicate, should one be inspired to do such a thing. Unlike the 1966 readings, which were part of the Evenings for New Music series, this fell under the Creative Associates Recitals program. Cardew was already involved in this series as both performer and composer, having been introduced in both roles in November 1966, and continuing to contribute compositions (such as *Solo with Accompaniment* and *Schooltime Compositions*) as well as performing piano works by numerous contemporaries in 1967. At the time of the April 15, 1970, performance, he was back in England, completing the major work *The Great Learning* and developing his involvement with the Scratch Orchestra, which was to consume much of his attention in the following years. Thus, it was left to the members of the Creative Associates to interpret the piece anew, and they did so by overlaying it with other recent compositions. The performers in this case were Gwendolin Sims, soprano; Petr Kotík, flute; Diane Williams, viola; Mary Lane, violoncello; Miroslav Vitous, double bass; William Furioso, percussion; and Jan Williams, percussion. The concert included one additional work with identical performing forces, Prague-born Rudolf Komorous's brief *Olympia*.

---

[65] Thomas D. Svatos, "Sovietizing Czechoslovak Music: The 'Hatchet-Man' Miroslav Barvík and his Speech *The Composers Go with the People*," *Music and Politics* 4, no. 1 (Winter 2010), 1–35.

THE "HACKER" MODEL   171

Unlike the 1967 performance, for which Cardew made interpretive decisions and performed with the ensemble, this version represents a different form of engagement. The interpretive labor here is even more closely aligned with hacking than in the first American version. Even in the most productive forms of hacking (e.g., open-source development), there must always be something being worked *against* (e.g., the capitalist corporate structure of proprietary software). In 1970, S.E.M. and guests produced their realization against their knowledge of Cardew's instructions and interpretive work. Without him there to supervise, they were both more free to introduce their own ideas, and simultaneously more responsible for the content they created. The *Buffalo Evening News* headline proclaims: "More Music Per Minute: Three Works at Once," and provides a flattering description of the event to be held two days later. Critic John Dwyer writes, "*Treatise* by Cardew is one of the most beautiful-looking scores in existence and could serve as an art exhibit. As sound it has an indefinite blend of erudition and irreverence, like a discussion of astro-physics in McClatchey's Blue Ribbon Bar & Grill. . . . As you can see, you're bound to have a good time."[66]

The resulting music from this three-work simultaneous performance lasts nearly two hours, with several stretches of relative silence sprinkled throughout. To some extent, the instrumentation and timing help to reveal what is happening at any given time, since the Cage score calls for many different styles of singing, and Kotík's piece is listed at 15' in his catalog and is designated for a specific set of instruments. The program does not specify who performs which piece, but the Kotík trio for viola, cello, and bass must have been played by Diane Williams, Lane, and Vitous. On the other hand, the shorter works could certainly have been divided up into sections and dispersed among sections of *Treatise*, and there is nothing to indicate even how much of the *Treatise* score was used for this performance. In addition, several instruments can be heard that are not listed on the program or in the Creative Associates Recitals catalog: harmonica, recorders playing dissonant intervals, and prepared piano. Throughout much of the performance, the texture remains sparse, with just one or two instruments playing at any given time. We hear virtuosic extended techniques, as well, from Sims's vocalizations to string harmonics and a number of sounds that are now impossible to identify definitively.[67]

---

[66] John Dwyer, "More Music per Minute," *Buffalo Evening News* (April 13, 1970).
[67] Creative Associates Recital (CA 275A-C), Domus Theater, Buffalo, NY (April 15, 1970), archival recording housed at the University at Buffalo Music Library (8 tracks, digitized May 1, 2015).

172   INTERPRETIVE LABOR

While some details about the performance have been lost to time, we do have a wealth of information about the individuals involved and about the sounds they created. In this group of performers, especially, I see an affinity for the "hacker ethic" discussed earlier in this chapter. Linus Torvalds, who created the Linux computer operating system, notes,

> The reason that Linux hackers do something is that they find it to be very interesting, and they like to share this interesting thing with others. Suddenly, you get entertainment from the fact that you're doing something interesting and you also get the social part. This is how you have this fundamental Linux networking effect where you have a lot of hackers working together because they enjoy what they do.[68]

This runs parallel to the phenomenon of performers of experimental music working in groups, such as the S.E.M. Ensemble. As those groups got to know one another and their various strengths as musicians, they could undertake increasingly challenging repertoire, up to and including performing multiple works at the same time. One might say, then, modifying Torvalds, "you have this fundamental *experimental-music* networking effect where you have a lot of *hacker-musicians* working together because they enjoy what they do." Even more directly, one might say that Kotík and the S.E.M. Ensemble hacked the "Creative Associates" institution itself, co-opting the recital series for new interests, such as promoting Kotík's own compositions. Without their CCPA positions and funding, these musicians would have been hard-pressed to develop their own programming, or—in the case of Kotík—even to be able to reside in the United States.

In addition, groups like S.E.M. and the individuals who drifted in and out of their networks formed a sort of culture unto itself. As noted by Eric Raymond,

> The "hacker culture" is actually a loosely networked collection of subcultures that is nevertheless conscious of some important shared experiences, shared roots, and shared values. . . . Because hackers as a group are particularly creative people who define themselves partly by rejection of "normal" values and working habits, it has unusually rich and conscious traditions for an intentional culture less than 40 years old."[69]

---

[68] Linus Torvalds, prologue to Himanen, *The Hacker Ethic*, xvii.
[69] Raymond, Introduction to *The New Hacker's Dictionary*, 1.

The Creative Associates and their affiliates, I submit, form one such hacker subculture, one that aligns both temporally and philosophically with the computer hackers of MIT and elsewhere. As suggested earlier, this creative, productive hacking is found within the Creative Associates, QUaX, the S.E.M. Ensemble, and all other groups who interpret indeterminate scores. Like open-source software developers, they form a community of like-minded workers, all contributing to a common goal. In this case, it happens to be producing realizations of experimental music.

On another level, the politics of *Treatise* are such that this composition comes to represent an entire mode of musical production. This type of hacking is distinct from the provocations of, say, George Maciunas or Nam June Paik. It was taken up by groups not simply to provoke or challenge, but instead to serve practical purposes such as building ensemble cohesion and establishing individuals as leaders within their musical communities. While *Treatise* could be read as just another example of graphic notation (albeit a particularly beautiful one), its real power lies in its capacity be whatever its realizers wanted it to be.

CARDEW, HACKER, VERSUS STOCKHAUSEN, VECTORALIST

McKenzie Wark's *Hacker Manifesto* (2004) introduces a new post-capitalist class division: the hackers versus the vectoralists. The latter term comes from the idea that

> [information], like land or capital, becomes a form of property monopolised by a class, a class of vectoralists, so named because they control the vectors along which information is abstracted, just as capitalists control the material means with which goods are produced, and pastoralists the land with which food is produced. This information, once the collective property of the productive classes—the working and farming classes considered together—becomes the property of yet another appropriating class.[70]

Toning down the rhetoric a bit, Wark's ideas claim that in late capitalism (or neoliberal capitalism), whoever controls the movement of information

---

[70] Wark, *A Hacker Manifesto*, 11.

174   INTERPRETIVE LABOR

actually yields a level of power analogous to the capitalists or landowners of prior ages.

The relationship between Cardew and Stockhausen parallels this hacker/vectoralist divide. Through their fraught artistic interactions, they manifest its divisive power. As I see it, the primary aspect of Stockhausen's affinity with the "vectoralist" class is that his compositions (particularly *Plus Minus* and *Carré*) presuppose the existence of producers other than himself.[71] To some extent, these musicians have just a metaphorical connection to the most recent class divide; Stockhausen is not actually controlling patents, copyrights, and so forth, of others' realizations, and there are certainly some distinctions to be made between a composer writing an indeterminate score and the neoliberal corporate culture of data control. Importantly, though, Stockhausen does exert authorial control in a way analogous to the controlling impetus of the vectoralist class. In fact, his work—and that of others creating similarly demanding works, such as Cage—could not exist without a group of other artists willing (or pressed) to adopt the potentially subservient role of cultural production. In this way, I see in Cardew and Stockhausen a microcosm of the broader hacker/vectoralist class division. Cardew explained the problem in typically polemical terms:

> Stockhausen's *Refrain*, the piece I have been asked to talk about, is a part of the cultural superstructure of the largest-scale system of human oppression and exploitation the world has ever known: imperialism. The way to attacking the heart of that system is through attacking the manifestations of that system, not only the emanations from the American war machine in Vietnam, not only the emanations from Stockhausen's mind, but also the infestations of this system in our own minds, as deep-rooted wrong ideas. And we must attack them not only on the superficial level, as physical cruelty or artistic nonsense or muddled thinking, but also on the fundamental level for what they are: manifestations of imperialism.[72]

Stockhausen's work, in Cardew's eyes, was not only the result of "muddled thinking" but also an actual product of the imperialist system. Like other political systems marked by a significant imbalance of power, imperialism meant wealth (or goods, or property, or prestige) for the few at the expense

---

[71] Again, this could be claimed for any composer of most any music conceived as a "work," but in these examples of challenging indeterminacy, they require extreme interpretive labor by others.

[72] Cardew, "Stockhausen Serves Imperialism," in Cardew, *Stockhausen Serves Imperialism*, 47.

THE "HACKER" MODEL   175

of the many. This might be reflected today in conflict between hackers (in the sense of creators or developers) and those who control the things they make. For example, royalties and licensing fees for musical recordings are paid to those who own the copyright, not necessarily those who wrote the songs or recorded them. This, too, runs in tandem with Wark's perceived division:

> The vectoralist class wages an intensive struggle to dispossess hackers of their intellectual property. Patents and copyrights all end up in the hands, not of their creators, but of a vectoralist class that owns the means of realising the value of these abstractions. . . . The time is past due when hackers must come together with workers and farmers—with all of the *producing classes* of the world—to liberate productive and inventive resources from the myth of scarcity.[73]

Technology companies like Spotify and Pandora, as well as companies that buy up batches of licenses, can potentially make huge profits while the songwriters providing their "products" receive little or no compensation.[74]

Finnish philosopher of information Pekka Himanen writes, "[T]he information economy's most important source of productivity is creativity, and it is not possible to create interesting things in a constant hurry or in a regulated manner . . . [I]t is important to allow for playfulness and individual styles of creativity since, in the information economy, the culture of supervision turns easily against its desired objectives."[75] Indeterminacy is, in fact, an information economy, or perhaps a small portion of the general information economy: a complex system in need of data analysis, storage, and translation. Musical works with indeterminate elements require data management; in this case, the data to be managed is primarily modes of operation for interpretive work. Himanen's discussion above brings to light another significant aspect of this problem: what he calls the "culture of supervision." The working conditions on *Carré* are likely the most direct example of this, but many other relevant connections can be found. For instance, percussionist Jan Williams—in addition to specific recollections about working with Feldman and others—recalls,

---

[73] Wark, *A Hacker Manifesto*, 7–8 (italics added).

[74] Eric Drott provides an account of some political and cultural implications of these services in "Music as a Technology of Surveillance," presented at the National Meeting of the American Musicological Society (Vancouver, BC, November 5, 2016).

[75] Himanen, *The Hacker Ethic*, 39.

176 INTERPRETIVE LABOR

In Buffalo, at the Center, there were always composers around. And between those composers-in-residence and those who came just to work on their pieces with us, we spent a lot of time working on pieces with the composers present. As a player, that certainly keeps you honest and adds a level of stress, good stress, because you have direct and immediate feedback from the composer on what and how you're doing. A string quartet playing Beethoven today does not experience that same type of stress, right? So, that puts an edge on things and makes things a lot more interesting and exciting.[76]

Not only did Stockhausen reinforce or enact a culture of supervision, then, but it was also a part of the general landscape of new-music performance at that time. Performers were accustomed to having composers weigh in on their realizations of works both indeterminate and not, and many were close collaborators with various composers. Some, like Cardew, came to resent that relationship, frustrated with the imbalance of power and recognition. Others, like Williams, identify a distinction between technical and creative work. In a discussion of working closely with Elliott Carter, he notes:

He [Carter] had the idea of getting harmonics on timpani; I suggested touching the head lightly in the center and striking the drum very close to the rim. It went back and forth like that until we figured it out. Harmonics ended up in the piece, but it was his idea, not mine. He "heard" harmonics in the piece, and I helped him decide if it would be possible. My input was only of a technical nature.[77]

As discussed previously, this was just one type of reaction to the challenges of working with living composers. Some performers welcomed it as an opportunity for collaboration, while others—Cardew, in particular—resented the idea of being watched over. Cardew's writings about Stockhausen and Cage also hint at a recent problem: the marked increase in surveillance, made possible by exponential growth of data. As more of our activities and interactions happen online and as more communication is made electronically, massive quantities of information are produced and stored, and become subject to

---

[76] Jan Williams in interview with Jonathan Hepfer, *Percussive Notes* 8 (February 2007), n.p.

[77] This context is also discussed in the "Executive" chapter. Jan Williams in interview with Jonathan Hepfer, n.p.

THE "HACKER" MODEL   177

oversight.[78] At the same time, this development is certainly more severe than even Cage's efforts at controlling performers; at least they knew who was watching them.

Cardew represents the hacker class—not just a hacker as someone who plays with expectations, but as a member of an emergent socio-political class. Because of this, his criticisms of Stockhausen and Cage suggest also the class issues within neoliberal capitalism. His most direct attack is found in the introduction to chapter 2 of *Stockhausen Serves Imperialism*:

> The American composer and writer John Cage, born 1912, and the German composer Karlheinz Stockhausen, born 1928, have emerged as the leading figures of the bourgeois musical avant garde. They are ripe for criticism. The grounds for launching an attack against them are twofold: first, to isolate them from their respective schools and thus release a number of younger composers from their domination and encourage these to turn their attention to the problems of serving the working people, and second, to puncture the illusion that the bourgeoisie is still capable of producing "geniuses." The bourgeois ideologist today can only earn the title "genius" by going to extreme lengths of intellectual corruption and dishonesty and this is just what Cage and Stockhausen have done. Inevitably, they try and lead their "schools" along the same path. These are ample grounds for attacking them; it is quite wrong to think that such artists with their elite audiences are "not doing anyone any harm."[79]

John Tilbury later notes that this criticism is manifested not only in Cardew's writings but also in his compositions. *Memories of You* (1964), ostensibly a tribute to Cage, uses "virtually the same notation" as Cage's *Concert for Piano and Orchestra*, and *Solo with Accompaniment* (1964) "seems to allude to Stockhausen's *Plus-Minus*."[80] If Tilbury is correct here, I see Cardew as kindred to composers of other subversive compositions, in line with Nam

---

[78] See, for example, discussion of NSA surveillance in David E. Pozen, "Privacy-Privacy Tradeoffs," *The University of Chicago Law Review* 83, no. 1 (Winter 2016), 221–47, and of information technology in Margaret S. MacDonald and Anthony G. Oettinger, "Information Overload: Managing Intelligence Technologies," *Harvard International Review* 24, no. 3 (Fall 2002), 44–48, and in Stephen Gill, "The Global Panopticon? The Neoliberal State, Economic Life, and Democratic Surveillance," *Alternatives: Global, Local, Political* 20, no. 1 (January–March 1995), 1–49.

[79] Cardew, *Stockhausen Serves Imperialism*, 33.

[80] John Tilbury, "Cornelius Cardew," *Contact* 26 (Spring 1983), 4–12. As noted elsewhere, Virginia Anderson reads this more strongly, as Cardew creating *Solo with Accompaniment* as a satire of *Plus Minus*. Anderson, "'Well, It's a Vertebrate,'" 300.

178 INTERPRETIVE LABOR

June Paik and Albert M. Fine. As will be discussed in greater detail in the next chapter, these artists played with the idea of the homage or tribute work, twisting it to convey their ambivalent attitudes toward better-known composers. In other words, they hacked the genre to do what they wanted it to do.

Along with artists like Paik and Fine, Cardew refused to accept the status quo of musical activity. In fact, he took it a step further by altering the established parameters even of existing texts. In a recent article, Roger Rothman argues for considering Fluxus artists as hackers, emphasizing "playful cleverness" (pace Richard Stallman) as the main condition of hackerism.[81] While there is much to be said for the connection between Fluxus and the MIT computer hackers—which coincided in time as well as in "spirit"—I would argue that it is only a small portion of a broader set of networks. Hacking, in short, is polyvalent. Rothman's work suggests acceptance of the usage becoming common today, that is, hacking as alteration. On magazine covers and websites like lifehacker.com, it is proclaimed that "hacks" exist for all manner of activity, from "easy dinner hacks" to "Ikea hacks" for creating furniture. This mainstreaming of the term, though, dilutes its original political power. Hacking, as I see it, is different when it involves a degree of subversion. Painting and adding trim to a cheap storage unit is mere alteration. It is a decorative procedure that does not fundamentally change our understanding of the object. The term "hack" has simply been co-opted for its cultural cachet as something slightly edgy.

I do not wish to limit the term by trying to define something like "true hacking," as this would weaken its multivalent strength. On the other hand, I do want to emphasize its more political aspects, focusing largely on the ways it connects to Cardew's practice. One area in which this is particularly fruitful is what Philip Lewis calls "abusive fidelity." This phrase perhaps uniquely captures what Cardew did when he snuck his own personality into Stockhausen's *Carré*, for example. Venuti explains,

> Derrida remains unsure about whether to apply the term translation to his rendering of Portia's line, "when mercy seasons justice." I want to suggest that it is indeed a translation, although one that exemplifies what Philip Lewis, influenced by Derrida's thinking, has called "abusive fidelity." This translation practice, Lewis observes, "values experimentation, tampers

---

[81] Rothman, "Against Critique," 794.

THE "HACKER" MODEL   179

with usage, seeks to match the polyvalencies and plurivocities or expressive stresses of the original by producing its own." It is demanded by foreign texts that involve substantial conceptual density or complex literary effects, namely, works of philosophy and poetry, including Derrida's own writing.[82]

I see Cardew's work as "abusive fidelity"—hacking the source text in a quite literal way in his work on *Carré*, but also in a metaphorical sense in his work after the mid-1960s more generally. By playing with the norms of experimental music and by undermining the authority of other composers, Cardew twisted his musical training and experience into a new form of engagement. This was made possible through this meddling translational work, driven by his emergent political affiliations.

MUSIC-MAKING AS HACKING

The argument in this chapter is the least straightforward among the five models of Interpretive Labor. In each of the first two models, under-recognized labor is produced when someone engages with indeterminate material: the composer in the "Scientist" Model and the assistant in the "Executive" Model. But here, I am claiming that performers have to deal with the indeterminacy in *Treatise*, and yet Cardew, the composer/creator, is also laboring in a way that has yet to be sufficiently theorized. It is not just realizing indeterminacy that signals an imbalance in labor. Instead, Cardew here uses indeterminacy as a tool to demonstrate his impatience with the status quo. He reappropriates the system to his own ends, namely, to trigger social change. At first sight, this is not at all revolutionary. Several artists working with chance, performer "freedom" and the like professed to be working toward "a situation in which no one told anyone what to do and it all turned out perfectly well anyway."[83] John Cage is now well-known for fostering just such a utopian ideal—or at least claiming to—up until the atrocities of the American involvement in Vietnam overwhelmed that naïve stance.[84] In an

---

[82] Lawrence Venuti, Introduction to Derrida's "What Is a 'Relevant' Translation?," 172.

[83] John Cage in conversation with Alan Gillmor, in Kostelanetz, *Conversing with Cage*, 78–79.

[84] This was certainly not unique to Cage; as Pisaro recounts, Cardew's own group, the Scratch Orchestra, was deeply affected by "the growing violence surrounding the opposition to the Vietnam War in America, the 1968 Paris riots, the Prague Spring, and the return of troubles in Northern Ireland," with some members shifting from an "urban folk" group to a "Communist rock group,

180 INTERPRETIVE LABOR

essay from around the same time that *Treatise* was being composed, Cage writes, "Art instead of being an object made by one person is a process set in motion by a group of people. Art's socialized. It isn't someone saying something, but people doing things, giving everyone (including those involved) the opportunity to have experiences they would not otherwise have had."[85]

So what is different about Cardew in this instance? Is his role different simply because he had different founding experiences shaping his approach? In what way is he not just taking on the "executive" persona for which I have taken Stockhausen (and Kreidler) to task? Primarily, I see an important distinction in the realm of authorship and recognition. In *Carré*, for example, or in *Fremdarbeit*, the composer takes sole credit for the artwork, despite the (real or fictional) collaboration with other artists. In Cardew's graphic-notation scores, as well as those of composers such as Cage and Brown, each performance is a new iteration. The Creative Associates did not work out a "definitive" version of *Treatise* in 1970, nor did anyone else in any other year. That composition is necessarily different every time it is performed. Because of this, the labor involved belongs to a different category than that of co-written works. To clarify: yes, the performers of *Treatise* absolutely labor to make their realization(s) of the score, and yes, it is possible to overlook their labor. However, it is not deliberately hidden away like the work of Cardew on *Carré*. A musician or audience member—especially one familiar with the score of *Treatise*—is confronted with realizers' labor during the performance itself (and experiences it again when listening to recordings); their work is inextricably bound up in the sounding of the piece itself. They become part of the work via their interpretive labor. In contrast, Cardew is part of *Carré*, but it is very easy to ignore that fact. His work was finished decades ago, it is not marked anywhere on the score, and we do not hear evidence of his sounding body when the piece is performed. His labor has essentially been erased.

Because of this paradigm—that is, laboring under erasure—Cardew had to find other ways to bring recognition to hidden work, both his own and, increasingly, that of others. As we have seen, this sometimes took the form

---

People's Liberation Music," and others leaving the orchestra altogether. Kathryn Gleasman Pisaro, "Music from Scratch: Cornelius Cardew, Experimental Music and the Scratch Orchestra in Britain in the 1960s and 1970s" (PhD diss., Northwestern University, 2001), 4–6.

[85] John Cage, "Diary: How to Improve the World (You Will Only Make Matters Worse) Continued 1967," in *A Year from Monday* (Middletown, CT: Wesleyan University Press, 1967), 145.

of literary interventions such as the essay "Stockhausen Serves Imperialism," but more often than not, it meant fighting for individuals in positions of decreased authority, as will be seen below. To borrow from Wark again, "The hacker class, being numerically small and not owning the means of production, finds itself caught between a politics of the masses from below and a politics of the rulers from above. It must bargain as best it can, or do what it does best—hack out a new politics, beyond this opposition."[86] In this way, Cardew's work leading up to the publication of *Treatise* aligns closely with the hacker ethic: his refusal to supply instructions is meant to spur productive difference in interpretation. By the time the *Handbook* went to press, though, he was already changing his approach. Instead of celebrating difference, he was beginning to lean toward a more communist political stance, and within the next two years, was actively supporting the workers' movement. This is not to suggest that any left-leaning artist cannot also be a hacker; to the contrary, some of the most important hacking serves the socialist aims of free information and concern for the welfare of the underprivileged or misrepresented.[87] What I claim here is that, for Cardew specifically in the role of composer, his work on *Carré* and *Treatise* illustrates the subversive form of hacking, while his later, overtly political songs, do not.

CARDEW'S POLITICS AFTER *TREATISE*

In the spring of 1963, Cardew was writing things like, "A composer who hears sounds will try to find a notation for sounds. One who has ideas will find one that expresses his ideas, leaving their interpretation free . . ." and "Notation is a way of making people move."[88] Just a few years later, he would admit, "I make no bones about having produced music just as backward as anything a Cage or a Stockhausen is capable of. . . . In my output I was preoccupied for

---

[86] Wark, *A Hacker Manifesto*, 17.

[87] A particularly rich example of this is the 2015 filming of the television show *Homeland*. As recounted by artist and doctoral fellow at the Berlin Graduate School of Muslim Cultures and Societies Heba Amin: for an episode depicting a Syrian refugee camp, artists were hired to "lend graffiti authenticity" to the set. Disturbed by the show's "inaccurate, undifferentiated and highly biased depiction of Arabs, Pakistanis, and Afghans, as well as its gross misrepresentations of the cities of Beirut, Islamabad, and the so-called Muslim world in general," the artists took the opportunity to "decorate" the set with anti-*Homeland* phrases: "The situation is not to be trusted," "#blacklivesmatter," and "Homeland is a joke, and it didn't make us laugh," among others. Heba Amin, "'Arabian Street Artists' Bomb Homeland: Why We Hacked an Award-Winning Series," October 14, 2015, hebaamin.com.

[88] Cardew, *Treatise Handbook*, iii.

182   INTERPRETIVE LABOR

several years with a largescale manifestation of this second disease [that is, the "aesthetic identity" of a musical score], the graphic score *Treatise*, and it is to this work that I wish to apply some more detailed criticism."[89] The following year, Cardew accepted a DAAD fellowship in West Berlin, where he participated in Erhard Grosskopf's concert series.[90] As noted by musicologist Beate Kutschke, "The proletarian turn of both composers [Cardew and Grosskopf] . . . manifest[ed] itself . . . in what one could call a more general change of artistic identity and interest. Music was not a purpose in itself anymore, but should rather serve the needs of the new allies, the workers."[91] While in West Berlin, Cardew actually served on the "battle committee" that opposed the government's plan to install an arts center in the former Bethanien hospital, arguing in part that to do so would drive out the poorer working-class residents of the area, and that those residents would be better served by a medical clinic for their children.[92] So, just a few years after completing *Treatise*, Cardew was already involved in direct political activism for workers' rights.

As alluded to earlier, despite Cardew's own alleged repudiation of his experimental works, I believe that it was through the process of working on *Treatise*, through his own interpretive labor in the form of hacking, that Cardew was also working through his emergent political beliefs. This process reflects his transition from subversive, self-interested work contra Stockhausen toward productive, community-interested work as a member of a group. The score itself was a springboard for group improvisation, as well as a tool for helping ensembles learn to work together. The accompanying notes throughout the *Treatise Handbook*, cited earlier, and Cardew's other writings, provide a window onto this development. Together, these artifacts suggest Cardew's shifting political stance. Tilbury notes, "[Cardew] began to identify with Marxism. The formation of the Scratch Orchestra was the culmination of Cardew's career within—or at least on the fringes

---

[89] Cardew, "Self Criticism: Repudiation of Earlier Works, (1972)," in Cardew, *Stockhausen Serves Imperialism*, 79, 81.

[90] "One of the channels through which the musician 'guests' ('prisoners' would be more appropriate) of the Programme can present their work to the public is 'Musikprojekte,' a concert series organised by the Berlin composer Erhard Grosskopf. Grosskopf, despite the economic discrepancy between him and the well-paid guest composers, realises the necessity of uniting where possible with the visitors on the basis of opposition to the cultural oppression of capitalist society." Cardew, "A Critical Concert," in Cardew, *Stockhausen Serves Imperialism*, 65.

[91] Kutschke, "Protest Music," 334.

[92] Ultimately, though, the Berlin government's plans prevailed and an arts institution was created. Kutschke, "Protest Music," 328–43.

THE "HACKER" MODEL   183

of—the musical establishment. His profound commitment to the democratic ideals of the Orchestra led inevitably to his, and several other members', politicisation."[93] This group was active between 1969 and 1974 and so largely coincided with—and contributed to—Cardew's political shift following the work on *Treatise*.[94] Tilbury continues, "His socialism was the logical consequence not just of his involvement with the Scratch Orchestra but of the experiences and direction of his life up to that point. His deeply rooted morality and tenacious humanism finally found a political purpose, which embraced and broadened previous preoccupations and achievements."[95] The "experiences and direction of his life" certainly included his lengthy engagement with creating and revising *Treatise*, and being involved in a number of its performances. To quote the "Caudwell" essay cited by Tilbury, "art is not in any case a relation to a thing, it is a relation between men, between artist and audience, and the art work is only like a machine which they must both grasp as part of the process."[96] Through his work on *Treatise* and other related works, then, Cardew began to lay the groundwork for his political activism of the 1970s.

CONCLUSION: MUSICAL HACKING

In a brief essay from 1972, Scratch Orchestra member Rod Eley writes,

> In the case of music, the claim that the reduction of manpower by new technology is to reduce "drudgery" is seen for what it really is in all fields—hypocritical rubbish! Today the opportunity for people with musical talent, or other artistic ability, to play a productive part in society is shrinking to [a] vanishing point. [. . .] Even in "serious" music orchestral players are ground down to a monotonous repertoire of eighteenth and nineteenth century classics, and often feel little better than hacks.[97]

In this instance, "hack" suggests the ancient meaning of one who lacks finesse, but gets the job done. Of course, this is only one small portion of the

[93] Tilbury, *Cornelius Cardew*, 9.
[94] Pisaro, "Music from Scratch."
[95] Tilbury, *Cornelius Cardew*, 9.
[96] Christopher Caudwell [pseud., Christopher St. John Sprigg], "D. H. Lawrence: A Study of the Bourgeois Artist," in *Studies in the [/a] Dying Culture* (London: Lawrence & Wishart, 1938), 11–13.
[97] Rod Eley, "A History of the Scratch Orchestra," in Cardew, *Stockhausen Serves Imperialism*, 14.

184 INTERPRETIVE LABOR

wealth of connotations. As demonstrated through the examples discussed in this chapter, there is a deep and significant connection between musical experimentalism and the so-called hacker ethic and hacker culture. This is evident not only in the sense of hacking as play or exploration but also in hacking as a way to trouble prevailing power structures. Hacking, in fact, is made manifest in indeterminacy, both musical and otherwise:

> The free and unlimited hacking of the new produces not just "the" future, but an infinite possible array of futures, the future itself as virtuality. Every hack is an expression of the inexhaustible multiplicity of the future, of virtuality. . . . [Property] cannot capture the infinite and unlimited virtuality from which the hack draws its potential.[98]

Indeterminacy—that is, endless virtuality—and hacking are inseparable. Cardew took this to the extreme, as illuminated in his thoughts on performer freedom: "Here we are in a similar situation to that where things are left 'free,' and then the composer tells the player afterwards that he played well or badly ('used' the freedom well or badly). If there exist criteria for making such a judgment, then there is no freedom."[99] Only in musical activity devoid of criteria is there a full measure of freedom, and only there do we find the "infinite and unlimited virtuality" to which the hack aspires.

Hacking must subvert power precisely because that power is oppressive. While the computer hackers of the Model Railroad Club at MIT were working around limitations on their access to machinery, the hackers of experimental music confronted limited ideas about what music could be, and about what sounds were welcome in their performances. For musicians like Cardew, challenging compositional control was a way, first, to expand the accepted universe of sounds, and second, to align their artistic practices with their broader political beliefs. One such aspect was the importance of taking responsibility for oneself and others. As Cardew writes, " 'Dynamics are free' does not mean that there are to be no dynamics, or one constant dynamic, but invites the player to ask himself 'what dynamic(s) for this sound?,' thus bringing him into the situation of having to *take care of the sound*, putting it in his charge, making him responsible."[100] In this, his aesthetic aligns with Heidegger's idea of Care. Thinking back to the fable of Care, Earth, and

---

[98] Wark, *A Hacker Manifesto*, 34.
[99] Cardew, "Notation: Interpretation, etc.," 30.
[100] Emphasis added. Cardew, "Notation: Interpretation, etc.," 31.

THE "HACKER" MODEL   185

Jupiter in *Being and Time*, we might be reminded that "[t]his pre-ontological document becomes especially significant not only in that 'care' is here seen as that to which human Dasein belongs 'for its lifetime' but also because this priority of 'care' emerges in connection with the familiar way of man as compounded of body (earth) and spirit. . . . 'Being-in-the-world' has the stamp of 'care' which accords it its Being."[101] Or, in Nicholas Dungey's words, "To care for, and be involved with, one's life, others, and the world, are all manifestations of dwelling. As the most primordial set of activities through which our care is expressed, dwelling signifies *who* we are and the *way* of our being."[102] Living with the *Treatise* project for several years—dwelling with it—brought Cardew into closer care for the interpretive practices it engendered. Tampering with the norms of compositional authority, then, enabled him to introduce a new level of caring for sound, a project well worth the political effort.

* * *

While Cornelius Cardew is the best-suited musician within my chosen network to fit the hacker model of Interpretive Labor, he is not alone in that distinction. At present, a number of individuals and groups active in new-music performance might be thought of as hackers in various ways. As musicians subvert power through their creative interventions, they hack the prevailing standards, and this can (and does) happen in a wide range of genres, including popular styles. For example, Radiohead made headlines in the mid-2000s for making its album *In Rainbows* available for download—for whatever price consumers wanted to pay—in exchange for the user's contact information.[103] They effectively circumvented the usual major-label and retailer procedures, and still achieved financial success, despite fans being able to pay only the credit-card processing fee if they wished, and despite the massive number of unauthorized downloads on file-sharing sites.[104] As digital media have changed in the past decade, many other artists have experimented with modes of transmitting and circulating their work, shifting such tests from hacks to new norms.

---

[101] Heidegger, *Being and Time*, 242–43, quoted in Bolt, *Heidegger Reframed*, 13–14.

[102] Nicholas Dungey, "The Ethics and Politics of Dwelling," *Polity* 39, no. 2 (April 2007), 239.

[103] Angela Monaghan, "Radiohead Challenges Labels with Free Album," *The Telegraph* (October 2, 2007).

[104] Will Page and Eric Garland, "In Rainbows, on Torrents," *Economic Insight* 10 (2008), www.mcps-prsalliance.co.uk/economics.

186 INTERPRETIVE LABOR

Within so-called art music, too, musicians have introduced new modes of operation. Returning to the organization known as AACM, I also see some affinities with their contemporaries, the early hackers. Founded in 1965 in Chicago, this "African American musicians' collective" represents, in its very construction, a type of experiment—a feature that connects them to the Scientist model—but much of their work has also expertly sidestepped perceived norms.[105] Their very construction shares the communitarian spirit of hacker groups. As a flexible group with various soloists and smaller ensembles (including the legendary Art Ensemble of Chicago), one of its stated goals has always been to "provide an atmosphere conducive to the development of its member artists and to continue the AACM legacy of providing leadership and vision for the development of creative music."[106] There is a strong commitment to creating original music and appreciation for stylistic eclecticism.[107] Many of their members' performances have featured lengthy group improvisations, including the concert discussed at the beginning of the Scientist chapter. I see this practice as a strong parallel with computer hacking, at least in its early iterations: one must thoroughly understand the underlying system (musical style/genre or computer code), have the creative capacity to subvert that system, and also possess the skill and artistic ability to actually do something with that creative thinking. This is a sophisticated form of interpretation through and through.

One might draw similar conclusions about the artists involved in Fluxus. As noted earlier, art historian Roger Rothman does make some compelling points in his argument for the similarities between Fluxus and aspects of the "hacker aesthetic."[108] Given the time at which computer-hacking play began, it is tempting to associate that phenomenon with contemporary playful experiments in art and music. However, as I will discuss in the next chapter, there are also some oversimplifications here that ought to be addressed, and the amorphous quality of Fluxus—whatever it is or may have been—makes it resistant to blanket comparisons.

[105] Lewis, "Experimental Music in Black and White," 100.

[106] "About AACM," https://www.aacmchicago.org/about-us, accessed June 29, 2020.

[107] Paul Steinbeck, "'Area by Area the Machine Unfolds': The Improvisational Performance Practice of the Art Ensemble of Chicago," *Journal of the Society for American Music* 2, no. 3 (2008), 399.

[108] Rothman, "Against Critique."

THE "HACKER" MODEL   187

Musicians and arts administrators have also hacked the material conditions of concerts. Since at least the 1960s, new-music festival organizers have programmed challenging works in unusual spaces. Following the capable lead of Charlotte Moorman, whose annual Avant-Garde Festivals of New York were held in such places as Grand Central Station (1973) and the Staten Island Ferry (1967),[109] other series have taken up residence in surprising places. At the 2015 Ostrava Days Festival, in addition to the mundane concert halls and theaters, concerts were also held in the Provoz Hlubina and Trojalí Karolina—a former coal mine and coking plant, respectively.[110] Also, while churches often house musical events, there was a subversive quality about the "Voices and Instruments" concert at St. Wenceslas, an early-14th-century structure near the Ostrava town square. A diverse set of compositions was presented there on August 27, 2015, including Rolf Riehm's dramatic *Adieu, Sirènes*, performed brilliantly by Annette Schönmüller. Her *sprechstimme* and clear mezzo-soprano voice cut through the crowded nave, packed with folding chairs, audio equipment, and new-music supporters. The work's frightening text and texture seemed to threaten the space itself, undermining its original purpose as a place of spiritual reprieve (see Figure 5.5). In this way, as with Moorman's festivals, artists hacked the spaces around them, not only repurposing them but actually diminishing their authority as sites for a particular function.

***

Moving along the spectrum of indeterminacy, I situate the hacker model toward the "free" or "open" end of the scale. To be sure, aspects of the composition or other musical entity are specified, at least to the extent that discrete works and practices can be identified. However, each intervention into the expected practice also twists it in some way, capitalizing on whatever aspect can be manipulated. This allows for all kinds of new ideas to flood in and destabilizes prevalent norms, sometimes permanently changing both perspectives and resulting actions. These characteristics make it an important mode of thinking about experimental music, and further reinforce that

---

[109] Complete list of festival dates, locations, and events can be found in Moorman, "History of the Annual Avant Garde Festival of New York."

[110] One truly appreciates the magnitude of transatlantic jet lag when immersed in a three-orchestra performance of Stockhausen's *Gruppen* inside a massive, resonant former factory building in an unfamiliar industrial center.

188　INTERPRETIVE LABOR

Figure 5.5a Interior view of a concert being set up in St. Wenceslas Church, Ostrava. Photograph by the author, August 27, 2015.

Figure 5.5b Interior view of Trojalí Karolina (Karolina Triple Hall), Ostrava. Photograph by the author, August 27, 2015.

Figure 5.5c Exterior view of St. Wenceslas Church, Ostrava. Photograph by the author, August 27, 2015.

key avant-garde musicians embody "the values of the hacker culture: the dedication, the irreverence, the respect for competence, and the intellectual playfulness that makes hackers such a stimulating group to be among."[111] In short, hacking is a form of interpretation. It involves creative engagement, expertise, and exploration, all underwritten by a productive sense of disruption. The interpretive labor of hacking, then, represents a way for socially conscious artists to react to problematic paradigms, as in Cardew's naïve efforts to bestow "freedom" on his performers. As will be argued in the following chapter, this approach is beholden to a broader, even more elemental function: play.

---

[111] Eric S. Raymond, "Hacker in a Strange Land," in Raymond, *The New Hacker's Dictionary*, xviii.

6

THE "GAMER" MODEL

GAMES, PLAY, AND OTHER LUDIC EXPERIMENTS

> In the enjoyment of music, whether it is meant to express religious ideas or not, the perception of the beautiful and the sensation of holiness merge, and the distinction between play and seriousness is whelmed in that fusion.
>
> —Johan Huizinga, *Homo Ludens* (1938)[1]

INTRODUCTION: EXPERIMENTAL MUSIC AND LUDOMUSICOLOGY

In three models of Interpretive Labor—the scientist, the executive, and the hacker—artists take on the work of realizing a musical score. In a way, all of these forms are a type of play, wherein the performers participate actively in shaping the composition. Gaming, then, is the broadest such model, encompassing many musical processes. Taking cues from Sherry Ortner's work on serious games,[2] I consider musical practices that challenge conventional modes of inquiry (e.g., Happenings, Fluxus events, and open-ended graphic and text notations, all of which trouble the fine line between work and play). A concert given by the Creative Associates at the University at Buffalo in 1970 provides a central case study, for which a Buffalo *Courier Express* reviewer hit the nail on the head with the headline "Games at UB Recital."[3] From this, I expand outward to consider a host of issues surrounding gaming and play. From the computer program development

---

[1] Johan Huizinga, *Homo Ludens: A Study of the Play-Element in [as] Culture*, trans. unknown (London: Routledge, 1949), 183.

[2] Sherry Ortner, *Anthropology and Social Theory: Culture, Power, and the Acting Subject* (Durham, NC: Duke University Press, 2006).

[3] Thomas Putnam, "[Review:] Games at UB Recital," *Buffalo Courier-Express* (October 22, 1970).

Interpretive Labor. Kirsten I. Speyer Carithers, Oxford University Press. © Oxford University Press 2025.
DOI: 10.1093/9780197698815.003.0007

THE "GAMER" MODEL   191

of *Fighter Maker* (PlayStation, 1999) to the free-range indeterminacy of *Dungeons & Dragons*, from hopscotch to chess, games—and the culture of play more generally—suggest new ways of thinking about artistic practices. In this chapter, I explore several related questions: do "avant-garde" artistic practices actually modify existing paradigms, and if so, how and to what extent do they do so? What kind of play is this, and why is this significant?

Scholars in the developing subfield of ludomusicology are working with the soundworlds in online gaming, rhythm games such as the *Guitar Hero* and *Rock Band* franchises, and numerous other types of "playful work and workful play."[4] As it turns out, concepts from gaming also illuminate the heightened political stakes of the repertoire with which I am most concerned, that is to say, issues of power, control, and authorship in experimental music. For example, much of the creative labor involved in realizing non-traditional notation can usefully be understood in terms of modding and user-generated content (to be defined below), with musicians and gamers making similar investments in their creative worlds. Likewise, thinking about avant-gardism in this way reveals the interconnectedness of these recent phenomena: both (video) games and experimental music are necessarily plural—art and craft, commerce and hobby, free and constrained. At present, the young subfield of ludomusicology is primarily concerned with accounts of music and sound in digital games. In what follows, I expand its present scope to encompass aspects of play and gaming in other creative practices, namely, experimental music. By considering indeterminacy in terms of modding, as I begin with below, we gain essential insight into its laden socio-cultural and political meanings.

At the same time, the present-day paradigm is such that real problems can easily be hidden behind game-like or otherwise playful masks. The most pervasive of these may be user-generated content (UGC) production by hordes

---

[4] Donovan and Katz, "Cookie Monsters," 209. For other examples, see Roger Moseley, *Keys to Play: Music as a Ludic Medium from Apollo to Nintendo* (Oakland: University of California Press, 2016); Roger Moseley, "Digital Analogies: The Keyboard as Field of Musical Play," *Journal of the American Musicological Society* 68, no. 1 (Spring 2015), 151–228; Cheng, *Sound Play*; K.J. Donnelly, William Gibbons, and Neal Lerner, eds., *Music in Video Games: Studying Play* (New York: Routledge, 2014); Mark Grimshaw, ed., *Game Sound Technology and Player Interaction: Concepts and Developments* (Hershey, PA: IGI Global, 2011); Kiri Miller, *Playing Along: Digital Games, YouTube, and Virtual Performance* (Oxford: Oxford University Press, 2012); Karen Collins, *Game Sound: An Introduction to the History, Theory and Practice of Video Game Music and Sound Design* (Cambridge, MA: MIT Press, 2008); Karen Collins, ed., *From Pac-Man to Pop Music: Interactive Audio in Games and New Media* (Aldershot, UK: Ashgate, 2008); and numerous articles on sound and music in specific video games and other interactive media.

192   INTERPRETIVE LABOR

of "volunteer" laborers. Just consider the following pitch from inbound-marketing[5] firm HubSpot:

> Tired of struggling to crank out the endless streams of content needed to appease today's consumers? You're in luck! There is an option for burned out business owners, and that's user generated content. This technique, in conjunction with the growth of popular social media websites, allows modern businesses to *delegate some of these brand-building responsibilities to an unlikely voice—their customer.*
>
> Having users contribute to your content creation efforts has another interesting advantage, as consumers are more interested in hearing the views of their peers than reading cleverly written sales messages. [. . . S]tudies show *consumers trust user generated content more than all other forms of media.*
>
> In light of these trends, there's never been a better time to start using user generated content to engage your readers and *build trust* with them.[6]

I'll return to the idea of exploitation later, but for now, I will just point out that the more entrenched digital media become in many people's everyday lives, the more carefully we need to keep a critical ear attuned to underlying inequalities. Media theorist/provocateur McKenzie Wark confronts readers with a bleak picture of this paradigm:

> "Play" was once a great slogan of liberation . . . Only look at what has become of play. Play is no longer a counter to work. Play becomes work; work becomes play. Play outside of work found itself captured by the rise of the digital game, which responds to the boredom of the player with endless rounds of repetition, level after level of difference as more of the same. Play no longer functions as a foil for critical theory. The utopian dream of liberating play from the game, of a pure play beyond the game, merely opened the way for the extension of gamespace into every aspect of everyday life.[7]

---

[5] This refers to a form of advertising in which consumers are drawn in to a company through its blogs, subscription content, social media, etc., in contrast to traditional outbound marketing (e.g., billboards, non-targeted direct mail, radio, etc.).

[6] Emphasis added. Eric Siu, "10 User Generated Content Campaigns That Actually Worked," *Hubspot* (blog), March 12, 2015, http://blog.hubspot.com/marketing/examples-of-user-generated-content.

[7] McKenzie Wark, *Gamer Theory* (Cambridge, MA: Harvard University Press, 2007), §016.

While Wark presents a number of thought-provoking insights throughout this text, I would like to suggest a way out of this pessimism: namely, by considering the ways artists have troubled the all-or-nothing fatalism so prevalent in dystopian accounts of the present. Through critical and affirmative play—in short, creative engagement—musicians and other artists have proven time and again that human agency will not so easily be overcome.

MODDING

A term frequently encountered in gaming, particularly within the context of digital games, is "modding." An abbreviation for *modifying*, it therefore suggests an underlying dissatisfaction with the game as published, and invites consideration of what it means when a player makes the effort to modify a given game. One simple example is altering the appearance and/or functionality of avatars within a video game, such as introducing a Marvel Comics superhero into Rockstar Games' popular *Grand Theft Auto* franchise.[8] Some of these alterations are much grander in scale, such as the Defense of the Ancients (DotA) map. This began as a modification to the massively multiplayer online role-playing game (MMORPG) *World of Warcraft*, via a tool called the World Editor. Using this tool (and its predecessor, the StarCraft editor), players develop 3D maps, "behavior scripts," link "indoor" and "outdoor" levels, and even create their own cut scenes by importing sound and video and controlling camera movement.[9] The entry on the Warcraft wiki site notes that its first development was done by a player in the United States (screen name Eul) and acknowledges nine additional designers for this modification, citing Eul, Quantum.dx, Fluffy_Bunny, Ryude, and Danite as the more prolific designers.[10]

---

[8] "This mod clearly gives you massive destructive power. It makes your character a functional superhero, able to take on an army of police officers and vehicles alone. Iron Man's arsenal of repulsor beams, missiles, and extremely powerful punches are usable in the mod, as well, letting you wreak havoc in Los Santos." Alex Newhouse, "GTA 5 Mod Turns Your Character into Iron Man," July 31, 2015, gamespot.com.

[9] Blizzard Entertainment (game publisher), "World Editor FAQ," posted on their proprietary game-management application Battle.net, accessible at us.battle.net.

[10] The page also includes the following disclaimer: "This article is about a fan created Custom Map designed on Warcraft III with the World Editor. The map contains non-Blizzard information, and events are not official. It should not be taken as representing official lore!" "Defense of the Ancients (Warcraft III map)," World of Warcraft (WOW) Wiki, http://wowwiki.wikia.com/wiki/Defense_o f_the_Ancients_(Warcraft_III_map).

194   INTERPRETIVE LABOR

Both of these interventions and countless other mods embody the characteristic labeled "reskinning" by digital humanities scholar Mary Flanagan, whose work on critical game design provides insight into a number of practices discussed in this chapter. Essentially, reskinning involves changing the appearance or other physical qualities of a game or toy—for example, war-era pinball game manufacturers selling kits to change their games into anti–Japanese-themed toys. Along with "unplaying" and "rewriting," this action makes up the core of her project, which is to identify characteristics of critical play.[11] Within a digital-game mod, reskinning serves to customize the gaming experience for the player, granting her or him greater control over the digital environment. Many players spend a substantial amount of time in these online gameworlds, often to the tune of several hours per day for months on end, so it makes sense that they would want to "own" a portion of the design.

Experimental composers, too, have played with modification. Audiences in Buffalo in 1966 were treated to a "test of nerves" presented by what one critic called the "new radical right wing in the sonic arts."[12] By this, he meant University of Michigan–based composers Robert Ashley and Gordon Mumma, along with David Behrman and Alvin Lucier, who gave a concert in conjunction with Henri Pousseur's Slee Lecture at the University at Buffalo. The group was known as the Sonic Arts Union, founded that year to "pool their resources and help one another with the performance and staging of their music."[13] Mumma and Ashley, especially, had by that time developed the ONCE Festival in Ann Arbor into an important site of musical experimentation, and they brought that energy to the Buffalo concert, performing works that altered typical conventions of vocalization and instrumental performance. Dwyer's review identifies only two compositions, but based on his descriptions, it seems likely that a version of Mumma's *Hornpipe* was also presented that evening. The composer later notes,

In 1961 I began a series of pieces for Horn, with various accompanying resources, culminating in late 1967 with the cybersonic piece *Hornpipe*. *Hornpipe* is a live-electronic work for French Horn with cybersonic console,

[11] Mary Flanagan, *Critical Play: Radical Game Design* (Cambridge, MA: MIT Press, 2009), 33.
[12] Dwyer specifies that he uses this term because "Europe has already given us the musical left, in Stockhausen and the groups in Darmstadt and Cologne . . . This, however, is an American populist movement." John Dwyer, "Dialed Music, or Whatever, Offers Stiff Test of Nerves," *Buffalo Evening News* (December 19, 1966).
[13] Liner notes, The Sonic Arts Union, *Electric Sound*, Mainstream Records (LP), 1971.

and is dedicated to Christian and Holly Wolff. The cybersonic console is a small metal box worn by the performer. This console contains electronic circuits of my own design which respond to the sounds of the Horn and to the acoustical resonances of the performance space. In *Hornpipe* the instrument is seldom played traditionally. Most of the sounds are produced with special double reeds, and the slides are rearranged so that sound is heard from different parts of the instrument.[14]

In late 1966, then, he would have been playing with the electronics that would soon be codified in the piece *Hornpipe*. As explained by Dwyer, Mumma "played a wired-up French horn, though used more as a modifying long-tube for the whispering or growling voice, and his colleagues made amplified vocal sounds through throat mikes."[15] The group also presented Ashley's now-(in)famous *The Wolfman* (1964).[16] This piece is "essentially a work about feedback—a microphone is positioned so close to the performer's mouth that changes in the size of the oral cavity bring about great changes in the feedback sound."[17] While the performer must actually produce sound extremely quietly, the amplification and feedback are arranged in such a way that the resulting sound can be painfully loud for the audience. Creative Associates program coordinator Renée Levine Packer recalls the Buffalo performance as "fierce amplified growls and yells emanating from the hall" near her office in Baird Hall.[18]

Thus, both Ashley and Mumma used electronics—microphones, circuitry, amplifiers—to create mods of their instruments and voices. Likewise, popular musicians have long altered their tools, and the Sonic Arts Union's work coincides with the rise of the do-it-yourself (DIY) ethic both within and outside music. Steve Waksman notes the "amnesia that has informed the punk appropriation of DIY as a term of resistance to dominant music industry practice," arguing instead for its origins in suburban assertions of

---

[14] Sonic Arts Union, *Electric Sound*, note by Gordon Mumma.

[15] Dwyer, "Dialed Music, or Whatever."

[16] Ashley later notes that this piece was premiered at the second annual Avant-Garde Festival in New York, organized by Charlotte Moorman in 1964, but—unlike Mumma's *Hornpieces* [sic], it does not appear on the printed program; likely, it was a late addition or substitution on the Mumma/Ashley concert on September 1, 1964. Programs in the Charlotte Moorman Collection, Northwestern University Special Collections.

[17] Alvin Lucier, "Origins of a Form: Acoustical Exploration, Science and Incessancy," *Leonardo Music Journal* 8, Ghosts and Monsters: Technology and Personality in Contemporary Music (1998), 5.

[18] Levine Packer, *This Life of Sounds*, 72.

196 INTERPRETIVE LABOR

masculinity via enthusiastic engagement with technology in the home.[19] For guitar makers like Les Paul and Leo Fender, altering instruments (tinkering) was not only a way to achieve the type of sound that they wanted but also served as "a mode of self-directed activity in which musicians have sought to carve out a sphere of 'independence' from the broader structures that govern the music and guitar-manufacturing industries."[20] By extension, experiments like Mumma's suggest a similar fascination with sonic technology and an effort at "emancipation."[21] Of course, this is somewhat different from the situation with *Grand Theft Auto* or *Warcraft*. The composers modified equipment for their own scores, which still had their names on them, unlike a videogamer modifying a weapon or character in a game produced on behalf of a corporation. What is similar, though, is the *why* behind the work. In each instance of modding, a participant is unsatisfied with the existing parameters, and takes matters into his or her own hands.

Why does this matter in a theory of labor? At its core, modding is a form of work: the player does the work of a programmer (or other creative laborer). One reason for this, I suspect, is that the act of modding (or reskinning) grants the player a more thorough form of agency than would otherwise be felt. In fact, there are some game mods that strongly testify to this phenomenon, for example, in Konami's *Pro Evolution Soccer* (PES) franchise for the PlayStation console. Historically, Konami has been unable or unwilling to secure licenses to portray leagues like the English Premier League, much to the dismay of players. Without their favorite real-life football squads, the game lacks the excitement of its rival, *FIFA* (produced by EA Sports, and named for the governing body Fédération Internationale de Football Association). In response, user communities have exploited the edit mode within PES, developing massive data files with the real teams' names and uniform designs, which can be ported into the game via large downloadable files. Game players can enter the edit mode within the game, apply their image files, and transform the visual aspects of the game to correspond to the official team "kits," advertisements within the stadiums, players' names, and other areas.

---

[19] Steve Waksman, "California Noise: Tinkering with Heavy Metal and Hardcore in Southern California," *Social Studies of Science* 34, no. 5, Special Issue on Sound Studies: New Technologies and Music (October 2004), 696.

[20] Waksman, "California Noise," 676–77.

[21] Dwyer notes that in the post-concert discussion, "Mr. Pousseur sought to establish a point of departure between the European continuity and this one, thus implying a relationship, even if a divorced one. The composers would have none of it. [. . .] To the populist, it is of the utmost importance to be sui generis, self-generating, purged of history." Dwyer, "Dialed Music, or Whatever."

This process is now much easier than in early versions of the game, in which each individual player used a pixel-level editing tool to design logos and other visuals, painstakingly creating uniform designs.

Even today, using the files readily available online, it takes several hours to revise the player images, team logos, jerseys, manager photos, uniform-number font colors, and so forth, for just one league, let alone all of the teams available within the game. When I asked a gamer friend why people would go to all the trouble to create these, particularly those who create the detailed mod files for others to use, he said, "I'm actually surprised at how many people do this, but if you can play in a real stadium with real teams, it's so much better. The gameplay mechanics in Pro Evo are a lot better than in FIFA, so people want to play the game anyway, and having the real teams just adds to the authenticity of the game."[22] As noted in a warning posted on a PES-themed forum, however, this only works well when players respect one another's contributions:

> Recently we have received some complaints regarding users failing to credit their sources, failing to obtain permission before using others' work and even stealing credit for other peoples' [sic] work. It shouldn't be necessary to caution users on this, however, it is entirely unacceptable to use others' work without permission or claim credit for something you have not produced yourself. An editing community cannot work successfully if people are unhappy to upload their work for fear of it being misused or misrepresented. Do not engage in this behaviour.[23]

This clearly resonates with the community aspect of hacker culture. In fact, we might wonder if modding is simply a specific type of hacking, as it too alters the parameters of a given world. This largely depends on how one defines "hacker"—as noted in the previous chapter, that term can range in meaning from mere alteration to complicated forms of subversive play. In general, I prefer to reserve "hacking" for a type of intervention that challenges the status quo, and I see this as distinct from the modifying activities of videogamers making new characters and uniforms. In the case of the DotA mod, for example, the newly created map and its mechanics became part of

---

[22] PlayStation user Superweak, interview with the author, June 5, 2016.
[23] User ID Original?, "Warning: Stealing Credit," on Pro Evolution Soccer Forum, May 1, 2011, pesgaming.com.

a later expansion pack, so while it was not technically sanctioned by Blizzard Entertainment (*World of Warcraft*'s publisher), it has become a commonly used part of its larger gameworld. With *Pro Evolution Soccer*, the gameplay remains unaffected; avatars are merely re-dressed or reskinned in a way that is not at all disruptive to the official game. Even Mumma and Ashley's playful mods of the horn and electronics failed to irreparably damage that specific concert experience. Instead, all of these participants engage in a form of critical play that allows them to control the *aesthetic* characteristics of their artistic and ludic environments.

THE WORK OF ART IN THE AGE OF USER-GENERATED CONTENT

In modding, players alter aspects of an existing game, changing parameters to suit their preferences. This represents just one type of UGC, a crucial paradigm within recent digital media writ large. It is found in social media, advertising, conventional and computer games, and a host of other interactive media. Most broadly, this is exactly what it sounds like: content generated by the individuals using a given platform. For example, this might include posting photographs on the photo- and video-sharing application Instagram or maintaining a personal blog (weblog) or—as will be discussed shortly—uploading midi files of original songs within an MMORPG. Perhaps the biggest game-changer in terms of the music industry has been the video-sharing platform YouTube. The now-ubiquitous site, launched in 2005 and purchased by Google the following year for $1.65bn USD, has over a billion users, who watch hundreds of millions of hours on the site daily.[24] This is a staggering number, placing it second only to Google's own search engine for visitors and pageviews, as of this writing.[25] While the company now has its own production facilities in six global cities, much of its content is still created and uploaded by non-affiliated individuals, both amateur and professional, and ranges from how-to videos for everything from home-improvement projects to hairstyling, to family-vacation and kids' dance recital videos that might be of interest to only a handful of relatives, to professionally produced movie trailers and music videos. In some ways, it is truly

---

[24] https://www.youtube.com/yt/press/statistics.html (accessed June 2, 2016).
[25] Amazon Alexa data analytics, "Top 500 Sites on the Web," http://www.alexa.com/topsites (accessed June 6, 2016).

democratic: anyone with a camera and an internet connection can potentially become known worldwide through its interface.[26] Scholars have begun to document its potential and its dangers in this regard, for example, noting the success of otherwise marginalized hip-hop artists and the use of original ballads posted online to send threatening messages to rival drug cartels, respectively.[27] Other researchers have noted the pedagogical uses of YouTube, including classroom use and individual music instruction.[28]

Beyond YouTube, other "social media" fully depend on the participation of users, who create and share their photographs, videos, and writing. Most readers are probably familiar with web-based applications like Facebook, Twitter, and Instagram, which seem to be the "big three" at present. As of March 2016, Facebook has almost 1.1 billion daily active users, 84% of whom are located outside the United States and Canada, as well as dozens of U.S. and international offices and several data centers, employing over 14,000 people as of June 30, 2016.[29] Like YouTube, its pages are increasingly populated by individuals and companies using the platforms for advertising; in fact, the company as a whole is now primarily an ad-distribution complex masquerading as a social network.[30] Their product is user data, and non-advertiser participants (users) either willingly or unwittingly provide it for free in exchange for the ability to communicate with distant friends and

---

[26] But see also the important caveat that such claims can be "idealistic fantasies of individuals who have the luxury of inhabiting these realms and propagating such optimistic theories." William Cheng, "Role-Playing toward a Virtual Musical Democracy in *The Lord of the Rings Online*," *Ethnomusicology* 56, no. 1 (Winter 2012), 43. Likewise, we ought to watch out for the "deceptive opposition between the passive recipient, couched in the rhetoric of 'old media,' and the active participant cast ideally as someone who is well-versed in the skills of 'new' media," which can undermine the varying levels of participation for those viewing, commenting, and creating within new media. José van Dijck, "Users Like You? Theorizing Agency in User-Generated Content," *Media, Culture and Society* 31, no. 1 (2009), 44.

[27] See Eun-Young Jung, "Transnational Migrations and YouTube Sensations: Korean Americans, Popular Music, and Social Media," *Ethnomusicology* 58, no. 1 (Winter 2014), 54–82 and John H. McDowell, "'Surfing the Tube' for Latin American Song: The Blessings (and Curses) of YouTube," *The Journal of American Folklore* 128, no. 509 (Summer 2015), 260–72, especially 264–65.

[28] For example, in a special issue of the journal *The Science Teacher* 81, no. 6, 21st-Century Tools and Skills (September 2014); Glynda Hull, John Scott, and Jennifer Higgs, "The Nerdy Teacher: Pedagogical Identities for a Digital Age," *The Phi Delta Kappan* 95, no. 7 (April 2014), 55–60; and Miller, *Playing Along*.

[29] http://newsroom.fb.com/company-info/ (accessed March 5, 2016).

[30] This becomes more apparent with each update of the desktop and mobile app. In early June 2016, they expanded its purview yet again: "Instead of just selling ads on Facebook, or on Facebook platforms (like WhatsApp and Instagram), Facebook is now selling ads everywhere, to everyone, whether or not you have a Facebook account. If you do have a Facebook account, though—like 1.6 billion other humans do—Facebook will also use your Facebook data to sell those ads." Kate Cox, "PSA: You Need to Update Your Facebook Privacy Settings Again to Opt Out of New Targeted Ads," *Consumerist*, June 2, 2016, https://consumerist.com/2016/06/02/psa-you-need-to-update-your-facebook-privacy-settings-again-to-opt-out-of-new-targeted-ads/.

200   INTERPRETIVE LABOR

family. While this presents some challenging questions (is it worth losing control over whatever data we share, in order to see what our friends are posting? How can we balance concerns about privacy with a desire for convenient online interaction?), it may be small potatoes compared to the new Facebook at Work version, or as one commentator puts it, "the latest way to keep us all chained to our jobs for the rest of eternity."[31] This gets us back to the heart of the matter for this chapter, and the book as a whole: namely, issues around creative labor. One key significance of this question is that, as in other forms of interpretive work, the participant/player is doing work not conventionally "assigned" to them: that of the composer, or programmer, or game designer, and so forth. This must be recognized as labor because, first, we ought to give credit where it is due, and more importantly, it tells us something about these participants. Why would they "voluntarily" invest their time and effort into these things? Are they being duped, or enacting agency in participating more deeply? If, as Eun-Young Jung has argued, "the story of social media ... deserves much greater attention ... for the equalizing opportunities they offer musicians, for the easy transnational dissemination of music and related forms of cultural expression they make possible, and for new patterns of production and consumption that are only beginning to emerge,"[32] they also warrant a critical eye toward the work involved.

User-generated content in social media, then, primarily exists for the benefit of the parent company. In other formats, though, it can produce a range of different effects. In conventional and computer games, players often create content to personalize or enrich their game experiences. As recounted by musicologist William Cheng, players of the MMORPG *The Lord of the Rings Online* (LOTRO) have created musical content that performs numerous functions. For example, many players have created music files using LOTRO's "ABC" system, in which musical information (pitches, rhythms) are mapped onto plain-text code and activated as fully formed audio files during gameplay. Groups formed within the game—for example, one calling themselves the Hobbiton Philharmonic—use several such files activated simultaneously to "perform" multi-part compositions.[33] Along with ABC mode, music can be created via mapping the computer keyboard to pitches, whereby the sounds are produced live during gameplay (called freestyle

---

[31] Sophie Kleeman, "What Is Facebook at Work and Do You Need to Care?" *Gizmodo*, March 4, 2016, http://gizmodo.com/what-is-facebook-at-work-and-do-you-need-to-care-1762754256.

[32] Jung, "Transnational Migrations and YouTube Sensations," 77.

[33] Cheng, "Role-Playing toward a Virtual Musical Democracy," 37–38.

THE "GAMER" MODEL   201

mode). Using both modes, players can create pleasant background music for their own enjoyment, arrange for "public" (in-game) concerts, or even "spam" other players with intentionally obnoxious audio pollution, as was the case with a group of bagpipers inside a small enclosed space.[34] While LOTRO has one of the most comprehensive music-making systems among digital games, other titles certainly make room for UGC of many types. All of these creative activities, of course, require an expenditure of time and energy.

This phenomenon is perhaps even more pronounced in the myriad experimental forms of musical indeterminacy explored in the 1960s and 1970s. Any piece with a substantial degree of indeterminacy demands that performers fill in the blanks, sometimes literally. To cite one such example, Fluxus artist Robert Filliou's *Teaching and Learning as Performing Arts*, a book from the middle of this period, includes writing space explicitly left open for readers.[35] "As Filliou puts it, this allows the reader to 'enter the writing game as a performer rather than as a mere outsider.' "[36] In the excerpt shown in Figure 6.1, he indicates games for the interested reader/participant.

On page 89, shown in Figure 6.1, not only is the book meant to be interactive as a whole but the content in that section is also meant to spur a ludic experience: "gap-filling investigations and games." Situated in the middle of a free-ranging (and frequently coarse) set of musings on art and economics, this section is one of a few with tables to be filled in by the interested reader.

This recalls the blank staves left on the pages of Cardew's graphic-notation magnum opus *Treatise*; the reader-performer is also emphatically a co-author (see also Figure 6.2). The text would not signify the associated work in quite the same way if there were no one playing along with Cardew or with Filliou.

Just as significant are musical scores that fail to overtly acknowledge the contributions of participant co-composers, because they, too, mask playful labor. These range from George Brecht's *Motor Vehicle Sundown (Event)* (1960), in which participants gather in automobiles in the early evening

---

[34] Cheng, *Sound Play*, 131–33.

[35] Atypically for the time, he also acknowledges all of the contributing authors, with the spiral-bound text attributed to "Robert Filliou and the reader, if he wishes, with the participation of John Cage, Benjamin Patterson, George Brecht, Allen Kaprow, Marcelle, Vera and Bjoessi and Karl Rot, Dorothy Iannone, Diter Rot [*sic*], Joseph Beuys. It is a Multi-book. The space provided for the reader's use is nearly the same as the author's own." Robert Filliou, *Lehren und Lernen als Auffuehrungskuenste [Teaching and Learning as Performing Arts]* (Köln and New York: Gebr. Koenig, 1970).

[36] Marc James Léger, "A Filliou for the Game: From Political Economy to Poetical Economy and Fluxus," *RACAR: revue d'art canadienne/Canadian Art Review* 37, no. 1 (2012), 71.

202   INTERPRETIVE LABOR

I suggest gap-filling investigations and games could follow the following schema :

	Traditional Educational Response	Usual Social consequences	Suggested Educational Response	Aimed at social consequences
GENERATION GAP				
TIME GAP				
PERSONALITY GAP				
INITIATION GAP				
POTENCY GAP				
SEXUAL GAP				
MIND GAP				
RESULT GAP				
PERFORMANCE GAP				
....				
....				
....				

Figure 6.1   Filliou, *Lehren und Lernen als Auffuehrungskünste* [*Teaching and Learning as Performing Arts*] (Köln and New York: Gebr. Koenig, 1970), 89. Reproduced with permission. © Estate of Robert Filliou. Courtesy the Estate of Robert Filliou & Peter Freeman, Inc., New York/Paris.

and perform activities such as turning on their cars' headlights, to Cage's *Variations IV*, whose score is made up of small dots and circles printed on transparencies, which are arranged at random on a drawing of the performance space, showing where sounds are to be made.[37] Many artists associated with the quasi-group Fluxus exploited these ideas, drawing attention to the gaps between score and performance. This term, Fluxus, encompasses visual artists, musicians, performing artists, and poets, many of whom worked in and around New York City beginning in the 1960s, and a sister group making art in Europe around the same time. It refers to performances, art and sound installations, and boxes of simple objects; it is also the name given to an effort to publish avant-garde scores. "Fluxus," as I use the term, refers to a group

---

[37] La Monte Young and Jackson Mac Low, eds., *An Anthology of Chance Operations*, 2nd ed. (N.p.: Heiner Friedrich, 1970); John Cage, *Variations IV*: Second of a group of three works of which *Atlas Eclipticalis* is the first and *0'00"* is the third: for any number of players, any sounds or combinations of sounds produced by any means, with or without other activities (New York: Henmar Press, 1963).

THE "GAMER" MODEL   203

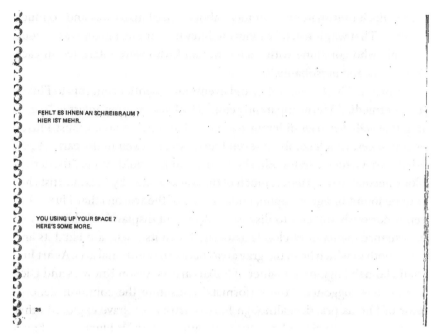

Figure 6.2 Filliou, *Lehren und Lernen als Auffuehrungskünste* [*Teaching and Learning as Performing Arts*] (Köln and New York: Gebr. Koenig, 1970), 25. Reproduced with permission. © Estate of Robert Filliou. Courtesy the Estate of Robert Filliou & Peter Freeman, Inc., New York/Paris.

of artists, rather than a specific direction or movement within contemporary art, although those involved typically considered it to be more complicated. In its early form, the group included George Maciunas, Nam June Paik, Ben Patterson, Emmett Williams, Alison Knowles, Wolf Vostell, Dick Higgins, and Bengt af Klintberg, who worked together to organize concerts in Europe in 1962.[38] They were joined by a number of others, including Jackson Mac Low, George Brecht, La Monte Young, Ben Vautier, Al Hansen, and Milan Knizak. As Ken Friedman explains in his introduction to *The Fluxus Reader*, a number of creative and intellectual genres contributed to the entity of Fluxus. Not only was it an art form; it was also "a way of viewing society and life."[39] One central artist, George Brecht, emphasizes it as a social

---

[38] Owen Smith, "Developing a Fluxable Forum," in *The Fluxus Reader*, ed. Ken Friedman (Chichester, West Sussex: Academy Editions, 1998), 5.
[39] Friedman, *The Fluxus Reader*, ix.

204   INTERPRETIVE LABOR

group: "Each of us had his own ideas about what Fluxus was and so much the better. That way it will take longer to bury us. For me, Fluxus was a group of people who got along with each other and who were interested in each other's work and personality."[40]

Intermedia, Fluxkit multiples, and events are essential concepts to Fluxus art. "Intermedia," a term apparently coined by Dick Higgins, refers to "something that falls *between* different media."[41] This encompasses most Fluxus performances, which combine several forms of art. Even in the early 1990s, Walker Art Center curator Elizabeth Armstrong would write, "the terminology needed to describe . . . much of the work created by Fluxus artists has yet to be found or agreed upon, and it is one of the reasons that Fluxus has been notoriously difficult to discuss, collect, and display."[42] Today, the two performance media most closely associated with its artists are Fluxkits and events, both of which lie in the gray areas between traditional arts. As art historian Hannah Higgins, daughter of Fluxus artists Alison Knowles and Dick Higgins, has suggested, "these [formats] constitute the common denominator of Fluxus practice, although Fluxus artists also have explored other formats, such as music and graphic and painted work."[43] Fluxkits are boxes filled with simple everyday objects and/or printed cards. The performance occurs when a person sifts through the items in the box, reading or playing or whatever they may be inspired to do. Performance, then, exists merely by way of being framed by the premise of performance. In other words, if a simple action takes place in a performance setting, or is merely intended to be a performance, then it is an artistic event, according to (at least some) Fluxus artists. In *American Avant-garde Theater*, Arnold Aronson offers an explanation:

> Theater is created by the simple act of framing an action. Not only does such a definition eliminate questions of hierarchical quality—an Elizabethan tragedy, a juggler on a street corner, and activity seen through a window take on equal weight—but it places the question of intention upon the

---

[40] Smith, "Developing a Fluxable Forum," 7–8.

[41] Michael Nyman, "Seeing, Hearing: Fluxus," in *Experimental Music*, 79.

[42] Elizabeth Armstrong and Joan Rothfuss, *In the Spirit of Fluxus* [catalogue] (Minneapolis, MN: Walker Art Center, 1993), 14, cited in John Held Jr., "A Living Thing in Flight: Contributions and Liabilities of Collecting and Preparing Contemporary Avant-Garde Materials for an Archive," *Archives of American Art Journal* 40, no. 3/4 (2000), 15.

[43] Hannah Higgins, *Fluxus Experience* (Berkeley: University of California Press, 2002), 12.

spectator. Thus, if a spectator places a mental frame around an activity it becomes theater for that observer.[44]

Theater, then, in musical terms, becomes a wide-open concept that can encompass all manner of activity, from staged and costumed presentations with scripted words and music—that is, conventional opera—to a pair of friends gathering to improvise sounds based on the smallest of inspirational sources.

Despite my reservations about art historian Roger Rothman's general theory of Fluxus as hackers, discussed in the previous chapter, there are resonant correlations such as this. Fluxus artists certainly do play with the dominant ideas about music and performance, causing shifts in their meanings. In this way, Fluxus *can* be thought of as hackers, modifying and subverting the norms of theater and other types of performance as they were usually understood at that time. On the other hand, Rothman associates their work with "a radically different principle [from 1960s critical movements], one that begins with affirmation rather than critique, and that sets out to operate within, rather than outside, the informational environment of post-industrial capitalism."[45] While several activities organized by Fluxus artists invite playful interaction, I am not convinced that this is not *also* a form of critique. The art of play effectively calls into question ideas that would otherwise be taken for granted. It reveals the potentially oppressive cultural "rules" governing activities, whether that be typical concert etiquette or whether or not to pour water into a tuba onstage.

The early members of the Fluxus collective had been, at least in part, brought together thanks to John Cage. In 1958, Cage taught a composition class at the New School for Social Research in New York City. Students included George Brecht, Dick Higgins, Allan Kaprow, Al Hansen, and Jackson Mac Low,[46] whose participation points toward two crucial facts: they were interested in the creative process, and they considered themselves musicians. Actually, these artists were more workshop participants than Cage's students. In this class, they used chance operations in musical and poetic experiments, working with available instruments and other objects. Following the performances, the class discussed the "philosophical and

[44] Arnold Aronson, *American Avant-garde Theater: A History* (London: Routledge, 2000), 35.
[45] Roger Rothman, "Against Critique," 790. Rothman identifies useful parallels between some artists associated with Fluxus and some aspects of hacker culture, but some comparisons are provisional at best. In general, I agree that some activities of the two groups align, but remain unconvinced that the political and aesthetic reasons underlying those activities are as wedded as he claims.
[46] Smith, "Developing a Fluxable Forum," 5.

206   INTERPRETIVE LABOR

practical implications of each piece."[47] Cage produced numerous indeterminate works in tandem with his teaching at the New School. In the previous year, he had begun his *Concert for Piano and Orchestra*, and 1958 saw the creation of the graphic/mobile-score work *Fontana Mix*, as well as his lecture *Indeterminacy*, among other works.

In the years immediately after he taught the future Fluxus artists, he created a number of theatrical works that make use of indeterminacy, including *Variations II–IV* (1961–63) and the aptly titled *Theater Piece* (1960). This work, for eight performers, uses a score consisting of numbers. The performers choose words, write them on cards, and then use the numbers in the score to determine which words to act out. Cage instructed the performers to choose the actions because he did not want to tell them to do anything they could not do. Here, a number of elements resonate with the Fluxus aesthetic of simplicity and accessibility. First, *Theater Piece* is theater. Many Fluxus performances are intended to be at least as focused on the visual as on the aural. Also, as in many Fluxus events, the performers are expected to do everyday tasks, and in this case, only ones with which they are comfortable. The nouns and verbs that made up the action in Cage's piece could be randomly selected from a dictionary,[48] and could theoretically be anything the performers chose, either intentionally or not. The performance emphasizes simple actions, which are essential to Fluxus events, and the manner of the performance is also nearly identical. For example, in some of George Brecht's pieces, the score consists of cards on which are printed words that determine the action. His score for *Drip Music (Drip Event)* reads, "For single or multiple performance. A source of dripping water and an empty vessel are arranged so that the water falls into the vessel. Second version: Dripping." Some scores are more ambiguous, such as his *Two Durations*: "red. green."[49] In each of Brecht's works, as with Cage's, the printed words comprising the score direct the performers' actions, but do not offer precise instructions of how to bring those actions into existence.

---

[47] Higgins, *Fluxus Experience*, 2.

[48] See John Cage, "Interview with Michael Kirby and Richard Schechner," *[Tulane] Drama Review* 10, no. 2 (Winter 1965), 63.

[49] See Nyman, "Seeing, Hearing: Fluxus," 77; and Geoffrey Hendricks, ed., *Critical Mass: Happenings, Fluxus, Performance, Intermedia and Rutgers University 1958–1972* (Catalog of an exhibition held at the Mead Art Museum, Amherst, MA, February 1–June 1, 2003 and Mason Gross Art Galleries, New Brunswick, NJ, September 29–November 5, 2003), 44.

THE "GAMER" MODEL 207

Following Cage's definition of theater ("something that engages both the eye and the ear"),[50] many works from this time period and within the so-called avant-garde are theatrical. Perhaps taking cues from their contemporaries in New York City, composers in residence at Buffalo began experimenting with events in similar ways. James Fulkerson, composer and trombonist and a member of the Center of the Creative and Performing Arts from 1969 to 1972, organized the Creative Associate recital held on October 21, 1970. A one-time program called "Spaces and Activities," this was a Fluxus-like set of events with the SEM Ensemble and members of the Center. Accompanying the program is a three-page typescript headed "Notes and Scores," which provides a glimpse into the experience shared by the participants—both audience and "Members of the Center." Fulkerson, at that time in his mid-20s and having just finished his MMus at University of Illinois at Urbana–Champaign, was also in 1970 a composer-in-residence with the New York program Creative Artists Public Service Program (CAPS).[51] Founded that year and funded by the New York State Council on the Arts, the National Endowment for the Arts, and private donations, CAPS was "the first statewide program . . . to provide financial support for individual artists."[52]

At the concert, they began with what Fulkerson called *Two Activities*, both of which are meant for the Buffalo-affiliated performers designated in the program. The score reads:

1) Find a substance, i.e., wool, steel, resin, rubber, wood, etc., and explore your instrument as a sound producing medium.

If you normally hold your instrument, you must suspend it or place it on a table, the floor, or a pedestal. If you normally sit at your instrument, you must walk around it, lie under/on or crawl over/under/around it. If you normally walk around your instrument, perhaps you should suspend yourself.

When you finish, leave.

---

[50] Here, I think Cage implies that theater, in contrast to other musical performances, *intentionally* "engages the eye" as well as the ear. Kostelanetz, *Conversing with Cage*, 107.

[51] "James Fulkerson," *The Living Composers Project* [website], ed. Dan Albertson (last revised January 3, 2016) http://www.composers21.com/compdocs/fulkersj.htm.

[52] Liner notes for *New American Music: New York Section, Composers of the 1970's* [sic], Folkways Records 33903 (1975).

208 INTERPRETIVE LABOR

2) Tell a true story of something which has happened to you or that you have witnessed. If things are funny—laugh; don't act, perform, or pretend. When you finish, leave.[53]

As described by critic John Dwyer, the second was apparently more successful. He writes,

> Earlier there were Mr. Fulkerson's "Two Activities." In one they fooled around with instruments and mikes in the time-honored John Cage manner. The second one was delightfully imaginative, a conversational fugue in which performers in sequence and ultimately all at once related personal experiences. You could listen to one, a few or all, as at a cocktail party. However it reads, it was unusual, capriciously and dramatically effective.[54]

In fact, both critics who reviewed this event compared it to a social gathering. Thomas Putnam used those terms more generally than Dwyer, noting that "there were several games on James Fulkerson's Creative Associate recital Wednesday night . . . It was like a party, only they didn't play Pin the Tail on the Donkey."[55]

Like Max Neuhaus's *Water Whistle*, which would be staged (swimming-pooled?) 18 months later, these pieces have an aspect of good-natured silliness about them, a playful reprieve from the more serious demands of much of the Creative Associates' repertoire.[56] While Dwyer seems to dismiss the first activity as "fool[ing] around," it closely aligns with the types of exploratory practices that engaged the artists affiliated with Fluxus and other avant-garde practices. As in other indeterminate pieces, each performer is responsible for figuring out exactly what to do within the constraints of the instructions, in this case using some physical material to produce amplified sound on, rather than with, their instruments. In the second activity, they have to select which short anecdote to share and how the story will be delivered. Here, the "music" is the resulting mixture of overlapping words

---

[53] James Fulkerson, *Two Activities*, printed in "Notes and Scores" (unpublished program notes), October 21, 1970.

[54] John Dwyer, "13 Chords Connect a Musical Stunt," *Buffalo Evening News* (October 22, 1970).

[55] Putnam, "[Review:] Games at UB Recital."

[56] Herman Trotter, "Underwater 'Music': A New Wave, or Did Audience Get Soaked?" *Buffalo Evening News* (April 19, 1972).

being spoken, and perhaps laughter or other reactions from the performers and audience.

Considering all of these cases of indeterminacy in experimental music—open-ended "scores" that question the very parameters of performance—we begin to build a picture of the work being done by performers (and sometimes by sympathetic audiences). Each instance requires a level of participation analogous to present-day UGC: individuals expressing their views in 140 characters or fewer, or parents posting photographs of their children on social media. In a very real and literal sense, then, most forms of indeterminacy demand UGC; they remain concept art without it.

With that in mind, I would argue that UGC is part of the game itself, and should be understood as central to it. If, with Johan Huizinga, we argue that the playful is a crucially important part of society ("civilization arises and unfolds in and as play"), this is a problem worth taking seriously.[57] Performers and/as players are entertained and challenged, investing their creative energy into their gaming or other performative experiences. What might inspire such behavior? Is a personalized Ie reward enough? I suspect that, in contrast to the aesthetic motivations underlying much modding activity, there is something else going on with other types of UGC. This, I believe, points to a deeper and more primal concern: namely, that of *belonging*. With creative labor, we buy into the gaming economy. The wages of interpretation are acceptance in a community of like-minded creatives. For the artists of the 1960s, that sense of place, of knowing who you are and what you are about, would have been especially vital. As has been well documented by scholars across the humanities, this was an era of student protests, developments in the civil rights movement, and other forms of cultural revolution, which—while urgently necessary—led to significant change. Injecting their personalities and selves into their practices gave artists a way to negotiate this challenge. Simultaneously, the work of creating content also contributes to a community of *makers*, a professional category that was otherwise losing ground. During the war years, the roles of factory worker and skilled laborer were respected and—in the United States, at least—viewed as doing their patriotic duty. In the postwar era, these jobs started losing their cultural capital[58] as industries shifted toward greater automation and speed,

---

[57] Huizinga, *Homo Ludens*, ix.
[58] This might be read more precisely as respectability, but I do see these types of jobs carrying a degree of cultural capital within the working class, at least.

210   INTERPRETIVE LABOR

and even became the targets of outright antagonistic attitudes as workers organized strikes in response to deteriorating working conditions.[59] Anticommunist sentiment and skepticism about socialist agendas lingered in the wake of McCarthyism, galvanizing those sympathetic with the New Left as a community apart.

Beyond the need for a sense of camaraderie, artists may have also been motivated by another basic desire: recognition. Why else would George Maciunas have sent his announcements about terrorizing the art scene in New York to non-sympathetic outsiders?[60] If he had really wanted to organize propaganda actions as he claimed, he would have held meetings or otherwise communicated with those likely to join his mission. As it was, he instead produced only a publicity stunt, and one that nearly tore apart the U.S. branch of Fluxus as it existed at that time. Just as cynically, we might cite more recent events: the explosion of UGC on websites like YouTube and numerous music-sharing sites, where participants trade their work for a chance at fame and fortune. Or, as van Dijck puts it, "Although YouTube and many other video-sharing sites carefully nurture the concept of amateur home-made content, the actual myth driving this concept is the popular belief in 'rags to riches' stories. The UGC market increasingly relates to the professional Hollywood market as stock options relate to shares and bonds—a trade market in potential talents and hopeful pre-professionals."[61] Likewise, we see abundant UGC in the present badge economy; that is, "likes" and "shares" on social media, "top contributor" labels on forums, and so on. Without corresponding compensation in the form of economic or social cachet, this weak form of recognition mimics the exploitation prevalent in so-called reality television.[62]

---

[59] Cf., David Knoke et al., *Comparing Policy Networks: Labor Politics in the U.S., Germany, and Japan* (Cambridge: Cambridge University Press, 1996); Peter B. Levy, *The New Left and Labor in the 1960s* (Urbana: University of Illinois Press, 1994). The latter provides an insightful account of the overlapping networks fighting racial and labor inequality in the era.

[60] Cuauhtémoc Medina, "The 'Kulturbolschewiken' I: Fluxus, the Abolition of Art, the Soviet Union, and 'Pure Amusement,'" *Anthropology and Aesthetics* 48 (Autumn 2005), 181.

[61] van Dijck, "Users Like You?," 53. At that time (2009), it was not yet fathomable for someone to become famous merely via YouTube, but that paradigm has since changed.

[62] Of course, this is a different type of exploitation than that of underpaid factory workers. Individuals who agree to participate in "reality" programming are frequently aiming to break into show business, and engage in potentially demeaning or embarrassing situations hoping for that chance. I categorize this as exploitation because of the extreme financial disparity built into the system: while contestants may receive some prize money or other rewards, the telecom companies producing them typically earn many times that in advertising income. For example, as noted by Denham and Jones, "it took CBS the equivalent of one minute in advertising revenues to recoup

THE "GAMER" MODEL   211

Elsewhere, artists who engaged seriously with indeterminate art-games found their labor validated through recognition of that work—or at least recognition of the resulting artistic or musical experience. I would argue that this is a different type of recognition than the sort associated with mainstream celebrity, though. In this case, I posit that musicians such as Fluxus artists or the Creative Associates may have felt validated for their investments, without necessarily aiming for some broad conception of fame. Here, there is a close connection with the development of community as discussed above. These artists may not have become rich from their efforts with, for example, Fulkerson's *Two Activities*, but they (performers and audience alike) were thus initiated into a club of sorts, in which art was fun and worthwhile. Generating content was an enjoyable challenge, and one that encouraged sharing among the group.

EXPERIMENTAL MUSIC AS A SHARING ECONOMY

Imagine that, one chilly October evening, you attend a recital at the university in town. Having read about the artists in the local papers, you have a general sense that you might be surprised or even bothered by some of what is presented, but curiosity has gotten the better of you and you find yourself in Baird Hall. It is 1970 in Buffalo, and unbeknownst to you, you are about to become an avant-garde performer. After a pleasant start to the concert, watching and listening as people on stage behave strangely with musical instruments and then tell short stories, things get a little more far-out: the musicians and a dancer improvise for fifteen minutes, while strobe lights are projected onto screens. Suddenly, a staffer asks you to put on a blindfold, along with the rest of the audience. The most conventionally game-like score on this recital, James Fulkerson's *Pathways*, thus recalls the children's party game Pin the Tail on the Donkey.[63]

In this case, the (mostly amenable) audience were led from one room to another. The notes read:

---

the $1 million prize it offered a victor on *Survivor*" in its first season. Bryan E. Denham and Richelle N. Jones, "Survival of the Stereotypical: A Study of Personal Characteristics and Order of Elimination on Reality Television," *Studies in Popular Culture* 30, no. 2 (Spring 2008), 81.

[63] As mentioned by critic Thomas Putnam, cited earlier. Putnam, "Games at UB Recital."

YOU ARE BLINDFOLDED
FIND A PATH INTO THE NEW PERFORMING SPACE
FIND A NEW SEAT

T
E
X
T
U
R
SPACES
O   S
U
N
D
S

PLEASE REMAIN BLINDFOLDED
IF YOU CANNOT WALK BLINDFOLDED, TELL US[64]

There was a purpose to this activity, aside from the fun of seeing what would happen when a concert audience was asked to walk around with artificially impaired vision. For the last two pieces, Fulkerson and his crew had set up their instruments in the blacked-out band room, and needed to move the audience there from nearby Baird Hall. Staff members assisted the audience, now active participants in the event whether they liked it or not, and helped them find blindfolds and move into the other room. Like the first two activities, it seems to have been received well, with only one audience member preferring to opt out of the game and being helped further by a member of the Center.[65] By 1970, such performance practices were no longer terribly provocative, as Fluxus artist-practitioners had been experimenting with game-like activities for several years, and the versions mounted in Buffalo tended to be tamer than some of the earlier concept pieces. For example, in Benjamin Patterson's *Please Tell Me about Your Face; Or If You Prefer, about*

---

[64] James Fulkerson, *Pathways*, printed in "Notes and Scores."
[65] Putnam, "Games at UB Recital."

My Face (1964), two performers slap one another's cheeks in alternation. As with Fulkerson's *Pathways*, Alison Knowles's *String Piece* (also 1964) involves the audience, but in this case they are tied up with twine by the performers, invoking a sense of moderate peril.[66] In a piece like *Pathways*, in contrast, this is more about a shared experience than any rebellious, discomfiting practice.

Following that active performance, a group of 13 pianists across the world joined together to play designated chords, which sounding together covered all keys of the instrument. In the dark band room, where the blindfolded audience was led, Petr Kotík held out his portion of the group chord. This musical game involves a dual sharing: the ensemble of performers who cannot hear one another but perform in faith that the others are doing so; and the audience-turned-participants who become attuned to the sonic event. Critic John Dwyer notes that "the globe-girdling mass chord was felt, so to speak, by a blindfolded audience . . . [creating a] vast, implied space effect and spiritual rapport."[67] Fulkerson's notes for this piece, called *Space Music*, read in part, "At 9:20 PM (Buffalo time) October 21, 1970, play this chord as softly as possible on a piano. Hold it until it completely dies away./ As you play this chord, people in the following locations are also playing assigned chords which collectively form an 88-note tone cluster (entire piano range). *Try to sense a connection with everyone involved at that exact moment of playing.*"[68] Just a few months earlier, the University at Buffalo faculty composers had had to move their recital from campus to the downtown Buffalo library at the last minute, because their usual home, Baird Hall, had been tear-gassed and was uninhabitable. As noted by newspaper writer Carol Steiner, "It seemed to give [the audience] something added to think about during the performance of Carlo Pinto's 'Tre Frammenti di Guerra,' songs of the Resistance movement in Venice during World War II."[69] A communal chord, then, may have provided welcome respite from the bombardment of violent and troubling events outside the doors. Fulkerson's *Space Music* is also reminiscent of one of Nam June Paik's more charming compositions, *Half-time:*

---

[66] Various authors/artists, "Fluxus" [foldout section with images and scores/descriptions of pieces], *The Tulane Drama Review* 10, no. 2 (winter 1965), 100.

[67] Dwyer, "13 Chords Connect a Musical Stunt."

[68] Emphasis added. James Fulkerson, program notes for *Spaces and Activities* concert, University at Buffalo (October 21, 1970), 2.

[69] Carol Steiner, "UB Composers Adjust Quickly, Head Downtown," *Buffalo Evening News* (May 9, 1970).

214   INTERPRETIVE LABOR

half-time

or

a piece for the peace.

play on the first July

12 o'clock noon (Greenwitch mean time)

the tonika-accord of c. major

for

10 minutes.

thinking that

someone, somewhere

in the world

is

playing

exactly same time

exactly same sounds[70]

Both Paik and Fulkerson, in these compositions, evoke an imagined ensemble of performers who work together to achieve a musical goal. In this case, the labor is distributed across a network in such a way that the main performer does not even know if anyone else is acting in support.

To some degree, this idea of a shared musical experience relates also to the concept of music as a gift. Rather than forming a temporary community, though, this involves a complex set of interrelationships that may be separated temporally and geographically. As Danielle Fosler-Lussier has shown, music itself—in recordings and live performances—can be given by one cultural institution to another as a way to foster diplomatic relations, for example, through musicians being sent on tours to politically important locations. As discussed in her work on the United States government's Cultural Presentations program during the Cold War, she notes, "The circulation of gifts delineates social relationships, including power relations. The recipient of a gift can incur particular obligations or a lowering of social status, and even gifts that appear to be free can be given in self-interest. [...] the gift of classical music defined social and power relationships among nations much as a gift might link neighbors."[71] In these cases—that is,

---

[70] All spelling and punctuation as in the manuscript. Nam June Paik, *Half-time*, John Cage Notations Project Manuscript Scores, Folder B-197, Northwestern University Music Library.

[71] Danielle Fosler-Lussier, *Music in America's Cold War Diplomacy* (Oakland: University of California Press, 2015), 26.

THE "GAMER" MODEL   215

"classical" (including avant-garde) musicians performing in Eastern Europe, Africa, Asia, and elsewhere—the performances carried a degree of prestige, increasing with the perceived sophistication of the repertoire. In this way, there was a two-way street: the United States tried to demonstrate its cultural erudition by showing off its best artistic representatives, and the hosting states were honored (or were assumed to have been honored) by being considered worthy of that quality. While the precise circumstances of each tour varied, of course, most events were deemed successful at improving perceptions abroad, and modernist and avant-garde music was particularly well received.[72] Music as a gift, then, is a type of economy in which the labor of performers can serve a direct purpose, in addition to the aesthetic pleasures of listening: advancing the cause of American political power.

Subversive Sharing/Subversive Play

Sharing a gift can also be imposed on someone else in a way that threatens the stability of the relationship. We see this in two provocative text scores created in the 1960s, both of which purport to celebrate John Cage while simultaneously challenging his professed aesthetics of discipline and detachment. In what follows, I explore the peculiar tension between homage and provocation within the context of a sharing economy, and bring this tension into conversation with broader questions of play.

At this time, there is little published information about the composer, visual artist, and poet Albert M. Fine, who was affiliated with the Mail-art movement and other sorts of peripheral artistic movements. He had studied with Boulanger in Paris and Persichetti at Juilliard, at about the same time as Philip Glass, and in the 1960s, he composed in multiple genres such as neo-Classical ballet scores, chamber works, and minimalist piano pieces for David Tudor.[73] During this time, he also participated in the activities of Fluxus. Fine's *Experiment for John Cage*, like many of his creations, relies on verbal instructions rather than

---

[72] Fosler-Lussier notes that there were several reasons for this, including that it appealed to intellectuals and young people abroad, and it implied social/political freedom. *Music in America's Cold War Diplomacy*, 31–33.

[73] The University of Iowa Libraries, "MsC 518: Manuscript Register, Alternative Traditions in the Contemporary Arts, The A. M. Fine Collection," Special Collections Department, University of Iowa Libraries.

216   INTERPRETIVE LABOR

conventional or pictographic notation. Written on a postcard and stamped April 26, 1966, it reads:

> Experiment for John Cage:
> Try projecting a strong "emotion" (silently) onto sensitive recording material. Then realize the pattern of waves thus produced in terms of sound [by electronic means applied to the recording material]. Apply identical recording _ in realization to different "projections." Vary and etc.
>
> A.[74]

The *Experiment for John Cage* is a striking example of a work that presupposes no external audience. In fact, it may have been intended literally only for John Cage; in that case, it may never be performed "accurately" again. If the title merely refers to an experiment devised in honor of Cage, though, one *could* perform the piece at any time, provided the appropriate equipment is available and the performer is capable of a strong emotional state. In addition, a performer may realize the work by altering the parameters as indicated by the phrase "vary and etc.," perhaps silently projecting emotions onto someone's voicemail, for example. On the surface, this is an innocuous, perhaps even respectful attempt to engage with the older composer.

In contrast, Korean-born composer and video artist Nam June Paik was a well-known provocateur, notorious for frequently incendiary performance art. Having met Cage at Darmstadt in 1958, Paik began trying to ingratiate himself to Cage, injecting himself into the elder composer's professional and personal world and creating several artworks whose titles refer to Cage. His *Gala Music for John Cage's 50th Birthday* exists in multiple forms, all written in text/verbal notation. The document that appears to be the earliest version is a sheet of crumpled paper glued to cellophane, on which the text is typed. Even a cursory glance will suggest that performance is impossible, if the words are meant to be prescriptive for a performer's actions. It begins: "on Monday sleep with Elizabeth Taylor; on Tuesday sleep with Brigitte Bardot; on Wednesday sleep with Sophia Loren," and so forth.[75] Paik created at least one other document with similar text. This handwritten version, undated

---

[74] Albert M. Fine, John Cage Notations Project Correspondence, Northwestern University Music Library, Box 5, Folder 5.

[75] Nam June Paik, *Gala music for John Cage's 50th birthday* (n.d.), John Cage Notations Project Manuscript Scores, Folder B-197, Northwestern University Music Library.

THE "GAMER" MODEL   217

but estimated to be from 1962,[76] reads "Gala music (nichi nichi kore konichi) for John Cage's 50.5 Birthday." It is subtitled "Music for gentlemen," and has mostly same text as the *Gala Music*, although there are a few variants, some of which are quite troubling: "on Saturday sleep with Malyrin [*sic*] Monroe—if possible," and the even more problematic "on Wednesday sleep with Princess Soraya and make a child," and "on Thursday sleep with a [breeding] street girl," and also adds "et c.—repeat (ad lib)."[77]

Paik was certainly no stranger to making audiences uncomfortable, with theatrical and conceptual works that defied conventions of performance. Part of a broader performance-art moment, his pieces like *One for Violin Solo* and the *Danger Music for Dick Higgins* series play with the idea of the taboo. This is a form of concept art, almost certainly not intended for translation into performance. Incidentally, Cage's third Darmstadt lecture from 1958 opens with the phrase "Nichi nichi kore konichi," conventionally translated as "every day is a good day." Among the wealth of surviving correspondence, including holiday cards, updates about performances, and requests for connections, visits, introductions, and financial connections for himself and others, is a note that reads, "1967 is the 9 years anniversary of our friendship and I am happy that I was acquainted with you just in time. My present for your 61st birthday will be my realization of your complete works (of course, only such pieces which allow realization)."[78] Judging by the documents that Cage preserved, theirs was an ambivalent relationship. Paik frequently conveys his admiration for and appreciation of Cage, but this occasionally seems disingenuous, or at least possibly exaggerated.[79]

---

[76] Estimated date refers to folder and document order within the Notations Collection and its finding aid.

[77] If this manuscript dates from the second half of 1962, it would have been written just after Monroe's death, and four years after Soraya's husband, Shah Mohammed Reza Pahlavi of Iran, divorced her for failing to produce an heir. Nam June Paik, John Cage Notations Project Correspondence, Northwestern University Music Library, Box 10, Folder 4 [1961–Oct. 1966]. In the version published in *Kalendar*, "breeding" is changed to "bleeding." In other correspondence, Paik sometimes uses "r" and "l" interchangeably, for example, writing to Cage, "1967 is the 9 years anniversaly of our friendship," and "my poor English vocaburary," suggesting that either term may have been intended. Box 10, Folder 5 [Nov. 1966–1973].

[78] Paik, John Cage Notations Project Correspondence, Box 10, Folder 5 [Nov. 1966–1973], Northwestern University Music Library.

[79] For example, in the early 1970s he was arranging a public-TV appearance, and claimed that if Cage did not participate, he would commit suicide. He writes, "By some reason, you don't appear, I will stage the world first televised REAL video-harakiri by myself . . . therefore if you don't want to go into the troubles of writing a necrologue of N.J. Paik and attend his funeral, please, come rather to your birthday party here at WGBH." Paik, John Cage Notations Project Correspondence, Box 10, Folder 5.

218   INTERPRETIVE LABOR

For all the communication between Cage and Paik, I have been able to find no evidence of the dedicatee's reaction to the *Gala Music*. The "music for gentlemen" version was filed with other letters and documents that Cage had collected in the early 1960s, and we know the first version had been submitted (but not used) for the *Notations* book, but in 1964 Paik wrote, "I enclose the galamusic for your 50th birthday and hope that you don't mind it," suggesting that either he had not enclosed it in the earlier letter or that he forgot and re-sent it, or that Cage had simply not responded. The following year, a postscript in another letter notes that the piece was printed in the 1965 issue of the avant-garde art periodical *Kalender*, and that he would present it to Cage if he did not have it. There is some inconsistency in this dating of the *Gala Music's* publication: the Everson Museum of Art identifies it as having been published in the 1962 edition, but the Bonotto foundation lists it in the 1965 issue, corroborating Paik's letter. In any case, Paik contributed to both volumes, and since the letter dates from the middle of the decade, it seems likely that Cage still had not given any indication that he had received a copy of the score earlier. Given Cage's rejection of other eroticized art and performances, especially of his own works, he may have been not at all amused by having his name connected with Paik's work. In this way, I see Paik's provocations as a form of subversive play—a way of imposing his ideas on other artists. While the *Gala Music* and related scores are not games per se, Paik seems to have approached the entire encounter as game-like: he foisted the problematic documents onto Cage, perhaps just to see what would happen.

As with Paik, written correspondence between Cage and Albert Fine had been going on for some time. A postcard dated February 1966 indicates that the young composer had already started to lay the groundwork for his *Experiment* piece, in the somewhat absurd language found in a number of his works. He writes,

> John: it is not enough to suggest silence—but to understand [and utilize] the possibilities of projection through the silence—then, concentrating "silently" on an F# I project a different nexus of intention than, say, a silent projection of a dish of spaghetti . . . (variations of appetite—projections of sauce subtleties, etc.). Properly rehearsed & combined with the actualities, the world of art will be thoroughly expanded.[80]

---

[80] Fine, John Cage Notations Project Correspondence, Box 5, Folder 5, Northwestern University Music Library.

THE "GAMER" MODEL   219

On another card, postmarked the same date as the score, he writes, "John, have you ever worked directly & exclusively with sound vibrations above & below the audible hearing range?"[81] To be sure, Fine's pieces are part of a larger practice of text-based scores. His *Experiment* dates from a few years after the rise of event scores by other avant-garde artists like Yoko Ono and George Maciunas. George Brecht's *Water Yam*, partly organized by Maciunas, was compiled in 1963, and Brecht became a key figure in this hybrid genre, which was simultaneously poetry, musical score, visual art, and trigger for action. Liz Kotz notes the "conceptual ambiguity" of these texts, arguing that "when they are read at all, these 'short form' scores are seen as tools for something else . . . scripts for a performance or project or musical piece which is the 'real' art—even as commentators note the extent to which, for both Brecht and Ono, this work frequently shifts away from realizable directions toward an activity that takes place mostly internally, in the act of reading or observing."[82] Fine's composition may inhabit both aspects: it could be used as instructions for action, but is also effective as a thought experiment. Most of Paik's word scores, on the other hand, are shocking in their utter impracticality for performance. They, I think, reside closely to Kotz's "alternate poetics," in which "the instructions themselves [become] poetic material."[83]

Many of the activities of Fluxus—however that group is defined—run counter to an aesthetics of discipline, rigor, and adherence to a system. Specifically, the *Experiment for John Cage* and *Gala Music for John Cage's 50th Birthday* push up against Cage's professed philosophy. Following a period of expressive composition in the 1940s, Cage had pulled away from the separation of art and life that he perceived among Abstract Expressionist artists. Cage ultimately rejected what Bernstein calls the "overwrought emotionalism and heroic existentialist narcissism that characterized the abstract expressionist aesthetics."[84] In stark contrast to this turn, the *Experiment* instructs its performer to project strong emotions. Its entire essence is affective: without the personal, even sensual investment of the participant, it fails. Likewise, the *Gala Music* evokes the embodied self: a thought experiment grounded in the erotic. This would likely have been unthinkable for

---

[81] Fine, John Cage Notations Project Correspondence, Box 5, Folder 5.
[82] Liz Kotz, "Post-Cagean Aesthetics and the 'Event' Score," *October* 95 (Winter 2001), 57.
[83] Kotz, "Post-Cagean Aesthetics," 61.
[84] David Bernstein, "John Cage and the 'Aesthetic of Indifference,'" in *The New York Schools of Music and Visual Art*, ed. Steven Johnson (New York: Routledge, 2002), 118.

220 INTERPRETIVE LABOR

Cage. Following a 1975 performance of *Song Books* at the June in Buffalo festival, for example, Cage was so disturbed by Julius Eastman's sexualized realization of *0'00"* that he regretted having composed the piece.[85] As Ryan Dohoney argues, Eastman's performance enacted critical camp as part of a broader theatrical, homoerotic practice, rather than as an attack on Cage.[86] However, the composer was disturbed to the point of giving a lecture the next day about the problems of the offending performance. Eastman's performance, then, "revealed the limits of Cagean acceptance and the degree to which Cagean freedom was contingent on performers having internalized Cage's own tastes and preferences," and those preferences clearly excluded the risqué.[87]

The *Gala Music* and the *Experiment*, in short, evoke the erotic and the affective. Their language-based scores convey personality: hardly the dispassionate, disciplined self championed by Cage. This issue of personality is raised in a 1963 interview between Robert Ashley and Morton Feldman.[88] Ashley belabors the point somewhat, trying to push an idea that a new generation of composers were capitalizing on the images of Cage, Feldman, and others. Feldman's responses are especially illuminating here. In discussing a performance of one of his graph pieces, in which musicians had intentionally circumvented his aesthetic motivations, he likens their actions to "homicide" of the piece, and wonders aloud whether Nam June Paik brings "an element of violence" that may have been implied in Cage but that was exploited to serve Paik's own ambitions.[89] This provocation is evident particularly in the *Gala Music* but also subtly active in Fine's *Experiment*. Both composers antagonize Cage though their uncomfortable closeness to the emotional, embodied being. In some ways, they really are *for* John Cage: they can be read as aligning with his own work, and especially with his ambivalence between aesthetics and authorship. At the same time, they introduce an ethical question by being promoted as homages to Cage while violently antagonizing his carefully crafted image. My sense is that all three men—Cage, Paik, and Fine—struggled with a desire to break with convention, to question the limits of music, and to embrace new ideas, while simultaneously needing some of

---

[85] Steve Schlegel, "John Cage at June in Buffalo, 1975" (MA thesis, State University of New York at Buffalo, 2008).

[86] Dohoney, "John Cage, Julius Eastman," 39–62.

[87] Dohoney, "John Cage, Julius Eastman," 47.

[88] Morton Feldman and Robert Ashley, "Around Morton Feldman," March 1963, Morton Feldman Collection, Paul Sacher Foundation.

[89] Feldman and Ashley, "Around Morton Feldman," 14.

THE "GAMER" MODEL   221

those conventions to support their more experimental projects. Paik's *Gala Music* and Fine's *Experiment* not only challenge Cage's carefully managed aesthetics, they also demonstrate that he was unable to achieve his ideal of detachment. They shine a spotlight on the inherent tension between his attempted disinterest and the regulated parameters of performance that he held close. His systematic, controlled approach already always grates against chance and contingency; this is the real Cagean paradox. Works like these try to draw the unwilling Cage out of that control, opening up an ethics of possibility from which he would continue to retreat. Beyond the cognitive labor of engaging with these inaudible works, Cage is also faced with the disciplinary labor of resistance: to emotions, to the body, and to personality.

To return to the related but unequal ideas of the sharing economy and the (perhaps unwanted) gift, we might consider Yoko Ono's well-known *Cut Piece*, which calls for participants from the audience to approach the performer and cut off bits of her or his clothing with scissors. Works like Ono's, Rothman argues, "make it clear that social production demands acceptance of vulnerability. Sharing can only take place in an environment in which individual participants willingly suspend their autonomy and thus their instinct for self-preservation."[90] In the case of the *Gala Music* and possibly the *Experiment*, Cage apparently refused to participate, effectively shutting down Paik and Fine's problem-laden attempts to share. Thinking about experimental music as sharing, then, opens up a wide world of playful activity: playing with roles within a group, altering parameters of performance and participation, and shifting the old performer-audience divide. It also immediately suggests a closeness among those present that may be absent in some other types of musical events, for example, a symphony performance. While I acknowledge the connections felt between audiences and performers in operatic and orchestral performances, there is typically a physical distance and a separation of the two groups' activities that precludes the same sort of participation that happens when an audience is, say, tied up by the performers or led blindfolded through the performance space. In a sharing economy, creative labor is distributed among the network—so, it is necessarily a more equitable form of work, as long as all agree democratically. On the other hand, as we have seen, there are cases where sharing becomes an imposition of values, at which point the game loses its appeal. In highly

---

[90] Roger Rothman, "Fluxus, or the Work of Art in the Age of Information," *symplokē* 23, no. 1–2 (2015), 322.

222   INTERPRETIVE LABOR

networked environments (e.g., computers, Fluxus, experimental music as a whole, maybe even most if not all modern systems), sharing is the essence of the landscape. Without connected nodes, the network fails.

As suggested by pieces like Paik's *Gala Music for John Cage's 50th Birthday*, musical playfulness can be used toward subversive ends. Play itself can be a critical, interventionist act both within and outside music, and has been employed for "artistic, political, and social critique and intervention."[91] While art historian and digital humanities researcher Mary Flanagan's project emphasizes using alternative games to build a theory of avant-garde game design specifically (especially "activist game design"), her ideas benefit from adaptation and expansion to other playful artistic practices. One key point of departure between her work and Rothman's is in their respective conceptions of Fluxus. That group, Flanagan argues, "saw the forces of critical play—unplaying, reskinning, and rewriting—as the most urgent quality of art itself. . . . Opposed to seriousness and the ossification of art as object, Fluxus artists sought a new art practice, one that was open to humor, intimacy, player agency, and various aspects of performance."[92] Of course, this generalizes a bit, as there have been numerous artists affiliated with Fluxus over a few decades, with diverse ideas and approaches. However, I agree that—for the most part—most Fluxus artists *were* doing critique. Through game-like events, Happenings, kits, and other works (plays?), they defied expectations and revised what it meant to be an artist.

To some extent, this continues to mirror Cardew's relationship with Stockhausen's compositions. In his realization work on *Carré*, Cardew was playing with the score and instructions from his mentor. As discussed in a previous chapter, this increasingly took on a subversive motive as he felt subjugated by the elder composer. Likewise, many artistic games created by Fluxus and the Creative Associates function as embodiments of a critical posture. Thinking back to the S.E.M. Ensemble and Guests recital held September 30, 1970, for example, Kotík and his crew effectively rewrote the norms of concert attendance. By placing musicians in three separate rooms, the audience had to actively participate by moving through the space, or limit themselves to only one set (or, as suggested in the program, "take a break from listening and go to the basement for some refreshment, to play

---

[91] Flanagan, *Critical Play*, 2.
[92] Flanagan, *Critical Play*, 96.

ping-pong or bowl.")[93] The 1972 *SEM Gives a Lecture* event, too, turned the lecture-recital on its ear by eating dinner onstage, then sharing dessert with their bemused audience. (In the resonant words of critic Tom Putnam, "Dull routine is a monster easily slain on Center programs."[94]) Most of the musical events and happenings discussed throughout this text, in fact, involve some sort of critical play. The interventions made by these artists, especially within new experiments in indeterminacy, simultaneously expand our understanding of music and introduce new questions about creative and interpretive labor.

CONCLUSION: MUSICAL GAMES AS TECHNOLOGIES

Musical games, sometimes, are exactly what they seem. Take John Zorn's *Cobra*, for example, which by 1993 would be cited as "a favored pastime among New York improvisers."[95] In contrast to Cardew's approach with *Treatise* a couple of decades earlier, Zorn did create rules for the piece, although—like Cardew—he chose not to publish any guidelines for it. Zorn biographer John Brackett notes that

> Even with the scattered and incomplete information relating to *Cobra* that began to appear in print in the early and mid-1990s, the work has remained somewhat of an enigma. The enigmatic aura surrounding *Cobra* is, I believe, intentional and can be traced back to Zorn's reluctance to publish a complete and detailed account of the work, preferring instead a desire for *Cobra* (and his other game pieces) to exist and persist as part of an oral tradition.[96]

Zorn's series of game pieces, his best-known works from the 1970s and 1980s, involve various types of rule sets that inform improvised sounds and actions by the performers. Elsewhere, Brackett has noted that these experiments were likely inspired, if not directly influenced, by Zorn's experiences with

---

[93] Petr Kotík, S.E.M. Ensemble, & Guests, "Creative Associate Recital I" program, State University of New York at Buffalo Department of Music (September 30, 1970).
[94] Tom Putnam, "UB Arts Center Slays 'The Usual,'" *Buffalo Courier-Express* (September 13, 1970).
[95] Ann Powers, "All-Girl Cobra: Knitting Factory," *New York Times* (February 4, 1993).
[96] John Brackett, "Some Notes on John Zorn's *Cobra*," *American Music* 28, no. 1 (Spring 2010), 47.

224 INTERPRETIVE LABOR

members of the Black Artists' Group (BAG) and Chicago's AACM while attending Webster College in St. Louis; Zorn carried that interest in improvisation with him when he returned to New York in the mid-1970s.[97] Following a performance in 1989, a critic explains,

> Like many of Mr. Zorn's works, *Cobra* (first performed in 1984) is a semi-improvisatory piece that draws its structure and substance from an elaborate set of rules rather than from a score. To direct the work, Mr. Zorn held up cards bearing symbols. What was performed was a function not only of the symbol but also of how high Mr. Zorn held it, how quickly he lowered it, and whether he was wearing his baseball cap.[98]

The score itself, now available online despite the composer's wishes, raises more questions than it answers: the left side lists body parts (e.g., mouth, nose, eye, etc.), with lists of what appear to be roles, actions, and other categories listed beneath each. The right side is a bit more clear, with some icons noting hand cues and operations (marked "squad leader ONLY").

Without an accompanying set of explanations for each of these cryptic symbols and short phrases, an ensemble wishing to realize this score would be in trouble. Some terms suggest possible musical interpretations (duos, drone, coda) but others are more mysterious—cartoon trades? Spy? Guerrilla? It helps to know that the title comes from another diversion: a war-simulation game based on the 1944 battle at Normandy, first printed in 1977 and released in expanded form in 1984 by the company that produced *Dungeons & Dragons*.[99] In the musical version of *Cobra*, some related actions are possible, such as a player going "rogue" and forming a "guerrilla" squad to temporarily take over the proceedings. In practice, this only works well when everyone involved takes the game seriously, respecting the rules and the actions of others in the group and paying close regard to the prompter, who serves as intermediary among the performers and the directions.[100]

---

[97] Zorn also admired much of the work of New York avant-gardists Earle Brown and others, whom Brackett cites as further inspiring the game pieces. John Brackett, *John Zorn: Tradition and Transgression* (Bloomington: Indiana University Press, 2008).

[98] Allan Kozinn, "Review/Music: John Zorn and 'Cobra,'" *New York Times* (September 3, 1989).

[99] Brackett, "Some Notes on John Zorn's *Cobra*," 44–45.

[100] A videotaped performance was given in 2014 at New England Conservatory. Performers of this version were Anthony Coleman, prompter; Eden MacAdam-Somer, violin; Alexandra Simpson, viola; Breanna Ellison, french horn; Leo Hardman-Hill, trumpet; Mariel Austin, trombone; Wendy Eisenberg, Will Greene, electric guitar; Damon Smith, keyboard; Evan Allen, piano; Kirsten Lamb, electric double bass; Simon Hanes, electric bass; Aaron Edgcomb, drums. Recorded November 4, 2014, at NEC's Jordan Hall; available at youtube.com/watch?v = UdNdSJUf_8I&t = 154s.

Zorn himself is adamant about the importance of the group dynamic. Regarding choosing performers, he has noted, "You want to pick someone not just because they can play well, but because they have a good sense of humor, or they get along with the guy across the room . . . because they have a lot of compositional ideas (and maybe play awful) but they're going to make good calls. There's a lot of reasons to call someone into the band in a game piece."[101] And elsewhere, "Whether we like it or not, the era of the composer as autonomous musical mind has just about come to an end. . . . Over the past 40 years, many of the great composers have worked with collaborators. Ellington had Billy Strayhorn as well as his amazing band, John Cage had David Tudor and Takehisa Kosugi . . . Philip Glass and Steve Reich work closely with their ensembles. The collaborative aspects of the recording process make this even clearer."[102] *Cobra*, then, represents the sort of democratic ideal to which critical play might aspire. Neither utopia nor anarchy, because there is still one individual at the center who may ignore requests from the other players, *Cobra* is a physical and sonic embodiment of the messy procedures of social play. *Cobra*'s reception suggests that this is its most important aspect, inspiring another generation to rethink the porous boundaries between work and play—perhaps even prompting 21st-century phenomena like live coding.[103] Like laptop ensembles modifying algorithms on stage, or like soccer players shifting formations on the fly, rules-based improvisation demands quick thinking and deep communication. To cite Zorn once again,

> The game pieces are meant for improvisers working in a live situation. They weren't really meant to be recorded because they're like a sport—It's an exciting thing to see, it's very visual when all the musicians are making signs at each other, trying to get each other's attention . . . My role there was to set up rules so that the people in the band have to make decisions, have to communicate.[104]

---

[101] John Zorn interview with Cole Gagne, *Soundpieces 2: Interviews with American Composers* (Metuchen, NJ: Scarecrow Press, 1993), 521, cited in Brackett, "Some Notes on John Zorn's *Cobra*," 48.

[102] John Zorn, liner notes to *Spillane*, Nonesuch 979 172-1 (1987).

[103] Composer-programmer Nick Collins cites *Cobra* as one possible precedent for this phenomenon ("programming on the spot, typically for an audience in a concert setting"). Nick Collins, "Live Coding of Consequence," *Leonardo* 44, no. 3 (June 2011), 207.

[104] John Zorn, cited in Gene Santoro, "Music: John Zorn," *The Nation*, (January 30, 1988).

226 INTERPRETIVE LABOR

Through game-like compositions such as Zorn's *Cobra*, we continue to be confronted with many of the issues raised in this chapter: what it means to participate in game-like artistic movements, the necessity of critical play, and the ways in which labor can so easily be obscured by playful practices.

***

Play and playfulness suggest a way of interacting with the world that is marked in some way. In Huizinga's formulation,

> Play is distinct from "ordinary" life both as to locality and duration . . . Play begins, and then at a certain moment it is "over". It plays itself to an end. While it is in progress all is movement, change, alternation, successions, association, separation. [. . .] All play moves and has its being with a play-ground marked off beforehand either materially or ideally, deliberately or as a matter of course. . . . The arena, the card-table, the magic circle, the temple, the stage, the screen, the tennis court, the court of justice, etc., are all in form and function play-grounds, i.e., forbidden spots, isolated, hedged round, hallowed, within which special rules obtain. All are tempo-rary worlds within the ordinary world, dedicated to the performance of an act apart.[105]

Within the temporary world, actors are a bit more free to experiment. Avant-garde music's world, perhaps, is double-walled: music as a whole is itself already playful, and many iterations of this play take the form of games. With that in mind, Flanagan's provocative suggestion becomes all the more resonant with music: "Games can be thought of more productively as situations with guidelines and procedures. Perhaps games are *themselves* a technology."[106] Certainly, if we think about games and, by extension, music-making as technologies, we bring these questions into conversation with other technologies, highlighting once again issues of work and labor in (especially) the digital age.

As Christopher Leslie notes in an insightful review, "new media employ traditional forms of exploitation. The way that media owners have co-opted the labor power of their customers is seen as far back as when telephone companies trained their customers to dial their own numbers instead of

---

[105] Huizinga, *Homo Ludens*, 9–10.
[106] Flanagan, *Critical Play*, 7.

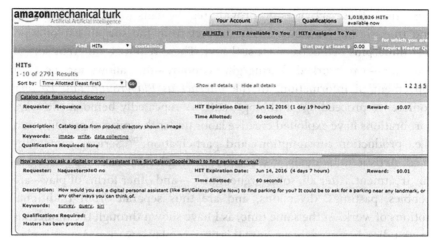

Figure 6.3 Amazon Mechanical Turk interface from 2016 showing 2,791 microjobs available. Screen capture by the author.

using an operator."[107] Now we create much of the content that occupies our "free" time, in the form of blogs, photographs, and videos. Likewise, on microwork platforms (the best known being Amazon Mechanical Turk), laborers complete "human intelligence tasks" (HITs) such as "transcribing a snippet of handwritten text, . . . rating the relevance of a search engine result, and selecting the most representative frame in a video clip."[108] For this labor, registered workers receive fractional compensation (often $0.01 USD per HIT; see Figure 6.3).

In the present media-rich environment, then, all of our tiny contributions of UGC add up to form a massive (mostly online) networked world, made possible by labor from across a spectrum of formats. Looking to the practices of experimental artists from Paik to Zorn, Fulkerson to Filliou, we recognize traces of a conception of labor that continues to problematize the line between work and play. This playful work—encompassing activities like interpreting graphic notation, modifying a map in a video game, or competing against others to decode word puzzles as quickly as possible—runs the risk of masking the very effort that makes it exist. At the

[107] Christopher Leslie, "Review: Trebor Scholz (ed.) *Digital Labor: The Internet as Playground and Factory*," *Media, Culture, and Society* 36, no. 4 (2014), 552.
[108] Eliane Bucher and Christian Fieseler, "The Flow of Digital Labor," *New Media and Society* 19, no. 11 (November 2017), n.p.

228   INTERPRETIVE LABOR

same time, these activities do provide real benefits to their participants, and thus should be conceptually distinct from the sort of exploitation that underpins orthodox Marxist theory. These require a different sort of economy—a networked sharing/gift economy—that allows for the fluid movement of information. In the *Internet as Playground and Factory* conference-proceedings anthology, authors repeatedly bemoan the ways corporations have exploited creative labor under the guise of prosumption (i.e., production-consumption) and participation.[109] Serious games, indeed. Artistic individuals, it seems, are particularly prone to poor or unfair treatment. After all, some argue, music—and other forms of play—are hobbies, pastimes, diversions, and are thus separate from traditional notions of work. At the same time, as I have shown through the numerous case studies discussed throughout this project, play is work and work is play, especially when the (musical) work demands interpretation.

---

[109] Trebor Scholz, ed., *Digital Labor: The Internet as Playground and Factory* (New York: Routledge, 2012).

CONCLUSION

INTERPRETIVE LABOR BEYOND EXPERIMENTALISM

After working as a performer myself after a long absence, I began to see the hope of a new ensemble music being a voluntary, rather than a coercive, affair. . . . If chamber music is going to be anything more than cut-rate orchestra music, more and more responsibility has to be given to the people who really make the thing happen on stage. Otherwise, why not replace them with a computed and precise taped-sound-source? This position leads, of course, to the writing of a different kind of music, both more "abstract" and more "figurative," in which the chief means used by the composer consists precisely in those human qualities that only a live performer, and one who is *involved*, can infuse into the part before him on the stand.

— Michael Sahl[1]

In the spring of 1967, a group of musicians gathered in an art gallery in Buffalo, New York, to present new works by Elliott Carter, William Albright, and others. The final piece on the program, *Plus Minus* (1963), brought together composer-pianist Cornelius Cardew and percussionists Edward Burnham and Jan Williams. One of the more demanding compositions in the avant-garde repertoire, *Plus Minus* in this instance has prompted Williams to convert just a fraction of its complicated guidelines and symbols into dozens of pages of new score material, resulting in a performance that lasts more than 30 minutes.[2] The same year, in West Germany, the QUaX

[1] Emphasis in original. Michael Sahl, program note for *Ensemble '65* (February 19, 1966), Albright-Knox Art Gallery Auditorium, Buffalo, NY (University at Buffalo Music Library).
[2] Personal communication with Jan Williams (May 5, 2016); "Evenings for New Music Catalog 1964–1980," University at Buffalo Music Library, 18; Evenings for New Music, concert program, Albright-Knox Art Gallery Auditorium (April 29, 1967), Special Collections, University at Buffalo Music Library.

Interpretive Labor. Kirsten I. Speyer Carithers, Oxford University Press. © Oxford University Press 2025.
DOI: 10.1093/9780197698815.003.0008

230 INTERPRETIVE LABOR

Ensemble gave the premiere of Czech musician Petr Kotík's *Kontrabandt*, commissioned by Stockhausen as head of the Electronic Music Studio at Westdeutschen Rundfunk (WDR) Cologne.[3] Neither composer provided a playable score; instead, performers were tasked with translating their markings into a working document from which to perform.

Kontrabandt and *Plus Minus*, then, make serious demands on their performers. This is better stated, of course, by saying that the *creators* of these works make time-deferred demands on those who perform them, as do other composers of all manner of experimental music.[4] This raises the important question of hierarchy among participants in this repertoire. John Cage stated in 1967 that "

[a]rt instead of being an object made by one person is a process set in motion by a group of people. Art's socialized. [...] [M]usic is a social art, social in the sense that it has consisted, formerly, of people telling other people what to do, and those people doing something that other people listen to. What I would like to arrive at, though I may never, what I think would be ideal, would be a situation in which no one told anyone what to do and it all turned out perfectly well anyway.[5]

Despite Cage's utopian vision, these social interactions are never truly balanced. Performers—both within and beyond avant-garde movements—labor to navigate their relationships to the score and to the composer, their work obscured by the conventions of artistic recognition. The investigations undertaken for this project reveal time and again that, even in the most "free" of improvisatory and indeterminate works, someone is always telling someone else what to do.[6]

***

As I sit down to write this conclusion, in the middle of 2023, I am struck by the degree to which labor issues have gained mainstream attention. From the backlash against Starbucks' alleged union-busting to the solidarity between writers

---

[3] Kotík, "Petr Kotík Biography" (personal communication provided February 23, 2016); program notes, "S.E.M. Ensemble Plays Cage, Wolff, and Kotík" (December 3, 2010), ISSUE Project Room, Brooklyn, NY.

[4] By this I mean that the composers' demands are not necessarily connected to the time of composition. A performer in 2023 desiring to interpret an indeterminate piece from 1965, for example, may have no direct contact with the composer (who may no longer be available for such a consultation) but those requirements are still an integral part of that work's identity.

[5] Cage, "Diary," 145; interview with Alan Gillmor, in Kostelanetz, *Conversing with Cage*, 78–79.

[6] Portions of the preceding two paragraphs appeared previously in my "Stockhausen as CEO: The Executive Model of Interpretive Labour," *Contemporary Music Review* (2022): 1–2.

CONCLUSION 231

and actors in the WGA and SAG-AFTRA strikes, "hot labor summer" seems to be going strong. Of course, if workers were treated well and compensated fairly, there would be no need for such actions. I suppose that statement reflects my motivations and biases driving both this specific project and my research overall: in drawing attention to activities that may not previously have been theorized as "work," I aim to demonstrate the myriad ways experimental/ avant-garde art, which may feel inaccessible or superfluous to some, is actually not so different from other forms of creativity. This project also engages with labor history/labor studies more broadly, which thus far has largely excluded creative work, and shows how ideas from one particular idiom might shed light on others. Experimentalism's practitioners may rely on different codes and norms than most classical or popular musicians, but the underlying work that individuals do to create, understand, prepare, and produce it is actually quite ordinary. At the same time, because this music did not have the benefit of normative performance practice (in contrast to genres like Baroque sonatas, American musical theater, or late-Romantic symphonies, for example), the work involved was often more pronounced, and sometimes took unusual forms, when it was first being developed. In documenting the practices of a broad cross-section of musicians, we gain a better understanding of processes of interpretation and of those who choose to invest their time and resources into such pursuits. The story of Interpretive Labor, therefore, demonstrates the value of a marriage between labor studies and music studies. Without considering labor-related issues, I would argue, we musicologists simply reinforce hegemonic structures and other inequitable systems.

Throughout this book, I have made a case for considering labor-related issues alongside the aesthetic, structural, and sonic questions frequently addressed in studies of "experimental" music. As I hope to have demonstrated at the close of each chapter, the concept of Interpretive Labor and its various forms can be instructive to anyone whose work involves some degree of creativity, from computer programmers to social-media influencers, interior designers to event planners, and—of course—musicians. Looking ahead, industries such as filmmaking and music production seem to show no sign of returning to a slower, more deliberate pace. If anything, technological tools are crowding out human participants, as seen in some of the concerns brought forth in recent contract negotiations.[7] Given the rapid pace of

---

[7] For example, "the Writers Guild is asking that their contract include language stipulating that every credited writer be a human person, that screenplays, treatments, outlines, and other 'literary material,' in industry parlance, can't be written by ChatGPT or its ilk. Also, they're asking that AI

232   INTERPRETIVE LABOR

development and current lack of meaningful oversight, one might rightfully be concerned about what this all means for the future of creative work.[8] Will a majority of new songs be AI-generated?[9] Will we be able to tell if something was made by actual people? Will writing as we know it become obsolete?

In the meantime, Interpretive Labor gives us a toolkit for understanding acts of performance—both musical and economic. Each model of Interpretive Labor, and its representative case studies, demonstrates a unique but interrelated form of engagement with the work—the often hidden or under-examined effort—of being a contemporary artist. This text has been structured along an axis of control, with the first model most closely tied to the composer's "intentions," and the latter models illustrating more open-ended interpretive practices. From the boss-like Executive calling the shots to the Scientist exploring new ways of engaging with music and its technologies, the Administrator making sure events happen on time and on budget, the Hacker subverting a given system, and the Gamer making a new system entirely: all of these characters, and their characteristics, make up a rich network of working methods that can help us understand creative work more broadly.

To be sure, the specific compositions, ensembles, and experiences discussed throughout are meant to illustrate these different forms of work; at the same time, most could just as easily be applied to other models, and other examples could have been selected to demonstrate how each model functions in practice. This project has benefited greatly from the perspectives of individuals in numerous roles and identity groups, in order to present a range of case studies that connect to broader considerations of work, such as racial and gender-based pay gaps and the 21st-century gig economy.

[artificial intelligence] not be used to generate source material or be trained on work created by WGA members." Angela Watercutter, "AI, the WGA Strike, and What Luddites Got Right," *Wired*, May 5, 2023, https://www.wired.com/story/wga-strike-artificial-intelligence-luddites/.

[8] During a recent discussion about this project, a particularly insightful colleague—Devin Burke—asked a question that gave me pause: what happens to interpretive labor when it's done by a non-person? My first instinct is to say that such a thing is not, in fact, interpretive labor—that (at least at present) data modeling and "smart" computing are not (yet) capable of true interpretation. Already, though, this feels like a defensive reaction. More time and research are needed to investigate the implications of technologically generated work on the theories and practices laid out throughout this book.

[9] Kris Holt, "Spotify Has Reportedly Removed Tens of Thousands of AI-Generated Songs," *Engadget*, May 9, 2023, https://www.engadget.com/spotify-has-reportedly-removed-tens-of-thousands-of-ai-generated-songs-154144262.html.

As noted earlier, interpretation in experimental music also reveals hidden forms of labor. For example, institutional administrators and composers' assistants have expended significant amounts of effort and energy to help their colleagues succeed; however, their work has historically been under-recognized, if it is discussed at all. I hope that participants in such areas will be served by a deeper understanding of labor's connections to institutions like the academy, entrepreneurial ensembles, and other crucial nodes in new-music networks. Notably, many of these groups are actively shaping both higher-education curricula and professional music industries today, so I see Interpretive Labor as applicable to teachers, performers, university administrators, development officers, and so on. A thorough understanding of these processes sheds valuable light on labor issues within and beyond the arts.

INTERPRETATION AS LABOR

Writing in 1938, Johan Huizinga could not have predicted the wild new directions music would take in the following decades. Still, his discussion of what he calls the play-element or play-quality of music remains relevant:

> Like play, music is based on the voluntary acceptance and strict application of a system of conventional rules: time, tone, melody, harmony, etc. This is true even where all the rules we are familiar with have been abandoned.... In this inner diversity of music, therefore, we have renewed proof that it is essentially a game, a contract valid within circumscribed limits.... The need for strenuous training, the precise canon of what is and what is not allowed, the claim made by every music to be the one and only valid norm of beauty—all these traits are typical of its play-quality. And it is precisely its play-quality that makes its laws more rigorous than those of any other art. Any breach of the rules spoils the game.[10]

The specific components of music's play-quality have changed drastically since the interwar era, largely through the experiments of avant-garde musicians. By questioning the validity of parameters like strenuous training, the musical canon, and even the very notion of beauty, these artists formed

[10] Huizinga, *Homo Ludens*, 214.

234   INTERPRETIVE LABOR

a new paradigm for musical play itself. At the same time, the notion of play serves as a foil for the notion of work. Through the many case studies presented throughout this book, I have become convinced that we are now in an era in which the work/play division is especially porous, and that this is especially evident in musical performance. This porosity makes it particularly urgent to be mindful of the politics of these artistic practices, which threaten to conceal their demanding, multi-faceted interpretive labor.

In short, in this project I have restaged interpretation *as* labor. The procedures of interpreting a musical text (typically, a score) are conceived as a form of labor (the expenditure of effort/energy). For much of the labor discussed, this can also be conceived as the work of performance practice, such that the theory of Interpretive Labor actually radicalizes performance practice as a mode of production. To consider Wark one more time: "Production meshes objects and subjects, breaking their envelopes, blurring their identities, blending each into new formation. Representation struggles to keep up, to reassign objective and subjective status to the products of production. Production is the repetition of the construction and deconstruction of objectivity and subjectivity in the world."[11] Is this so abstract as to be devoid of meaning, or is Wark perhaps on to something here? How might musical interpretation repeat the construction/deconstruction of objectivity and the construction/deconstruction of subjectivity? The act of interpretation—the *work*—creates a musical object (an iteration), and simultaneously deconstructs and destabilizes the previous understanding of the work-concept beholden to that score up until that point. Likewise, interpretive work shapes the subjectivity of the composer and performer (and, if assigning agency to inanimate entities in line with actor-network theory, also of the musical work in the sense of an artistic entity). We seem to need this playful use of language—the shades of meaning of "work" and even "musical work"—to get at the heart of this question: that is, what does musical interpretation *mean* and what does it *do*?

***

In reflecting on this project as a whole, I might consider whether and how my own practices—researching, writing, learning—are driven by interpretation. I remain unconvinced by Wark's criticism that "many of the conflicts within higher education are distractions from the class politics of knowledge.

[11] Wark, *A Hacker Manifesto*, 69.

CONCLUSION   235

Education 'disciplines' knowledge, segregating it into homogenous 'fields,' presided over by suitably 'qualified' guardians charged with policing its representations. [. . .] From this containment of the desire for knowledge arises the circular parade of false problems of discipline and the discipline of false problems."[12] This, to me, is unnecessarily cynical; however, I do recognize that musicology, like other academic disciplines, has been slow to embrace "outside" perspectives and methods. Looking back over conference programs from the last decade and a half suggests a recent and welcome explosion of diversity within and across fields, though, and I am genuinely excited about these new directions. Any interdisciplinary work—and I aim for this to be so—is at least in part a hack of the conventional divisions within academe. (At the same time, interdisciplinarity itself is becoming the ruling class, so perhaps I am not actually hacking at all.)

Thinking of Gertrude Stein's provocative 1935 poem-essay on masterpieces, I see a parallel with the continuously contested disciplinary boundaries in music research itself. Toward the end of the piece, she writes, "When you are writing before there is an audience anything written is as important as any other thing and you cherish anything and everything that you have written. After the audience begins, naturally they create something that is they create you, and so not everything is so important, something is more important than another thing, which was not true when you were you." [13] I find this to be a powerful idea: for writers, perhaps an idea – or rather, an iteration of an idea – is "concretized" once it is shared with an audience. It is reified into a *thing*, and that thing's impact is largely determined by the disciplinary schema in which it is read. Music functions the same way. While the field of musicology has (happily) experienced a rapidly expanding scope in genre, geography, and explanatory theory, it remains distinct from its "sister" field, ethnomusicology. There are historical reasons for this, well-documented by scholars in both fields, though it is encouraging to see many colleagues involved in multiple academic societies (the American Musicological Society, the Society for Ethnomusicology, and numerous subdisciplinary institutions), and conducting research and teaching across now-permeable boundary lines that would have been firm just a couple of decades

[12] Wark, *A Hacker Manifesto*, 28.
[13] I thank Petr Kotík for his opera based on this text for prompting this line of thinking. Gertrude Stein, "What Are Master-Pieces and Why Are There So Few of Them," reprinted in *The American Poetry Review* 27, no. 4 (July/August 1998), 9–10.

236   INTERPRETIVE LABOR

ago. Musicology, though, still struggles to define itself, as was made painfully clear in a 2016 debate over the language used in a blog post sponsored by the AMS.[14] We might ask: why do departments and schools of music still teach courses called "Western Art Music," when all forms of music-making have deep, important meaning? What makes something qualify as "art" music, anyway? Is it, as Burkholder argues, those pieces composed "for contemplation as works of art," which, as he rightly notes, would leave out much of what is now pedagogically canonical?[15] What is, or should be, the primary objective of our field: understanding the entity (through score study, formal analysis, and related text-based methodologies) or understanding the identity (through interviews, participant-observation, and related person-based methodologies)?[16] These sorts of questions have defined the debates shaping music research for decades. In my view, the study of Interpretive Labor is an example of how all of these methods can be put to use to develop a close reading of a particular musical phenomenon: exploring both the texts and the contexts provides a fuller picture of the experience of performing indeterminacy. Again, this is not especially innovative (scholars have been doing this work for decades), but it is a deliberate component of how and why this book is framed as it is.

As suggested earlier, experimental concepts, particularly musical indeterminacy and—more broadly—experimentalism, are difficult to define in a meaningful way. By this I mean that their meanings have been established,

[14] See Pierpaolo Polzonetti, "Don Giovanni Goes to Prison: Teaching Opera behind Bars," *Musicology Now* (blog), https://musicologynow.org/don-giovanni-goes-to-prison-teaching-opera-behind-bars/ and, more importantly, the myriad conflicting responses it prompted, including comments on the AMS blog itself; the "Brown AMS Avenger" blog and comments posted there (http://brownamsavenger.livejournal.com/612.html), and Twitter posts classified with #AMSSoWhite. Cf. also Tamara Levitz, "Decolonizing the American Musicological Society," a colloquium talk given at NYU on February 18, 2016, available online at http://music.as.nyu.edu/object/music.colloquium.levitz.

[15] Not to mention the question of what could possibly be meant by "Western" in the 21st century, and why that might be a relevant scope. J. Peter Burkholder, "Music of the Americas and Historical Narratives," *American Music* 27, no. 4 (Winter 2009), 400.

[16] C.f. Erica Mugglestone, "Guido Adler's 'The Scope, Method, and Aim of Musicology' (1885): An English Translation with an Historico-Analytical Commentary," *Yearbook for Traditional Music* 13 (1981), 1–21; *Ethnomusicology* 41, no. 2: Special Issues in Ethnomusicology (Spring–Summer 1997); Kay Kaufman Shelemay, "Crossing Boundaries in Music and Musical Scholarship: A Perspective from Ethnomusicology," *The Musical Quarterly* 80, no. 1 (Spring 1996), 13–30; James Currie, "Music after All," *Journal of the American Musicological Society* 62, no. 1 (Spring 2009), 145–203; Roger W.H. Savage, "Crossing the Disciplinary Divide: Hermeneutics, Ethnomusicology and Musicology," *College Music Symposium* 49/50 (2009/2010), 402–8; Tamara Levitz et al., "Musicology beyond Borders?" *Journal of the American Musicological Society* 65, no. 3 (Fall 2012), 821–61; Gabriel Solis, "Thoughts on an Interdiscipline: Music Theory, Analysis, and Social Theory in Ethnomusicology," *Ethnomusicology* 56, no. 3 (Fall 2012), 530–54; and many others.

CONCLUSION   237

contested, and re-drawn even in the few decades in which they have been considered within musical scholarship. Nearly every individual author puts forth a unique explanation, making these concepts especially salient for a post-Derridean sort of investigation. If meaning is always ambiguous because each person brings his/her/their own set of contexts to the project, it is further muddied by disagreement on even basic concepts. In this way, "indeterminacy" may function as a *pharmakon*: it points toward other terms, carries with it traces of mid-century experimentalism, and signals a point in history in which it was common practice to presuppose an evolutionary narrative in music.[17]

In the end, my own interpretive labor as a historian and writer runs the risk, and reaps the rewards, of rewriting history. To quote Rheinberger: "Historial [*sic*] thinking . . . has to accept such recursive forces as being inherent in any hindsight—and hence, in the interpretation, or iterative action on the part of the historian."[18] Over the course of these chapters, I have examined the act of interpretation and the meanings inherent within it, and brought indeterminate-music practices into alignment with developing theories of labor. In considering the executive, scientist, administrator, hacker, and gamer roles and their attendant models of Interpretive Labor, it becomes necessary to rethink creative work. Now, much of our work as artists and scholars involves playing with labor and working with interpretation: a productive performance practice, indeed.

---

[17] A pharmakon is both remedy and poison; it enables the coming into play of oppositions without allowing itself to be fully encompassed by them. Likewise, its ambiguity/instability threatens dialectics. See Jacques Derrida, "Plato's Pharmacy," in *Dissemination*, trans. Barbara Johnson (Chicago: University of Chicago Press, 1981), 61–171.

[18] Rheinberger, *Toward a History of Epistemic Things*, 178.

Bibliography

Abrams, Muhal Richard and John Shenoy Jackson. "Association for the Advancement of Creative Musicians." *BlackWorld* 23, no. 1 (November 1973): 72–74.

Adorno, Theodor. *Philosophie der neuen Musik*. Frankfurt-am-Main: Europäische Verlagsanstalt, 1958.

Anderson, Virginia. "'Well, It's a Vertebrate . . .': Performer Choice in Cardew's *Treatise*." *Journal of Musicological Research* 25, no. 3–4 (December 2006): 291–317. https://doi.org/10.1080/01411890600840578.

Aronson, Arnold. *American Avant-Garde Theater: A History*. London: Routledge, 2000.

Asplund, Christian. "Frederic Rzewski and Spontaneous Political Music." *Perspectives of New Music* 33, no. 1/2 (1995): 418–41.

Austin, Larry, John Cage, and Lejaren Hiller. "An Interview with John Cage and Lejaren Hiller." *Computer Music Journal* 16, no. 4 (1992): 15. https://doi.org/10.2307/3680466.

Aytes, Ayhan. "Return of the Crowds: Mechanical Turk and Neoliberal States of Exception." In *Digital Labor: The Internet as Playground and Factory*, edited by Trebor Scholz, 79–97. New York: Routledge, 2013.

Babbitt, Milton. "The Composer as Specialist (1958)." In *Collected Essays of Milton Babbitt*, edited by Stephen Peles, 48–54. Princeton, NJ: Princeton, 2003.

Bakla, Petr. "Ostrava Days 2007: Institute and Festival of New Music." *Czech Music* 3 (April 2007): 26–31.

Bakla, Petr. "Ostrava 2007—A Backward Look." *Czech Music* 3 (July 2007): 30–34.

Bakla, Petr. "Petr Kotík: As a Composer, I've Always Been a Loner." *Czech Music* 2 (2011): 5–6.

Barbash, Jack. "The Work Humanization Movement: U.S. and European Experience Compared." In *Labor Relations in Advanced Industrial Societies: Issues and Problems*, edited by Benjamin Martin and Everett M. Kassalow, 184–195. Washington, DC: Carnegie Endowment for International Peace, 1980.

Barron, Stephanie, and Sabine Eckmann, eds. *New Objectivity: Modern German Art in the Weimar Republic, 1919–1933*. Los Angeles: Los Angeles County Museum of Art, 2015.

Battcock, Gregory, ed. *Breaking the Sound Barrier: A Critical Anthology of the New Music*. New York: E.P. Dutton, 1981.

Beal, Amy C. "A Place to Ply Their Wares with Dignity: American Composer-Performers in West Germany, 1972." *The Musical Quarterly* 86, no. 2 (2002): 329–48.

Benjamin, Walter. *Selected Writings, Vol. I, 1913–1926*. Edited by Marcus Bullock and Michael W. Jennings. Cambridge, MA: Harvard University Press, 1996.

Benjamin, Walter. "The Work of Art in the Age of Mechanical Reproduction [1935]." In *Illuminations*, edited by Hannah Arendt, translated by Harry Zohn, 217–252. New York: Schocken Books, 1969.

Berliner, Paul. *Thinking in Jazz: The Infinite Art of Improvisation*. Chicago: University of Chicago Press, 1994.

Bermann, Sandra, and Catherine Porter, eds. *A Companion to Translation Studies*. Blackwell Companions to Literature and Culture. Chichester, England: Wiley-Blackwell, 2014.

Bidet, Jacques, and Anne Bailey. "Questions to Pierre Bourdieu." *Critique of Anthropology* 13–14 (1979): 203–8.

Bohlman, Philip V. "Translating Herder Translating: Cultural Translation and the Making of Modernity." In *The Oxford Handbook of the New Cultural History of Music*, edited by Jane F. Fulcher, 501–22. New York: Oxford University Press, 2011.

240 BIBLIOGRAPHY

Bohn, James Matthew. "An Overview of the Music of Lejaren Hiller and an Examination of His Early Works Involving Technology." PhD diss., University of Illinois, 1997.

Bolt, Barbara. *Heidegger Reframed: Interpreting Key Thinkers for the Arts*. London: I.B. Tauris, 2011.

Borgo, David. "Negotiating Freedom: Values and Practices in Contemporary Improvised Music." *Black Music Research Journal* 22, no. 2 (Autumn 2002): 165–88.

Born, Georgina. "For a Relational Musicology: Music and Interdisciplinarity, beyond the Practice Turn: The 2007 Dent Medal Address." *Journal of the Royal Musical Association* 135, no. 2 (2010): 205–43.

Born, Georgina, ed. *Music and Digital Media: A Planetary Anthropology*. Chicago: UCL Press, 2022. https://doi.org/10.14324/111.9781800082434.

Born, Georgina. "On Musical Mediation: Ontology, Technology and Creativity." *Twentieth-Century Music* 2, no. 1 (March 2005): 7–36. https://doi.org/10.1017/S147857220500023X.

Bourdieu, Pierre. *Distinction: A Social Critique of the Judgement of Taste* [1979], trans. R. Nice. Cambridge, MA: Harvard University Press, 1984.

Bourdieu, Pierre. "The Forms of Capital." In *Handbook of Theory and Research for the Sociology of Education*, edited by J.G. Richardson, translated by R. Nice, 241–258. New York: Greenwood Press, 1986.

Boyer, Robert. "Pierre Bourdieu, a Theoretician of Change? The View from Regulation Theory." In *The Institutions of the Market: Organizations, Social Systems, and Governance*, edited by A. Abner and N. Beck, 348–97. Oxford: Oxford University Press, 2008.

Brackett, John. *John Zorn: Tradition and Transgression*. Bloomington: Indiana University Press, 2008.

Brackett, John. "Some Notes on John Zorn's *Cobra*." *American Music* 28, no. 1 (April 1, 2010): 44–75. https://doi.org/10.5406/americanmusic.28.1.0044.

Bravve, Elina, and Megan Bolton. "Out of Reach: America's Forgotten Housing Crisis." Washington, DC: National Low Income Housing Coalition, March 2012.

Brooks, William. "In re: 'Experimental Music.'" *Contemporary Music Review* 31, no. 1 (February 2012): 37–62.

Brown, Earle. "The Notation and Performance of New Music." *The Musical Quarterly* 72, no. 2 (1986): 180–201.

Brown, Ronald A., and Alok Kumar. "The Scientific Method: Reality or Myth?" *Journal of College Science Teaching* 42, no. 4 (March–April 2013): 10–11.

Bucher, Eliane, and Christian Fieseler. "The Flow of Digital Labor." *New Media and Society* 19, no. 11 (November 1, 2017): 1868–86. https://doi.org/10.1177/1461444816644566.

Buettner, Stewart. "Cage." *International Review of the Aesthetics and Sociology of Music* 12, no. 2 (December 1981): 141–51.

Burkholder, J. Peter. "Music of the Americas and Historical Narratives." *American Music* 27, no. 4 (Winter 2009): 399–423.

Burnett, D. Graham. "The Objective Case: A Review of 'Objectivity.'" *October* 13 (2010): 133–44.

Caernarven-Smith, Patricia. "Hackers Are Bad for Business." *Technical Communication* 35, no. 2 (1988): 143–45.Cage, John. "Interview with Michael Kirby and Richard Schechner." *[Tulane] Drama Review* 10, no. 2 (Winter 1965): 50–72.

Cage, John. *Silence: Lectures and Writings*. Middletown, CT: Wesleyan University Press, 1961.

Cage, John. *Variations IV*. New York: Henmar Press, 1963.

Cage, John. *A Year from Monday*. Middletown, CT: Wesleyan University Press, 1967.

Cardew, Cornelius. "Notation: Interpretation, etc." *Tempo, New Series*, no. 58 (1961): 21–33.

Cardew, Cornelius. "Report on 'Carré': Part 2." *The Musical Times* 102, no. 1425 (November 1961): 698–700. https://doi.org/10.2307/949169.

Cardew, Cornelius. "Report on Stockhausen's 'Carré.'" *The Musical Times* 102, no. 1424 (October 1961): 619–22. https://doi.org/10.2307/951181.

BIBLIOGRAPHY 241

Cardew, Cornelius. *Stockhausen Serves Imperialism, and Other Articles*. London: Latimer New Dimensions Limited, 1974.

Cardew, Cornelius. *Treatise Handbook*. London: Hinrichsen, 1971.

Carithers, Kirsten L. Speyer. "Musical Indeterminacy as Critical and Affirmative Play." *Journal of the Association for the Study of the Arts of the Present* 8, no. 1 (January 2023): 119–142.

Carithers, Kirsten Speyer. "Stockhausen as CEO: The Executive Model of Interpretive Labour." *Contemporary Music Review* 41, no. 2–3 (2022): 155–171. https://doi.org/10.1080/07494 467.2022.2080453.

Carlos, Wendy. "Tuning: At the Crossroads." *Computer Music Journal* 11, no. 1 (1987): 29–43. https://doi.org/10.2307/3680176.

Caudwell, Christopher [pseud., Christopher St. John Sprigg]. "D. H. Lawrence: A Study of the Bourgeois Artist." In *Studies in the [/a] Dying Culture*, 11–13. London: Lawrence & Wishart, 1938.

Chan, Chak Kwan, and Zhaiwen Peng. "From Iron Rice Bowl to the World's Biggest Sweatshop: Globalization, Institutional Constraints, and the Rights of Chinese Workers." *Social Service Review* 85, no. 3 (September 2011): 421–45. https://doi.org/10.1086/662328.

Chantler, Abigail. "Revisiting E. T. A. Hoffmann's Musical Hermeneutics." *International Review of the Aesthetics and Sociology of Music* 33, no. 1 (June 2002): 3–30. https://doi.org/ 10.2307/4149784.

Cheng, William. "Role-Playing toward a Virtual Musical Democracy in *The Lord of the Rings Online*." *Ethnomusicology* 56, no. 1 (February 1, 2012): 31–62. https://doi.org/10.5406/ethn omusicology.56.1.0031.

Cheng, William. *Sound Play: Video Games and the Musical Imagination*. Oxford: Oxford University Press, 2014.

Childs, Barney, Christopher Hobbs, Larry Austin, Eddie Prévost, Keith Rowe, Derek Bailey, Harold Budd, Lee Kaplan, Vinny Golea, Elliott Schwartz, Larry Solomon, Malcolm Goldstein, John Silber, Davey Williams, and Pauline Oliveros. "Forum: Improvisation." *Perspectives of New Music* 21, no. 1/2 (Autumn 1982–Summer 1983): 26–111.

Clague, Mark. "ONCE.MORE.: An Introduction." *University Musical Society (UMich)* (blog), October 28, 2010.

Clarke, Michael, and Peter Manning. "The Influence of Technology on the Composition of Stockhausen's *Octophonie*, with Particular Reference to the Issues of Spatialisation in a Three-Dimensional Listening Environment." *Organised Sound* 13, no. 3 (December 2008): 177–87. https://doi.org/10.1017/S1355771808000277.

Coenen, Alcedo. "Stockhausen's Paradigm: A Survey of His Theories." *Perspectives of New Music* 32, no. 2 (1994): 200–225. https://doi.org/10.2307/833609.

Cohen, Brigid. "Boundary Situations: Translation and Agency in Wolpe's Modernism." *Contemporary Music Review* 27, no. 2–3 (April 2008): 323–41. https://doi.org/10.1080/ 07494460801951439.

Cohen, Brigid. *Musical Migration and Imperial New York: Early Cold War Scenes*. Oxford: Oxford University Press, 2022.

Coleman, E. Gabriella. *Coding Freedom: The Ethics and Aesthetics of Hacking*. Princeton, NJ: Princeton University Press, 2013.

Collins, Karen, ed. *From Pac-Man to Pop Music: Interactive Audio in Games and New Media*. Aldershot, UK: Ashgate, 2008.

Collins, Karen. *Game Sound: An Introduction to the History, Theory and Practice of Video Game Music and Sound Design*. Cambridge, MA: MIT Press, 2008.

Collins, Nick. "Live Coding of Consequence." *Leonardo* 44, no. 3 (June 2011): 207–11. https:// doi.org/10.1162/LEON_a_00164.

Collins, Nick, and Julio d'Escriván, eds. *Cambridge Companion to Electronic Music*. 2nd ed. Cambridge: Cambridge University Press, 2017.

Corrin, Lisa Graziose, and Corinne Granof, eds. *A Feast of Astonishments: Charlotte Moorman and the Avant-Garde, 1960s–1980s*. Evanston, IL: Northwestern University Press, 2016.

242 BIBLIOGRAPHY

Currie, James. "Music after All." *Journal of the American Musicological Society* 62, no. 1 (April 1, 2009): 145–203. https://doi.org/10.1525/jams.2009.62.1.145.

Daston, Lorraine, and Peter Galison. *Objectivity*. New York: Zone Books, 2007.

de Bértola, Elena. "On Space and Time in Music and the Visual Arts." *Leonardo* 5, no. 1 (1972): 27–30. https://doi.org/10.2307/1572468.

de Man, Paul. "'Conclusions' on Walter Benjamin's 'The Task of the Translator' Messenger Lecture, Cornell University, March 4, 1983." *Yale French Studies*, no. 97 (2000): 10–35. https://doi.org/10.2307/2903212.

Demers, Joanna. *Listening through the Noise: The Aesthetics of Experimental Electronic Music*. Oxford: Oxford University Press, 2010.

Denham, Bryan E., and Richelle N. Jones. "Survival of the Stereotypical: A Study of Personal Characteristics and Order of Elimination on Reality Television." *Studies in Popular Culture* 30, no. 2 (Spring 2008): 79–99.

Derrida, Jacques. *Dissemination*. Translated by Barbara Johnson. Chicago: University of Chicago Press, 1981.

Derrida, Jacques. *Specters of Marx: The State of the Debt, the Work of Mourning and the New International*. Hoboken, NJ: Taylor and Francis, 2012.

Derrida, Jacques, and Lawrence Venuti. "What Is a 'Relevant' Translation?" *Critical Inquiry* 27, no. 2 (2001): 174–200.

Desan, Mathieu Hikaru. "Bourdieu, Marx, and Capital: A Critique of the Extension Model." *Sociological Theory* 31, no. 4 (December 2013): 318–42.

di Laccio, Gabriella. *Equality and Diversity in Global Repertoire*. England: Donne UK, 2022. Accessed July 24, 2023. https://donne-uk.org/wp-content/uploads/2021/03/Donne-Rep ort-2022.pdf.

Dohoney, Ryan. "The Anxiety of Art: Morton Feldman's Modernism, 1948–1972." PhD diss., Columbia University, 2009.

Dohoney, Ryan. "John Cage, Julius Eastman, and the Homosexual Ego." In *Tomorrow Is the Question: New Directions in Experimental Music Studies*, edited by Benjamin Piekut, 39–62. Ann Arbor: University of Michigan Press, 2014.

Donnelly, K. J., William Gibbons, and Neal Lerner, eds. *Music in Video Games: Studying Play*. New York: Routledge, 2014.

Donovan, Gregory T., and Cindi Katz. "Cookie Monsters: Seeing Young People's Hacking as Creative Practice." *Children, Youth and Environments* 19, no. 1 (2009): 197–222.

Dörries, Matthias. "Life, Language, and Science: Hans-Jörg Rheinberger's Historical Epistemology." *Historical Studies in the Natural Sciences* 42, no. 1 (February 1, 2012): 71–82. https://doi.org/10.1525/hsns.2012.42.1.71.

Dungey, Nicholas. "The Ethics and Politics of Dwelling." *Polity* 39, no. 2 (April 2007): 234–58.

Feldman, Morton. *The King of Denmark*. Glendale, NY: C.F. Peters, 1965.

Felski, Rita. "Critique and the Hermeneutics of Suspicion." *M/C Journal* 15, no. 1 (November 26, 2011): n.p. https://doi.org/10.5204/mcj.431.

Filliou, Robert, et al. *Lehren und Lernen als Auffuehrungskuenste [Teaching and Learning as Performing Arts]*. Köln and New York: Gebr. Koenig, 1970.

Flanagan, Mary. *Critical Play: Radical Game Design*. Cambridge, MA: MIT Press, 2009.

Flanagan, Robert J. *The Perilous Life of Symphony Orchestras: Artistic Triumphs and Economic Challenges*. New Haven, CT: Yale University Press, 2012.

"[Foldout]: Fluxus." *The Tulane Drama Review* 10, no. 2 (1965): 100. https://doi.org/10.2307/ 1125235.

Forster, Michael N. "Herder's Philosophy of Language, Interpretation, and Translation: Three Fundamental Principles." *The Review of Metaphysics* 56, no. 2 (2002): 323–56.

Fosler-Lussier, Danielle. *Music in America's Cold War Diplomacy*. Oakland: University of California Press, 2015.

BIBLIOGRAPHY 243

Fosler-Lussier, Danielle. "Review of Jakelski, Lisa, *Making New Music in Cold War Poland: The Warsaw Autumn Festival, 1956–1968*." H-Diplo, H-Net Reviews. April 2017. https://www.h-net.org/reviews/showrev.php?id=48728.

Foss, Lukas. "The Changing Composer-Performer Relationship: A Monologue and a Dialogue." *Perspectives of New Music* 1, no. 2 (Spring 1963): 45–53.

Fox, Christopher. "Stockhausen's Plus Minus, More or Less: Written in Sand." *The Musical Times* 141, no. 1871 (2000): 16–24. https://doi.org/10.2307/1004650.

Frader, Laura L. "Labor History after the Gender Turn: Transatlantic Cross Currents and Research Agendas." *International Labor and Working-Class History* 63 (April 2003): 21–31. https://doi.org/10.1017/S014754790300005X.

Frederickson, Jon, and James F. Rooney. "The Free-Lance Musician as a Type of Non-Person: An Extension of the Concept of Non-Personhood." *The Sociological Quarterly* 29, no. 2 (1988): 221–39.

Friedlander, Joshua P. "Year-End 2020 RIAA Revenue Statistics." Recording Industry Association of America, 2020.

Friedman, Ken, ed. *The Fluxus Reader*. Chichester, West Sussex: Academy Editions, 1998.

Froneman, Willemien. "'Composing According to Silence': Undecidability in Derrida and Cage's *Roaratorio*." *International Review of the Aesthetics and Sociology of Music* 41, no. 2 (December 2010): 293–317.

Gadamer, Hans-Georg. *Philosophical Hermeneutics*. Translated by David E. Linge. Berkeley: University of California Press, 1976.

Gadamer, Hans-Georg. *Truth and Method*. Translated by Joel Weinsheimer and Donald G. Marshall. 2nd rev. ed. New York: Continuum, 1994.

Gann, Kyle. "Petr Kotík's *Many Many Women*: A Monument from the 1970s." CD liner notes for remastered album *Petr Kotík: Many Many Women*. Dog W/A Bone, 2000.

Gill, Stephen. "The Global Panopticon? The Neoliberal State, Economic Life, and Democratic Surveillance." *Alternatives: Global, Local, Political* 20, no. 1 (1995): 1–49.

Goehr, Lydia. *The Imaginary Museum of Musical Works: An Essay in the Philosophy of Music*. Rev. ed. Oxford: Oxford University Press, 2007.

Gontarski, S. E. "'What It Is to Have Been': Bergson and Beckett on Movement, Multiplicity and Representation." *Journal of Modern Literature* 34, no. 2 (2011): 65–75. https://doi.org/10.2979/jmodelite.34.2.65.

Gracyk, Theodore. "Who Is the Artist If Works of Art Are Action Types?" *Journal of Aesthetic Education* 35, no. 2 (2001): 11–23. https://doi.org/10.2307/3333669.

Granat, Zbigniew. "Open Form and the 'Work-Concept': Notions of the Musical Work after Serialism." PhD diss., Boston University, 2002.

Grant, Morag Josephine. "Experimental Music Semiotics." *International Review of the Aesthetics and Sociology of Music* 34, no. 2 (2003): 173–91.

Gray, Nicholas. "Of One Family? Improvisation, Variation, and Composition in Balinese Gendér Wayang." *Ethnomusicology* 54, no. 2 (Spring/Summer 2010): 224–56.

Grazian, David. "Neoliberalism and the Realities of Reality Television." *Contexts* 9, no. 2 (2010): 68–71.

Gregg, Melissa. *Counterproductive: Time Management in the Knowledge Economy*. Durham, NC: Duke University Press, 2018.

Griffiths, Paul. "A Stockhausen Survey." *The Musical Times* 118, no. 1614 (August 1977): 637–39. https://doi.org/10.2307/960277.

Grimshaw, Mark, ed. *Game Sound Technology and Player Interaction: Concepts and Developments*. Hershey, PA: Information Science Reference, 2011.

Groesbeck, Rolf. "Cultural Constructions of Improvisation in Tāyampaka, a Genre of Temple Instrumental Music in Kerala, India." *Ethnomusicology* 43, no. 1 (Winter 1999): 1–30.

Gronemeyer, Gisela. "Seriousness and Dedication: The American Avant-Garde Cellist Charlotte Moorman." In *Charlotte Moorman: Cello Anthology*, n.p. Alga Marghen (audio CD box set), Milan, 2006.

244 BIBLIOGRAPHY

Grubbs, David. *Records Ruin the Landscape: John Cage, the Sixties, and Sound Recording.* Durham, NC: Duke University Press, 2014.

Guck, Marion A. "Analysis as Interpretation: Interaction, Intentionality, Invention." *Music Theory Spectrum* 28, no. 2 (October 2006): 191–209. https://doi.org/10.1525/mts.2006.28.2.191.

Haefeli, Sara Heimbecker. "Review: *This Life of Sounds: Evenings for New Music in Buffalo.*" *American Music* 30, no. 1 (April 1, 2012): 105–7. https://doi.org/10.5406/americanmusic.30.1.0105.

Haight, Marjorie May. "Value in Outsourcing Labor and Creating a Brand in the Art Market: The Damien Hirst Business Plan." *The American Economist* 56, no. 1 (Spring 2011): 78–88.

Hamlin, Cynthia Lins. "An Exchange between Gadamer and Glenn Gould on Hermeneutics and Music." *Theory, Culture and Society* 33, no. 3 (May 2016): 103–22. https://doi.org/10.1177/0263276415576218.

Hanna, Joseph F. "The Scope and Limits of Scientific Objectivity." *Philosophy of Science* 71, no. 3 (July 2004): 339–61. https://doi.org/10.1086/421537.

Hanoch-Roe, Galia. "Musical Space and Architectural Time: Open Scoring versus Linear Processes." *International Review of the Aesthetics and Sociology of Music* 34, no. 2 (2003): 145–60.

Hara, Kotaro, Abigail Adams, Kristy Milland, Saiph Savage, Chris Callison-Burch, and Jeffrey P. Bigham. "A Data-Driven Analysis of Workers' Earnings on Amazon Mechanical Turk." In *Proceedings of the 2018 CHI Conference on Human Factors in Computing Systems*, edited by Regan Mandryk and Mark Hancock, 1–14. Montreal, QC, Canada: ACM, 2018. https://doi.org/10.1145/3173574.3174023.

Harbinson, William G. "Performer Indeterminacy and Boulez's Third Sonata." *Tempo*, New Series, no. 169 (50th Anniversary 1939–1989, June 1989): 16–20.

Havelková, Tereza. "Petr Kotík's Umbilical Cord." *Czech Music* 2003-1 (January/February 2003): 8–11.

Hedges, Stephen A. "Dice Music in the Eighteenth Century." *Music and Letters* 59, no. 2 (1978): 180–87.

Heidegger, Martin. *Being and Time.* Translated by Joan Stambaugh, revised by Dennis J. Schmidt. Albany: State University of New York Press, 2010.

Heile, Björn. "Musical Modernism, Sanitized." *Modernism/Modernity* 18, no. 3 (2011): 631–37. https://doi.org/10.1353/mod.2011.0055.

Held, John. "A Living Thing in Flight: Contributions and Liabilities of Collecting and Preparing Contemporary Avant-Garde Materials for an Archive." *Archives of American Art Journal* 40, no. 3/4 (2000): 10–16.

Helmbold, Lois Rita, and Ann Schofield. "Women's Labor History, 1790–1945." *Reviews in American History* 17, no. 4 (December 1989): 501–18. https://doi.org/10.2307/2703424.

Henderson, Andrew D., and James W. Fredrickson. "Top Management Team Coordination Needs and the CEO Pay Gap: A Competitive Test of Economic and Behavioral Views." *The Academy of Management Journal* 44, no. 1 (February 2001): 98–99.

Hendricks, Geoffrey, ed. *Critical Mass: Happenings, Fluxus, Performance, Intermedia and Rutgers University 1958–1972* (Catalog). Amherst, MA and New Brunswick, NJ, 2003.

Hepokoski, James. "The Dahlhaus Project and Its Extra-Musicological Sources." *19th-Century Music* 14, no. 3 (Spring 1991): 221–46.

Hesmondhalgh, David, Ellis Jones, and Andreas Rauh. "SoundCloud and Bandcamp as Alternative Music Platforms." *Social Media and Society* 5, no. 4 (October 2019): 1–13. https://doi.org/10.1177/2056305119883429.

Higgins, Hannah. *Fluxus Experience.* Berkeley: University of California Press, 2002.

Hiller, Lejaren A., Jr., and Leonard M. Isaacson. *Experimental Music: Composition with an Electronic Computer.* New York: McGraw-Hill, 1959.

BIBLIOGRAPHY   245

Himanen, Pekka, ed.. *The Hacker Ethic and the Spirit of the Information Age*. New York: Random House, 2001.

Holm-Hudson, Kevin. "Outside of Time: Ideas about Music." *American Music* 29, no. 1 (May 1, 2011): 125–28. https://doi.org/10.5406/americanmusic.29.1.0126.

Hoogerwerf, Frank W. "Cage contra Stravinsky, or Delineating the Aleatory Aesthetic." *International Review of the Aesthetics and Sociology of Music* 7, no. 2 (December 1976): 235–47.

Huizinga, Johan. *Homo Ludens: A Study of the Play-Element in [as] Culture*. Translator unknown. London: Routledge, 1949.

Hull, Glynda, John Scott, and Jennifer Higgs. "The Nerdy Teacher: Pedagogical Identities for a Digital Age." *The Phi Delta Kappan* 95, no. 7 (April 2014): 55–60.

Husarik, Stephen. "John Cage and LeJaren Hiller: HPSCHD, 1969." *American Music* 1, no. 2 (1983): 1–21. https://doi.org/10.2307/3051496.

Iddon, Martin. "The Haus That Karlheinz Built: Composition, Authority, and Control at the 1968 Darmstadt Ferienkurse." *The Musical Quarterly* 87, no. 1 (2004): 87–118.

Iddon, Martin. "Outsourcing Progress: On Conceptual Music." *Tempo* 70, no. 275 (January 2016): 36–49. https://doi.org/10.1017/S0040298215000613.

James, Richard S. "ONCE: Microcosm of the 1960s Musical and Multimedia Avant-Garde." *American Music* 5, no. 4 (1987): 359–90. https://doi.org/10.2307/3051447.

Jean-Francois, Isaac. "Julius Eastman: The Sonority of Blackness Otherwise." *Current Musicology* 106 (Spring 2020): 9–35. https://doi.org/10.52214/cm.v106i.6772.

Johnson, Steven, ed. *The New York Schools of Music and Visual Art*. New York: Routledge, 2002.

Johnston, Ben. "Letter from Urbana." *Perspectives of New Music* 2, no. 1 (Autumn–Winter 1963): 137–41.

Johnston, Jill. *Secret Lives in Art: Essays on Art, Literature, Performance*. Chicago, IL: a cappella books, 1994.

Jones, Kevin. "Compositional Applications of Stochastic Processes." *Computer Music Journal* 5, no. 2 (Summer 1981): 45–61.

Jung, Eun-Young. "Transnational Migrations and YouTube Sensations: Korean Americans, Popular Music, and Social Media." *Ethnomusicology* 58, no. 1 (February 1, 2014): 54–82. https://doi.org/10.5406/ethnomusicology.58.1.0054.

Jůzl, Miloš. "Music and the Totalitarian Regime in Czechoslovakia." *International Review of the Aesthetics and Sociology of Music* 27, no. 1 (June 1996): 31–51.

Kim, Rebecca Y. "In No Uncertain Musical Terms: The Cultural Politics of John Cage's Indeterminacy." PhD diss., Columbia University, 2008.

Kim, Rebecca Y. "John Cage in Separate Togetherness with Jazz." *Contemporary Music Review* 31, no. 1 (February 2012): 63–89. https://doi.org/10.1080/07494467.2012.712284.

Kirzinger, Robert. "75 Years of New Music at the Tanglewood Music Center." 2015. www.bso. org/tmc/history.

Kitcher, Philip. "The Division of Cognitive Labor." *The Journal of Philosophy* 87, no. 1 (January 1990): 5–22. https://doi.org/10.2307/2026796.

Klepal, Boris. "Ostrava Days—Long Concerts You Never Want to End." *Czech Music* 3 (2013): 21–27.

Klumpenhouwer, Henry. "Late Capitalism, Late Marxism and the Study of Music." *Music Analysis* 20, no. 3 (2001): 367–405.

Knoke, David, et. al. *Comparing Policy Networks: Labor Politics in the U.S., Germany, and Japan*. Cambridge: Cambridge University Press, 1996.

Kohl, Jerome, Christoph Von Blumröder, Rudolf Frisius, Winrich Hopp, Michel Rigoni, and Christoph Von Blumroder. "Four Recent Books on Stockhausen." *Perspectives of New Music* 37, no. 1 (1999): 213–45. https://doi.org/10.2307/833632.

Kostelanetz, Richard, ed. *Conversing with Cage*. New York: Routledge, 2003.

Kotík, Petr. Liner notes to *Cornelius Cardew, Treatise [1967 live recording]*. QUaX Ensemble. Mode Records 205, 2009.

246 BIBLIOGRAPHY

Kotík, Petr. *Many, Many Women*. Unpublished manuscript, 1978.

Kotz, Liz. "Post-Cagean Aesthetics and the 'Event' Score." *October* 95 (Winter 2001): 54–89.

Kowalski, Elizabeth. "New Music Network." *CoA + A Community* (2018): 38–41.

Kraft, James P. "Artists as Workers: Musicians and Trade Unionism in America, 1880–1917." *The Musical Quarterly* 79, no. 3 (1995): 512–43. https://doi.org/10.1093/mq/79.3.512.

Kramer, Jonathan D. "Moment Form in Twentieth Century Music." *The Musical Quarterly* 64, no. 2 (1978): 177–94.

Kutschke, Beate. "Protest Music, Urban Contexts and Global Perspectives." *International Review of the Aesthetics and Sociology of Music* 46, no. 2 (2015): 321–54.

Lachenmann, Helmut. "The 'Beautiful' in Music Today." *Tempo, New Series*, no. 135 (1980): 20–24.

Landres, Sophie. "Indecent and Uncanny: The Case against Charlotte Moorman." *Art Journal* 76, no. 1 (2017): 48–69.

Latour, Bruno. "Coming out as a Philosopher." *Social Studies of Science* 40, no. 4 (2010): 599–608.

Latour, Bruno. "Why Has Critique Run out of Steam? From Matters of Fact to Matters of Concern." *Critical Inquiry* 30, no. 2 (January 2004): 225–48. https://doi.org/10.1086/421123.

Léger, Marc James. "A Filliou for the Game: From Political Economy to Poetical Economy and Fluxus." *RACAR: Revue d'art Canadienne / Canadian Art Review* 37, no. 1 (2012): 64–74.

LeMenager, Stephanie, and Ken Eklund. "Site-Specific Forecasting Games and Serious Play: An Interview with Ken Eklund." *ASAP/Journal* 2, no. 3 (2017): 509–20. https://doi.org/10.1353/asa.2017.0045.

Lerner, Gerda. "Placing Women in History: Definitions and Challenges." *Feminist Studies* 3, no. 1/2 (Autumn 1975): 5–14.

Leslie, Christopher. "Review: Trebor Scholz (ed.) *Digital Labor: The Internet as Playground and Factory*." *Media, Culture, and Society* 36, no. 4 (2014): 551–557.

Levine Packer, Renée. *This Life of Sounds: Evenings for New Music in Buffalo*. Oxford: Oxford University Press, 2010.

Levine Packer, Renée, and Mary Jane Leach, eds. *Gay Guerrilla: Julius Eastman and His Music*. Eastman Studies in Music. Rochester, NY: Boydell & Brewer/ University of Rochester Press, 2015.

Levitz, Tamara et al. "Colloquy: Musicology beyond Borders?" *Journal of the American Musicological Society* 65, no. 3 (December 2012): 821–61. https://doi.org/10.1525/jams.2012.65.3.821.

Levitz, Tamara. "Syvilla Fort's Africanist Modernism and John Cage's Gestic Music: The Story of *Bacchanale*." *The South Atlantic Quarterly* 104, no. 1 (Winter 2005): 123–49.

Levy, Peter B. *The New Left and Labor in the 1960s*. Urbana: University of Illinois Press, 1994.

Levy, Steven. *Hackers: Heroes of the Computer Revolution*. New York: Anchor Press, 1984.

Lewis, George E. "Experimental Music in Black and White: The AACM in New York, 1970–1985." *Current Musicology* 71–73 (Spring 2001–Spring 2002): 100–57.

Lewis, George E. "Improvised Music after 1950: Afrological and Eurological Perspectives." *Black Music Research Journal* 16, no. 1 (1996): 91–122. https://doi.org/10.2307/779379.

Lewis, George E. *A Power Stronger Than Itself: The AACM and American Experimental Music*. Chicago: University of Chicago Press, 2008.

Lewis, George, and Amina Claudine Myers. "Interview: Amina Claudine Myers." *BOMB* no. 97 (Fall 2006): 54–59.

Lewis George E., and Benjamin Piekut, eds. *The Oxford Handbook of Critical Improvisation Studies, Volume I*. Oxford: Oxford University Press, 2016.

Littlefield, Richard. "The Silence of the Frames." In *Music/Ideology: Resisting the Aesthetic*, edited by Adam Krims. Critical Voices in Art, Theory, and Culture. Saul Ostrow, series editor. Amsterdam: G + B Arts, 1998.

BIBLIOGRAPHY   247

Lochhead, Judith, Andrea Moore, Marianna Ritchey, Judy Lochhead, John R. Pippen, and Anne C. Shreffler. "Boundaries of the New: American Classical Music at the Turn of the Millennium." *Twentieth-Century Music* 16, no. 3 (October 2019): 373–455. https://doi.org/10.1017/S1478572219000288.

Lochhead, Judy. "The New Music Scene: Passionate Commitment in the Twenty-First-Century Gig Economy." *Twentieth-Century Music* 16, no. 3 (2019): 412–24.

Lucier, Alvin. *Music 109: Notes on Experimental Music.* Middletown, CT: Wesleyan University Press, 2012.

Lucier, Alvin. "Origins of a Form: Acoustical Exploration, Science and Incessancy." *Leonardo Music Journal* 8 (1998): 5–11. https://doi.org/10.2307/1513391.

Luque, Sergio. "The Stochastic Synthesis of Iannis Xenakis." *Leonardo Music Journal* 19 (2009): 77–84.

MacDonald, Margaret S., and Anthony G. Oettinger. "Information Overload: Managing Intelligence Technologies." *Harvard International Review* 24, no. 3 (2002): 44–48.

Maconie, Robin. *Other Planets: The Music of Karlheinz Stockhausen.* Lanham, MD: Scarecrow Press, 2005.

Maconie, Robin. *The Works of Karlheinz Stockhausen.* 2nd edition. London: Oxford University Press, 1990.

Malcomson, Hettie. "Composing Individuals: Ethnographic Reflections on Success and Prestige in the British New Music Network." *Twentieth-Century Music* 10, no. 1 (March 2013): 115–36. https://doi.org/10.1017/S1478572212000436.

Malcomson, Hettie. "Cuban Flute Style: Interpretation and Improvisation." *Ethnomusicology Forum* 24, no. 3 (Fall 2015): 478–80.

Malpas, Jeff. "Locating Interpretation: The Topography of Understanding in Heidegger and Davidson." *Philosophical Topics* 27, no. 2 (1999): 129–48.

Manovich, Lev. "The Practice of Everyday (Media) Life: From Mass Consumption to Mass Cultural Production?" *Critical Inquiry* 35, no. 2 (January 2009): 319–31. https://doi.org/10.1086/596645.

Margolis, Joseph. "Relativism and Interpretive Objectivity." *Metaphilosophy* 31, no. 1/2 (2000): 200–226.

Marx, Karl. *Capital: A Critique of Political Economy, Vol. I: The Process of Capitalist Production.* Translated from the 3rd German edition by Samuel Moore and Edward Aveling, edited by Frederick Engels. New York: International Publishers, 1967.

Mauceri, Frank X. "From Experimental Music to Musical Experiment." *Perspectives of New Music* 35, no. 1 (1997): 187–204. https://doi.org/10.2307/833684.

Mawyer, Alexander. "Review Article: The Game's Afoot, Watson: Culture and Crisis in Play: Mary Flanagan, *Critical Play: Radical Game Design.* Cambridge, MA: The MIT Press, 2009. Larissa Hjorth and Dean Chan (Eds), *Gaming Cultures and Place in Asia-Pacific.* New York: Routledge, 2009. Anikó Imre, *Identity Games: Globalization and the Transformation of Media Cultures in the New Europe.* Cambridge, MA: The MIT Press, 2009." *New Media and Society* 13, no. 5 (August 2011): 843–47. https://doi.org/10.1177/1461444811406399.

McCormick, Richard W. *Gender and Sexuality in Weimar Modernity: Film, Literature, and "New Objectivity."* New York: Palgrave Macmillan, 2001.

McDowell, John H. "'Surfing the Tube' for Latin American Song: The Blessings (and Curses) of YouTube." *The Journal of American Folklore* 128, no. 509 (Summer 2015): 260–72.

Medina, Cuauhtémoc. "The 'Kulturbolschewiken' I: Fluxus, the Abolition of Art, the Soviet Union, and 'Pure Amusement.'" *RES: Anthropology and Aesthetics,* no. 48 (2005): 179–92.

Mellers, Wilfred. "The Avant-Garde in America." *Proceedings of the RMA,* 90th Session (1963–1964): 1–13.

Meyer, Leonard B. "The End of the Renaissance? Notes on the Radical Empiricism of the Avant-Garde." *Hudson Review* 16, no. 2 (Summer 1963): 169–86.

248   BIBLIOGRAPHY

Michalski, Sergiusz. *New Objectivity: Painting, Graphic Art and Photography in Weimar Germany 1919–1933*. Köln: Taschen, 2003.

Miller, Kiri. *Playing Along: Digital Games, YouTube, and Virtual Performance*. Oxford: Oxford University Press, 2012.

Miller, Kiri. "Schizophonic Performance: *Guitar Hero, Rock Band*, and Virtual Virtuosity." *Journal of the Society for American Music* 3, no. 4 (November 2009): 395–429. https://doi.org/10.1017/S1752196309990666.

Miller, Leta E. "ONCE and Again: The Evolution of a Legendary Festival." Essay in booklet accompanying *Music from the ONCE Festival, 1961–1966*. New World Records 80567-2, 2003.

Monson, Ingrid. *Saying Something: Jazz Improvisation and Interaction*. Chicago: University of Chicago Press, 1996.

Moore, Andrea. "Neoliberalism and the Musical Entrepreneur." *Journal of the Society for American Music* 10, no. 1 (February 2016): 33–53. https://doi.org/10.1017/S175219631500053X.

Moorman, Charlotte. *Cello Anthology*. 4-disc set, NMN 064BOX. Italy: Alga Marghen, 2006.

Morrison, Matthew D. "Race, Blacksound, and the (Re)Making of Musicological Discourse." *Journal of the American Musicological Society* 72, no. 3 (Fall 2019): 781–823.

Moseley, Roger. "Digital Analogies: The Keyboard as Field of Musical Play." *Journal of the American Musicological Society* 68, no. 1 (Spring 2015): 151–228.

Moseley, Roger. *Keys to Play: Music as a Ludic Medium from Apollo to Nintendo*. Oakland: University of California Press, 2016.

Mugglestone, Erica. "Guido Adler's 'The Scope, Method, and Aim of Musicology' (1885): An English Translation with an Historico-Analytical Commentary." *Yearbook for Traditional Music* 13 (1981): 1–21.

Munday, Jeremy. *Introducing Translation Studies: Theories and Applications*. New York: Routledge, 2001.

Nettl, Bruno, and Melinda Russell, eds. *In the Course of Performance: Studies in the World of Musical Improvisation*. Chicago: University of Chicago Press, 1998.

Nooshin, Laudan. "The Song of the Nightingale: Processes of Improvisation in dastgāh Segāh (Iranian Classical Music)." *British Journal of Ethnomusicology* 7 (January 1998): 69–116.

NY Creative Artists Public Service Program. *New American Music: New York Section, Composers of the 1970's* [sic]. Folkways Records 33903, 1975.

Nyman, Michael. *Experimental Music: Cage and Beyond*. Music in the Twentieth Century. Cambridge: Cambridge University Press, 1999.

O'Grady, Terence J. "Aesthetic Value in Indeterminate Music." *The Musical Quarterly* 67, no. 3 (1981): 366–81.

Oram, Daphne. *An Individual Note: Of Music, Sound and Electronics*. London: Galliard, 1972.

Ortner, Sherry. *Anthropology and Social Theory: Culture, Power, and the Acting Subject*. Durham, NC: Duke University Press, 2006.

Page, Will and Eric Garland. "In Rainbows, on Torrents." *Economic Insight* 10 (2008), https://www.mcps-prsalliance.co.uk/economics.

Parsons, Michael. "The Scratch Orchestra and Visual Arts." *Leonardo Music Journal* 11 (2001): 5–11.

Patteson, Thomas. *Instruments for New Music: Sound, Technology, and Modernism*. Oakland: University of California Press, 2015.

Peirce, Charles Sanders. "A Sketch of Logical Critics." In *The Essential Peirce: Selected Philosophical Writings, Vol. 2 (1893–1913)*, edited by the Peirce Edition Project, 451–462. Bloomington and Indianapolis: Indiana University Press, 1998.

Piekut, Benjamin. "Actor-Networks in Music History: Clarifications and Critiques." *Twentieth-Century Music* 11, no. 2 (September 2014): 191–215. https://doi.org/10.1017/S1478572214000005X.

BIBLIOGRAPHY 249

Piekut, Benjamin. *Experimentalism Otherwise: The New York Avant-Garde and Its Limits.* Berkeley: University of California Press, 2011.

Piekut, Benjamin. "Sound's Modest Witness: Notes on Cage and Modernism." *Contemporary Music Review* 31, no. 1 (February 2012): 3–18. https://doi.org/10.1080/07494 467.2012.712279.

Piekut, Benjamin. *Tomorrow Is the Question: New Directions in Experimental Music Studies.* Ann Arbor: University of Michigan Press, 2014.

Piirimäe, Eva. "Berlin, Herder, and the Counter-Enlightenment." *Eighteenth-Century Studies* 49, no. 1 (Fall 2015): 71–76.

Pippen, John R. "The Boundaries of 'Boundarylessness': Revelry, Struggle, and Labour in Three American New Music Ensembles." *Twentieth-Century Music* 16, no. 3 (2019): 424–44.

Pisaro, Kathryn Gleasman. "Music from Scratch: Cornelius Cardew, Experimental Music and the Scratch Orchestra in Britain in the 1960s and 1970s." PhD diss., Northwestern University, 2001.

Polanyi, Michael. *Science, Faith and Society.* Chicago: University of Chicago Press, 1964.

Pontara, Tobias. "Interpretation, Imputation, Plausibility: Towards a Theoretical Model for Musical Hermeneutics." *International Review of the Aesthetics and Sociology of Music* 46, no. 1 (2015): 3–41.

Potter, Keith. "Boulez and Stockhausen, Bennett and Cardew." *The Musical Times* 122, no. 1657 (March 1981): 170. https://doi.org/10.2307/962850.

Pozen, David E. "Privacy-Privacy Tradeoffs." *The University of Chicago Law Review* 83, no. 1 (2016): 221–47.

Prévost, Eddie. "The Arrival of a New Musical Aesthetic: Extracts from a Half-Buried Diary." *Leonardo Music Journal* 11 (2001): 25–28.

Pritchett, James. "The Development of Chance Techniques in the Music of John Cage, 1950–1956." PhD diss., New York University, 1988.

Pym, Anthony. "On Indeterminacy in Translation: A Survey of Western Theories." Unpublished manuscript, Version 2.0. 2008.

Racy, Ali Jihad. "The Many Faces of Improvisation: The Arab Taqāsīm as a Musical Symbol." *Ethnomusicology* 44, no. 2 (Spring 2000): 302–20.

Ralston, Meredith. *Slut-Shaming, Whorephobia, and the Unfinished Sexual Revolution.* Montreal: McGill-Queen's University Press, 2021.

Raymond, Eric S., comp. *The New Hacker's Dictionary.* 3rd edition. Cambridge, MA: MIT Press, 1996.

Regelski, Thomas A. "Scientism in Experimental Music Research." *Philosophy of Music Education Review* 4, no. 1 (1996): 3–19.

Reynolds, Roger. "Indeterminacy: Some Considerations." *Perspectives of New Music* 4, no. 1 (Autumn/Winter 1965): 136–40. https://doi.org/10.2307/832533.

Rheinberger, Hans-Jörg. *Toward a History of Epistemic Things: Synthesizing Proteins in the Test Tube.* Stanford, CA: Stanford University Press, 1997.

Riccardi, Alessandra, ed. *Translation Studies: Perspectives on an Emerging Discipline.* Cambridge: Cambridge University Press, 2002.

Ritzer, George, and J. Daniel Schubert. "The Changing Nature of Neo-Marxist Theory: A Metatheoretical Analysis." *Sociological Perspectives* 34, no. 3 (September 1991): 359–75. https://doi.org/10.2307/1389516.

Robinson, Julia. "From Abstraction to Model: George Brecht's Events and the Conceptual Turn in Art of the 1960s." *October* 127 (March 2009): 77–108. https://doi.org/10.1162/octo.2009.127.1.77.

Rodgers, Tara. *Pink Noises: Women on Electronic Music and Sound.* Durham, NC: Duke University Press, 2010.

Rose, Sonya O. "Gender and Labor History: The Nineteenth-Century Legacy." *International Review of Social History* 38, no. S1 (April 1993): 145–62. https://doi.org/10.1017/S00208 59000112349.

250 BIBLIOGRAPHY

Rothfuss, Joan. *Topless Cellist: The Improbable Life of Charlotte Moorman*. Cambridge, MA: MIT Press, 2014.

Rothman, Roger. "Against Critique: Fluxus and the Hacker Aesthetic." *Modernism/Modernity* 22, no. 4 (2015): 787–810. https://doi.org/10.1353/mod.2015.0059.

Rothman, Roger. "Fluxus, or the Work of Art in the Age of Information." *Symplokē* 23, no. 1–2 (2015): 309–25. https://doi.org/10.5250/symploke.23.1-2.0309.

Rowlinson, Michael, and John Hassard. "Marxist Political Economy, Revolutionary Politics, and Labor Process Theory." *International Studies of Management and Organization* 30, no. 4 (2001): 85–111.

Rupprecht, Philip. " 'Something Slightly Indecent': British Composers, the European Avant-Garde, and National Stereotypes in the 1950s." *The Musical Quarterly* 91, no. 3–4 (September 1, 2008): 275–326. https://doi.org/10.1093/musqtl/gdp003.

Sabatini, Arthur J. "Robert Ashley: Defining American Opera." *PAJ: A Journal of Performance and Art* 27, no. 2 (2005): 45–60.

Sansom, Matthew. "Imaging Music: Abstract Expressionism and Free Improvisation." *Leonardo Music Journal* 11 (2001): 29–34.

Saunders, James, ed. *The Ashgate Research Companion to Experimental Music*. Burlington, VT: Ashgate, 2009.

Savage, Roger W. H. "Crossing the Disciplinary Divide: Hermeneutics, Ethnomusicology and Musicology." *College Music Symposium* 49, no. 5 (2010): 402–8.

Schettler, Jordan. "Wendy Carlos's Xenharmonic Keyboard." *Mathematics Magazine* 92, no. 3 (2019): 201–12.

Steve Schlegel. "John Cage at June in Buffalo, 1975." MA thesis, State University of New York at Buffalo, 2008.

Scholz, Trebor, ed. *Digital Labor: The Internet as Playground and Factory*. New York: Routledge, 2012.

Schonfield, Victor. "New Music." *The Musical Times* 111, no. 1525 (March 1970): 276. https://doi.org/10.2307/957505.

Scranton, Philip. "None-Too-Porous Boundaries: Labor History and the History of Technology." *Technology and Culture* 29, no. 4 (October 1988): 722–43.

Seidenberg, Steven. "Copyright in the Age of YouTube: As User-Generated Sites Flourish, Copyright Law Struggles to Keep Up." *ABA Journal* 95, no. 2 (2009): 46–51.

Semuels, Alana. "The Internet Is Enabling a New Kind of Poorly Paid Hell." *The Atlantic*. January 23, 2018.

Shelemay, Kay Kaufman. "Crossing Boundaries in Music and Musical Scholarship: A Perspective from Ethnomusicology." *The Musical Quarterly* 80, no. 1 (Spring 1996): 13–30.

Sherman, Howard J., and Paul D. Sherman. "Why Is This Cycle Different from All Other Cycles?" *Journal of Economic Issues* 42, no. 1 (2008): 255–68.

Skempton, Howard. "The Wiggly Lines and Wobbly Music of Cornelius Cardew." *The Guardian*. May 26, 2011.

Smalley, Roger. "Stockhausen's *Gruppen*." *The Musical Times* 108, no. 1495 (September 1967): 794–97. https://doi.org/10.2307/952487.

Soares, Janet. *Martha Hill and the Making of American Dance*. Middletown, CT: Wesleyan University Press, 2009.

Solis, Gabriel. "Thoughts on an Interdiscipline: Music Theory, Analysis, and Social Theory in Ethnomusicology." *Ethnomusicology* 56, no. 3 (Fall 2012): 530–54.

Solis, Gabriel, and Bruno Nettl, eds. *Musical Improvisation: Art, Education, and Society*. Urbana: University of Illinois Press, 2009.

Sonic Arts Union. *Electric Sound*. Mainstream Records (LP), 1971.

Spencer, David A. "Braverman and the Contribution of Labour Process Analysis to the Critique of Capitalist Production—Twenty-Five Years On." *Work, Employment and Society* 14, no. 2 (June 2000): 223–43.

BIBLIOGRAPHY 251

Stein, Gertrude. "What Are Master-Pieces and Why Are There So Few of Them." *The American Poetry Review* 27, no. 4 (July/August 1998): 9–10.

Steinbeck, Paul. "'Area by Area the Machine Unfolds': The Improvisational Performance Practice of the Art Ensemble of Chicago." *Journal of the Society for American Music* 2, no. 3 (August 2008): 397–427. https://doi.org/10.1017/S1752196308080127.

Stillman, Amy Ku'uleialoha. "Textualizing Hawaiian Music." *American Music* 23, no. 1 (Spring 2005): 69–94.

Stockhausen, Karlheinz. *Carré.* Vienna: Universal Edition, 1960.

Stockhausen, Karlheinz. *Carré für 4 Orchester und Chöre, Werk Nr. 10, Manuskript- und Skizzen-Kopien.* Kürten: Stockhausen-Verlag, 1983.

Stockhausen, Karlheinz. *Gruppen/ Carré.* Mauricio Kagel, Karlheinz Stockhausen, Andrzej Markowski, and Michael Gielen, conductors; Chor und Sinfonie-Orchester des Norddeutschen Rundfunks Hamburg. Deutsche Grammophon 137 002, 1960.

Stockhausen, Karlheinz. *Plus Minus: 2 x 7 Seiten für Ausarbeitungen.* Vienna: Universal Edition, 1963.

Stockhausen, Karlheinz, and Jerome Kohl. "Electroacoustic Performance Practice." *Perspectives of New Music* 34, no. 1 (Winter 1996): 74–105. https://doi.org/10.2307/833486.

Stockhausen, Karlheinz, and Robin Maconie. *Stockhausen on Music: Lectures and Interviews.* London: Marion Boyars, 1989.

Stubbs, David. *Future Sounds: The Story of Electronic Music from Stockhausen to Skrillex.* London: Faber & Faber, 2018.

Svatos, Thomas D. "Sovietizing Czechoslovak Music: The 'Hatchet-Man' Miroslav Barvík and his Speech *The Composers Go with the People.*" *Music and Politics* 4, no. 1 (Winter 2010): 1–35.

Tanenbaum, Leora. *I Am Not a Slut: Slut-Shaming in the Age of the Internet.* New York: Harper, 2015.

Taylor, Timothy D. "Moving in Decency: The Music and Radical Politics of Cornelius Cardew." *Music and Letters* 79, no. 4 (November 1998): 555–76.

Taylor, Timothy D. *Music and Capitalism: A History of the Present.* Chicago: University of Chicago Press, 2016.

Thomas, Philip. "Review: Cardew: *Treatise* by Sonic Youth, Art Lange and Cornelius Cardew." *Tempo, New Series*, no. 218 (October 2001): 59–62.

Thomas, Philip. "Understanding Indeterminate Music through Performance: Cage's *Solo for Piano.*" *Twentieth-Century Music* 10, no. 1 (March 2013): 91–113. https://doi.org/10.1017/S1478572212000424.

Tilbury, John. "Cornelius Cardew." *Contact* 26 (Spring 1983): 4–12.

Tilbury, John. *Cornelius Cardew (1936–1981): A Life Unfinished.* Essex, UK: Copula, 2008.

Turkle, Sherry. *The Second Self: Computers and the Human Spirit.* Cambridge, MA: MIT Press, 2005.

United States Census Bureau. *American Community Survey.* 2013–2017.

United States Census Bureau. *Statistical Abstract of the United States.* 2010.

United States Department of Labor. *1965 Handbook on Women Workers: Women's Bureau Bulletin*, no. 290. 1965.

United States Government Accountability Office. Report GAO-23-106041: "Women in the Workforce: The Gender Pay Gap Is Greater for Certain Racial and Ethnic Groups and Varies by Education Level." 2022.

University Musical Society. "ONCE. MORE. Tour: 1960s Ann Arbor in Memory and Imagination." Accessed July 20, 2023. ums.org/2010/10/29/once-more-tour-1960s-ann-arbor-in-memory-and-imagination/.

Valle, Andrea. *Contemporary Music Notation: Semiotic and Aesthetic Aspects.* Translated by Angela Maria Arnone. Torino: De Sono Associazione per la Musica, 2018.

252 BIBLIOGRAPHY

van Dijck, José. "Users like You? Theorizing Agency in User-Generated Content." *Media, Culture and Society* 31, no. 1 (January 2009): 41–58. https://doi.org/10.1177/016344370 8098245.

Venuti, Lawrence. "Introduction." *Critical Inquiry* 27, no. 2 (Winter 2001): 169–73.

Venuti, Lawrence, ed. *The Translation Studies Reader.* 2nd ed. New York: Routledge, 2004.

von Herder, Johann Gottfried. *Philosophical Writings.* Translated and edited by Michael N. Forster. Cambridge: Cambridge University Press, 2002.

Waksman, Steve. "California Noise: Tinkering with Heavy Metal and Hardcore in Southern California." *Social Studies of Science* 34, no. 5 (October 2004): 675–702.

Wark, McKenzie. *Gamer Theory.* Cambridge, MA: Harvard University Press, 2007.

Wark, McKenzie. *A Hacker Manifesto.* Cambridge, MA: Harvard University Press, 2004.

Watson, Scott B., and Linda James. "The Scientific Method: Is It Still Useful?" *Science Scope* 28, no. 3 (November–December 2004): 37–39.

Wedgewood, Mary. "Avant-Garde Music: Some Publication Problems." *The Library Quarterly* 46, no. 2 (April 1976): 137–52.

Whitesell, Lloyd. "White Noise: Race and Erasure in the Cultural Avant-Garde." *American Music* 19, no. 2 (Summer 2001): 168–89. https://doi.org/10.2307/3052612.

Williams, Jan, and Jonathan Hepfer. "Interview with Jan Williams." *Percussive Notes* 8 (February 2007): n.p.

Williams, Sean. "Interpretation and Performance Practice in Realizing Stockhausen's *Studie II.*" *Journal of the Royal Musical Association* 141, no. 2 (2016): 445–81. https://doi.org/10.1080/02690403.2016.1216059.

Wilson-Kovacs, Dana. "*Objectivity* [review]." *Critical Quarterly* 51, no. 3 (October 2009): 123–125.

Wimsatt, W.K., Jr., and M.C. Beardsley. "The Intentional Fallacy." *The Sewanee Review* 54, no. 3 (1946): 468–69.

Winn, Peter. "Labor History after the Gender Turn: Introduction." *International Labor and Working-Class History* no. 63 (Spring 2003): 1–5.

Wivagg, Dan. "The Dogma of 'The' Scientific Method." *The American Biology Teacher* 64, no. 9 (November–December 2002): 645–46.

Wolff, Christian. "Experimental Music around 1950 and Some Consequences and Causes (Social-Political and Musical)." *American Music* 27, no. 4 (December 2009): 424–40. https://doi.org/10.2307/25652228.

Young, La Monte, and Jackson Mac Low, eds. *An Anthology of Chance Operations.* 2nd edition. New York: Heiner Friedrich, 1970.

Zagorski, Marcus. "Carl Dahlhaus and the Aesthetics of the Experiment." *Acta Musicologica* 87, no. 2 (2015): 249–64.

Zorn, John. *Spillane* liner notes. Nonesuch 979 172-1, 1987.

Index

For the benefit of digital users, indexed terms that span two pages (e.g., 52–53) may, on occasion, appear on only one of those pages.

Tables and figures are indicated by an italic *t* and *f* following the page number.

0′00″ (Cage), 219–20
4 Systems (Brown), 30–31
1750 Arch Records, 88–89

AACM (Association for the Advancement of Creative Musicians), 7–9, 86–89, 186, 223–24
Abrams, Muhal Richard, 9, 87–88, 88*f*
"abusive fidelity" (Lewis), 178–79
Adieu, Sirènes (Riehm), 187
administrator model (Interpretive Labor), 12, 121–22, 124–26, 136–37, 139–44
advertising, 191–92, 199–200, 210–11n.62
affective labor, 12, 16, 136–37
agency, 132–34, 152–53, 196–97, 199–200
Akademie der Musik und Darstellende Kunst (Vienna), 92–93
aleatory, 31–32, 90–91
    See also chance; indeterminacy
Alsina, Carlos, 161–62
Amacher, Maryanne, 161–62
Amazon Mechanical Turk, 226–27, 227*f*
America Online (AOL), 24
American Symphony Orchestra, 131–32
AMM, 157–58
Anderson, Virginia, 69
Apple, Inc., 40–41
archival work, 131, 136
Aria (Cage), 161, 170–71
Arkansas State Symphony, 131–32
Armstrong, Elizabeth, 204
Aronson, Arnold, 204–5
artificial intelligence, 153, 231–32
arts administration, 127–31, 134–37, 187
    See also administrator model (Interpretive Labor)
Ashley, Robert, 88–89, 194–96, 197–98, 220–21
assistant role, 41–43, 54–55, 79–85, 233
    See also Cardew, Cornelius; *Carré* (Stockhausen/Cardew)

Association for the Advancement of Creative Musicians (AACM). *See* AACM
Atlas Eclipticalis (Cage), 29, 115–16
audiences, 14–16, 48–50, 166, 211–13, 221–23
Austin, J. L., 76–77
authorship, 42, 57–61, 180, 191
Avant-Garde Festivals, 12, 134–36, 187, 195n.16
Aytes, Ayhan, 29

Bakla, Petr, 94–95, 98–99
Battle, Laura, 83–84
Bauwens, Michel, 30
Beardsley, M.C., 152
Behrman, David, 135, 194
Benjamin, Walter, 56–57, 76–77, 78
Bermann, Sandra, 3–4, 46–47, 61–62, 76–77, 78
Black Artists' Group, 223–24
Black musicians and the avant-garde, 7–10
    See also AACM (Association for the Advancement of Creative Musicians)
Blum, Eberhard, 162
Bohemian National Hall (New York), 87, 88*f*, 88–89
Bohlman, Philip V., 61–62, 78
Bolt, Barbara, 18–20
Borgo, David, 32–33
Boulez, Pierre, 31–32
Bourdieu, Pierre, 26–27, 28
Bowling Green State University, 1–2
Brackett, John, 223–24
Braverman, Harry, 26
Brecht, George, 201–4, 205–6, 219
Brown, Earle, 30–32, 134–35
Bryars, Gavin, 75
Buckner, Thomas, 87–89
Burdocks (Wolff), 148
Burkholder, J. Peter, 235–36
Burnett, D. Graham, 103–4

254 INDEX

Burnham, Edward, 67–69, 69f, 70f, 161–62, 229–30
Butcher, Kayleigh, 141

Cage, John
0'00," 219–20
and African American art forms, 7–8, 9
Aria, 161, 170–71
Atlas Eclipticalis, 29, 115–16
and the Avant-Garde Festivals, 134–36
Cardew on, 150, 176–77
and the composer–performer relationship, 10, 80–81, 97–98, 148–49, 179–80, 230
Concert for Piano and Orchestra, 205–6
on experimental music, 105, 219–21
and Fluxus, 205–6
Fontana Mix, 161, 170–71, 205–6
HPSCHD (with Hiller), 113–15
on indeterminacy, 53, 90–91, 96, 150, 179–80
and Kotík, 90–91, 92–93, 96, 97–98, 100–1, 107–10
on music as a social art, 230
Music of Changes, 107
and Paik, 216–18, 220–22
in scholarship, 8–9, 34
Theater Piece, 206
Variations, 201–4, 206
works dedicated to, 215–17, 218–22
Calle, Sophie, 18–19
capital (Bourdieu). *See* cultural capital (Bourdieu)
capital (Marx), 24–28
Cardew, Cornelius
account of *Carré*, 44–45, 47–48, 50, 53–56, 57–61
in AMM, 157–58
on Cage, 150, 176–77
and the Center of the Creative and Performing Arts / Creative Associates, 67–69, 126–27, 159, 161–67, 170–73
and the composer–performer relationship, 10, 150–53, 157, 160, 164–67, 176–77
The Great Learning, 156–57, 170
as hacker, 12–13, 147, 148–49, 150, 154–56, 177–81, 184–85
on interpretation, 21, 31–32, 149–53, 166, 184
and Kotík, 167, 169
Memories of You, 177–78
on notation, 145, 148–53, 160, 181–82
as performer in *Plus Minus* (Stockhausen), 43–44, 67–71, 69f, 70f, 76, 229–30

performing *Treatise*, 161–62
political ideology of, 147–49, 156–57, 177, 181–83
Schooltime Compositions, 170
and the Scratch Orchestra, 170, 179–80n.84, 182–83
self-critique by, 148–49, 156–57, 166, 181–82
Solo with Accompaniment, 69, 170, 177–78
on Stockhausen, 47–48, 55, 57–61, 174–75, 176–77
as Stockhausen's assistant, 11–12, 41–42, 44–45, 50–56, 57–62, 78–79, 146–47, 222–23
See also *Carré* (Stockhausen/Cardew); *Treatise* (Cardew); *Treatise Handbook* (Cardew)
Carlos, Wendy, 117–18
Carnegie Hall, 68, 161–62, 163
Carré (Stockhausen/Cardew)
Cardew's account of, 44–45, 47–48, 50, 53–56, 57–61
Cardew's role in, 44–45, 50–154, 178–79, 180, 222–23
performance history of, 43, 55–56
performing forces and setup for, 43, 48–50, 55–56, 57–58
power imbalance involved in, 41–42, 54–55, 79–81, 222–23
scholarship on, 50–53
scores and notation of, 48–50, 49f, 51f, 52f, 54–55, 57–61
Stockhausen's role in, 41–42, 48–55, 57–61, 79–81, 180
and translational labor, 11–12, 39, 44, 56–62, 78–79
Carter, Elliott, 67–68, 176, 229–30
Case, Kevin, 21–22
CCPA. *See* Center of the Creative and Performing Arts (Buffalo)
Center for Computer Research in Music and Acoustics (CCRMA) (Stanford University), 119
Center of the Creative and Performing Arts (Buffalo), 12, 67–68, 93–94, 115–16, 126–31, 170–73, 211–13
See also Creative Associates (University at Buffalo); Kotík, Petr; S.E.M. Ensemble
Cerha, Friedrich, 92–93
chance, 12, 30–32, 90–91, 100–1, 103–6, 116, 205–6
See also indeterminacy
Chantler, Abigail, 21
Charlotte New Music Festival, 141
Cheng, William, 200–1

INDEX 255

classical music
  gender representation in, 141–42
  interpretive procedures in, 1–2, 5, 15–16, 44–45, 151, 230–31
  labor issues in, 21–23
  Moorman's background in, 131–32
  performer–audience relationship in, 221–22
  primacy of the composer in, 37
clerical work, 128–29, 137–39
Cobra (Zorn), 223–26
co-composition, 43, 55, 67–68, 76, 165–66
  See also composer–performer relationships
codetermination, 28–29
Coenen, Alcedo, 73–74
cognitive labor, 5, 16–17, 29, 67, 146–47
Cohen, Brigid, 46–47, 61–62, 78, 118–19
Cold War, 14, 93, 115–16, 167, 169–70, 214–15
Coleman, Gabriella, 145–46, 155–56
collaboration, 28–29, 41–43, 50–53, 58–61, 79, 176–77, 225
Cologne New Music Courses, 62
Columbia-Princeton Electronic Music Center (CPEMC), 118–19
commissions, 25, 48, 81–82, 88–89, 229–30
communism, 26, 147–49, 156–57, 169–70, 180–81
community, 145–46, 153–54, 172–73, 186–87, 209–11
compensation, 21–24, 40–41, 83, 88–89, 130, 138, 174–75
  See also recognition
composer, role of, 37, 50–53, 116, 151–53, 154–55, 162, 174–75, 193
composer–performer relationships
  and audiences, 14–16, 166
  Cage and, 10, 80–81, 97–98, 148–49, 179–80, 230
  Cardew and, 10, 150–53, 157, 160, 164–67, 176–77
  as co-composition, 43, 55, 67–68, 76, 165–66
  demands of, 14–16, 39, 55–56, 76, 175–77
  freedom and control in, 10, 55, 150–53, 162, 164–67, 175–77, 230
  Kotík on, 96–98
  Williams on, 55, 175–77
  See also interpretation; realization; translation
composer–performer–audience relationships, 14–16, 166
computer programming, 111–15, 114*f*, 117, 153–56, 172–73
Concert for Piano and Orchestra (Cage), 205–6
content creation, 14, 24
  See also user-generated content (UGC)

Corner, Philip, 132–33, 134–35
Cornish School (Seattle), 7–8
Cowell, Henry, 7–8, 30–31
Creative Artists Public Service Program (CAPS), 207
Creative Associates (University at Buffalo)
  and administrative work, 127–28, 130
  Cardew and, 67–69, 159, 161–67, 170–73
  Kotík and, 93–94, 115–16, 170–73
  repertoire and performances of, 67–69, 115–16, 161–67, 170–73, 190–91, 207–8
  See also Center of the Creative and Performing Arts (Buffalo); Kotík, Petr
critical theory, 4–5, 37–38, 122, 192
crowdsourcing, 29, 226–27
Crumb, George, 126–27
cultural capital (Bourdieu), 25, 26–27, 28, 209–10
"culture of supervision" (Himanen), 175–77
Cut Piece (Ono), 133–34, 221–22
Czech Center New York, 87

Danger Music for Dick Higgins (Paik), 217
Darmstadt Internationale Ferienkurse für Neue Musik, 43, 115–16, 216–17
Dasein (Heidegger), 18–20, 184–85
Daston, Lorraine, 103–4
de Bértola, Elena, 50–53
Demers, Joanna, 118–19
Derrida, Jacques, 4–5, 18–19, 37–38, 76–78, 178–79, 236–37
Desan, Mathieu, 24–25, 26–27
digital media, 16, 29, 185, 191–92, 193–94, 198–201, 226–28
  See also user-generated content (UGC); video games
disciplinary boundaries, 234–36
Dohoney, Ryan, 219–20
do-it-yourself (DIY), 62, 195–96
Donne, Women in Music, 141–42
Donovan, Gregory T., 147, 154
Dörries, Matthias, 5–6
Dramatic Arts Council (DAC), 125
Dream (Maxfield), 36
Drip Music (Drip Event) (Brecht), 206
Dungeons & Dragons, 190–91
Dungey, Nicholas, 184–85
Dupouy, Jean, 161–62
Dwyer, John, 171, 194, 195, 208–9, 213

Eastman, Julius, 99–100, 131, 219–20
Eidsheim, Nina, 119–20
El-Dabh, Halim, 118–19

256 INDEX

electronic music, 111–15, 114f, 116–19, 194–96
Eley, Rod, 183
embodiment, 34, 219–21
Emmett Williams's Ear (Higgins), 35–36
Ensemble Dal Niente, 81–82, 142–43
Ensemble Intercontemporain, 48–50
Ensemble Musikfabrik, 43
entrepreneurship, 143–44
erasure, 61–62, 180–81
    See also recognition
ethnomusicology, 32–33, 235–36
executive model (Interpretive Labor), 11–12,
    41–43, 45, 47–48, 50–56, 69–71, 78–85,
    180
Experiment for John Cage (Fine), 215–16
experimental music
    demands on audiences for, 14–15
    as fruitful site for Interpretive Labor inquiry,
        6–7, 230–33
    as hacking, 154–56, 172–73, 183–89, 205
    lack of institutionalized training in, 14–15
    as modding, 190–91, 194–96, 197–98
    racial exclusion in, 7–10
    role of notation in, 14–15, 34–37
    scholarship on, 5–10, 31–35, 236–37
    as sharing economy, 214–15, 221–22
    as term, 6–7, 105–6
    See also indeterminacy
exploitation, 23, 26–27, 79–85, 142–44, 192,
    210, 226–28

Facebook, 199–200
facilitator role, 121–22, 136–37, 138–39, 140–
    41, 142–43
    See also administrator model (Interpretive
    Labor)
Feldman, Morton, 35–36, 67, 135, 162, 221–22
Field, The (Ichiyanagi), 36
FIFA (video game), 196–97
Fighter Maker, 190–91
figural scores, 36–37
Filliou, Robert, 201, 202f, 203f
financial work, 125, 128–29
    See also administrator model (Interpretive
    Labor); arts administration
Fine, Albert M., 36, 177–78, 215–16, 218–19,
    220–21
Flanagan, Mary, 194, 222, 226
Fluxkits, 204
Fluxus
    as gaming/play, 13, 201–6, 210–11, 212–13,
        219–20, 222
    as hacking, 178, 186

Folio (Brown), 30–31
Fontana Mix (Cage), 161, 170–71, 205–6
Fort, Syvilla, 7–8
Fosler-Lussier, Danielle, 214–15
Foss, Lukas, 67–68, 126–28
Fosso, Paolo, 141
Foucault, Michel, 18–19, 41
Fox, Christopher, 66–67, 74–76
free and open-source software (F/OSS), 145–
    46, 155–56, 172–73
Fremdarbeit (Kreidler), 81–82, 83–84
Friedman, Ken, 201–4
Fulkerson, James, 207–8, 211
Fuller, R. Buckminster, 92–93, 98–99, 106–7
funding, 9, 88–89, 125, 126–27, 129–31,
    142–44
    See also commissions
Furioso, William, 170

Gadamer, Hans-Georg, 4–5, 37–38
Gala Music for John Cage's 50th Birthday (Paik),
    36, 216–17, 218, 219–22
Galison, Peter, 103–4
game pieces (Zorn), 223–26
gamer model (Interpretive Labor), 13, 158,
    190–93, 199–200, 226–28
gaming, 190–91, 193–94, 196–98, 200–1,
    209–10
    See also gamer model (Interpretive Labor);
    modding
Gann, Kyle, 101, 106–7
gender pay gap, 138–40
gender representation, 122–24, 141–42
gendered labor, 12, 121–26, 128–29, 137–40,
    141–42
genre, 44–45, 96, 230–31
gifts, 214–15, 221–22
gig economy, 13, 142–44, 232
Godard, Barbara, 76–77
Goethe-Institut Chicago, 81–82
Google, 198–99
Granat, Zbigniew, 50–53
Grand Theft Auto, 193
Grant, Morag Josephine, 21
graphic scores, 30–31, 35–36, 37, 148–49, 150
    See also *Carré* (Stockhausen/Cardew); *Plus
    Minus* (Stockhausen); *Treatise* (Cardew)
Great Learning, The (Cardew), 156–57, 170
Gregg, Melissa, 140
Grosskopf, Erhard, 181–82
Grove Music Online, 31–32, 91–92
Gruppen (Stockhausen), 99–100
Guitar Hero, 191

INDEX 257

Habermas, Jürgen, 37–38
hacker class, 146–47, 177, 180–81
hacker model (Interpretive Labor), 12–13, 75, 79, 146–49, 179–81, 183–89
hacking
   as community, 145–46, 153–54, 172–73, 186–87
   definitions of, 12–13, 145, 147, 150, 153–56, 178, 183–84, 197–98
   as distinct from modding, 197–98
   experimental music as, 154–56, 172–73, 178, 183–89, 205
   hacker/vectoralist divide, 173–75
   in science fiction, 145–46
   as subversion, 37, 145, 154–56, 184–85
   Wark on, 145–46, 180–81, 184
   See also Cardew, Cornelius; *Treatise* (Cardew)
Half-time (Paik), 36, 213–14
Hanna, Joseph, 103–4, 109–10
Hansen, Al, 201–4, 205–6
Hassard, John, 26
Havelková, Tereza, 109–10
Heidegger, Martin, 4–5, 18–20, 91, 184–85
Hembold, Lois Rita, 123–24
Herder, Johann Gottfried von, 18, 61–62, 91
hermeneutics, 4–5, 17–18, 20–21, 37–38, 91, 95, 116
   See also interpretation
hierarchy, 27–28, 230
   See also power
Higgins, Dick, 35–36, 201–4, 205–6
Higgins, Hannah, 204
highSCORE Festival, 141
Hill, Martha, 127
Hiller, Lejaren, 12, 91–92, 93, 103–4, 111–16, 114*f*
Himanen, Pekka, 175
Hirst, Damien, 80–82
homage, 177–78, 215–21
Hornpipe (Mumma), 194–96, 197–98
HPSCHD (Hiller/Cage), 113–15
HubSpot, 192
Huizinga, Johan, 209–10, 226, 233
Hynčica, Jan, 168

Ichiyanagi, Toshi, 36
Iddon, Martin, 83–84
Illiac Suite (Hiller), 112–13, 114*f*
Imaginary Landscape No. 5 (Cage), 7–8
improvisation, 2–10, 31–33, 157–58, 166, 223–26
income inequality, 23–24

indeterminacy
   and authorship, 180–81
   Cage on, 53, 90–91, 96, 150, 179–80
   defined, 14–15
   as element of all performed music, 10–11, 150–51
   as experimentation, 104–6, 107
   and hacking, 173, 179–80, 183–84, 187–89
   history of, 30–32
   as information economy, 175–77
   in scholarship, 2–3, 5–6, 31–33, 236–37
   spectrum of, 42–43
   as user-generated content, 201–9
   See also aleatory; chance
influence, 107–9
Institute of Sonology (The Hague), 117
intentional fallacy, 152–53
intentions, 54–55, 152–53, 232
intermedia, 204
International Computer Music Conference, 81–82
interpretation
   by administrators, 124–26, 136–37
   Cardew on, 21, 31–32, 149–53, 166, 184
   by composers, 90–92, 104, 107, 116, 179–80
   as dialectics, 44–45, 96–97, 116
   foundational knowledge needed for, 1, 50–55, 110–11
   Kotík's view of, 90–92, 94–98
   as labor, 5, 6–7, 16–17, 37–39, 234
   Margolis on, 95–96
   theories of, 17–21
   See also composer–performer relationships; Interpretive Labor; interpretive procedures; realization; translation
Interpretations series, 87, 88–89
Interpretive Labor
   avenues for further research on, 3–4, 5–7, 13, 231–33, 237
   defined, 3, 234
   guiding questions for, 38–39
   models of, 11–13, 232, 237
   paralleled in other systems of labor, 14, 230–32
   theoretical framework for, 4–5, 14–15, 16–20, 24–30, 37–38
   See also administrator model; executive model; gamer model; hacker model; scientist model
interpretive procedures
   analysis of, 17–18
   in chance compositions, 14–15, 90–91
   in classical music, 1–2, 15–16, 44–45, 78–79, 230–31

258 INDEX

interpretive procedures (*cont.*)
in jazz, 5
lack of critical engagement with, 2–3
as production, 30
See also interpretation
Isaacson, Leonard, 112
Ives, Charles, 30–31

Jackson, John Shenoy, 9
Jarman, Joseph, 7–8
jazz, 5, 7–8, 9–10
Jelinek, Hans, 92–93
Jennings, Terry, 71–72
Johnston, Jill, 133–34
Judson Hall (New York), 135–36
Juilliard School, 127, 131–32, 215–16
Jung, Eun-Young, 199–200
Jůzl, Miloš, 169–70

Kalender (periodical), 218
Kaprow, Allan, 71–72, 135–36, 205–6
Katz, Cindi, 147, 154
Kim, Rebecca, 2–3, 7–8, 10, 34
King of Denmark, The (Feldman), 67, 162
Klavierstuck XI (Stockhausen), 31–32, 35
Klein, Howard, 68
Klepal, Boris, 121
Klintberg, Bengt af, 201–4
Knizak, Milan, 201–4
knowledge as capital, 27–28
Knowles, Alison, 36, 133–34, 135–36, 201–4,
    212–13
Kohl, Marie-Anne, 84–85
Komorous, Rudolf, 109, 170
Konami, 196–97
Konczyna, Kristýna, 121, 141
Kondelík, Pavel, 168
Kontrabandt (Kotík), 169, 229–30
Kotík, Charlotta, 93–94
Kotík, Petr
    and the AACM, 86–89
    biography of, 91–94
    and Cage, 90–91, 92–93, 96, 97–98, 100–1,
        107–10
    on the Center of the Creative and Performing
        Arts, 115–16
    on composing, 100–3, 109–11
    compositional output and processes of, 39,
        98–104
    and interpretation, 21, 90–92, 94–98
    Kontrabandt (Contraband), 169, 229–30
    Many Many Women, 106–7, 108f
    Music for 3, 161, 170–71

Music in Two Movements, 102–3
    in new-music networks, 86–89, 92–94, 121,
        141, 169, 213, 222–23
    Nine + 1, 86–87
    on originality, 86
    performing Cardew's *Treatise*, 19–20, 161,
        167–69, 170–72
    Reiterations and Variables, 102–3
    and the scientist model of Interpretive Labor,
        12, 103–4, 106–11
    There Is Singularly Nothing, 102–3
    Variations for 3 Orchestras, 99–100
    See also Center of the Creative and
        Performing Arts (Buffalo); Creative
        Associates (University at Buffalo)
Kotz, Liz, 219
Kowalski, Elizabeth, 141
Krafft, Scott, 136
Kramer, Jonathan, 50–53
Kreidler, Johannes, 81–82, 83–85
Kuklová, Michaela, 121
Kurzwellen (Stockhausen), 73
Kutschke, Beate, 181–82

labor
    affective, 12, 16, 136–37
    cognitive, 5, 16–17, 29, 67, 146–47
    in concert music, 21–23
    gender and, 12, 121–26, 128–29, 137–40,
        141–42
    history of, 123–24, 137–38, 209–10,
        230–31
    interpretation as, 5, 6–7, 16–17, 37–39, 234
    in late capitalism / neoliberalism, 14, 21–24,
        40–41, 230–31
    in online activity, 24, 29, 191–92, 226–27
    physical, 16–17, 50–134
    realization as, 41–44, 54–62, 73–75, 76–77,
        78–79, 148–49, 180
    theories of, 16, 24–30
    translation as, 43, 44, 56–62, 76–79,
        146–47
    "voluntary," 13, 24, 191–92, 200–1. *See also*
        user-generated content (UGC)
    See also Interpretive Labor
labor process theory, 26
labor theory of value (LTV), 26, 82–83
Lane, Mary, 170, 171
late capitalism, 14, 84–85, 173–75
    See also neoliberalism
Le Nozze di Figaro (Mozart), 1–2, 15–16
Leslie, Christopher, 226–27
Levine, Jesse, 127

INDEX 259

Levine Packer, Renée, 12, 91–92, 93, 127–31, 137, 195
Levitz, Tamara, 7–8, 10, 34
Levy, Steven, 150
Lewis, George E., 8–10, 32–33, 87–88, 88*f*, 141–42
Lewis, Philip, 178
Liang, Lei, 119–20
Linux, 172
literary theory, 18, 46–47
Littlefield, Richard, 10–11
Lochhead, Judy, 142–43
Lord of the Rings Online, The (LOTRO), 200–1
Loriaux, Michael, 17, 20
Lucier, Alvin, 88–89, 194
ludomusicology, 191

Mac Low, Jackson, 201–4, 205–6
Maciunas, George, 71–72, 173, 201–4, 210
Maconie, Robin, 50–53, 62, 69–70, 79
Many Many Women (Kotík), 106–7, 108*f*
Margolis, Joseph, 95–96
Marxist critique, 24–28, 37–38, 82–83, 147–49, 227–28
Massachusetts Institute of Technology (MIT), 153–55, 173, 178, 184–85
Mauceri, Frank, 106
Maxfield, Richard, 36
Mayo, George Elton, 28–29
Memories of You (Cardew), 177–78
Meyer, Leonard, 105–6
Michii, Makoto, 161–62
Miller, Leta, 125
Mitchell, Roscoe, 87–88, 88*f*
MMORPGs (massively multiplayer online role-playing games), 193–94, 197–98, 200–1
mobile scores, 31–32, 35, 37
modding, 191, 193–98
modular scores. *See* mobile scores
Monson, Ingrid, 10
Moore, Andrea, 21–22, 143–44
Moore, Peter, 71–72
Moorman, Charlotte, 12, 43–44, 69, 71–73, 73*f*, 131–37, 187
Morrison, Matthew D., 10
Mostly Modern Festival, 141
Motor Vehicle Sundown (Event) (Brecht), 201–4
Mumma, Gordon, 194–96, 197–98
Music Academy (Prague), 92–93
Music for 3 (Kotík), 161, 170–71
Music in Two Movements (Kotík), 102–3
Music of Changes (Cage), 107

musical experimentalism. *See* experimental music
musicology, 234–36
Mutable Music, 88–89

National Endowment for the Arts, 129
neoliberalism, 11–12, 21–24, 40–41, 173–75, 177
    See also late capitalism
neo-Ricardian economics, 82–83
Nettl, Bruno, 32–33
Neue Sachlichkeit (New Objectivity), 91–92
Neuhaus, Max, 37, 71–72, 208–9
New Left, 123, 146–47, 209–10
New School for Social Research, 29, 205–6
New York Philharmonic, 21–22
New York School, 30–31
New York State Council on the Arts, 129
Niblock, Phill, 88–89
Nine + 1 (Kotík), 86–87
notation
    Cardew on, 145, 148–53, 160, 181–82
    and composer intent, 59–60, 97–98, 146–47, 152–53, 160
    demands on interpreters, 14–41, 42, 44–45, 47–48, 67, 74–77, 148–49, 166
    as source code, 155
    as subversion, 37, 154–55
    translation of, 50, 54–55, 56–61, 62–67, 76–79
    types of, 30–32, 34–37
    See also *Carré* (Stockhausen/Cardew); *Plus Minus* (Stockhausen); *Treatise* (Cardew)

objectivity, 56–57, 91–92, 95–96, 103–4, 234
Olympia (Komorous), 170
ONCE Festivals, 12, 13, 194
ONCE Group, 125
One for Violin Solo (Paik), 217
Ono, Yoko, 133–34, 219, 221–22
Opera Sextronique (Paik), 132
oral traditions, 14–15, 34, 223
Oram, Daphne, 111
Orchestra of the S.E.M. Ensemble, 86–88, 98–99
    See also S.E.M. Ensemble
orchestras, labor issues in, 21–23
Originale (Stockhausen), 135
Ortner, Sherry, 190–91
Ostrava Center for New Music, 87, 121, 141
Ostrava Days, 8–9, 87–88, 121, 141–42, 187, 188–89*f*
Ostravská Banda, 86–88
outsourcing, 11–12, 40–42, 81–82, 83–84

260 INDEX

Packer, Renée Levine. *See* Levine Packer, Renée
Paik, Nam June
    and Cage, 177–78, 216–18, 220–22
    Danger Music for Dick Higgins, 217
    Gala Music for John Cage's 50th Birthday, 36,
        216–17, 218, 219–22
    Half-time, 36, 213–14
    and Moorman, 43–44, 69, 71–73, 73f, 76, 132,
        133–34
    One for Violin Solo, 217
    Opera Sextronique, 132
Paterson, Robert, 141
Paterson, Victoria, 141
Pathways (Fulkerson), 211–212
Patterson, Benjamin, 201–4, 212–13
peer-commons production (Bauwens), 30
Peirce, Charles Sanders, 37
Penn, William, 161–62
performance art, 81–82, 83–85, 132–34, 204–8,
        211–14, 216–17
    See also Fluxus
performance practice. *See* interpretive
        procedures
physical labor, 16–17, 50–134
pictograms. *See* graphic scores
pictorial scores. *See* graphic scores
Piekut, Benjamin, 34
Pippen, John, 142–43
play, 192–93, 205, 209–10, 218, 221–23, 225–28,
        233–34
    See also gamer model (Interpretive Labor);
        gaming; modding
*Please Tell Me about Your Face; Or If You Prefer,
        about My Face* (Patterson), 212–13
Plus Minus (Stockhausen)
    Cardew/Rzewski performance of, 43–44,
        69–71, 76
    Fox/Snijders performance of, 66–67, 74–76
    Moorman/Paik performance of, 43–44, 69,
        71–73, 73f, 76
    QUaX performance of, 169
    realization process of, 65–67, 73–75, 76–77,
        78–79
    score and notation of, 62–67, 63f, 64–65f,
        66f, 69f
    and translational labor, 11–12, 43–44, 76–79,
        146–47
    Williams/Burnham/Cardew performance of,
        67–69, 69f, 70f, 76, 229–30
poetic scores, 36–37
Polanyi, Michael, 109
Pontara, Tobias, 21
Porter, Catherine, 46–47

portfolio careers, 143–44
    See also gig economy
Pousseur, Henri, 194
power, 26–28, 42–43, 55, 61–62, 79, 146–47,
        174–75, 184–85
    See also hierarchy; subversion
Practice-based Experimental Epistemology
        (PEER) Lab (University of California, Los
        Angeles), 119–20
Prague Conservatory, 92–93
Prague Spring (festival), 87–88, 99–100
precarity, 130, 143–44
Pro Evolution Soccer (Konami), 196–98
product placements (Kreidler), 83–85
Projection 1 (Feldman), 35–36
Putnam, Thomas, 67–68, 208, 222–23

Qualcomm Institute (QI) (University of
        California, San Diego), 119–20
QUaX, 93, 161, 167–70, 229–30

radical difference, principle of, 18
Radio Hamburg, 48, 55–56
Radiohead, 185
Raymond, Eric, 172
realization
    of *Carré* (Stockhausen/Cardew), 41–42, 54–62
    as labor, 41–44, 54–62, 73–75, 76–77, 78–79,
        148–49, 180
    of *Plus Minus* (Stockhausen), 65–67, 73–75,
        76–77, 78–79
    as subset of interpretation, 11–12, 44–45
    of *Treatise* (Cardew), 148–49, 162–66, 180
    See also interpretation; translation
recognition, 14, 25, 38–39, 79, 83, 116, 210–11, 233
recordings, 68–69, 163–66, 167, 170–71
Refrain (Stockhausen), 174
Reiterations and Variables (Kotík), 102–3
research centers, 119–20
reskinning, 194, 196–97
Reynolds, Roger, 31–32
Rheinberger, Hans-Jörg, 110, 237
Riehm, Rolf, 187
Robertson, David, 48–50
Rock Band, 191
Rockefeller Foundation, 126–27, 129
Rodgers, Tara, 118–19
Rose, Sonya O., 137–38
Rothman, Roger, 154, 178, 186, 205, 221–22
Roulette Intermedia, 87
Rowlinson, Michael, 26
Rychlík, Jan, 92–93, 100
Rzewski, Frederic, 37, 43–44, 69–71, 75, 134–35

INDEX 261

Sahl, Michael, 229
Sansom, Matthew, 32–33
Sapp, Allen, 67–68, 127–28
Schedel, Margaret, 117
schematics, 37
Schettler, Jordan, 117–18
Schieske, Karl, 92–93
Schneeman, Carolee, 37
Schofield, Ann, 123–24
Schönmüller, Annette, 187
Schooltime Compositions (Cardew), 170
scientist model (Interpretive Labor), 12, 90–92,
  94, 103–15, 116–20, 158
Scranton, Philip, 123
Scratch Orchestra, 170, 179–80n.84, 182–83
Seaman, Norman, 134–36
S.E.M. Ensemble, 19–20, 86–89, 93–94, 99–100,
  106–7, 170–73, 222–23
  See also Center of the Creative and
    Performing Arts (Buffalo); Kotík, Petr;
    Orchestra of the S.E.M. Ensemble
semiotics, 36–37
sharing economy, 214–15, 221–22, 227–28
Sherman, Howard J., 23–24
Sherman, Paul D., 23–24
Sims, Gwendolyn, 126–27, 170, 171
Skálová, Barbora, 141
Snijders, John, 66, 74–76
Snows (Schneeman), 37
social media, 199–201, 209, 210
Solo with Accompaniment (Cardew), 69, 170,
  177–78
Sonata for Cello and Piano (Carter), 67–68
Sonic Arts Union, 194–96
Sonic Laboratory at SARC studios (Belfast), 117
Soper, Kate, 141–42
Space Music (Fulkerson), 213
spatialization, 48–53
  See also Carré (Stockhausen/Cardew)
Spiral (Stockhausen), 73–74
Spisarová, Renáta, 121, 141
Šrámek, Vladimír, 92–93, 109
St. Wenceslas Church (Ostrava), 187, 188*f*, 189*f*
Steele, Guy, 153–54
Stein, Gertrude, 98–100, 106–7, 108*f*, 235–36
Steiner, Carol, 213
Stillman, Amy, 34
Stockhausen, Karlheinz
  Cardew on, 47–48, 55, 57–61, 174–75, 176–77
  Gruppen, 99–100
  Klavierstuck XI, 31–32, 35
  Kotík commissioned by, 229–30
  Kurzwellen, 73

as manager, 11–12, 41–44, 50–56, 69–71,
  78–81, 174–75
Originale, 135
Refrain, 174
role in *Carré*, 41–42, 48–55, 57–61, 79–81, 180
role in *Plus Minus*, 62–67, 63*f*, 64–65*f*, 66*f*, 69*f*
Spiral, 73–74
  See also Carré (Stockhausen/Cardew); *Plus
    Minus* (Stockhausen)
"Stockhausen Serves Imperialism" (Cardew),
  47–48, 55, 174–75, 177
String Piece (Knowles), 212–13
Strongin, Theodore, 163
studios, 116–17
subversion, 37, 145, 147, 154–56, 184–85, 218,
  222–23
Supermarket Song for George Brecht (Fine), 36
surveillance, 176–77

Tanglewood Music Center, 141–42
Taylor, Timothy, 21–22, 41
Teaching and Learning as Performing Arts
  (Filliou), 201, 202*f*, 203*f*
theater, 84, 204–5, 206–7
Theater Piece (Cage), 206
There Is Singularly Nothing (Kotík), 102–3
Third Piano Sonata (Boulez), 31–32
Thomas, Ronald, 72–73
Thompson, William, 130
Threadgill, Henry, 87
Tilbury, John, 75, 157–58, 167, 177–78, 182–83
TIME:SPANS, 141
Torvalds, Linus, 172
Tower, Joan, 141–42
Toyama, Michiko, 118–19
transformance (Godard), 76–77
translation
  as labor, 43, 44, 56–62, 76–79, 146–47
  of notation, 50, 54–55, 56–61, 62–67, 76–79
  theories of, 11–12, 17–18, 43, 45–47, 61–62,
    76–79, 178–79
  See also interpretation; realization
Treatise (Cardew)
  Cardew's involvement in performing, 161–62
  and Cardew's political ideology, 148–49,
    156–57, 181–83
  Cardew's rejection of, 148–49, 156–57, 166,
    181–82
  composition of, 157–60
  and the executive model, 150n.13
  as hacking, 12–13, 147, 154–56, 171–73
  labor involved in performing, 19–20, 39,
    146–47, 148–49, 201

262 INDEX

Treatise (Cardew) (*cont.*)
  performed in Buffalo and New York City
    (1966), 161–67
  performed in Prague (1967), 161, 167–70
  performed in Buffalo (1970), 161, 170–73
  recordings of, 163–66, 167, 170–71
  score and notation of, 101, 149*f*, 159*f*, 159–
    60, 163–66, 164*f*, 165*f*
Treatise Handbook (Cardew), 145, 160, 180–81,
  182–83
Trojalí Karolina (Ostrava), 187, 188*f*
Tudor, David, 57–58, 97–98, 134–35, 215–16
Two Activities (Fulkerson), 207–8, 211
Two Durations (Brecht), 206

unions, 21–23, 230–31
University at Buffalo. *See* Center of the Creative
  and Performing Arts (Buffalo); Creative
  Associates (University at Buffalo)
University of Illinois, 111–12, 115–16
U.S. Department of Labor, 24, 137–38
user-generated content (UGC)
  as exploitation, 24, 191–92, 199–200, 226–28
  indeterminacy as, 13, 201–9, 227–28
  motivations for, 209–11, 227–28
  in social media and video games, 198–201

Valle, Andrea, 35
van Dijck, José, 210
Varèse, Edgard, 94, 134–35
Variations (Cage), 201–4, 206
Variations for 3 Orchestras (Kotík), 99–100
Vautier, Ben, 201–4
vectoralists, 27–28, 145, 173–75
Vejvoda, Josef, 168
Venuti, Lawrence, 178–79
verbal scores, 36–37, 215–17, 219
video games, 191, 193–94, 196–98, 200–1
Vitous, Miroslav, 170, 171
"voluntary" labor, 13, 24, 191–92, 200–1
  See also user-generated content (UGC)
Vostell, Wolf, 201–4

Waksman, Steve, 195–96
Walmart, 40–41
Walshe, Jennifer, 141–42
Warburton, Dan, 168–69
Wark, McKenzie
  on education, 234–35
  on hacking, 16, 145–46, 180–81, 184
  on play, 192–93
  on production, 16, 173–74, 175, 234
  on the vectoralist class, 27–28, 145, 173–74,
    175
Warsaw Autumn (festival), 167
Water Whistle (Neuhaus), 208–9
Web 2.0, 24
Wehrer, Anne Opie Counselman, 125
Wehrer, Joseph, 125
Wernick, Richard, 127–29
Westdeutschen Rundfunk Cologne, 229–30
White, Andrew, 67–68, 161–62
Williams, Diane, 170, 171
Williams, Emmett, 201–4
Williams, Jan, 55, 67–69, 69*f*, 70*f*, 161–62, 166–
  67, 175–76, 229–30
Wimsatt, W.K. Jr., 152
Wolff, Christian, 87, 88–89, 148
Wolfman, The (Ashley), 195
Wolpe, Stefan, 46–47
"women and music," 122–23
"women's work." *See* gendered labor
"work humanization" movement, 28–29
work-concept, 10–11, 37, 50–53, 151, 234
World of Warcraft, 193, 197–98
Wrochem, Kalus von, 161–62

Yarn/Wire, 142–43
Young, La Monte, 201–4
YouTube, 198–200, 210

Zahradník, Václav, 168–69
Zonn, Paul, 161–62
Zorn, John, 223–26
Zwerin, Michael, 9

The manufacturer's authorised representative in the EU for product safety is Oxford
University Press España S.A. of El Parque Empresarial San Fernando de Henares,
Avenida de Castilla, 2 – 28830 Madrid (www.oup.es/en or product.safety@oup.com).
OUP España S.A. also acts as importer into Spain of products made by the manufacturer.

Printed in the USA/Agawam, MA
August 1, 2025

891350.006